Soul of a People

OTHER BOOKS BY THE AUTHOR

A Family Haggadah
Psalms That Hallow the Sabbath
Old Testament Lore
MANTRA

Soul of a People

A Lantern to the Past and a Lamp for the Future Nishmat Ha Am

NORMAN M. CHANSKY

RESOURCE *Publications* • Eugene, Oregon

SOUL OF A PEOPLE
A Lantern to the Past and a Lamp for the Future Nishmat Ha Am

Copyright © 2022 Norman M. Chansky. All rights reserved. Except for brief quotations in critical publications or reviews, no part of this book may be reproduced in any manner without prior written permission from the publisher. Write: Permissions, Wipf and Stock Publishers, 199 W. 8th Ave., Suite 3, Eugene, OR 97401.

Resource Publications
An Imprint of Wipf and Stock Publishers
199 W. 8th Ave., Suite 3
Eugene, OR 97401

www.wipfandstock.com

PAPERBACK ISBN: 978-1-6667-1077-9
HARDCOVER ISBN: 978-1-6667-1078-6
EBOOK ISBN: 978-1-6667-1079-3

08/10/22

Cover Art: King David by Adamo Tadolini. ShutterStock.com. Image#86557216

I dedicate this book to my sisters Sonya and Lois, to Sophie Mulugeta Gordon, and to my late, dear wife, Elissa, may our lives be an example to them.

Norman Chansky

And thou shalt teach the sacred law unto thy children
And they will to theirs for all generations

Give me your tired, your poor,
Your huddled masses yearning to breathe free,
The wretched refuse of your teeming shore.
Send these, the homeless, tempest-toss't to me.
I lift my lamp, beside the golden door.

—EMMA LAZARUS

We are your tired and poor
Breathing to be free
Lift your lamp and let me enter the golden
door of sapience.

PERSONS OF VALOR

Persons of valor augment and exalt the world
    By their efforts, courage, and humility.
Their strength guides them and others through each day.
    They are defined by their deeds that illuminate dreams.
Every deed is colored by heroism, by bravery, by courage.
    Their valor is golden, sparkled, and joyful.
They stand up to challenges no matter the barrier.
    Valor can't be held back or defined by age, race, or sex.
Persons of valor make the world change.
    For valor's not the belonging of the young or the old
But by the deeds of the heart that give and unfold.
    Its merit and honor that hold no disguise
Like the creation of being in the blessed Holy One's Eyes.
    For valor is the color of the song of the soul.
As people change, they create and turn light into gold.
    Divine is who they are as God's chosen people.
Their strength guides untold generations
    By the actions that bring light to all dreams.
        Valor is something that's defined by one's efforts.
            Welcome to the elite
                Who augment and exalt the world.

Contents

Introduction | xix
Petition | xxi

I: In the Beginning: From Entropy to Structure, Pattern, Light, and Life

The First Seven Days | 7
God's Creative Powers | 12
The First Seven Days: Another Version | 13
Undefinable Creation | 15
Conceiving Adam and Eve | 16
The First Humans: Another Version | 18
Adam and Eve: Yet Another Version | 26
The First Dawn | 27
Adam's Fear of the Dark | 28
Loss of Paradise | 29
Paradise Forfeited | 30
The Asp's Lament | 33
Lilith, Queen of the Night | 34
The First Family | 35
The Beginning of Evil | 39
The Budding First Family | 39
Genesis of Hate | 39
Endless Echoes of Murder | 40
The Final Kiss: Adam's Decline | 42
Out of Evil Cometh Good-In Time | 45

II: Legendary Heroes

Fallible Persons of Uncommon Valor | 49
Noah's Flood | 51

Dance of the Arbor: The End of the Flood | 53
Seven Noahide Laws of a Stable Society | 54
The Fate of Sodom | 55
Abraham, Abraham | 57
Isaac at the Mound | 59
Sarah's Death | 60
Hagar and Sarah | 61
Isaac's Place in History | 62
Abimelech Teaches the Patriarchs | 63
A Father's Blessing | 65
Jacob's Mysterious Dream | 68
The Contract with Laban | 69
P'nay Ayl: The Face of God | 70
Joseph and His Brothers | 72
Jacob's Last Will and Testament | 74
Israel's Plight in Egypt | 76
Moses Briefly: In the Bulrushes | 77
History of the Exodus from Egypt | 78
Miriam's Dance | 85
Moses' Song | 86
The Amalekites: The Perennial Foes | 88
Not a Curse But a Blessing | 90
Not as Grasshoppers But as Heroes | 91
Joshua | 92
The Red Thread | 93
Sisera and Ya-El | 95
Your God Is My God | 96
Gideon, the Deliverer | 97
Jephtha, the Deliverer | 100
Samson, the Deliverer | 102
What's-Her-Name, the Levite's Concubine | 105
Eli's Confession | 107
The Philistines Panic | 109
Ruth and Naomi | 110
Saul Becomes King | 111
David and Goliath | 113
Saul's Decline and Death | 114
Rizpah Guards the Dead | 115
Amnon and Tamar | 116

Absalom | 118
David's Final Moments | 119
David, David Beloved King | 122

III: Historical Figures and Events

The Fabric of the Nation Frays and Is Rewoven | 125
Amos | 127
The Words of Hosea | 129
The Legend of Jonah | 132
Micah | 134
Isaiah's Vision | 136
Isaiah Entreats Zion | 137
Isaiah's Prophesy | 137
These Words Came to Isaiah | 137
Jeremiah's Mission   138
Jeremiah Reveals God's Anguish | 140
Ezekiel's Vision | 142
Zephania | 143
Nahum's Proclamations | 145
Nahum Talks to God | 146
History Is Written on the Temple Wall: A Poem for Two Voices | 147
Tish'a B'av 586 B.C.E. | 151
The Vision of Obadiah | 153
Judith's Victory Over the Assyrians | 154
Susanah | 156
Jerusalem, the New | 157
Return from Exile | 157
Cyrus | 158
Renewal in the Days of Ezra and Nehemiah | 159
Ezra | 160
The Words of the Lord to Joel | 161
Haggai | 162
Visions of Zechariah | 163
Still Another Vision | 164
The Mission of Malachi | 164
Job's Suit | 165
Antiochus's Last Will and Testament | 167
Where are the Prophets? | 169
Golden Sayings of Solomon | 171

The Will of Kohellet | 173
A Codicil to the Will of Kohellet | 175
Tobit, a Good Man, as Seen from the Eyes of His Best Friend | 176
Good Living: A Guide My Grandfather Willed to
Me: A Midrash on Ecclesiasticus | 179
Eugulogy for Onias | 191
Lament of Aristobulus | 193
Alexander Yannai | 194
In Praise of Salome Alexandra | 195
Eulogy for Julius Caesar | 196
Asaac Ben Maier | 198
Legacy of the Sadducees | 200
John, the Baptist | 200
John, Baptist Immortal: A Dream | 201
Pilate in Jerusalem-Alone | 202
What Is Hateful to You Do Not to Others Do | 203
Lord! Send Us a Savior | 205
The Messenger from the North | 206
Who Is That Man of Nazareth? | 207
The Ministry of Jesus | 208
Helena of Adiabene | 210
Paul: Apprentice, Apostate, Apostle, Martyr | 211
Grandeur in Rome | 216
Civil War in Jerusalem: Murder in the Temple | 217
Mayhem in Caesarea. 66 C.E. | 218
The Lion Chases the Wolf: Jerusalem 66 C.E. | 219
The Lion Bites Itself: Jerusalem 70 C.E. | 220
The Pack of Wolves Bite the Lion Here, There, and
Everywhere: Jerusalem 70 C.E. | 221
We Have Lost Hope | 223
Mourning But No Corpses | 224
Elegy in the Temple Courtyard | 225
A Letter from Titus My Dearest Berenice | 227
The Epitaph | 229
Masada 73 C.E. | 230
First the Lion Bit the Wolf Then the Wolf Tamed the Lion | 232

IV: Post Biblical History

The Jew Is Redefined | 237
One Era Ends and Another Begins | 239
Yesterday, Today, Tomorrow | 239
Bedrock of Judaism   239
After the Destruction of the Second Temple | 240
The Heroes of Yesterday | 241
Wisdom of Ben Zoma | 241
Legacy of Ben Sirach | 241
Ethics of the Fathers: A Midrash | 242
Ethics of the Fathers: The Meanings of Four | 243
Ethics of the Fathers: The Meanings of Three | 245
Ethics of the Fathers: The Meanings of Two | 246
Ethics of the Fathers: The Meaning of One | 247
Bruria Bat Hanania   248
Enoch | 249
Battle of the Proof Texts | 251
The Trinity: Eusebius, Augustine, John Chrysostom | 252
Julian, Emperor of Rome 361 CE | 254
Why Are These Times Different from All Other Times? | 255
Maimonidean Degrees of Charity | 257
Theobold, the Apostate | 258
Nicholas Donin, the Apostate | 259
A Karaite K'tubah | 260
Reb Mendel's Amulets | 261
The Law of Return   263
Nathan, the Mute | 264
But Your Holiness the Jews Already Confessed: The Black Death | 265
Purim in Castille, 1339 | 268
Converso Lament | 269
Massacre in Mashad Iran March 1839 | 270
The Centuries Darkened Our Paths | 271
Other Faiths Seen from the Eyes of a Buddhist | 272
The Exorcism of Sarah Bas Plony | 273
Martin Luther: Friend and Foe | 276
Foul Called the Rabbis | 279
The Earthquake | 231
So Grand Is God | 285

Eulogy for the Rambam, Reb Moshe Ben Maimon | 286
Rabbi Nachmanides and the Apostate Pablo Christiani | 287
Happy Are They Who Listen Not to the Wicked | 289
Dear Lord, I Must Confess a Grievous Fault | 289
My Pain Overflows Like a River | 290
Almighty God, Merciful and True | 290
Almighty God, Blessed Be Your Name | 291
In Silent Pauses | 291
From Chief Rabbi to Bishop: The Conversion of Ha Levi
to Pablo De Santa Maria, Bishop of Burgos | 292
The Spanish Inquisition: Seed, Root, Stem, and Flower: An Essay | 293
Converso Reaffirmation | 300
Do We Have Messiahs? | 301
Cherem | 304
Lesser Purim Holidays | 306
Natural Calamities | 307
War | 308
Reb Yankel's Son, Mendel, the Schnorrer | 309
Witness to Creation: Kabbalat Shamayim | 311
Seven Chasidic Stories | 315
Eulogy for Moses Mendelssohn: The Great Emancipator | 321
Mr. and Mrs. Mortara. This Jew Is a Catholic | 323
Shtetl Life | 325
Monday Market | 329
My Bris Circumcision | 331
A Death | 336
The American Experience | 344
The First Minyan in New Amsterdam | 346
The First Professor of Hebrew At Harvard Used to Be a Jew | 347
The First Hebrew Teacher in Philadelphia | 348
Philip Minis of Savannah | 350
Becoming An American in 1837 | 351
In Honor of Rebecca Gratz | 354
A Tribute to Grace Aguilar 1816–1847 | 355
Ellis Island | 356
A Letter Home | 358
Last Will and Testament of Irving Née Itzik | 363
Genealogy of An American Jewish Family | 366

The First Graduation of the Reform Jewish
Seminary in Cincinnati | 366
The Little Yid and Santa Claus | 367
Kishinev's House of Eternity | 369
A Boxing Lesson for Barney Rosofsky | 371
Owed to Mort Levine | 373
Gastronomic Logic | 374
Jewish Sense of Humor | 374
It Takes a Shtetl: A Reminiscence | 375
Jewish Antisemites of the Nineteenth Century | 376
Hayyim Heine On Heinrich Heine | 378
Heine and Marx | 379
Who Is the Rebel? | 379
Montagu, the Anti-Zionist Jew | 379
Like a Gimel | 380
Emma Lazarus and the Immigrants | 381
There and Here: An Immigrant's Dilemma | 381
No One from My Tribe | 382
Tatteh I Won't Say Kaddish for You. | 383
The Excommunication of Rabbi Mordecai | 385

V: The Holocaust Period

Jewish Ashes Cloud the Firmament | 389
Spreading Darkness | 390
The Ashes of History | 392
N'ka-Mah | 393
Ode To Hannah Senesh | 395
The Righteous Ten Booms | 396
Roumania, Roumania, Roumania, Roumania, Roumania | 398
Righteous Gentiles | 399
Two Consuls and an "Ambassador": A Tryptich Essay on Visas | 400
Kapo Keinrich Schulz | 404
A Tribute to Misha Veksler | 406
A Tribute to the Memory of Anton Schmidt | 407
The Lore of Chelm: Amusing And Tragic | 408
Foon Brawchiz Tsu K'lawliz | 409
General Patton: We've Been to Camp | 410
Joseph, Joseph You're My Brother | 410
You are Our Brothers | 411

Dear Lillian | 411
The Light of Israel Beckons | 412
I Survived | 413
How I Yearn to Return | 414
I Survived Auschwitz | 415
Dear Mr. Eichmann | 416
A Letter From Latrun | 417
Jerusalem. The New | 419
Brothers Forever Now | 420
My Brother's Weeper | 421
Lost Youth. Gained Liberté | 422
Last Night the World Was Filled With Rage | 424
Aftermath of the Yom Kippur War | 425
Remembering Prime Minister Rabin | 425
Heaven's Gift | 426
Israel, Land of Beauty | 426
One Kid May He Rest in Peace | 427
Omri Jadah: Za Ts Al | 429
Israel Despite Your Faults You Have My Love | 430
The Lemba Petition | 431
Sarajevo, 1998 | 432
A Drop of Oil Am I: The Holocaust Experience | 433
Ingathering of the Remnants of Israel | 433
There Was No Holocaust. But There Was! | 434
My People Is Like a Kaleidoscope | 435
Israel Survives | 435
My People Is Evolving | 436
As Israel Kept the Sabbath So Has the Sabbath Kept Israel | 437
Blessed are the Candles | 437
Shabbat and the Earth Has Finished Its Daily Round | 438
Mother Whispers Her Prayers | 439
As Shabbat Draws Near | 440
The Sparkling Candles Illuminate Our Way | 441
On Sabbath We Pause from Daily Routine | 441
Blessed are We With Sabbath Beauty | 441
Not By Mystic Chariot | 442
Welcome Sabbath We Sing Together | 442
How Good It Is to Celebrate This Sabbath | 443
Silently Sets the Auric Sun | 443

Miriam's Daughters Join Hands | 443
As the Sabbath Day Is Growing Nigh | 444
Six Days Each Week We Toil | 444
When Work for The Week Is Done | 445
'Round the Sun the Earth Has Spun | 446
My Mother's Sabbath Candlesticks | 447
The Weekly Quest for Shabbat | 448
Fill Every Empty Space | 448

VI: Figments

Sundries | 451
Where There's a Will | 451
Miriam Is Sunshine | 477
When Sorrele Found Itzig: A Taste of Honey | 477
A Tale of Jail | 492
One for Here and One More to Go | 493
A Contemporary Song of Love | 495
Put Wings on It | 502
My Cousin's Funeral | 524
The Soft, Silvered Tongue of Avon | 525
Hark! Hark! How Splendid to Watch | 527
Request | 527
Grown Up at Nine During World War II | 528

Introduction

Soul of a People

A Mosiac Tapestry of Law, Lore, and Vita of the Jewish People

Soul of a People is a canopy of variegated images, rhymes, and rhythms that spreads over the Jewish heritage. Under that canopy is a rich lore of a people struggling to remain alive, to achieve some semblance of dignity, and to transmit God's message from Mount Sinai Resisting memory's urge to fade, these stories live on. This collection provides access to those moments of meaning through the medium of poetry as seen by a modern eye. It is a journey of the tree that my people planted. A tree: roots, branches, buds, flowers, pests, fire, and renewal. The poems are written, not to retell history, but to awaken interest in the fiber and fabric of my people in everyone. It recalls halcyon days as well as storms they withstood. Through the ages we have not only survived despite obstacles, but we continue to evolve and to branch

Included herein are poems that ignite the mystery and awe of Creation, relive human trial and error as the Jewish people grew up, celebrate glorious victories over relentless foes, fill the Sea of Anguish with tears from the travails of dispersions and pogroms, and understand the relief and exhilaration of each liberation. They will also sweat with the pioneers who rebuilt a homeland despite infested swamps and hostile neighbors, grieve over the internal struggles that split one branch of Judaism from another, quell the internal struggles that plunder inner peace, and join hands in community with brothers and sisters of different color, native tongue, garb, and religious practices. Readers will find the wisdom of the sages teaching us moral ways to live, experience the delight and serenity the Sabbath

Introduction

bestows, rekindle the ardor sensed when praying, drink a draught of kindness poured by a compassionate God, etch in memory the wisdom, love, and sacrifice of those who came before us, and, finally, kindle a candle of hope to guide those who will follow us in making this a better world.

The Hebrew word for SOUL is "N'shamah." It is derived from the verb "to breathe." Only the living breathe. The Soul is alive. Each new generation recasts its patina but not its essence. The Jewish soul, though, embracing many varieties of Judaism, has a unique signature. Some of the changes it undergoes are due to new ways of looking at text as permutations in human evolution. It is a Jewish tradition to interpret. This is called "*Midrash*." *Soul of a People* is a selection of my midrash, my interpretation, my reconstruction of the history and lore of my ancestors and contemporaries spanning centuries of good times and struggles. As the Jewish people evolved, it became clear that some writings in The Bible were metaphoric. To this day scholars plumb their meanings. This volume contains many a *Midrash* about Jewish history; the victories and defeats; the saints, scoundrels, sages, unlettered, heroes, cowards, oppressors, and rescuers. It not only addresses struggles, but the mission to raise the spiritual level of humanity.

Readers are invited to place themselves in the life and times of the characters and events in this collection as I have done. I begin with a prayer.

PETITION

Help us plumb our souls, Oh God! Elohim!
    Deep within lie-tangled lanes of memory
Drifting in bewildering arrays of yesterdays.
    In the Very Beginning there was Nothing filled with Everything:
Protons, Electrons, Neutrons, Light, Darkness, Land, Seas,
    Flora, Fauna, Man, Woman,
The Ordinary, the Sacred, the Daily, the Sabbath,
    Language, Thought, Devotion,
Evil and Mercy, Goodness and Wickedness.
    Then followed a Flood, then Farming, then Sheep herding,
The Matriarchs: Sarah, Rebecca, Leah, and Rachel
    And The Patriarchs: Abraham, Isaac, Jacob, and Joseph.
A Kidnapping, Famine, Emigration to Egypt, Slavery, Freedom,
    Wanderings in the Desert, Sacred fires, The Law, The Covenant with You,
And Our Impatience, The Golden Calf, Moses' wrath,
    The breaking the Tablets of the Law,
Attack of foes, Fright: Flight, Fight. Rededication to Noble aims,
    Sin, Divine Inspiration, Pettiness, Wisdom, Ignorance;
        Love of You, Your Forgiveness,
Building of The Holy Temple consecrated to You,
    Alliances with strangers; Adoption of alien ways;
        Exhortation of the prophets, Destruction of the Temple.
Exile, Silencing of the prophets, Your Silence, Through
    Whom will You Speak?
        Are we mere human beings Your Prophets today?
Do You now speak through us rededicated to Your Noble aims?
    The hands of Heaven hover about our heads
        And consecrate us to Your purposes.
Still there are constant curses of foes and they sear our souls,
    But Your Blessings through song and dance heal.
Exile and Dirges; Distrust of Strangers; Rededication to Your Holy purpose.

Heroes who rose above their circumstances;
martyrs who succumbed to them.
    Rebuilding Your Sacred Temple. Again drifting away from You.
Again destruction of The Temple. Again and again infernos.

Fires that consumed us because of our unswerving faith in You.
    Teachings of the Masters. Rededication of Noble aims
in every generation.
Tides of history rise like black storms then ebb in the soft
    silence of sunshine.
                      Life, Death, and Rebirth.
And we, particles of dust in Thy Creation, seek alliance with You
    To find You in all that is good and merciful within us.
Rupture of the Old and its reconstructions, over and over.
    A patchwork of history is woven into our souls filling us with Holes.
Incomplete we will always be. Striving for the ideal is our destiny.

        Norman M. Chansky, Ph.D.
        PROFESSOR EMERITUS
        TEMPLE UNIVERSITY

I

IN THE BEGINNING
From Entropy to Structure, Pattern, Light, and Life

Curious but blind are we to the mysteries of the universe. What does the universe consist of? How did it come into being? Of what use and value are its elements? We ask what is the place of the humans in the cosmos? What is *my* place in particular? What does God Want of me? Each culture has its own creation story to fix one's place in history and to define one's destiny. According to a Crow Indian myth, in the beginning there was only water and ducks. Then the Sun, the Creator, merged with the Coyote. The Creator told the ducks to dive into the water and from the mud on the webbed feet the Earth was created and peopled. Early Egyptians explained that dry land appeared out of a primordial ocean. Atum, the Sun god later named Ra, father of all other gods, arose from an abyss. In Mesopotamia, creation also took place from a watery abyss, Apsu. But the world came into being from a violent clash between older and younger gods. Marduk made the sky and earth from two halves of the body of Tiamat, a dragon personifying evil. In Persian cosmology, Ahura Mazda was THE creator of Man as well as the determiner of natural events such as the course of the moon. All cultures have creation stories. They form sacred truths of that culture. In several gods, people often manifest themselves in male and female forms. A creature lumbers through hole in primeval sea and deposits earth upon which a society begins life. It is a time of sacred musings out of which societies grow. Such stories are found throughout the world: In Egypt, China, even among the aborigines of Australia, Good and Evil, twin attributes of his character, contended for superiority. In the end righteousness defeats evil. The gods of the Greek and Roman pantheons are well known. Zeus and Jupiter are chief gods. But neither were creators. These narratives do not include planets or meteors or expanding Space.

The Quran, the holy book of the Muslims, proclaims that God created the world and the cosmos, made all the creatures that move. He made angels, and the solar system. Rain fell in torrents, and broke up the soil to bring forth flora and fauna; Before God created humans, other creatures inhabited the world. Humans were created from earth, sand, clay and water. God breathed into that mix and the mortals began to live.

The first human was Adam who lived in Utopia. There Adam learned the names of flora and fauna. But Satan lured Adam to disobey, and this led to his expulsion.

God placed Adam in a beautiful garden in Paradise, telling him that he could eat whatever he wanted except the fruit of a forbidden tree. Satan tempted Adam to disobey God and eat the fruit. When Adam disobeyed God, God cast Adam out of Paradise. Muslim scholars are divided whether the Paradise from which Adam was expelled is the paradise in the heavens awarded to the righteous at the day of judgment or a paradise on earth. Man is forever tempted to rebel against God. Unlike the Hebrew version, Eve is not mentioned.

In sharp contrast is the God of the Hebrews. Creation did not come into being through violence, nor is there a pantheon of lesser gods. There is only one God Who created the cosmos, by fiat, through words not brutality. They named that God Elohim. A plural word with singular theme. "Let there be light!" was the command. And there was Light. Furthermore, Elohim of the Hebrews has no dual nature. Although the heavens and earth were created from an abyss, it was the Spirit of God that hovered over the deep dividing light from darkness. Elohim is in complete control of the creative process: day, night, vegetation, lower animals, and higher animals. Man is created with the mandate to protect all manner of life. Then on the seventh day, God rested and gave the Sabbath to humanity. The God of the Hebrews, a nomadic people, was portable unlike neighboring peoples who worshipped Baal, a stone god.

The Old Testament of The Bible presents two accounts of creation: the P or priestly account (Gen i and ii, 1–4) and the J account (Gen ii 4b-24). The differences are slight. In the former, God is called "Elohim"; in the latter, the ineffable sometimes transliterated "Yahweh." In the former, animals were created before Man; in the latter, they were created after Man. In the former, man and woman were created simultaneously; in the latter, woman was taken from Adam's rib. This instance is not an isolated one but a template for other narrations in the Bible. Multiple versions of the same event are not uncommon, giving The Bible an additional aura of the recondite. Reconciling the version of the same "event" are quite common, giving The Bible an aura of the recondite. Reconciling the versions and finding the deeper meanings of single accounts has been an undertaking of scholars of many faith communities for many centuries. Scholars find meaning through the distinctive lens they look through.

The creation poems that follow are reconstructions of the Hebrew biblical accounts from a lens ground with the grit of Biblical inspiration, scientific observations, a sense of the sacred, in a landscape of the mysterious, and guided by poetic imagination.

Shakespeare wrote in *A Midsummer-Night's Dream*

> ... The poet's eye, in a fine frenzy rolling,
> Doth glance from heaven to earth, from earth to heaven;
> And as imagination bodies forth
> The forms of things unknown, the poet's pen
> Turns them to shapes, and gives to airy nothing
> A local habitation and a name ....

It can apprehend some joy, imagine some fear, and turn a bush into a bear.

The poet combs a jungle of words until the mot juste is found to append to some subtle human enterprise, some stupendous feat, and, especially, quotidian undertakings that are taken for granted.

This book is a collection of works that enables me to make sense out of my heritage. That heritage is filled with contradictions, power plays, abuses, terror, triumphs, tragedies, theomachy as well as sciamachy, blemishes, confessions of worthlessness, yet the solace and beauty in being part of a prayerful people ever seeking Truth and human betterment.

Each poem in the collection is a midrash, an interpretive commentary, a perception of Jewish history and culture—an impression of forces and events that shaped my persona and that of others in this time, in eras past, and in generations to come. It is anchored in the Old Testament (O.T.). Many poems are introduced by passages of the O.T. Out of the original blossoms, flowers of poesy. There was no single literary technique that

I employed. Sometimes the rhyme is obvious; sometimes the rhythm; sometimes, the images. Some poems are lengthy epics; others, are 7-5-7 Haiku distillations of an idea. All deal with some twig of that branch of civilization given the name Judaism.

THE FIRST SEVEN DAYS

In the very beginning there was a sacred Source To be called GOD,
    Holy it was, and perfect and without equal.
First cause it was; Idea, anchor of love, Final judge, Fabricator.
    Amorphous it was containing endless, dark, multicolored,
Particles of divinity.
    Silently it stretched its vastness and wrapped around the Sacred Source.
Then did God Bless the expanding space.

God exists in Space and Space reflects God's Infinity.

Day 2

Gasses formed. Rising vapors and prisms coalesced.
    Then God Gathered clusters of gasses
And Compressed them until multicolored fires ignited
    And scattered them to bring forth suns and stars.
Volcanoes erupted, earth quaked and galaxies were launched.
    Each shone God's dazzling radiance;
Each spread God's thermonuclear warmth.
    Pleased with the divine astronomy God Blessed it.
Then orbs of fire released many kinds of dust,
    Each with its own electrical charge.
Some dusts drifted without plan;
    Others slammed with force into one another and formed mass;
Some hardened into mountains of rocks;
    Others melted into oceans of metal.

God exists in suns and stars, sands and rocks and they reflect
    God's creative fires.

Day 3

Then God Gathered and combined emerging gasses and dusts
    And engineered planets, each with its own distance from the Sun;
Each with its own motion:
    Each with its own orbit according to an ordained schedule.
No planet falling; no planet failing; each held in place by gravity.
    Then were the planets and their seasons blessed
For they were all good to God.

God exists in planets and their seasons reflect God's peerless design.

Day 4

Gasses spread and surrounded the Earth planet,
    Admitting Light so that Creation's works could be seen
Yet providing a protective shield to the eyes
    And allowing warmth to pass through the atmosphere
While protecting all creatures from burning.
    The Sun illuminated the spinning Earth by day and the Moon
By Night. Newly emerging gasses collided, separated and broke away
    And recombined to form seas where life would flourish.
And gasses rising from the seas joined other elements
    To form air for breathing.
Moving land masses collided to make majestic mountains
    Rise from the seas
Hiding minerals beneath the great depths.
    Then God Blessed the Earth planet.

God exists in planet Earth whose seas, air, and hills reflect God's grandeur.

Day 5

Proteins, dusts, sodium, zinc, ammonia, cesium,
    And cobalt were drifting idly
When God Whirled these elements in mystic dance.
    Then God Made an ocean vent rise and warm the salty broth

Until the elements combined.
    And then there was Life.
Bacteria. Cells. Mitochondria! Messengers of God!
    Then did God Create amino acids:
Adenine, thymine, cytosine, and guanine.
    Then did God Twist the helix of amino acids
And rearranged them in infinite patterns,
    Bridging them with sugars and phosphates in spiraling ladders.
The emerging proteins became the endless fonts of life.

Mitochondria, fixing themselves to mother's generative cells,
    Energized the helix.
Then God's messengers breathed life into the generative cells
    And gave each creature a sacred voice and a sacred rhythm for all time.
And God Choreographed life on Earth
    With crawling animals and walking animals;
There were fruit trees for fruit eaters;
    Herbivores and carnivores; procreators and scavengers.
Parasite and epiphyte.
    Each absorbed God; each extended the Divine Genius of creation.

Then appeared all manner of flora:
    Those that grow in the sea, those that grow in the air,
Those that grow on the land.
    Those that flower, those that bring forth fruit; those that bear nuts.
Those that are eaten; those that are merely admired.
    Those that complete their cycle in one season;
Those that survive for centuries.

Firs with needles; cacti with thorns; trees with leaves;
    Each plant producing its own kind for all generations;
Each plant transmitting its seeds to continue its species;
    Each seed unfolding new and unique qualities;
And each used mixing with others of the same species
    To build a new family.
New combinations of proteins brought forth all manner of fauna.
    Insects that crawl and those that fly.

All manner of birds were brought forth.
    Those that float; those that fly; and those that walk on land.
All manner of fish were brought forth;
    Those living in caves; those living in trees; and those living in the wild.
Those that are fleet; those that are slow.
    Then God Blessed the plants and the animals.

God's Genius exists in flora and fauna, and they reflect
    God's living presence.

Day 6

After careful meditation
    God's Genius rearranged spiraling amino acids, phosphates and sugars.
Each new helical twist brought forth a different human family:
    The tall, the short; the dark, the light; the narrow, the stout.
Each was endowed with The Holy Spirit;
    Each was chosen to protect Nature.
Each was chosen to discover order in and extended
    The unfolding worlds of Nature.
Each was chosen to bring order to the worlds of Nature.
    Each was endowed with the intelligence to study Nature's secrets.
Each was endowed with the power to preserve and extend Creation.
    Each was endowed with the choice of conserving Nature or destroying it.
Within each human, God Inscribed the Sacred Knowledge
    Of Right and Wrong
To balance destructive, generative, and protective impulses.
    To each new generation was revealed Nature known since antiquity;
To each new generation was revealed Nature unknown to its forbears.
    Each human was given the power to think and extend;
Each human was given power to construct and reflect.
    Each human was given the seeds of mercy and forgiveness;
Each human was given the resolve to serve others through
    Sacred Inspirations.
To God each human is holy; no one is more treasured than another.
    Each is a child of the Sacred Source.

When the mechanisms were in place for all Creation
    To be good for all Time,
Each was gifted with the Essence of Divinity giving all of Nature
    Its distinctiveness and its connection with one another.
God blessed the human families and assigned them the duty
    To preserve creation.
God's Grace exists in human families and human families
    Reflect God's Infinity.

Day 7

When the patterns of Nature were completed, God Rested and Found Peace.
    So it was with heavenly hosts circling eternity: a time to give light,
A time to renew.
    So it is with the seas which rage today and whimper in the morrow.
So it is with the trees which awake in Summer and sleep in Winter.
    So it is with all manner of life, seeking food and shelter for days
Then resting to prepare for the next quest.
    So is with God, glittering in glory and with ardor created
The cosmos in six constituents
    And rested on a seventh Time component to contemplate
On its wonders and remember them.
    God Ordained that humans work six days and restore themselves
On the Sabbath.
    Since that First Day of Rest has God Blessed each Sabbath day
And made it Holy
    And that holiness permeates all of creation.
Slithering between all that is Good is Evil.
    God's Glory glitters in cycles of Creation and Rest and exists
In all of Nature.
    And all of Nature reflects harmoniously rhythmic continuity.

GOD'S CREATIVE POWERS

Almighty God alone is stretching
    The firmament throughout space;
Almighty God with splendid hand
    Gilds sparkling stars with grace.

Almighty God alone in spinning
    The terrestrial ball about the sun.
Almighty God alone silvers the inert moon
    When each day is done.

Almighty God alone from seeds unfolds the beauty of a flower!
    Almighty God alone imbues each creature with Divine Power.
The endless grandeur of God stems not from just building mountains
    Or filling seas
But from enwrapping souls with Hope and Love spun
    From celestial melodies.

THE FIRST SEVEN DAYS: ANOTHER VERSION

Within each particle throughout the vast
That has no present and had no past
Dwelled God, enshrined in endless time,
Circled by depths and heights sublime.

All was hot and dark and still,
When swiftly dawned The Creator's will,
Launching lightning in all directions,
Pursued by thunder's ricocheting reflections.

It was then that Time began
And when Space, as well, spread out its span.
Light eddied from a fiery sun
And rings of planets in the cosmos spun.

Distant stars, jewels of the night,
Watched Earth born 'midst showers of light.
Gasses mixed and moisture spread
And living matter then was bred.

From the waters seas formed
To wash the world and as
Heavens stormed and baptized cells as they arrived
And fed them, too, so they survived.

Plants grew up, both short and tall,
With flowers and fruits to feed us all.
Mountains rose to a majestic size
Reaching to the swelling skies.

All manner of fish swarmed the seas
Spreading rainbowed fantasies.
Animals roved the land to find
The havens which God to them assigned.

Birds in the sky would daily scout
Nesting places all about.
Each bird chirped its very own song,
And animals and trees sang along.

Plainly lacking was a human pair
To tend to all with loving care.
Moments after Divine Meditation,
Humans arose to crown creation.

Woman and Man did God then fashion
Complete with every human passion.
Adam, the man, and Eve, the wife,
Were placed on Earth to honor life.

To their souls did God convey
The laws of kindness to obey
"Plants and animals with care do tend
And Nature's frail you must mend."

God Ordained, when all was
done, a Sabbath day, a holy one,
A day of prayer, a day of rest,
A day The Mighty God had Blessed.

UNDEFINABLE CREATION

Mystery and chance play dice with the universe
    And scoff not at Science.

CONCEIVING ADAM AND EVE

God Sought the counsel of angels, partners in causation.
    "Let a race of creatures crown creation.
A race who will respect My Authority
    And preserve and extend creation's immensity."

The Consenters advised, "Create a creature
    With a Mind like Yours capable of learning,
With a Soul like Yours sprouting righteousness,
    With a Heart like Yours overflowing with mercy."
The Dissenters advised, "such a creature
    Would have a mind teeming with ignorance,
Would have a spirit sprouting wrongdoing,
    Would have a heart flowing with malice."
Because what creature can be as perfect as God?

But God Accepted the advice of the Consenters.
    "You will rue this day," scoffed the Dissenters!
In a thrice sown genes in God's laboratory mutated
    And from the essence of God were fashioned humans:
Men and Women,
    Not too many, as humanity was still an experiment.
Adam and Eve, closest to God in mind, soul,
    And heart were endowed with free will.
God said, "live upon My creation, enjoy it, and improve upon it
    But you must be obedient and be responsible for your actions."
God Placed them side by side in Paradise, the epicenter of Creation,
    And consecrated their marriage, pronouncing them
Husband and Wife.
    Each was the complement of the other; each the help mate
of the other.
    A choir of the Consenters filled the heavens with sweet songs

Which wafted to Paradise and is heard today in the arias of birds.
    The hearts of the newlyweds were filled with rapture.
But the vexed Dissenters brewed cannons of thunder
    Which rumble even today.
The newlyweds sought shelter from the tantrums of the Dissenters.
    Rain drowned their ecstasy.
In time Adam and Eve learned what hunger is and how to satisfy it,
    What thirst is and how to slake it,
What heat and cold are and how to protect their bodies.
    What beauty is and how to admire it;
What comfort is and how to enjoy it.
    What knowledge is and how to increase it.
They learned how to make babies:
    How to feed them, comfort them, and how to teach them to survive.
But they also discovered need, greed, and evil.

They surrendered to temptations and engaged in actions prohibited by God.
    They disobeyed The Commandment and then knew guilt and shame.
They knew remorse and God's forgiveness but also exile from Paradise.
    The refugees learned about the work of life and the permanence of death.
They built houses protecting them from the elements
    And bracing them from foes;
They sewed garments shielding their skin.
    They composed songs celebrating God's Creation; they
painted visions of history.
    They witnessed murder and learned to grieve to console, and to endure.
They taught their lessons to their descendants
    And to other humans in Creation.
And the Consenters who advised God to create humans were vindicated
    And so were the Dissenters.

THE FIRST HUMANS: ANOTHER VERSION

I

The biota of Eden were thriving
And daily new species were arriving.
Blooms were on every manner of plant:
Fruit bearing and flowers that enchant.

Striped animals at great speed were running
Leather-hide animals stretched out were sunning
Spotted animals through brush were leaping
Daytime animals lay in tree branches sleeping.

Birds nesting in all kinds of trees
Were chirping enchanting melodies;
And fish were swimming hither and yon;
Catch a glimpse and then they are gone.

Angels on high, God's adjutants—
Planners, designers, confidantes—
Marveled at the roots of God's Creation,
The very cause of cosmic causation.

But as they gazed upon the works they'd schemed
Something was missing to them it seemed.
Lacking was a bridge to God above:
A force of wisdom, of justice, of love

Who could preserve the Creation that was wrought.
Someone who would forge links, they sought,
Between the Sacred and the norm:
Someone who would Creation transform.

For many eons at length they debated
And for many more they meditated.
Finally, they developed a strategy
And formed a plan to which all could agree:

Chimpanzees were charming and clever as well
And at solving problems they did excel.
Let us take an ovum from the primate, the very best,
Mutate it, and with Divine seed it then invest.

In a sacred amniotic stream the angels immersed
Themselves and their imperfections were dispersed.
At the moments that they were purified,
The spirit of God in them did abide.

Seeds of life from the Angelic race
Sped toward the ovum in a random pace.
When the seed and the ovum at last had met
The two curved and whirled as in a minuet.

Then one seed to the ovum was invited
And the two gametes were united.
A zygote divinely human was spun
And what had been two now was one

Absorbed into an angel's womb
A human creature began to bloom.
Nurtured by the Sacred Water
The human would become God's first daughter.

Surrounding the ovum in empyrean mystique
The angels watched the ovum grow week by week.
Then after what seemed like an interminable time
Out of its nest a human did climb.

Its body somewhat resembled the chimpanzee
But its soul resembled The Deity.
The babe who from a labyrinth had crawled
Was someone whom the angels enthralled.

When the woman was fully grown,
The radiance of God upon her shone.
Her fingers were agile, her posture was erect,
Her brain was of superior intellect.

She was Eve, exuding life and cheer,
Ready to conquer every new frontier.
From her celestial abode
Along sacred waters she strode

Until she reached heaven's gate
Which opened to Eden's utopian estate.
There she beheld a sylvan wonder,
Opaque lightning and silent thunder.

There was warmth to bathe the skin
And mercy to nourish the soul within.
When she would taste any manner of food,
She thanked God in gratitude.

But lonely she was and lonely she'd be-
What kind of companion is a gnarled olive tree?
She petitioned the angels to send her a friend
To be her husband with whom she would blend.

II

The angels set out to create a HE
That would complement Eve, the SHE.
In the sacred amniotic stream angels again submerged
And their imperfections again were purged.

At the moment that they were purified
The spirit of God in them did abide.
Then from another chimpanzee an ovum was extracted
That to the Divine seed would be attracted.

Seeds of life from the Angelic race
Sped towards the ovum in a random pace.
When the seed and the ovum at last had met
They curtsied and whirled as in a minuet.

The two gametes were united
When one seed to the ovum had been invited.
Again a zygote divinely human was spun
And what had been two now was one.

Absorbed in an angel's merciful womb
A human creature began to bloom.
What a remarkable deed the angel had done
And the human grew into a God's first son.

Erect like Eve with a comparable brain
He was ready to explore the Divine Domain.
He wandered until he reached heaven's gate
Which opened to Edens utopian estate.

He looked about and was struck by awe
And gave a name to whatever he saw.
Then in a stream he saw his reflection
And noticed that he had a reddish complexion.

From the language that he had improvised
The sound "Adam" he then verbalized.
To him "Adam" meant red,
The color he saw upon his head.

Wherever he traveled, wherever he went
When he saw God's Creation he said "excellent."
He wandered for many a week;
Then one morning he heard a shriek.

He was as frightened as was Eve,
Another human to perceive.
A sound from his throat was then unchained
Which would not ever be regained.

It was amazing; a beguiling mystery
And the beginning of history:
Once an act is dispatched and done
Its memory is stored and lingers on.

III

He remembered the shriek as did she
And HE and SHE then became WE.
Each lonely creature reached for the other
And walked hand in hand like sister and brother.

The mystery of voice was tantalizing
And they spent many days speech analyzing.
Together they attached leaning to each uttered sound:
For events mundane, for adventures profound.

Together they would taste the rain,
Watch the moon on the wane.
Together they were awed by the golden sun,
And chirped with the birds just for fun.

They climbed the branches of the linden tree
Whose heart shaped leaves were poetry.
But the simian branches, now in the dozens,
Evoked tenderness and joy in the human cousins.

They gamboled like deer from place to place
And copied the gorilla in fond embrace.
Eve saw colors in poignant hues:
Ambers, crimsons, and azure blues.

These were the colors of the fire on the hill
Which they daily watched just for the thrill.
One day they put a squash inside the heat
And found the squash meat tasty to eat.

They discovered what else can be done by the fire:
Melt things, fuse things, and make wet things drier.
Every day was another epiphany,
Revealing God's creative supremacy.

There was so much to learn of God's sacred plan
By Eve, the woman, and Adam, the man.
Adding words to their vocabularies
Blessed Creation's awesome mysteries.

How fragrant was the bed of spices. Step nearby and it entices
Each to taste the cinnamon, curry, thyme, and cloves
And to learn how to grow such treasure troves.

Their ears were filled with all kinds of sounds.
Like the crying of cats, the yelping of hounds
Whispering trees, and palm fronds clacking,
Hands clapping, wet lips smacking.

Birds chirping,
Stomachs burping,
Horses neighing,
Donkeys braying.

Lions roaring,
Water pouring,
Ruminants bleating,
Elephants eating.

Adam blew wind into the horn of a ram
Trumpeting a sound that awakened his lamb.
Eve cut thickets and twisted their vines
And decorated Eden in exquisite designs.

The Sun shone by day warming the land;
At night Moon and Stars glowed by God's command.
Day was the time to learn and see;
Night was the time for ecstasy.

They gathered old leaves into a heap
And lay upon them preparing to sleep.
Adam reached for Eve's curly hair,
Smoother than silk and twisted with flair.

His fingers lingered on her swan-like neck
And his tongue licked a speck
Of pollen from an apple tree
That had been overlooked by a honey bee.

Eve placed her hand upon Adam's head
And ran it through his hair of red.
Adam caressed Eve's little ear
And kissed her eye trickling a tear.

At long last their mouths invented the kiss
And they discovered the meaning of bliss.
The evening was cool and both trembled with chill;
They embraced one another and twisted with thrill.

They quivered.
They shivered.
Their hearts skipped a beat
And soaring in both were surges of heat.

Their love reached higher than the linden tree's crown
Whose trunk was softer than eider down.
The two warm bodies combined as one
And what was begun could not be undone

His manly stamen, now tumescent,
Planted seeds inside her unfolding crescent.
First they communed
Then they swooned.

Together they said of their moment sublime
That transcended Space and surpassed Time.
And they gave thanks to God who gave life
To Adam, the husband, and Eve, the wife.

Jasmine blossoms perfumed the air
And nightingales were heard everywhere.
The host of angels in heaven above
Sang anthems extolling connubial love.

And every woman, possesses the water,
Which nurtured Eve, God's first daughter.
And every man to this very day
Carries within him Adam's DNA.

ADAM AND EVE: YET ANOTHER VERSION

It was the dawn of history-
In ways still wrapped in mystery-
That God created man and wife,
Companions and help mates meant for life.

Each was granted a special gift
God's holy world to uplift.
Adam, the man, of earth was he;
Eve, the woman, of life was she.

Equals were they before God;
Together they strolled paths untrod.
Eden, their abode, burst with bliss,
All was by plan, nothing amiss.

Wonder shone wherever they turned;
Awe and marvel within them burned.
Lions and lambs gamboled about
Their voices echoed in Eden throughout.

Adam's voice joined theirs in a song
And birds in the trees sang along.
He returned to Eve ev'ry night
And held her closely with delight.

Passion flowed from his manly frame
And a font of love she became.
She soothed his spirit with a psalm;
His wounds she soothed with her balm.

They engraved their stories on parchment scrolls.

THE FIRST DAWN

Slowly did slats of sunshine break through the dark
And songs of morning sprung from the meadow lark.
Eve gazed at Adam; Adam gazed at Eve
And together they said, "For the blessings we receive

Thank You, Lord." And at dawn they were renewed
And from each there did exude
Ribbons of bounty from Heaven above
Sent to Earth from God with Love.

And the two found it fitting to begin each day
Thanking God in the very same way.
And this legacy they bequeathed to all:
Listen with your heart to the Lord God's
Call:

Make this world a better place
And crown it with the glory of God's Holy Grace.

ADAM'S FEAR OF THE DARK

Adam watched the white sleek frames of egrets
    Drifting in the twilight sky,
Bars of dappled crimson were turning gray.
    A fear seized Adam that he was losing his sight;
He had not known night before.
    His heart beat faster than a fly's wings; his hands were wet as rain.
In a panic he summoned The Maker.
    After having seen Your magnificent Creation,
Am I forever to be in darkness?
    Will I ever again see azure clouds? trees stretching their arms?
Birds in flight?
    Will I ever again see mountain peaks?
The turquoise blue of rolling rivers?
    Will I forever be without light? Adam asked.
Worry not, God calmed Adam, the darkness was made for sleep.
    Most living creatures sleep in the darkness then awake in the light.
It is their rhythm. Lions, sheep, elephants,
    Crows have it as do all living creatures.
This is your time, Adam, to sleep, to renew yourself.
    Yours has been a busy day naming and cataloging all of the animals.
Adam prepared piles of thatch: one for him and one for Eve.
    They laid their heads upon them.
Their eyes stared at the silver crescent glowing in the sky
    And scanned the sprays of twinkling stars dotting the dark night.
As he listened to the coo-cooing of the owl,
    And the wolves playful howl and the sonar pulses of bats on the prowl,
About to ask God why in the dark they must sleep
    Angels into their eyes slumber did sweep.

LOSS OF PARADISE

The sly serpent, it is said,
Planted an idea in Woman's head,
To eat of the fruit of the Tree
That would make her wise and make her free.
But instead of gaining wisdom
She and Adam lost their freedom
And would forever pay the price
Of their trespass in paradise:
Both saw they were without any clothes
And shame colored their faces as red as a rose.

PARADISE FORFEITED

Adam asked, "Eve where are you hiding? I'll find you."
    A tortoise lumbered toward him and he climbed on its back.
They wandered hither and yon seeking Eve.
    As the sun was setting over the sapphire sea,
The skies were turning orange and pink.
    Then a red cloud passed by and opened its windows
Raining, iridescent, beads of pearls.

Yellow finches swarmed about to catch them.
    The beads dropped to the ground and grew into tall trees
with spindly branches.
    On each branch was a savory golden fruit.
Eve! There you are! Come out of hiding. Do not pick the fruit!
    Is it sweet? Does its nectar burst in your mouth?
"Let me taste it," he said. "What ecstasy!"
    What's happening? My hands tremble. My legs are frozen.
My loins scream.

My arms are heavy with sleep. My soul is slipping away.
    I am no longer Adam. "I am Man."
Eve answered, "I lusted after the fruit but did not taste it
    Until the sly serpent cajoled me to do so."
The serpent told me that he is the deputy of the Creator.
    Whatever is in the garden is ours.
I bit the skin and sweet nectar trickled on to my tongue then down my throat.
    My breasts titillated; my eyes sparkled;
My hands trembled; my legs froze. I looked at me then looked at you
    And we were both naked. I was so ashamed.
Lightning branches scudded through the darkening skies.
    My arms are heavy with sleep and my soul is slipping away.
I am no longer Eve. I am Woman.

In the morning when we awake
    We will pluck leaves from the umbrella plant and wrap ourselves in them."
The two moved toward one another
    Their skins tingled with the touch of the other.
Each bonded to the other sensuality, joy, and shame
    Then lapsed into fitful sleep.

When the sun melted the night,
    Adam awoke. Eve was no longer next to him.
He called to her. His voice trilled like a flute echoing throughout the valley.
    "Where is your hiding place? Are you behind a rock?
Come out. Let's gambol by the stream
    Let's stand beneath the waterfall
And wash away the heat of the morning."

"My hands will comb your silken curls.
    My lips will taste them; my nose will sip your delicate fragrance.
Your gazelle pines for you.
    The zephyr rises and will cool your breasts.
Let us again drink of the sweet nectar of the peaches."

Adam was no longer in a familiar place.
    Eden was a dream that evaporated.
Eve stepped out of the woods clothed in the leaves of the umbrella plant.
    She handed Adam a leaf to cover his loins.

Hand in hand they walked away from the Valley of Yesterday.
    God's angry words etched in their brains followed them all through the day.
"You disobeyed my commandment. Enmity will cleave you from others.
    With ebbing strength you will sow your seed and reap your harvest.

With the sweat of your brows will you eat your bread.
    Your sorrows will multiply.
Never forget your disobedience and err never again.
    Teach your children to obey and their children will learn from their example.

You and your children will know no rest until, lifeless,
    You rejoin the dust of Earth

From whence you sprang. From dust you came
    And to dust will you return.
You are blessed and you are cursed.
    The bridge between us is cracked.
You and all of your descendants will spend their lives repairing it.
    I AM THE LORD!"

THE ASP'S LAMENT

The lowly asp slithered slowly down
The Tree of Life in Eden's Wood.
Swaggering through the rock-strewn path,
Adam, First Man, of flesh and mind,
Of earth and sea, of joy and tears
Was teaching beasts his moral laws
Which he never comprehended,
Or without hope of reward,
Ever practiced. Thou shalt; thou must;
Do not; must not. But he and Eve
Did God's Commandment ignore and sinned
And with cunning projected blame
On guileless me. I, first victim,
In history accuse thee Man
Of duplicity. The tale you altered
So you would look pure. You called me "snake"
In derision. What's done is done!
I forgive you. Before losing
My power of speech, to you I say,
Admit the truth 'though it may
sting.'
Could I, an asp, with a brain inferior
Persuade you, man with the brain superior
To disobey God's Commandment?
For acts of your own design be
Responsible. Amen. Amen.

LILITH, QUEEN OF THE NIGHT

Lilith, a winged demonic spirit in Semitic legends flies about at night with thousands of pernicious angels. Jewish women wore amulets to protect their families from her. One legend depicts her as Adam's first wife from whom monsters issued. She sought equality with him. Rejected, she flies off into the night speaking God's ineffable name. There is, however, only one reference to her in the Bible and that is in Isaiah 34:14. She is referred to as a spirit who lays waste the land for centuries.

Lilith, Queen of the Night, slyly slithers into the human heart
    And germinates seeds of passion
Sown by the Creator at the beginning of Time.
    In a cosmic burst she opens the gates of carnal pleasure
And steals the blues, greens, and reds
    Hiding within the black curtain,
Separating fleeing Apollo from Saturn's grasp,
    And mixes them as they coalesce into an epiphany of angles,
lines and arching curves.
    Percolating lightning, she twists tongues of orange flame and flings them at Man and his Woman
    Who helplessly writhe in pleasure
Enchanted, deceived, and destroyed.

THE FIRST FAMILY

Adam and Eve under one another's spell
Dissolved in passions neither could quell.
They coupled while watching stars at night
And coupled, too, when the sun was bright.

Then within her most secret place
A creature grew from only a trace of life.
Her monthly blood stopped its flow
And she felt a heaviness down below.

Her pelvis was strong enough to withstand strain
As well as the movements of the unborn Cain.
But many a morning she'd wake up queasy
Whatever was happening was not easy

On her digestion. She began to worry
That Adam might catch it in a hurry-
The problem that within her was brewing.
So she asked him to stop what he was doing

And pray to God for information
Or, perhaps, some confirmation
That whatever it was she was undergoing
Was within her realm of knowing.

She should, after all, understand her state
Given that she forbidden fruit once ate,
The one that on her bestowed intuition
Should have explained her indisposition

And her weight gain—but did not.
Adam prayed. God answered the fact you have sought
Is this: within Eve a creature is growing
From the ecstasy you both were knowing.

One instant when fathoming her did you together conceive
A new life: one part Adam and one part Eve.
What features that creature will possess I must confess.

I cannot predict because when sperm and ovum do their dance
What happens next is due to chance.
Eve will feel heavy, her breasts will swell,
And there are a few more things I must tell

You. Like a melon round will she be
And she'll feel a strain about each knee.
This will make her walk like a duck.
But that is truly a stroke of luck

Because it means the child inside
Is growing long as Eve is growing wide
Yet she will feel beautiful, just like a queen,
The first human mother that has ever been.

Eve sparkled with a rosy glow
As her hand guided his to show
What they both had done
One moment under a palm tree shading the sun.

There was much to do to build a nest
And furnish it with the very best.
Trees to be cut and stones to be hewn.
Together they built a safe cocoon.

Then one day Eve felt an urgent strain;
There were tears of joy mixed with stabs of pain.
Dear husband, she said, drawing near is the time
For us to witness a moment sublime.

Rotating slowly, without making a sound,
The being in her womb turned upside down.
A head first pushed its way towards the light
And was sliding from her canal with all its might.

Eve pushed and puffed in the heat of the day
And a round hairy headed inched its way
From between her legs. It's a pear with hair
Adam said of him who was to become his son and heir.

But Eve was dizzy with sweat and pain
From the arduous effort as well as the strain
Of giving birth. Her mind conjured images of the garden fruit,
The seductive serpent, the eviction, and the route

Out of Eden. But the memories were jumbled.
The images were clotted and Eve's lips mumbled
Thoughts which were spinning, spinning, spinning
In her brain like a circle without end, without beginning.

When it seemed that her energy was spent
She touched Adam's face who over her was bent.
Suddenly there was an urgent rush
And the child oozed out in a reddish gush.

Eve shouted Thank you Lord!
With a palm frond Adam sawed the cord
That connected mother with child.
He knotted the cord and smiled.

Then he stroked the child's back.
It expelled mucous that within its mouth had welled.
It breathed a hardy cry
Resounding as it spiraled toward the sky.

Amazed beyond belief,
Adam mopped the brow of Eve, his love,
With a patch of wool sent from the Lord above.
He washed the child and wrapped him in a leaf.

"It's a miracle," he said to Eve
"For us to receive
A child who is one part yours and one part mine
Sent to us by the Lord Divine."

They held each other's hands to pray
To God for the blessing they received that day.
Thank you Lord for the gift of life
That grows from the love of husband and wife.

Eve cradled the babe in her soft, warm arms
And sang to him with all of her charms,
"May peace and goodness into your being flow,"
And the voice of God whispered, "Let it be so."

THE BEGINNING OF EVIL

When the sons of the all powerful ones
Looked upon the daughters of mortals
Their hearts pounded with delight
And their knees melted from passion.
They took these daughters as their wives
And from their offspring proceeded evil.

THE BUDDING FIRST FAMILY

From the seeds of passion's flower buds of joy unfold
    And smile at the world about.
The fruit of the womb ripens exuding beauty unparalleled in the past.

GENESIS OF HATE

Evil roams the heart like asps
Lurching at the chaste
And infecting them with hate.

ENDLESS ECHOES OF MURDER

A tear dropped a million years ago from a mother's eye
    And fell into the sea of grief where mothers go to cry.
*Havah of us all, having borne two sons in woe   *Havah (Eve)
    Fed them her milky breasts from which her love did flow.

She taught them to acknowledge God who Created everything
    And from their abundant bounty a thanks offering to bring.
*Havel offered fattened sheep; *Kayin, scraps of the field.   *Havel (Abel)
    When God favored Havel's gift, a rage in Kayin reeled.   *Kayin (Cain)

Kayin grabbed a pointed rock and crushed his brother's skull.
    Then Havel slumped to the ground—bloodied, lifeless, null.
Havah's eyes filled up with tears, bitterly she cried.
    He who swam inside her womb lay lifeless by her side.

Her fingers touched the bleeding wound, then caressed the teats that fed
    The innocent shepherd, Havel, prostrate before her, dead.
Kayin reached out to touch her hand but she turned away in pain
    And staggered to be free of him who had his brother slain.

Kayin raised the rigid corpse onto his sweating back.
    And blood droplets dripped from the skull that sustained the crack.
He walked in sun, he walked in rain; no shelter did he find
    A heavy heap of Havel lay on his shoulder and on his mind.

Kayin wandered east of Eden, his sorrowing shoulders sagged
    With his rigid brother Havel, a burden to be dragged.
Kayin shrieked, "Forgive me," every night in his terror-dreams.
    But Havel made no sound at all 'though Kayin heard his screams.

Weary worn at dawn he'd 'wake and traveled by the light,
    And fought off attacking vultures until dusk met the waiting night.
The stench of Havel filled the air, no longer did Kayin eat.
    He felt his strength was ebbing and a swelling in his feet.

His back was bent and drooping low when his feet toyed with the sea
    And as he stepped into a wave Havel slipped off quietly.
Kayin was not aware that Havel dropped into the deep,
    His shoulders sensing a heavy load causing him to creep.

He crawled along the edge of Time although the light was dim
    And saw his mother Havah and toward her began to swim.
"Mama, mama, comfort me! I'm dying for what I've done."
    Kayin pleaded with Havah, losing another son.

But Havah trembled and turned away, her body in a chill.
    There was no forgiveness for a son who would his brother kill.
Kayin's keening filled her ears, Ever she wept bitter tears.

THE FINAL KISS: ADAM'S DECLINE

Eve bent over Adam and lovingly closed her own eyes, wet with grief.
    She drifted into nostalgia. How many tides, she mused,
Has the moon pulled in its journey through our lives.
    How many sunrises have there been to bring on the day;
How many sunsets, the night. Time deserts us.
    Brushing wisps of his sparse silver hair, she spoke to Adam,
His face blue with death,
    These past few months have been especially hard for you,
Your manhood was stolen; your incontinence, embarrassing;
    Your nausea, constant.
The little you ate came back up.
    Remember how tenderly I washed your face
And changed your clothes? Your cough still echoes in my ears.
    I heard each rasp. My fright returns to me.
Staring at me blankly, you seemed to be asking, "Who am I?
    Where am I? How did I get this way? What will happen next?"

The man I admired had shriveled. Your mind was confused,
    Filled with forgetting yet remembering what never happened.
You blamed God for entrapping us to sin in the garden.
    You thought that Seth murdered Abel
And that it was he who wandered East of Eden.
    When he came to visit, you called him Cain.
We both knew that meaning had drifted out of your life.
    You were drowning in a sea of anguish.
I wish I had eaten from the Tree of Life instead
    Of from the Tree of Knowledge.
Maybe you would still be with me. But once done an act
    Cannot be reversed! Can anyone alter History?
To cheer you, I told you stories about your kindness, your virility,
    Your passion. You smiled an empty smile.

How roused you were to pity when a frail horse had fallen along the way.
    How your hands lovingly caressed my face, my arms, my breasts.

I swoon thinking about how beautiful it had been to make babies together.
    I felt young again. You nodded blankly.
Did you understand the words of my heart?
    How tender you had been to Cain and later to the baby Abel.
Both drank of my milky breasts. I tingled with joy as they nursed at my teats.
    You held each babe in your arms;
In a voice like the nightingale sang hymns to God.
    How, frightened yourself, you confronted the wild cat
Poised to menace our babies.
    When they grew up you taught them so much:
How to sow, how to reap, how to build, and above all, how to pray.
    How pained you were when Cain took Abel's life away.
Can any difference between Children of God
    Be so chafing as to justify murder?
We lost a child. What did Cain gain?
    Marked by God, he wandered in fear, in guilt, and in grief.
You hurt, too, but you wanted to be with him to soften his pain.
    They were such dear children. Heartaches they gave us, though.
They were a crucible mixing jealousy, strife, and rage.
    Seth made up for the two of them.
We could count on him to make us smile.
    The jokes he would tell the tiger and the leopard.
And he made us feel proud, too. So gentle, so methodical, so wise.
    Abel never left your mind, though.
You must have been sensing your oncoming death,
    Hugging a dead donkey lying along the path and calling it Abel.
Your eyes clouded up and droplets of tears fell to the ground.
    I, too, had a foreboding,
But I did not know when would be your last breath.
    God keeps us guessing, or, perhaps, has us cling to a thin thread of hope
That we still can be of use tomorrow.
    We are to make every moment count.
    And how useful you had once been!
Your hands were not always so calloused.
    In Eden they had been as smooth as rose petals.

After we were ejected, they became rough making axes
    And calloused felling trees, stripping bark, building a home.
How arduous it was to break clods of earth,
    Muddy from the seasonal rains.
But you did all those things.
    By the sweat of your brow did you plant and reap grain.
By the sweat of your brow did we eat bread.
    Then there were sheep to shear and clothes to sew.
How cleverly you planned for the cold and the drought.
    You did all things without complaint and with no
Thought of receiving praise.
    Praise God, you would say. Thank God, you would proclaim.
It was for the family's welfare that you labored.
    That was True Love and I will cherish your memory
Until stars lose their glitter.
    Eve kissed Adam's stone, cold lips and sobbed,
"Good bye, best friend."

OUT OF EVIL COMETH GOOD-IN TIME

The penitent Cain took a wife who begat Enoch
    Whose son, Irad, cleansed his father's sin and begat Mehujael
Who cleansed his grandfather's sin and begat Methushael
    Who cleansed the world of his great grandfather's sin
And begat Lamech, the pure,
    Who begat three sons who expanded God's Creation:
Jabal, breeder of horses and cattle;
    Jubal who taught the world to play the harp and flute;
And Tubal who worked bronze and iron.
    From these three grew fundamentals of a society:
Economics, art, and science.

II

LEGENDARY HEROES

FALLIBLE PERSONS OF UNCOMMON VALOR

In ancient Greek lore, the hero, either a human elevated to the status of the Divine or a demoted divine, was revered as a demigod. Often he was perceived as a ghost to be appeased. In contrast, the hero in Biblical literature was no demigod nor someone to be feared. Noah is the exemplar of the Biblical hero. He was a man righteous in his generation but fallible. To the ancient Israelites, heroes were persons of valor. As humans they erred but as heroes they transcended the ordinary.

From the very beginning, the humans that God Created had cavorted with truancy. Adam and Eve were disobedient and Cain took his brother's life. Generations to come developed the arts and technology, but they also lived by stealth. Jealous of one another, the cattlemen tried to vanquish shepherds. Herdsmen fought with farmers. It is apparent that the series God created could destroy itself. God, it appears, became so repulsed by the human that creation was inundated by a flood. Noah, a man righteous in his generation, was spared so that a new and more moral civilization would take root. God regretted having flooded Creation and decided never to repeat that error. However, even after the flood waters subsided, the descendants of Noah could not cleanse their inclinations of evil. Noah, moreover, the righteous gentile, got drunk and had sexual relations with his daughter-in-law.

Abraham, a righteous man, honest in his commercial dealings, lied to the king about the status of his comely wife, Sarah. This same Abraham, though, tried to negotiate with God about saving lives in the wicked cities of Sodom and Gemorrah. Sarah, an otherwise pious woman, after cajoling her husband to father a son by her maid, Hagar, then evicted her. She sent her out to fend for herself in the desert. Isaac also lied to a king about his comely wife, Rebecca, who herself planned to deceive her blind husband. Jacob, that son, knowing the fraud, did not protest. Jacob, righteous in his generation, a model of hard work and enterprise, had sexual relations with his daughter-in-law. Joseph, his son, abandoned by the very brothers who would later head tribes of Israel, avenged their selling him into captivity.

Moses of the tribe of Levi was chosen by God because he, too, was righteous in his generation. He led the Israelites out of Egypt and taught them the commandments of God, guides to righteous living. His temper was violent, and he disobeyed God. He was never to see the land which God had promised to Israel. After him came Joshua. A prostitute helped Joshua trap a foe who was then murdered. After Joshua there was no central government. Instead there were people of exceptional valor whose heroic deeds saved the Children of Israel from their foes. The offspring of one prostitute became a hero. High birth did not assure righteousness; low birth did not guarantee ignominy. Jephtah, another hero, caused the death of his own daughter; Deborah was involved in murder, Samson whored after a Philistine woman, and David seduced the wife of one of his soldiers and later sent him to certain death in the battlefield. This was a time when brothers humiliated brothers who were offspring of prostitutes and even killed them. Anarchy did not reign, yet the Mosaic laws were ignored.

In summary, Biblical heroes performed righteous deeds but were not without flaws. When the situation called for heroism, though, they rose to the call. Do not we all?

NOAH'S FLOOD

When the world was still young in years
And each land was explored by pioneers,
New plants and creatures were still arising
In lovely forms, at times, surprising.

Some years the hot sun burned the land
And dried the rich soil to sparkling sand.
In other years the rains each day
Would wash the roots of crops away.

During the times with little to eat,
Life was bitter and rarely sweet.
But instead of working with one another,
People cheated and stole from each other.

They were greedy and selfish as well,
Their very own children they would sell.
This is not what God had in mind
When the humans were first designed.

Then there arose within God's plan
A humble hero, a righteous man.
This modest mortal, Noah, his name,
Sought no glory and sought no fame.

God called to Noah, "Listen with care.
A flood will come. You must prepare."
Noah felt a shiver. He was a river of chill
When called upon to serve God's Will.

God had planned to bring on a flood
And bury the sinners in heaps of mud.
At God's command, Noah built a ship
And brought the provisions for his trip.

All manner of life did he take,
From land, from sea, and from the lake.
The only mortals who would be saved
Were Noah and his kin who were not depraved.

After many days of endless rain,
A brilliant sun dried the muddied terrain.
A dove went forth, his journey brief,
And returned to Noah with an olive leaf.

This was the sign for which Noah had waited.
The waters, he knew, had now abated.
Then the ship docked and the entire crew
Cleansed the land and built homes anew.

DANCE OF THE ARBOR: THE END OF THE FLOOD

Twigs twist and boughs bend as the zephyr pirouettes
    With the rustling leaves.

God laid down seven laws to cleanse the world of evil
    And to move the tribes toward a stable world.
These are known as the Seven Noahide laws which govern
    Social behavior in a civil society. Meeting these seven
Obligations is the foundation of a moral society
    Ethics desperately needed to be rebuilt.

SEVEN NOAHIDE LAWS OF A STABLE SOCIETY

1. Establish a court system where justice will be dispensed mercifully.
2. Prohibit Blasphemy
3. Prohibit idolatry. Worship God, the Creator, only.
4. Prohibit incest among family members
5. Do not eat the raw flesh. Slaughter animals first.
6. Proscribe robbery
7. Outlaw Murder

By abiding by these rules a society will be fruitful, multiply,
    And progress.

A corollary to these rules is to show kindness to everyone
    And not be adversarial.

This will guarantee quality relationships among a society's members
    And will promote a civil civilization, much needed
After the dregs of an uncivil society lingered.

Sodom exemplified the need for these laws. The people of Sodom
    Worshipped idols, blasphemed, had no courts, murdered,
Ate raw flesh and committed adultery.

THE FATE OF SODOM

The people of Sodom, renowned for guile
Attacked every stranger in ways quite vile.
They robbed, they knifed, and set homes on fire-
And against their own kin would often conspire.

"They've scorched my land," God tearfully spoke
"And defiled what is sacred just as a joke."
God urged them to treat all creation with kindness,
But they just poked about, causing infections and blindness.

God's laws the Sodomites ignored,
No matter the mercy with which He them implored.
God judged it best Sodom to raze.
To rid the world of its evil ways.

Was such a verdict just and right?
God sent messengers to Sodom before the fall of night.
They stayed with Lot, Abraham's kin,
Who, though better than most, was not without sin.

They sought proof that Sodom should be saved.
But what they found, instead, was a community depraved.
The saddened angels found no reason to believe
That the people of Sodom deserved a reprieve.

In fact the people of Sodom set out snares
Against anyone whose ways were different from theirs.
They banged at Lot's door to kill the messengers God sent,
But Lot pushed them away to thwart their intent.

With heavy heart, God decided the fate
Of the city of evil and exporter of hate.
God thought the matter over. It was carefully reviewed.
Then advised Abraham how Sodom would be subdued.

"Abraham," reported God, "Sodom will burn.
I must be just but I must also be stern.
Let all peoples learn that God despairs
Of those who harm others whose ways differ from theirs."

Abraham knew Sodom was a blight on the land
But destruction would reduce Sodom city to sand.
Why raze a city and kill both the good and the bad
Abraham asked himself in a mood that was sad.

Humbly Abraham asked if God really would waste
Those who are guilty as well as those who are chaste?
He asked God if, perhaps, fifty righteous were found,
Would Sodom be burned right down to the ground?

God replied, "If fifty righteous were found,
Sodom city would not burn to the ground."
"were the number of righteous but forty-five,"
Abraham asked modestly, "Would they remain alive?"

God replied that if the number of righteous were but forty-five,
He would save Sodom and that city would thrive.
"But what if the number equals the fingers on each hand,"
Bargained Abraham meekly, "Would You, then, let Sodom stand?"

God Replied if the righteous of Sodom numbered but ten,
Spared would be Sodom's women and men.
But only self-righteous were found in the city,
And a stony fire consumed Sodom without any pity.

ABRAHAM, ABRAHAM

God searched the world for a righteous soul
To pattern in history the patriarch's role:
Teacher to every generation
And a model of goodness to every nation.

Such a man must obey
God's commands without delay.
To judge if Abraham was that very one,
God asked him to give up his son.

"My Isaac? my dearest one?"
"If he is gone, I'll lose Sarah's son."
Thus Abraham questioned The Voice,
But the Wind whispered, "He's My choice."

Up the mountain Abraham and Isaac trod,
According to directions received from God.
Isaac saw wood for the fire
But no lamb that offerings require.

"God will provide," Abraham told his son,
As fires for the offering had already begun.
Then Abraham bound Isaac to the alter site
And unsheathed his knife, flashing with light.

"Abraham, Abraham" was heard from above
In a sobbing Voice filled with merciful love,
"Hurt not your son; cause him no harm!"
And midair stopped Abraham's arm.

Abraham wept copious tears
On that day and for the rest of his years
And so did God whose cruel request
Was a lesson to the world, not just a test.

ISAAC AT THE MOUND

What son who had already reached the age of knowing
    Would climb the dusty, sacred mound with his father
As he sensed from the firestone and knife in his father's hand
    And the wood he carried for the fire that there was no lamb
For the sacrifice? A trusting one.

What father who waited until he was 100 years old to realize his seed
    Climbed the dusty, sacred mound with his son,
The only child of his beloved Sarah,
    And with palms wet with sweat held firmly to the Firestone
And to the unsheathed knife scintillating in the hot sun while the lad
    Carried the wood, both knowing there was no lamb for the sacrifice?
An obedient one.

What God would ask of Abraham to give up his son,
    The first Hebrew circumcised
At eight days, risking extinction of the line at the dusty, sacred mound,
    As the father seized the Firestone and the unsheathed knife
scintillating in the hot sun
    While the son carried the wood, all three knowing
There was no sacrificial lamb? A young One.

What God, wet with tears and regretting the assignment to the first patriarch,
    Caused Abrahams's hand to stop midair at the dusty sacred mound
So it touched not Isaac, the patriarch to be, on the altar of the dusty,
    Sacred mound? A contrite One.

SARAH'S DEATH

As Abraham raised his hand holding the scintillating knife,
A mob of ravens circles above awaiting Abraham to take Isaac's life.
Anticipating the kill they swooped down on the youth
And sped away to tell Sarah what they saw was the truth.

Three baby ravens remained watching from a tree
And saw the knife stop according to God's decree.
But the gang of ravens winged their way to Sarah, Abraham's wife,
With the news that Abraham had taken Isaac's life.

Sarah, distraught at the news, heard a lambkin bleating.
Isaac, she thought, and her heart stopped beating.
The ravens arrived the news to update
But Sarah had died; the news was too late.

HAGAR AND SARAH

A hoarse voice despondently wailed, "Hagar! Hagar!"
No sound was heard but for the silence of passing Time. "Hagar! Hagar!"
No sound was heard but for the peace of those in eternal rest. "Hagar! Hagar!"
No sound was heard but for the echoes of quiet despair. "Hagar! Hagar!
I have searched for you for thousands of years
In the caves of Judea; in the desert of Arabia; in the wilderness of Africa.
How well I understand your hurt, your anger, your vengeance.
History, too, has hurt me, angered me, made me vengeful.
I look in the mirror and see your woe-stricken face, ashen and punctured.
My soul anguishes because I have brought you such pain.
I was selfish to want Abraham's seed to be inside of me only
To be heir to the land. I was cruel to ask Abraham to send you and Ishmael away
To live in the sandy wilds. Let your heart hear my sorrow. I hurt you. I sinned.
I swim in a sea of contrition. History gnaws at me. I repent. Forgive me.
The mirror shows that we are twin sisters. You, too, are a princess."
The winds that tore the two souls to shreds
Encircled the deteriorating fragments
And united Hagar deaf with rage
To Sarah grieving with guilt.
Each Sister, an Ur mother,
Forgave the other
And became
One.

ISAAC'S PLACE IN HISTORY

God! I assured You of my faith and constancy at the dusty, sacred mound.
 Why is it that I, the first of Your eternal line,
Alone among the patriarchs to be monogamous,
 Alone among the patriarchs to hold fast to my given name,
Laughable as it was,
 Have so little told about me in Your Holy Writ?
Am I merely a chasm separating my father and my own seed?
 Bushes glowed with the Spirit of the Lord
Zephyrs whispered the Divine Words
 Birds grew silent; lions stifled their roars.
The universe was still; torrents of clouds had halted their rolling paths.
 With every pulse of his heart and every breath of his lungs
Isaac heard God's message, "You are
 The dawn that brings on the day light,
The dusk that brings on the darkness of night,
 The spark that ignites the fire, the idea that precedes the tool,
The nerve prod that moves the muscles.
 Not a chasm are you Isaac but the bridge across
Time connecting father Abraham and the covenant with posterity.
 Judge not the importance of souls by how much is written about them
But how their existence changed history." So said the Lord.

ABIMELECH TEACHES THE PATRIARCHS

From his palace window high above the town
Abimelech gazed at Sarah and her billowing gown.
What an alluring figure; what a comely face
What regal carriage; what style; what grace.

    He hungered for her, so comely and so fair
    To sire through her womanhood a royal heir.
    But the royal bed was filled with woe,
    His river of semen refused to flow.

An eerie dream filled his aching head;
Stricken with fear, he lay like stone in his bed
Because the Hebrew God, in ghostly disguise,
Unmasked Abraham and his lies.

        Not a sister was Sarah but his wife-
        He had practiced deceit to save his own life.

    Abraham! Abraham! Listen to this *"goy" *Gentile
    I was led astray by your cowardly ploy.
    Have the courage to speak the truth
    Less than that would be uncouth.

Many years later—Abimelech was old-
He was watching Rebecca as she strolled.
What an alluring figure; what a comely face
What a regal carriage; what style; what grace.

    How he did for her young body pine
    To renew his youth and enrich his line.
    But Isaac called her "sister", though she was his wife,
    Lying like his father to save his life.

Isaac! Isaac! This Philistine goy,
Is more honest than Abraham or his boy.
Isaac you learned not what you aught
I will teach again what your father I taught.

    Taint not the truth.
    Speak no lie but paths of virtue beautify.

A FATHER'S BLESSING

A dusky curtain dropped inside Isaac's eyes.
Only shadows of memory did he see:
The glitter on his father's knife;
The sheen on the face of Rebecca, his wife.

And his soul was filled with anguish.
His remaining days were few.
Who will care for Rebecca, so fine?
Who will continue the Abrahamic line?

There was Esau who hunts,
Liable to be mauled by his prey
And Jacob who the sheep tends
Yet on his mother depends.

But the first born Esau, by custom,
Should inherit the land.
Yet Jacob, so refined,
Was more toward home inclined.

Isaac, perplexed, spoke to God
Who illumined his soul.
God replied, "Isaac. It has already been decided.
Worry not. Rebecca will be well provided.

Since blindness descended upon him
Isaac's sense of smell had grown sharper.
One day he noticed the aroma of stew
And a gnawing hunger within him grew.

Who is preparing the mutton?
"It is I, Esau, father," a faked gruff voice said.
His hearing had also grown more acute
And the "I, Esau" he wanted to refute.

"Come closer," Isaac urged.
And the figure of Jacob drew near.
Isaac stroked the youth's new beard
To which pieces of horse hair had adhered.

"Coarse like Esau's," Isaac mused.
And then he inhaled Jacob's clothes
Which had been rolled on by the forest floor.
That forest smell he had known before.

"Esau, my son," Isaac asked
"Let me taste of your mutton stew."
Jacob gave him a spoon to lick
And Isaac found the sauce thick

Just like Esau always prepared.
Then Isaac placed his hands upon Jacob's head.
"Bless you my son, my heir."
And no longer did Isaac feel despair.

He had fulfilled his paternal duty;
He blessed his son as Abraham had blessed him.
But guilt shot through Jacob's soul
It was his brother's birthright that he stole.

He quivered, he shivered.
He stuttered, he muttered.
His own father he had deceived;
His own father his lies believed.

Energy filled his legs.
"G-G-Good bye father, I must leave."
Away he ran, his innocence slain,
And on his soul a bright red stain.

"Rebecca! Rebecca!" Isaac hoarsely cried,
"Give Jacob some gold for his journey."
He had known from the tremor in the voice
That Jacob was the son who was God's choice.

JACOB'S MYSTERIOUS DREAM

Rebecca sent Jacob to her older brother.
Tell Laban, she said, that you were sent by your mother.
He will provide you with shelter and with food
But never forget Jacob, he's wily and shrewd.

    Jacob trekked eastward in the dark of the night,
    So Esau would not chase him while he was in flight.
    He recalled what he to Isaac had said,
    Father languish not with fever there in your bed.

Eat of the savories that I, Esau, prepared,
Jacob's heart was thumping, his lie made him scared.
Blind Isaac blessed Jacob there and then,
You are God's chosen and he blessed him again.

    Jacob, now panting with a heaving chest,
    A rock for a pillow, he lay down to rest.
    Ropes of stars scintillated in the sky
    And choruses of angels sang a lullaby.

In a dream, a ladder appeared for him to climb
And he peeked into heaven for a moment sublime.
As he to the top had carefully trod
He heard from a distance the sweet voice of God.

    Bless you Jacob My nation to be
    Extending from desert to the shores of the sea.
    When Jacob awoke to continue his trail,
    He consecrated the rock and named it *Bayt Ayl. *House of God

THE CONTRACT WITH LABAN

As his legs reached Haran, some shepherds he spied.
Know ye Laban, my kinsman? We do, they replied.
Approaching with sheep is Rachel, his daughter,
She comes every day to give her sheep water.
This woman he dreamed about during his life;
This is the woman he wanted as a wife.
Laban gave Jacob shelter and food
And made him a deal that would include
Seven years of work for his daughter to wed
As well as her maid to lie in his bed.
He worked his time and was ready Rachel to wed
But was given as husband to sister, Leah, instead.
Seven more years he labored in the fields of his kin
And in the end Rachel's heart did he win.

I have another deal said Laban to Jacob one day:
You want sheep and goats, I'll tell you the way.
Tend my sheep a little while longer
And I'll give to you those animals that are the stronger.
Jacob replied, white goats and black sheep are what I will take
That's the deal with you I will make.
Such goats and sheep are hard to find
Agreed to by Laban of treacherous mind.
Then one day Jacob gathered his wives and his sons
And took Laban's animals, the very best ones.
Laban discovered that he had been cheated
And at his own game had been defeated.

P'NAY AYL: THE FACE OF GOD

A curtain of thick darkness filled the night;
Only a dim light from a distant star was in sight.
Each night at this time Jacob had been confessing
The sin he committed to receive Isaac's blessing.
Lord, he asked, "What will happen to me?
And what will happen to my progeny?
Esau, fast approaching, is consumed with rage
Like a wild animal escaped from his cage.
There will be a grave calamity.
And my clan and I will only know misery.
I deserve his hatred. I deceived and cheated.
It was base of me the way I had Esau treated.
My soul hemorrhages with every tormenting accusation
And throbs without relief of expiation."
A figure approached out of the black.
"Is that you, Esau, about to attack?"
No voice was heard but he saw sparkling eyes
Scintillating like the stars high in the skies.
The stranger grabbed hold of Jacob's thigh,
A struggle between them did intensify.
They were battling hard when dawn's threads of light
Cast shadows on the combatant's ardent fight.
"Let me go," Jacob heard the cry.
"If I don't return, I will surely die."

Jacob knew he had struggled with the Divine
Who wanders the Earth until the sun shows its shine.
I will release you when you bless me,
Came Jacob's decree.
"You shall be called 'Israel,'" the stranger replied
Because with God this night you had vied.

A sacred silence was stilling Time
And Creation resounded in a moment sublime.
Pulling Jacob's thigh the stranger evaporated
But Jacob's pain never abated.

Beginning then and beyond today,
As if God's messenger to repay,
Israel limps through history,
Struggling with God, its nightly destiny.
But when the gates of morn open wide,
Israel is blessed and purified.

JOSEPH AND HIS BROTHERS

Rachel, his lamb, bore Joseph to Jacob's delight.
Upon this son shone God's sacred light.
Because his brothers were jealous of the favored one,
They planned to rid Rachel of her only son.
Chaining him, they spat on his face
And shouted epithets, his soul to debase.
They threw him into a slimy pit, expecting he would die
When a caravan of merchants happened by.
Let's sell to the merchants our worthless half-brother,
Make a small profit and report to his mother
That we were waylaid and Joseph was killed,
Surely that would be what Yahweh had willed.
What will you give us for this runaway slave?
The brothers bartered Joseph and his life thus did save.
Despite the brothers' mean spirit and guile
Joseph prospered in the land of the Nile.

It came to pass a drought dried Jacob's land;
There was too little food for his burgeoning band.
So he sent his sons to Egypt to buy grain,
Enough to last until the next season's rain.
The brothers left with bags of gold,
They were willing to pay at least sevenfold.
Joseph was now The Food Commissioner
And to the needs of all peoples did administer.
The brothers did not recognize
Joseph, who was now tall in size.
But Joseph remembered how he had been mistreated
And how his loving parents had been cheated.
Joseph said I'll sell you grain in return for this young one,
Pointing to Benjamin, Rachel's other son.

No not that one, they protested, our father's heart will break
Pick from any of us someone to take.

We've lost one brother and Jacob, our father, nearly died.
Upon hearing his father's name Joseph cried,
"Judah, Reuben, Gad, Dan" all you others
Although we're of different mothers
We are kin, I am Joseph whom the Lord did save
From the pit you threw me to be my grave.
The brothers were filled with guilt and with shame.
We are surely to blame
For the misery we've done
To Jacob, our father, and to you Joseph, his son.
Joseph forgave his brothers the misery they had done
To Jacob, their father, and to him, Joseph, his son.
And all of the brothers wept torrents of tears
They regained one another but had lost too many years.

JACOB'S LAST WILL AND TESTAMENT

Jacob's beard was ragged; his breakfast stuck to its hairs.
His voice was thin but resolute as he called together his heirs.
They gathered around his bed to hear him speak his last
What they feared the very most was he'd review their past.
Don't strain yourself dear father they whispered to silence him
As they gazed into his eyes already growing dim.
    But Jacob trumpeted each word into each anxious ear.
    What he said was loud enough for posterity to hear.

Reuben, my eldest, proud and strong,
You dishonored my bed and did me wrong!
When I think of what you've done wrath rises inside of me
And I will never forgive you or ever set you free.
You lay with your brothers' mother for pleasure's sake,
Your destiny will be paltry because you played the rake.
    I had expected much, much more of my very first;
    Now forever, Reuben, you are damned and you are cursed.

Reuben received no pardon for his heinous deed,
Jacob-Israel expected virtue from a son who would lead.
Simeon and Levi, you are killers, acting out of your rage
Neither Reason nor Justice would either of you assuage.
You and your descendants will be scattered in a holy land
Just as summer winds scatter sifting grains of sand.
    The brothers objected to what their father decreed;
    But Jacob-Israel expected virtue from sons who would lead.

Dan! You are cunning, fit to rule
Be fair and just, act not a fool.
Gad! You're a magnet to those who waylay.
You will pursue robbers and drive them away.

Although no mantle, a fitting fate they agreed
Jacob-Israel expected virtue from sons who would lead.
    Asher! Your land will grow the food for the table of a king
    And a bountiful harvest each year to priests you will bring.

Naphtali! You are handsome and fleet as a deer
And will sire children of beauty deep not just veneer.
Happiness and beauty will make their breed;
Jacob-Israel expected virtue from sons who would lead.
    Joseph! God will bless you with all His mighty power
    And will give you water, cattle, children, grains and flowers.

Benjamin! You are like a vicious wolf, wily and strong of will.
Morning and evening you'll hunt, then devour the kill.
Jacob-Israel had no worries that these brothers would others feed;
Jacob-Israel expected virtue from sons who would lead.
    Judah! Judah! Clever as a fox; strong as a lion,
    Your name will be praised forever in Zion.

Jacob-Israel had named the son whose virtue did exceed
His very own and would the patriarch succeed.
"Children of Israel, forever . . ." sighed Jacob with his last swell of breath
But before his thought had ended, he was embraced by Death.
    To wrestle with God was to be Israel's bequeathed estate
    And wrestling with God has been his children's fate.

ISRAEL'S PLIGHT IN EGYPT

Joseph ben Jacob was soon forgotten
And the gains of his kin, though fairly gotten,
Were despised by Egypt's newest ruler
Whose reign was even crueler
Than marauding jungle cats
Ripping prey in their habitats.
As the world around contentedly slept
Israel's children lamented, and they wept.
Egyptian whips delivered their thwacks
One after another upon their backs.
The lashes making bloody prints made
God on high cringe and wince.
How Israel moaned;
How Israel groaned.
"Abandon us not in this hour of needing,"
Israel prayed as their wounds were bleeding.
Then into history, a moment dark and grave,
Arose a Moses his people to save.

MOSES BRIEFLY: IN THE BULRUSHES

Hidden among the flotsam waiting to be
   seen
Was a light unto the world.

WITH PHARAOH:
Stamm'ring on many a word he made his appeal,
   "L-Let my p-people go."

PHARAOH'S REPLY:
   "Moses, my treasured one, you and your people will stay!"

HISTORY OF THE EXODUS FROM EGYPT

In the Holy Scrolls there is engraved
    The story of a people once enslaved
By an Egyptian Pharaoh who without remorse
    Inflicted pain with a brutish force
On the innocent Children of Israel
    Who cried in misery but without avail.
He ordered their healthy as well as their lame
    To build red fires of the hottest flame
And to bake him sturdy bricks
    From a clay and crushed straw mix.
This ruthless Pharaoh then decreed
    To shape the bricks with greater speed.
And those who worked no faster
    Were whipped on the back by a cruel task master.
How they did lament and wail
    Then Pharaoh ordered each first born male
To be found and the be killed
    And the blood of babies to be spilled.
Decrees like these wore away their pride
    And a furious rage arose inside.
They prayed, pleaded, and humbly appealed
    But Pharaoh's law was not repealed.

What Pharaoh's men did instead
    Was to beat the Israelites until they bled.
He also multiplied the brick making quota,
    Their tormenting pain mattered not one iota.

Anguished cries rose throughout the nation.
    Pharaoh called it "insubordination"

And provided even less food to eat.
    "I am a god," he said with great conceit,
"Whatever I do is right and just
    And The Children of Israel must in me show trust."
He was indifferent to their lack of food
    And turned his back in a vengeful mood.
As Pharaoh continued to shout and curse,
    Living conditions grew even worse.

There had been born under Egyptian noses
    An Israelite son given the name of Moses.
Because he was drawn from Egypt's Nile
    And brought to the unhappy world a Godlike smile.
He was schooled in a princely way:
    He studied law and how to pray.
He felt the pain of each brick cutter
    But bit his tongue so as not to stutter.

In his heart, though, he truly knew
    There was something that he must do.
"Save us God!" he would pray
    Not just once but three times each day.
As Moses' prayers reached God's ears,
    The Almighty's eyes were filled with tears.
Yes God would Sigh
    And then would Cry
Wherever the just had no voice
    And easing others was the only choice.

While walking one day Moses had seen
    A bush aflame but yet stayed green.
He stopped and stared.
    Then became quite scared
When a voice austere
    Breathed, "Draw near. Draw near."
"I have a plan Israel to save;
    No people should suffer the pain of a slave.

You will know this very well,
    And Israel will for generations retell
"That from this land you will them lead."
    This is what God, The Just, decreed.
But then Moses, a person humble,
    Said, "O God, I'm afraid I'll stumble."
Then God replied, "I'll help you carry
    This heavy burden. So no longer tarry!"
Humbly did Moses beg of Pharaoh
    "Let my people go. Let my people go!"

At first the Pharaoh did agree
    And even gave his guarantee.
But on a whim he changed his mind
    And increased the work he assigned.

So Moses went to The Pharaoh, and spoke in a voice polite,
    Let my people go. Relieve their plight.
Pharaoh said looking him in the eye, "My princely son,
    I'm in a fix. I ask you who will the mortar mix?"

I have this dream to populate Pithon and Ramses,
    Two cities to scintillate with solar rays.
Moses interpreted Pharaoh's dream,
    And said "Pharaoh forget your theme.

My people came here briefly to sojourn
    Now it is time. For their return
To their God-promised land. You
    must understand."

Such words Pharaoh could not bear,
    His heart grew hard as a granite rock,
And plagues came from everywhere
    Before Moses led out his flock.
The plagues befell the Egyptians of old
    And punished them a thousand fold.

They suffered from boils and then from lice;
    Vermin devoured all of their rice.
Millions of frogs upon them did prey
    And there was darkness for one whole day.
Fire swarmed around their beaded brows
    And diseases spread to their cows.
There were locusts, rains, and rivers of mud
    And water that tasted like human blood.
One plague did all of their crops destroy
    And the last one killed each first born boy.
Slaying Egypt's first-born sons ended its tyranny
    And Moses exclaimed "We are free. We are free."
That night in the midst of a clamor,
    "We leave," he said without a stammer.

With matzah only, the unleavened bread,
    The Children of Israel from Egypt fled.
Ten drops of wine we toss and spray
    To remember Pharaoh's judgement day
For making Israel lowly slaves
    Then beating them with prickly staves.
The sharp sting of their whips
    Lives in history on our finger tips.
Through marshy highways
    Moses raced according to the plan that was traced
By God on high who was his guide
    And Who never for a moment left his side.
Pharaoh's soldiers were in hot pursuit
    And followed each step of the Mosaic route.
They met where waters were gently flowing
    And rows of reeds in mud were growing.

Lightning branches filled the air
    And thunder came from everywhere.
The sea of reeds then was parted
    And the Children of Israel to dry land darted.
As they reached the drying ground,
    The pursuing soldiers then were drowned.

In the desert Moses' kin felt free
    Just as they dreamed was their right to be.
But soon they complained to him about who led,
    "Tell us how we'll *now* be fed."
"God will provide."
    God never leaves our side.
Moses knelt down in the heat of the day.
    All of Israel heard him pray.
"Elohim, O God! I humbly entreat,
    Our people are hungry. What will they eat?"
Then from the Heavens manna fell
    This tasty food they all ate well.
But there were more complaints that made Moses despair.
    And he was also aware
That the people he'd led had become unruly.
    And one another were treating cruelly.

So God taught Moses The Holy Laws
    To stem the growth of human flaws.
These did Moses to the entire people release
    To bring them hope as well as peace.

    "I am the Lord Thy God Who led you out of Egypt land."
    Worship not an idol fraud. That is My command!
    Never profane My Sacred Name, carry it always in your breast;
    Six days every week are for work but the seventh is a day of rest.
    Children, honor your parents no matter their age.
    Never do another slay. Always curb your rage!
    Do not steal. Do not envy what your neighbors own.
    Perform good deeds with modesty; for wayward ways atone!
    Husbands and wives adore each other; love your children, too.
    Pass these rules etched in our lore to each generation anew!

There was silence; the air was still
    When Israel accepted the Lord God's will.
The earth quaked and the mountain spun
    And Israel proclaimed Adonai is One.

The laws which You gave to us today
    We accept and will obey.
It was then they understood creation;
    It was then they became to God a nation,
Transformed from a people without an aim
    To one directed by The Eternal Flame.
Each babe from every tribe and race
    Is born with the Light of Heaven's grace.
And every person with faults and flaws
    Becomes perfect by heeding God's holy laws.

Moses felt the barbs of those who railed as well as the pain
    Of those who ailed.
Still he knew he must proceed if his mission was to succeed.
    With deep conviction he said, "Have hope; our future lies ahead."
There were people who wanted very much to believe.
    But there were others who asked to leave
And return to Egypt where a bed would be a treat
    And there'd be meat for them to eat.
No matter how hard they might yearn for Egypt
    It was too late to return
Moses insisted. And the Israelites persisted.
    To realize their dream one day to be free they had to find esprit
Which in their souls they would sow and there would
    Give it time to grow.
So they struggled and they coped and they prayed and they hoped
    That soon they would enter the land
That Moses' scouts had scanned.
    It happened one day under a shining sun
That a vision occurred to everyone.
    Lightning flashed round a nearby mount.
There were thunderclaps too many to count.
    How could this mystery be explained?
Is this what God had ordained?
    They thought it must be the Lord God's wrath
But walking down the mountain path
    Was Moses aglow with rays from above carrying

With him God's rules of love
    Carved in slabs of cold, gray stone.
Hundreds of rams horns then were blown
    To announce the gift Moses was bearing.
The gift which he with the world was sharing.

In a subdued voice that trembled, Moses proclaimed to all assembled:
    Man, wife, and child of every station in every place
And every generation.
    "These laws I today unveil will forever prevail
To guide humanity in its passage through life
    In seeking joy and in avoiding strife."
Every soul was electrified and awed by this bequest
    From their loving God.
Israel accepted what God had gifted, their sagging spirits
    Becoming uplifted.
But what they discovered on that very day is that freedom
    Comes to those who stay
The course. In each loving heart beats a promised land
    Whether one climbs a mountain rock or treks on desert sand.
Life is a journey beyond the lowly to discover within us what is holy.
    We are pious pilgrims all ready to answer God's tacit call.

MIRIAM'S DANCE

The curtain of heaven wrapped around the sun in a golden mystery.
Another day its course had run and trickled into history.
Lying in a watery grave was Egyptian warrior with horse
Sentenced there by Almighty God with sadness and remorse.

Miriam watched the rolling seas, the moon beamed upon her face.
With outstretched arms she beckoned the Light of Heaven's Grace.
Her soul gleamed with the flame of God, a flute-like voice left her lip
Giving thanks for victory and for breaking the Egyptian whips.

Her voice was reaching distant stars when night breezes gave its call,
Head held high she stepped in dance, her shadow growing tall.
Then out of every tent there danced maidens on to the sand
To join Miriam beneath the moon in a song sublime and grand.

They spread their arms towards heaven as Miriam before had done
Then circled the mystic prophet and sang together as one,
"Thank You Lord, O mighty God, Who our enemy defeated."
And silhouetted against the moonlit sky to a timbrel beat they retreated.

MOSES' SONG

By day they sweltered in the desert sun; by night they shivered
    In the chill desert air. The relentless winds parched their throats;
Swarms of gnats bit their faces.
    Their starving young stifled their cries; the stoic elderly
Succumbed to the ordeal. The refugees from Egypt
    Wandered into the plague of the wilderness.
Having punished the Egyptians, God was careening
    The Israelites to their doom.
Moses, the nomads complained, our garments are tattered!
    Our dreams are shattered.
Our stomachs have cramps; our kidneys burst.
    Our mouths parched with thirst.
Did we need to roam this desert to die?
    Weren't there enough graves in Egypt?
Moses checked his anger, he held back his tears.
    The burden of leadership was too heavy.
He was caught between a struggling
    God and a hurting people.
God, he humbly whispered, these are hard times.
    There's no food or water.
The children of Israel, Your people, judge me incompetent.
    Lord what can I do? They complain and fret.
Yet aren't their grievances warranted?
    If the people You chose accepted Your covenant,
Why do they now suffer so?
    Do you want them to know that wandering
And suffering is to be their eternal destiny?
    Zebulon fights with Judah and the families
Of Judah quarrel amongst themselves.
    Husbands slap their wives; mothers spank their children;

And children hit each other.
    They are disappointed, distraught, and hot.
God replied, I, too, hear their murmurings.
    Who can anticipate every difficulty? Life is suffering.
They suffer and so do I.
    But there are always solutions, Moses. Tap that rock.
Moses whacked it with a great fury. Cool, sweet waters gushed out.
    The Children of Israel slaked their thirst and watered their cattle.
Then a flock of quail appeared on the desert floor.
    The Children of Israel saw the ruffled breasted birds.
Then the quail whistled, inviting the complaining band to join their feast.
    We are in the midst of a delusion or it is a miracle.
Two birds ambled toward Moses. They did not protest
    When Moses raised them high and said, Praise be to God.
A desperate mother grabbed the birds and stuck her face
    Into their soft feathers. Praise be to God, she cried.
The wanderers rushed the willing birds.
    Grabbing them, they sang Praise be to God.
They cooked the birds and ate heartily. When they finished eating
    Some said the birds were here by happenstance.
What will we eat tomorrow? And the next day?
    And the days after that one? Moses watched the sun
Set in a blaze of color and knew God's power.
    The Children of Israel saw the glory of God in the rainbowed cloud.
God, Oh God. Do not abandon us. Watch over us and grant us sustenance.
    The next morning the fading fog revealed scale-like matter
On the ground. Manna? What is this?
    The fascinated but frightened people asked.
Is it poison? Is this how our beloved leader wants to kill us?
    Again they murmured. Is this one of his magic tricks
Or is it a mirage brought on by our fever?
    A curious child scooped it up and licked it.
His parents, worrying that their child would die, ululated in grief.
    Scooping another batch the child beckoned to his parents to join him.
It's like honey he sang. The onlookers ate and called it a miracle.
    They wandered, knowing what they had lacked,
Treasured what they now had. Then they understood God
    And smiled but God understood Israel and wept.

THE AMALEKITES: THE PERENNIAL FOES

The midnight watchman fell asleep
    And did not hear the Amalekites creep.
Along the desert floor to gather where the quail stopped days before.
    They came by the tens; they came by the hundreds,
Hiding beneath their kaffiya draped heads.
    And blended in with the wavy dunes.
By dawn there was a thousand platoons.

The leader whistled; the soldiers ululated
    And rushed the Hebrew tents unabated.
At the dawning morning light,
    They slashed and burned everything in sight.
The stench of burning flesh filled the air HELP US,
    HELP US was heard in prayer.
In minutes infants, mothers, and aged were dead
    As Hebrew soldiers to their weapons sped.

Swords clashed, rocks were thrown,
    And Israel's losses had already grown.
Rest my arms upon these boulders bid Moses,
    Israel's fate upon his shoulders.
Why do You God test us so?
    Angrily Moses demanded to know.
Whenever his faith was flagging,
    Israel's fortunes were also lagging.

But when he realized men, not God, wage war
    His faith in God began to soar.
Then in a frenzy Israel defeated their foe
    And buried them in row after row.

The souls of Amalek, though, did not die,
    But tomorrow's wicked did brutify
And prey upon Israel in the dead of night,
    Ever killing with great delight.

NOT A CURSE BUT A BLESSING

Into Balak's heart hot desert winds seared a fear
    That the émigrés from Egypt, an enchanted people,
Would spread plagues of blood, boils, frogs, and darkness-
    Not to mention the killing of first born sons-
And would overtake his kingdom, destroying his gods,
    Those exquisite creatures lovingly formed out of clay
That brought fertility to his people, fecundity to his land,
    Seasons to years, and victories in war.
The fear spindled into anger and rasps of rage
    As when the heavens exploded with booming thunder.
A call went forth to Balaam, a prophet, an enchanter,
    A holy man who through his curse
Would cast a spell on the people of Israel whose fringéd shawls
    Danced in the breezes.
Fresh from a rebel from his jackass whom he abused
    And from the True God whom he revered, Balaam,
Handsomely paid for his efforts, opened his mouth.
    Clutching his cloak, Balak waited anxiously
To hear Balaam's prophesy.
    The voice was the voice of Balaam, filled with rapture,
But the words were of the True God.
    The winds carried the prophesy to the four corners of the world.
"How goodly are your tents, you children of Jacob;
    How magnificent are God's Temples.
You will be blessed with fertile valleys,
    You will be exalted among the nations.
Those who bless you will themselves be blessed;
    Those who curse you will themselves be cursed."
Upon hearing these words Balak prostrated himself and died.

NOT AS GRASSHOPPERS BUT AS HEROES

Twelve spies had gone to Canaan, one from every tribe had Moses sent,
    And returned months later, reporting how their time was spent.
Caleb said the land that God had promised to our ancestors one
    And all was filled with milk and honey
And with nuts and fruits that would enthrall.

Joshua agreed with Caleb, his words tingled in the air:
    The land had riches many for each of our tribes to share
Not so, scowled the others. There was nothing inviting about the land
    Because it was a place where giants slept
On rocks and washed in sand.

What we saw would terrify those in whom fear dwells not at all.
    To them, and us, we were like grasshoppers
Whom the giants tried to maul.
    But we managed to fly away, we barely got back unhurt,
Go not to Canaan and harm you will avert.

The Children of Israel trembled; they cursed Moses in their rage.
    Did you lead us put of Egypt giants in war to engage?
Then a voice came from the winds it spoke with words quite clear
    If you think of yourself as mere grasshoppers your name
You alone will smear.

You Children of Israel put aside your fears
    Your offspring will enter Canaan amidst trumpet calls and cheers.
And so it came to pass the children born in the desert felled the
    Canaanite foe and entered into the Holy Land
Where like giants they brought sorrow and woe.

JOSHUA

Moses was soaring toward his reward and glory,
    When God beckoned to Joshua to preserve the story
Of The Holy Writ and to transmit it
    To generations to come with an accelerated momentum.
"Dear God, not me!" Joshua said, his face beet red.
    "You want to give me the job to lead
The children of that unruly mob
    Who sinned at the sight of the molten calf.
And You want me to lead them on Your behalf?
    For me that's no task; from me it's too much to ask."
"Joshua, Joshua, patient and wise, you can the motley tribes civilize.
    Be their leader; I'll be your guide. You will never be alone;
I'll be by your side.
    I call upon you to lead My people to the Holy Land
And My mercy and justice to teach and expand."
    Reluctantly, Joshua agreed. When God calls you to lead,
You must accede!
    Together they studied The Sacred Law reverencing each other
With profound awe.
    God learned that the One who is sage must learn to control
Outbursts of rage.
    What Joshua learned that God's Law transcribed must in every heart
Become inscribed. This he taught to his nation for them
    To teach to each new generation:
From all false gods sinful ways must sever and spread
    Their sacred heritage for all and forever.

THE RED THREAD

Joshua sent two spies to reconnoiter The Land and report to him what
    They saw first-hand. Into the city of Jericho they stealthily crept
As the unsuspecting citizens languidly slept.
    But they had not gone unseen crawling about in a rugged ravine.
Soldiers chased them in quick pursuit. But the spies, chosen
    Because they were astute, ran from the soldiers into the house
Of Rahab, the whore, who hid them in flax stalks on the attic floor.
    When the soldiers came to Rahab's door, they shouted,
"Surrender the strangers, sodden whore."
    She said she knew nothing of spies; she only knew games
Where she was the prize.
    The soldiers snickered and heartily laughed, Rahab was known
Well for her exotic craft. She invited the soldiers to examine her grain
    Sacks and the attic floor where she kept stalks of flax.
Would she mention such places if the spies were there?
    They decided "no" and were caught in her snare.
The soldiers departed, chagrin in their eyes, and sang,
    "She plays games where she is the prize."
She knew many soldiers and their crafty ways.
    They would give up the search after a day or two,
Then change direction and begin their search anew.
    Rahab asked the spies to spare her kin an ill fate
When Joshua's army would raze Jericho's gate.
    On the window of your house hang a thread of red,
The spies told Rahab as they fled.
    The spies were saved thanks to Rahab's advice and reported
To Joshua their findings precise.
    Joshua prepared his band to leave, Jericho was the goal
They were to achieve.
    The priests placed their toes into the Jordan River;

And the waters stopped, not even a quiver.
    Then they their rams' horns mightily blew
And crossed the dry riverbed without much ado.

For seven days they marched around until the walls of the city
    Crumbled to the ground. Jericho surrendered to the
Soldiers of the Lord and Joshua stretched out his shining sword.
    This land we consecrate in God's Holy Name;
This land we consecrate in God's Holy Name;
    To this Land of Canaan do we lay claim.
The soldiers of Israel saw the red thread
    And rescued Rahab who had the spies sheltered and fed.
In Israel she lives to this very day as a spirit of virtue
    Who had once been a stray.

SISERA AND YA-EL

Sisera of Canaan addressed all his men: Israel had abandoned
    Yahweh again.
Now is the time to strike at its heart—they swagger about thinking
    No one else is smart. The captain heard cheers rise from each side,
thousands of men were bloated with pride. Nine hundred chariots
    Were ready to fight and utterly destroy every Israelite.
When we win, and for sure we will, an Israelite damsel for you each,
    Maybe even two, that's how the booty will be divided-
In Sisera's mind the war was already decided.
    The men ululated as they rode, thoughts of deeds heinous overflowed.
But the Lord's heart with anger was filled and Israelite soldiers
    The Canaanites killed. But Sisera escaped and ran into a tent
Begged Ya-el for water, his energy spent.
    She fed him milk and curds of cheese, a sign of friendship
Which set him at ease.
    But as he lay asleep in his bed Ya-el hammered a peg into his head.
His death was instant, there was only a sigh,
    The way every soldier hopes to die.
His form had been perfect a moment before; now it was lifeless,
    Just debris of a war. What wisdom he learned drawing his last breath,
How fragile is life, how final is death. Now in the hereafter where
    Soldiers tread Sisera staggers with a peg in his head.
"Ya-el killed me," he moans in disbelief, But Ya-el answers not,
    Ashamed in her grief. And his mother awaits him, so late to return,
And worries that bad tidings is what she will learn.
    Her maids gather round her to say Sisera's dead, ignominiously
killed with a peg in his head.
    She rent her robe and loudly keened, my son is no more,
His memory's demeaned. What good is a son when he is dead
    And six feet of earth over him is spread?

YOUR GOD IS MY GOD*

*Based on inscriptions at Ugarit

And we, the Children of Israel, say unto you, Children of Canaan,
    That your god, the aged sovereign of the pantheon, El: Merciful,

Benevolent, Creator, Kadosh, the holy one, will be our God.

GIDEON, THE DELIVERER

Israel whored after alien gods once more and a fiery wrath
    From The Eternal did pour:
How can I wipe away the sinful stains of those whose ancestors
    I freed from chains?
To stop the spread of moral blights, The Eternal submitted them
    To the Amalekites,
A marauding tribe who embittered their lives and sliced off
    Their heads with hunting knives.
As if the cruelty of Amalek had not been enough The Eternal
    Offered them to Midian, a tribe just as rough.
Year after year the formidable foes were wrecking the crops
    Israelites would sow.
People starved and babies died; and the merciful
    God and the angels sighed.
"Hear, O Israel,"
    The Eternal summoned them all. But they heard not a word;
No one answered God's call.
    Yet God heard their moans in caves where they slept; and Angels
Watched over as The Eternal had wept.
    They begged "God of compassion save the innocent;
Wait not for the parents to return and repent."
    God considered their request. When angels heard,
"Find Me a man of virtue!" they began their quest,
    Searching far and wide throughout the land,
They found a humble man, one who could take command.
    Gideon! Gideon! He is the man to lead Israel's people
And enact God's plan
    The angels looked into Gideon's face and he saw in them God's
Holy Grace. "Gideon! The Lord is with thee, You have been
    Chosen to set Israel free."

Hearing God's name, Gideon's young heart fluttered
   "B-Blessed is His Holy N-Name!" his lips stuttered.

Gideon was no coward nor was he a knave,
   An assignment from the Lord required someone brave.
Arguing with the angels, he asked,
   "Tell me why we are suffering so under God's watchful eye.
Did not Your Lord Almighty set Is-ra-el free
   From Egypt's cruel hand and made a covenant to give us this land?"
The Lord answered not his question but said,
   "There is nothing to fear; there is nothing to dread."
By your side I'll be and victory is yours and you'll put an end
   To murderous wars. Gideon, not easily convinced, tried out this test
He placed fleece on the ground that God had blessed.
   In the morning on that very special spot the fleece
Was wet but the ground was not.
   Dare Gideon fated to lead Israel's men test the Lord once again?
He petitioned God to reverse what He had done
   And in the morning when arose a fiery sun
Shining through a rich azure sky the ground was with dew
   But the fleece was dry. Gideon proclaimed, "You are, indeed, God.
The True." But he needed brave men the enemy subdue.
   Ten thousand volunteered to drive out the foe,
A force of that size could deliver much woe
   But could also suffer many losses.
His strategy called for a clever process: One with an element
   Of great surprise to be done by a force of a smaller size.
At the river's edge he ordered his men to drink. Many,
   Though, did not think
What was the purpose of this test and noisily drank
   Thinking this was a jest.
Those who quietly like a dog had lapped were the ones for his force
   That Gideon tapped.
Three hundred men formed companies three.
   When Gideon gave the signal they went on a spree.
Each man broke a pitcher then raised a flare and blasted rams' horns
   With a trumpeting blare.

Down the mountain at night they sped and awoke the enemy asleep in bed.
    Chaos broke out and the foe ran east and west, some ran in circles,
Alarmed and distressed.
    Whenever they ran Israel's men pursued slaying thousands until
Midian was subdued. But the tribe of Ephraim chastised Gideon,
    The hero who had just vanquished Midian.
"Cousin, we were there to help. Why didn't you ask?
    What's the matter, weren't we up to the task?"
Gideon replied it was God's proposition to send you
    On a more important mission:
To capture the kings of Midian and them to behead.
    Ephraim's pride was restored; their anger had fled.
Massaging their pride, Gideon asked how can my grapes
    Compare with Ephraim's vineyards, rarest of rare?
After his victories Gideon returned to his vines
    And consecrated to God a thanksgiving shrine.
The people sought a man who could lead, a man of great character,
    Of exceptional breed. Gideon was offered a regent's ring but
Refusing he said only God could be king.
    Grudges grew in jealous minds and flour of hate its grain mill grinds.

Among Israel there was a growing unrest;
    Among the very people who God had blessed.
Gideon, now aged, could no longer quell a moody spirit
    Which in Israel did dwell. Despaired and defeated Gideon then died.
What he united had become untied.
    In time, Israel's ways again became flawed forgotten were Moses,
Gideon and God. Perplexed angels rent their garments in grief
    As they watched war rob lives like a gluttonous thief.
How vexed became the heart of the Lord; when He saw
    His children worship the edge of the sword.

JEPHTHA, THE DELIVERER

Son of a whore, son of a whore, leave this house forevermore!
    So spoke to him Jephthah's brothers, offspring
Of different mothers.
    Through forest a field did Jephtha roam to build for himself
A hearth and a home.
    Relentless had been their searing refrain
Splattering hurts throughout his brain.
    Son of a whore, son of a whore, leave this house forevermore!
His mirror showed him a miserable clod until
    He turned for help to God.
Then within him rose a valor supreme that restored
    And rebuilt his self-esteem.
Each day he worked his grove and his vine
    And offered thanks to God, The Divine.
In time he wed and a daughter was born whom with shimmering
    Gems he did adorn. Then the soldiers of Amazon
Once again attacked and Israel's defense again had been cracked.
    The Elders of Gilead sought Jephtha out.
They had no doubt He could lead its warriors and in battle would succeed.
    Didn't you call me son of a whore and did you not my spirit gore?
Forgive us our cupidity, they replied. It was stupidity.
    Now our children have died by Ammon's ruthless bands
They will be mush in your able hands. Saddened
    By the fate of his kin Jephtha took command determined to win.
He tried to negotiate with Ammon's king, a peaceful settlement
    For all to bring. But the king refused to a peace to agree and
Jephtha and his men went of a spree
    And soundly defeated Ammon, the foe.
But Jephtha, an offering to God did owe.
    Who should it be but his own little girl, who greeted her father

With a swirl and a twirl.
    Isaiah why weren't you born centuries before to make a change
In Israel's lore? Burning flesh is not how we thank the Lord
    Nor do we give thanks by brandishing a sword.

A pure heart doing good is how God is praised.
    Jephtha knew this not and sacrificed the daughter he raised.
As they had done to Gideon before the men of Ephraim,
    Like lions did roar,
Why weren't we asked to join in the fight, do you think that
    We are afflicted by fright? But Jephtha had asked them
To offer their aid.
    Not e'en on the day that in your grave you are laid
Had been their surly reply as they spat in Jephtha's pleading eye.
    Jephtha reminded them of what they had said
And then attacked them and killed them dead,
    Leaving trails of blood on Israel's past,
Not for the first time nor for the last.

SAMSON, THE DELIVERER

Sadness fell like Winter rain upon the house where joy was slain
    By a silent killer who nightly crept into the bed where Manoah slept
With his wife of many years, who among Danite women had
    No peers in piety or in devotion to God. Yet she felt it very odd,
And could not be reconciled, though beseeching God, she had no child.
    The silent killer lurking in the night, with its insatiable appetite
For smiting gametes at their site,
    Had not quenched the fire of passion's flame, although
That had been his deliberate aim. The childless couple
    Were inspired to learn what it was that God required
For sperm and ovum to meet by chance
    And within the Danite's gates to do their dance.

Lost in reverie on one Sabbath day, as she 'neath a fig tree sat to pray,
    A stranger approached as in a dream.
His face was radiant and all abeam
    With a divine glow. A mother you will be within a year, said he.
Eat pure food only and drink no wine your child will be
    Consecrated to God Divine. But you must take special care
Never to cut his golden hair.
    He will be steadfast as the sun that shines
And he will vanquish the Philistines.
    The neighboring Philistines were a mighty foe,
Schooled in war they inflicted much woe
    Upon the men and women of Israel and in many a battle did prevail.
The woman did as the stranger said and made a child
    With the man she wed.
The child was fleet and canny and strong but decided himself what
    Was right and wrong.
He was stiff-necked with a willful streak whom women
    For pleasure was wont to seek.

The women he sought were not of his kind but enchanting Philistines
    With spells that bind.

To his father he spoke man to man and laid before him his marriage plan:
    I have found a woman of comely hue, her smile beckons
And she is soft as a ewe, Her hair is curly like ocean swells,
    And about her neck are perfumed smells.
Her body is lithe like a swan in flight and her eyes
    My eyes with yearning ignite.
When I gaze upon her flawless face, my knees buckle
    And my heart does race.
Samson felt faint from professing his love, the woman he cherished:
    His darling, his dove. Father! Go to her father to ask for her hand!
But Manoah refused Samson's demand.
    He replied, find a woman from your very own kin!
In rage Samson smashed jugs that whole had been.
    He returned to Philista to marry his love but a turn of fate
gave him a shove.
    The father of his bride to be had given her to another secretly.
Samson had trusted this man who winked with a smile behind
    Which he'd hidden his wile and his guile.
Samson's temper flared and he killed the men he saw,
    Yielding to passion, his villainous flaw.
Filling the field was corpse after corpse; filling his heart
    Was a flood of remorse.

Lord why must we our neighbors be killing?
    Lord why must they our blood be spilling?
If the game of life is "we must kill first" then civilization
    Will be doubly cursed.
Samson was brooding for many a day; then Delilah winked at him
    As she passed his way. Once again his heart was racing
And he longed for the woman that he was facing.
    She rekindled the flame that had gone out in his heart;
She excelled in love's secrets and practiced its art.
    Samson was amazed at the heights at which he rose to
And thought he found love, honest and true.
    But as she her fantasies did intricately weave she devised a plan

Samson to deceive. Tell me Samson, she whispered in his ear;
    Tell me Samson, tell me my dear,
What makes you so physically strong?
    My hair must not be cut; it must grow long.
That's what makes me the very best. He, with arrogance, to her confessed.
    He disclosed his secret at a moment weak-
When she kissed his lips and caressed his cheek.
    She cut his curls one night while he slept;
Then Philistine warriors about him swept.
    With a hot poker they burned out his eyes and black to him
Became the blue of the skies. To celebrate, a banquet was made
    In Dagon's Temple they built a stockade
And to its pillars Samson's hands were bound tight;
    No one could save him from his degrading plight.
Then with ebbing strength he pushed the pillars away
    And the Temple of Dagon began to sway.
Ceiling and walls came down with a crash.
    There was a fire; left only was ash.

The dying Samson spoke directly to God, why did You Choose me,
    A bungling clod
Afflicted with strength, lust, and rage, to end my days
    Like a bird in a cage?
Blindly I stumbled into Cupid's lair where my soul became shredded
    And now is threadbare.
God Looked down at the temple that had been laid waste where evil
    men Perished as well as the chaste.
"This was not meant to be the way you would die; yet great heroes act
    Bravely without asking why."

WHAT'S-HER-NAME, THE LEVITE'S CONCUBINE

Based of Judges Chapter 19

WHAT'S-HER-NAME, the Levite's concubine,
    Ran away to her father's house in Bethlehem
Where she wandered in craggy hills among the bleating sheep
    In utter empathy with them: face to face,
Breasts to breasts, womb to womb.
    Blithely bounding before the sacrifice, how little they knew
The fate awaiting them.
    She lifted a skipping lambkin, and cradled it in her arms,
Gently caressing its oily coat beneath the azure skies,
    As she was once loved and caressed,
When what's-his-name, the Levite from Ephraim,
    Who had pursued her and wooed her, now subdued her.
He, her man, was bringing his skipping ewe back home
    And she held the lambkin in her arms as a mother
Does her beloved child.
    Together they hiked the sun baked trails to the land of Ephraim,
A smile shone on what's-his-name's lips
    And leaden resignation lay on WHAT'S-HER-NAME's heart
And contentment filled the lambkin.
    Travel weary, they knocked at the door of an old man
At Gibeah in the land of Benjamin, hoping for kindness.
    The old man invited them in. As hospitality to strangers required,
He gave them food and drink, washed their feet, and fed their donkeys.
    Then there came a banging on the door. The town flotsam shouted,
"Send out the man, the Levite, so that we may empty our passion
    Inside of him." Incensed, the old man refused.
Ye men of broken commandments, he bellowed,
    This is no way to treat a son of Israel, a stranger, a guest,

A direct descendant of Moses himself.
    The base scoundrels, heady with desire
And energized by the shouting of their increasing numbers to do treachery,
    Demanded the Levite for their pleasure.

The frightened husband flung What's-her-name to the crowing crowd.
    She felt their claws ripping her robe and their paws tearing her thighs.
One after another they defiled her; one after another they tortured her;
    One after another they spat and cursed her.
WHAT'S-HER-NAME did not plead for mercy but begged for Death.
    Anger, compassion, fear, impotence collided like storm-filled clouds,
Lightning scudded through the labyrinth of the Levite's mind.
    "Yahweh! Stop these roguish Benjaminite whoresons!
And I will offer WHAT'S-HER-NAME's beloved lambkin
    As a sacrifice to You."
With each thud, each scream, each sob rising from What's-her-name's body,
    What's-his-name, the Levite from Ephraim,
Thumped his chest in rhythm with his pulsing heart.
    He, too, screamed and sobbed. He, too, felt pain.
But how could he know her pain?
    WHAT'S-HER-NAME, the Levite's concubine,
Shivered until dawn when Death wrapped itself around her
    Like a warm, safe blanket. Gleaning the last wisps of life
Scattered about her body,
    She crept toward the door and weakly knocked on it.
When the door was opened, she bleated, "baa!"
    And fell into the loving arms of God's cherubs
Who winged their way to an endless forever.
    The distraught Levite held her body, sliced it
And diced it into twelve parts, one for each tribal elder.
    To assuage his guilt, he sacrificed WHAT'S-HER-NAME'S
Lambkin to Yahweh.
    An estuary of history flows with blood that reddens
The shores of innocence to this day.
    And from the far reaches of Eternity can be heard
The sweet duet, "Baa!"

ELI'S CONFESSION

Eli's voice, gnarled with age, twisted his name from his lethargic tongue,
    "Sa-mu-el! . . . Sa-mu-el!" and Samuel came following
The voice twisting and tumbling
    Against the concrete walls in the silent night desperately
Trying to stay aloft.
    The lone lamp coaxed shadows of Eli's disfigured body onto the ceiling.
A swirl of moths hoarded the meager light. Samuel softly spoke
    To the silhouette rather than look at Death
Whose stench was spiraling in his nostrils.
    "Grasp my fingers," the ancient croaked.
"When I am gathered to our fathers make a sin offering for me:
    A bullock without blemish
Because I had not been without blemish."
    Samuel writhed in his chair.
Who was he a mere acolyte to minister to the master?
    Eli's tears were staining Samuel's fringéd shawl.
"I lived my life off the sins of others, like a leech.
    I wanted so to be holy but the smoke
Of the olive oil in the lamp is more pure.
    I hid my sins from everyone but the Lord.
Before you were born I accused your mother of being a drunkard.
    Not just accused her but chastised her
With all of the anger my heart could pour out.
    Would I have been as severe to a man?
But she was a woman and looked drunk to me.
    An uncurbed rage rushed from my lips like a waterfall.
But I had misjudged her. Little did I know that Penina,
    Your father's other wife, badgered her,
Taunted her. Called her names: cow, pig, slop overflow.
    Your dear pious mother, Israel's Hanna,

Rocked, muttered, and fought the pain of the snake
    Sucking the marrow of her soul and injecting it with disdain.
I judged her on what seemed to be rather than what truly was.
    And this coward whose gaze you now avert
Did not admit his error, too filled was he with false priestly pride.
    Our people expected me to be without blemish.
Still The Almighty rewards the virtuous
    You, Samuel, paradigm of righteousness, carry God's name.
Never did you perform service for personal gain.
    Never did you oppress the destitute.
Never did you set before God's holy alter
    A swirling, drunken prostitute. But my sons did.
Coward that I am, I did not repudiate them.
    Against my wishes they carried the holy ark into battle
And I did not stop them.
    The Philistines slew them then scattered their blood on the ark.
My own sons set a bad example for Israel;
    Priests should be held to higher standards.
You, Samuel, are what is best of the tribe of Aaron.
    Now I have confessed all; May God grant me amnesty.
Eli's body twitched convulsively as the Celestial Messenger clasped
    Eli's knobby fingers. His time had come.
The dimming vision in his eyes surrendered,
    The sagging sounds swimming in his ears
Were released to roam at random,
    The wobbly words languishing on his tongue were muted.
Hand in hand they strolled toward eternity.
    Samuel prepared the sin offering.
A flame consumed the unblemished bullock
    Then curled back toward heaven
Following the path Eli trod to meet the waiting God.
    Answering to the higher law of decency
Samuel cleaned the detritus of life expelled by the dying stomach,
    Washed the corpse, dressed him in a shroud, and then buried him.
Praising the name of God, Samuel purified himself
    And was holy in the sight of God and Israel.

THE PHILISTINES PANIC

Again, the people of Israel were enticed by false gods.
    Samuel called them together and said, "Cleanse your
souls. Worship sincerely the One True God, Creator of the universe."
    Humbly apologizing to God, they consecrated themselves
To the One True God
    With all their hearts, with all their souls, and with all their minds.
But at that sacred moment Philistine kings mounted an attack upon them.
    "Samuel, Samuel," they pleaded.
"Pray for us or the seed of Israel will wither."
    As they fasted to cleanse their hearts of their sins
The heavens shook with crashing blasts of thunder.
    Mountains rocked; waters rose; the skies became black as pitch.
Panic broke out in the Philistine camp.
    Many soldiers ran away,
But others, awed by the God of Israel, prostrated themselves
    Before Samuel, the High Priest,
And dedicated themselves to serve the One True God.

RUTH AND NAOMI

In her own eyes Naomi was bitter not sweet, what travail in her life did she not meet? She lived in Moab, strangers to her, where slurs toward her people were often astir. Her husband was dead; two young sons were dying. In her wrath her wits went flying and she disowned God Who had created a world slipshod. Thinking these thoughts made her feel shame. Why must God be the One given blame? Then disease devoured the bodies of her boys like a raging fire flares and then destroys.

Once again was she wed to her pain and a loss of hope inflamed her brain. A life of loneliness Naomi was to face when Ruth gave her a compassionate embrace. "Go home to your own," Naomi insisted. But her daughter-in-law had the entreaty resisted. "Wherever you go, there I shall follow. Where you will build your nest, there, too, shall I rest. The God Who is thine, will also be mine. And where you will die, there, too, will I." Hand in hand walked the sisters in grief, their love for the other gave each relief.

Arriving in Judah, both women were greeted, warmly welcomed as queens are feted. This was home, their hearts told them so, and never again from this land would they go. Ruth tended to Naomi's every need and looked for work with utmost speed. In Boaz's field did she barely glean when one day she was by Boaz seen. His eyes were moist; his heart did melt. Never before had he such passion felt.

Ruth found him kind; someone to admire who rekindled her heart with love's tender fire. Then one night while the world was asleep Ruth into his tent did quietly creep. In a moment sweetly sublime into Boaz's bed did the widow Ruth climb. There she lay by his side her love for him she could not hide. During the night he awoke to find Ruth, his kin, for whom he had pined. Gently he covered her so she would be warm and quelled the torment which within him did storm. In the morning when they awoke looking at Boaz, Ruth then spoke, "Take me dear Boaz as your loving bride." "Forever and ever," Boaz replied.

SAUL BECOMES KING

Samuel wandered from village to village bringing with him
    The word of God.
Towns once prosperous had been pillaged by the marauding Philistines.
    Many sheep and milch cows were slaughtered for sport.
Fields of grain had been torched for amusement.
    Too often did a family mourn an innocent child slain like game.
Butchery was rampant throughout the land.
    Corpses and carcasses covered the landscape;
The stench of refuse and decay filled the air.
    Samuel's mission was to offer comfort
To the bereaved and mercy to anguished souls to make
    Thanksgiving offerings.
But what was there to be thankful for? Grain had been burned;
    Cattle lay dead;
Houses keened in morning. Where was God?

The Children of Israel were unsettled.
    From Dan in the north to Beersheba in the south
They struggled with one another: Ephraim wanted to lord it over Judah;
    Joseph's tribes bickered with Simeon; and Ruben taunted Gad.
The Philistines, Amalekites, and Canaanites were strong
    Because the children of Israel were weak, scuffing with one another:
Stealing one another's women, plundering their lands,
    Besmirching their souls
And all in the name of God. Samuel silently prayed with a purpose
    Echoing in the caves of his heart, undistracted
By the raucous chatter of the birds,
    Or the crackling leaves; noticing neither the blue of the skies
Nor the fluttering gilded azure butterflies.
    He closed the door to all memory and buried its shadows

And scintilla in the dark mazes of mind.
    Invisible to himself Samuel prayed
That the dying soul of Israel be reborn,
    That he could learn wisdom to comfort the forlorn,
And that he build a nation that will serve God's holy mission.
    Then the Lord's thoughts grew in every part of his body
And he saw the divers cell shapes and locations
    Become one body crowned by God's Holy Law.
Samuel awoke transformed.
    Tears streamed helplessly from his cheeks.
For had he not spoken to God and had not God answered?

The children of Philistia, suckled at their mothers' teats on
    hate, were again ready to do battle with their immortal foe.
Samuel summoned the elders of Israel
    And told them of his vision. Israel would become one nation,
Great, admired, holy, and united under God's glorious crown.
    Saul of Benjamin, the least of the tribes, would be borrowed
From life to wear the crown. A tumult followed.
    The tribe of Benjamin exulted; the elders of the other tribes protested.
Why Benjamin, the most insignificant among Israel?
    Shouts of anger and shouts of joy sparked like clashing swords,
Sending snaking splashes of fire into the dark corridors of history.
    Samuel anointed Saul's head with oil
And proclaimed him king in Israel.
    Saul rallied his kinsmen's rage and marched
Into battle against Philistia. The Philistines were subdued.
    Both friends and foes lauded Saul, King of Israel.
But Samuel lauded God, King of the Universe.

DAVID AND GOLIATH

'Twas the middle of a summer's day, the sun above was hot,
When Goliath shouted across the field, "Send me the best you've got."
The Hebrews were not cowards but Goliath was a giant to be feared,
So they retreated a bit to strategize when through the brush appeared

David, a shepherd, a teenage lad, very short at that,
Who knew Goliath was strong though crude from the way he spat.
So when next the giant thundered in words terribly impolite,
"Come out you scummy cowards!" Little David stepped into sight.

Goliath laughed a giant's laugh, "You gotta be kidding me,
You sent this little urchin who hardly reaches my knee."
Goliath and David were face to face, the gigantic and the
Small, But David stared into the giant's eye, not afraid at all.

David drew his slingshot and gave a stone a ride.
Which pierced the head of Goliath who fell down there and died.
Jews are not a warlike group; they study day and night
But when their lives are threatened they must go out and fight.

And even though they're little, and like David, tend their flocks,
They always sing their psalms to God but carry rocks.

SAUL'S DECLINE AND DEATH

Saul lay in his bed forlorn watching clouds hide his star.
He tossed and turned 'till early morn when he heard Philistines from afar.
He had not been victorious for some time. He had suffered many a defeat.
No longer was he in his prime, his heroism was largely deceit.
Thoughts like these filled his brain, gloomy was his mood
Weighed down with Israel's pain, in anguish did he brood:
I never achieved a thing in life as father, soldier, or king.
I had no love for my wife; I sundered everything.
He left his bed wet with fright, frantically pacing like a lion
Who in Israel knew the plight of the king of a divided Zion?
And why was Samuel in such a rage? I don't understand his contempt.
For God's honor did I the battles wage; no priestly role to preempt.
And Jonathan and David, friends of the heart, how I loved them both.
I did not want to tear them apart; they had sworn an oath
To teach other of loyalty.
But they cheated me and my beloved Jonathan is dead.
And David, that jackal, is free to rule Israel in my stead.
The Lord left king Saul's side and the Philistines defeated the men Saul led.
Saul fell upon his javelin and died and the Philistines cut off his head.

RIZPAH GUARDS THE DEAD

For three years that David reigned there was a famine explained
    Only as that which God had willed because of the Gibeonites
Saul had killed.
    To appease the families of those who fell,
And the root cause of the famine to expel,

David approached the Gibeon folk and to them these words then spoke,
    "What would soothe your injured pride?" They said,
"To avenge the ghosts of those who died."
    David asked, "How shall I proceed?"
Give us seven men of King Saul's seed.
    Saul who in a frenzy a javelin had seized
And whose dark mood David then had eased
    Now lay dying, his name defamed, groaned
As his offspring were profaned.

For David agreed to the Gibeonite demand
    To destroy Saul's seven like contraband.
They strung them up in the scorching sun
    And stabbed their bellies one by one.
The corpses lay moldering in the cold
    And heat until Rizpah arrived with sackcloth sheet.
Weeping she covered the slaughtered ones including
    The bodies of her very own sons.

She chased the vultures when the day was bright
    And chased the beasts who prowled in the night.
She guarded the corpses, victims of crime.
    No merciful act is more sublime.

AMNON AND TAMAR

Ahinoam, the least of David's comely wives,
    Knew that a woman like her survives
Only by heaping love upon her son,
    And by forgetting the king who would her shun.
And so Amnon, the son, was indulged every whim,
    And thought himself born of Cherubim.
Around the palace he haughtily swaggered
    And drank all night until he staggered.

Handsome, desirable, a gift to the world.
    And before every lass was his maleness unfurled.
There was a lady fair for whom he pined,
    A virgin who was to the palace confined.
He thought of her as a snobbish prig;
    And she rated him below the pig.

To David, one day, he cunningly feigned a sallow face,
    One that seemed pained.
"Father, dear father! Send me cakes sweet
    And a sister who will wash my feet."

How David ached for this son bundled in ennui,
    So to Amnon's crafty plea did his father agree.
David sent Tamar, an innocent flower,
    Who Amnon did overpower.
He grabbed her and wrestled her onto his bed;
    Tamar was frightened and filled with dread.

And there she was taken while screaming "stop, stop."
    But she could not dislodge him so heavy on top.

He yowled and yowled with wanton rapture; Again and
    again he did her recapture.
Pressing and jabbing he drummed at her door
    And biting her face he called her a whore.
"This heinous deed to our house brings shame.
    You ravished your sister, and stained my name."

Amnon just laughed and chased her away
    Beating her like some dog, some wandering stray.
Her innocent body with his venom was filled;
    Her sadness and grief could not be stilled.
In mourning, she rented her dress and ashamed
    Her face in her distress.
Dazed and distraught she wandered away,
    Thinking of ways her half-brother to slay.

Stunned she meandered her and there,
    Remembering in horror her shock and her scare.
She arrived at the home of Absalom, her brother-
    They were children of the very same mother.
Absalom had guessed what had occurred
    And a surge of rage within him stirred.
But to his sister he wanted a comfort to be,
    A source of love and kindness was he.

"Little sister no wrong have you done,
    You are purest of women under the sun."
He washed her face and combed her hair
    And they joined their hands to offer a prayer:
Comfort us, O God, amongst Zion's oppressed.
    Her sad tears dried as she lay at his breast.
Many years later while shearing their sheep
    Absalom killed Amnon in a drunken sleep.

ABSALOM

When the news of Amnon's death arrived, David was distraught
    He had already forgiven him for all the shame he had brought.
Absalom, Absalom, Absalom, my son.
    How miserable my state had been:
One son, dead; another, fled and my face is filled with chagrin.
    Like a bird of prey you perched at the gates
And pounced on any opportunity
    To humiliate me, your father, Zion's king,
And sow slander and seeds of treachery.
    You were sowing rebellion and with malcontents conspired
Then anointed yourself king in Hebron and were in royal dress attired.
    How could the country resist your charms: strong, handsome,
And most clever with speech?
    But thousands were killed because of you.
My monarchy made ready to breach.
    I ran away when your men were approaching
And then before all my people's eyes
    One after another you took my concubines
And shamed me beneath the bright blue skies.

The people were saying that Zion was yours.
    Upon entering Jerusalem you claimed the king's whores.
As the palm fronds swayed in the wind and the moon the day benighted;
    Charioted horses stomped on the dead
And the mob dispersed you incited.
    And you, Absalom, too, are among the dead,
Your cause sped to oblivion.
    Now for you I sit and grieve Absalom, Absalom, my beloved son.
Then a plaintive voice rose from the grave,
    "Forgive me, father, against you have I sinned."
And David's heart welled up with tears
    Then banished the ghost to the wind.

DAVID'S FINAL MOMENTS

Solemnly David wrapped himself in his shroud,
    Soft and white like a downy cloud.
He was musing about his final rest, his soul rose high like an ocean crest.
    His life had been one long blessing and now his lips were expressing
Thanks to the Lord who had called him to lead and without
    Whom he would never succeed.
Golden light had been his domain but now and forever darkness will reign.
    As his life was ebbing away at the close of the Sabbath day,
Pictures of the past flashed wildly in his mind:
    Joy and pain together were entwined.
A raucous laugh rose from his throat, remembering battles
    Where he the foe smote
With a band of untutored men: debtors, runaway husbands,
    And those with a yen
For adventure. Imitating hyenas they raided desert tribes
    And doled out the booty, so wrote his scribes.
Then a picture popped up that froze him with fear.
    Saul threw a javelin, narrowly missing his ear.
Then he asked "was my modesty character or guise?"
    Bungling sword-girding seemed to be wise.
Of course, he knew how one girds a sword
    But Saul his betters had always abhorred
And to be on the good side of his superiors would
    Subordinate themselves and act like inferiors.
But that was Saul's failing! Unknowingly he, himself, was derailing
    His kingdom and as well as his power and his reign
Was unraveled like a petal plucked flower.
    In another flash David was a youth again admired
By the ladies and praised by the men.
    Handsome he was as he strutted about:

An ardent lover though sometimes a callous lout.
  Bath-Sheba! How special she was.

Rising in passion who better could innovate the love-making fashion?
  Palm trees swayed as their hearts would quiver;
He caressed her braids and their bare chests would shiver.
  Rapture rose to a height unknown;
For one moment with her he'd surrender his throne,
  Crowding his mind now were Jerusalem's hills
Whose mystical beauty still gave him the chills.
  Cheering voices proclaimed him king
And commoner and prince did together sing,
  "David, David King of Israel, You will live forever.
It is you we hail."
  Those fervent cheers were ringing in his ears
When a rage surged throughout his brain that howled
  And stormed like a hurricane.
There were voices, more than a few, saying that he, David,
  Was no authentic Jew.
Ruth, his saintly grandmother, Moabite ancestries,
  Adopted with gladness the sacred Jewish creed,
Upon her they spewed calumny and blame though
  Her Judaism glowed like The Eternal Flame.
Devout she was and truly pious, more righteous than those bellowing bias.
  Most zealots never be satisfied until they have others vilified?
Now unfolding before his eyes was the new map of Israel
  Of magnificent size
It began at the Euphrates and ran to the Nile.
  His pocked face filled up with a smile.
He had done it all through diplomacy and war;
  Now Judah's lion could lunge and roar.
Then came a picture with fading fringes—which his stalwart
  Eyes with tears unhinges.
"O Jonathan, devoted friend, I wish I could have reversed your unlucky end."
  Tears rolled down his craggy cheek and words were lacking
For him to speak.
  Then darker grew the pictures he saw painted

With anguish and filled with flaw.
    He saw thousands of killers and many more dead
Was there some other way to write history instead?
    "Why must it always be written in blood.
Why can't its beauty unfold from a bud?"
    Widows, orphans, maimed, and blind the costs of war to humankind.
Is all this heartache and pain for naught, is it all just in vain?
    He once put this question to Solomon, his son,
The wisest of men, barring none.
    This reply before his father he spread:
"It's true of the ignorant and of the well-bred.
    All is vanity. That is no mystery.
Nothing's new under the sun is human history.
    The meaning of life can be learned from the goat
Leaping craggy ledges to fill up his throat
    And when he reaches the mountain top he retraces
His steps searching grasses to crop."
    The Angel of Death then shaded David's head
But David ordered him "Wait," from the crown of his bed.
    The angel obediently stopped right there in its tracks,
Just like any loyal subject reacts.
    "Lord," David began, "You have my shepherd been,
And though I wandered into sin,
    You showed me the righteous path to walk
And brought me back to rejoin Your Flock.
    I do not fear what is to come; who is able death's meaning to plumb?
But Your Mercy will a comfort be today, tomorrow and for eternity."
    Then the Angel wrapped David soul in His shawl
And together they hearkened to God's last call.

DAVID, DAVID BELOVED KING

David, David beloved king.
In your memory we daily sing

Your psalms that reach heights sublime
That is not defined by partitions of time.

Brave you were and comely too.
With a love of God did you imbue
Our people then and yet to be.

And today we walk with dignity.

Imperfect you were as we all are

But also of righteousness were an avatar.
David, David, beloved king.

To your memory we'll ever sing.

III

HISTORICAL FIGURES AND EVENTS

THE FABRIC OF THE NATION FRAYS AND IS REWOVEN

Solomon was a political genius. He forged alliances with many of his neighbors and developed a mercantile system that enriched the populace. David, having been a conqueror of some reputation, subdued many nationalities. Integrating them into the mainstream was a challenge. By building a temple where all could come to make sacrifices on a regular basis provided all with the same religious identity. Priests were given the main religious role and were assisted by the Levites, auxiliaries to religious ceremonies. Solomon was in some ways ecumenical. Not only did he build a temple for the worship of Yahweh but built places of worship for wives not of the Jewish faith. He sowed seeds of enmity among priests practicing different rites. After his death his offspring warred with one another and the kingdom of Solomon was divided. Each division had its own royal house its own central place of worship. It was not too long before kings from either royal house wandered from its Mosaic roots. Not only were sacrifices made to alien gods, but the general moral tone decayed. At this point there arose "seers" invested with Divine inspiration. These prophets preached against the errant ways of the people. Some warned that the moral decay weakened the fabric of the Israelite nation and made it vulnerable to conquest. The themes of most prophetic writings are divinely inspired warnings of dire consequences from Israel's wayward behavior, punishment, atonement, and God's forgiveness. Also in evidence is that God disdains priestly sacrifice in favor of highly ethical behavior. Much of the exquisite Biblical poetry was composed by these prophets between the eighth and fifth centuries B.C.E. Their oratory resounds each Sabbath and Festival after the chanting of the Torah, the Mosaic scripture. Prophets were vindicated when the first temple was destroyed and many of the important Israelite citizens were deported to Babylonia. In time, many of the exiles, remnants of Zion, were allowed to return to Zion where strong political and moral authority was wrested from the royalty. The Temple was rebuilt and priests once again attained religious and political power. Inevitably, there were schisms. Some priests were more conservative; others, more adaptive to an evolving civilization. There were also conquerors who marched through Asia Minor and left their mark on that area, including Judea, the name for the land of the Israelites. So Israel became an amalgam of the Mosaic law as interpreted by varying priestly sects, Persian ideology, and Hellenic culture. There was a residual Persian influence when Alexander conquered Asia Minor and a Greek influence when the Romans conquered most of Greek held lands. By the time of the destruction of the second temple in 70 A.D., Judea was host to a variety of religious rites and ideologies, some indigenous and others imported and modified by the populous. Those were times of foment. Not only did groups rebel against alien thought but against those who enforced order by means of their military prowess.

AMOS

Amos wandered fields tending his sheep when
    God's pained voice rose from the deep.
Lightning sizzled in his sea-green eyes;
    And streak after streak sped through clear, blue skies.
That that Voice strange and remote nettled Amos's reticent throat
    Where it quivered and vibrated and every word humanity berated,
"Amos, Amos how sad am I that so many brutify
    My Creation and turn it into an aberration."
Instead of showing justice, nations afflict the needy;
    Instead of showing kindness, the rich are greedy.
Amos call them by name! Each of the are in shame!
    Edom, Ammon, and Philistia; Moab, Gaza, Tyre, and Syria.
But Israel and Judah, who accepted my laws
    Are themselves paragons of flaws.
How they once made my heart leap but now they make my eyes weep.
    Justice, justice is the duty of every nation;
In My Eyes there is no difference of station.
    And, now to My chagrin, destruction awaits everyone in sin.
"Oh God, my God" Amos appealed;
    "Speak to Israel," The Voice then said,
"Because you have stolen from the poor their bread
    And have adorned holy alters with ill-gotten gains
For sins such as these I'll withhold Spring rains."
    No need have I for silver or gold or smoldering bullocks
Or heroics bold.
    No need have I for the rites of priests or for burning sheep
To celebrate feasts. But feeding the poor and aiding
    The weak is worship sincere that I seek.
I speak to you whose ways are flawed; remember Me.
    I am Your God.

I am the spark of mercy in your soul and the warmth
    That flows from burning coal.

I am the thrust that moves the wind but also the judge
    Who sentences those who sinned.
I am the Lord *all* peoples share; I listen to every humble prayer.
    But if you My Laws disobey, fire and locusts will be your pay.
Grain will wither and grapes will dry; mothers will starve
    And babies will die.
Foes will conquer and will debase and you'll be exiled in disgrace."
    Silence rippled in Amos's heart, trembling
As God's message he did impart.
    His mouth spoke the words that he had heard
But Israel thought him quite absurd.
    They stoned him and sent him away and into sin they continued to stray.
Then the earth shook and the mountains quaked and the sun grew hot
    And the soil was baked.
Seeds that were planted refused to grow and juice from grapes
    Ebbed its flow.
Cattle died for want of food and the stench of death they did exude.
    Locusts came and Bethel caught fire and melted
In the flames of God's ire.
    The enemy burst through and killed young
And old just as God's words to Amos foretold.

As Amos the righteous path humbly trod he pleaded
    And prayed to Almighty God.
Enough! Enough! Israel has suffered too long.
    Merciful One forgive their wrong,
These are Your children, the heirs to Your Laws
    Who renounced their sins and righted their flaws.
Forgive their past, they now do as You willed, help them
    Your House with justice to build!

And God heard Amos' humble plea and once again set Israel free.

THE WORDS OF HOSEA

A vision came to Hosea, the Ephraimite seer;
    A distant Voice whispered in his Israelite ear.
Hosea! Succor, help, and savior, speak to Israel about its behavior.
    They have abandoned Me and dishonored My Name;
Instead, the virtues of a sculpted stone proclaim.
    Condemn them for their deceit; censure them for their conceit.
They swindle; they murder; they drink too much wine;
    Remind them Hosea that I fatten their kine.
They sell their daughters' virtue and they plunder, remind them
    Hosea that I command the thunder.
Ask them who brings the rains that make the grains grow.
    Inquire of them who protects them from woe.
Remind them Hosea that I freed them from slavery; enlighten them
    Who forgives their knavery.
Remind them Hosea that I soothe their pain;
    Enlighten them that it is I Who did Creation ordain.
Remind them Hosea that I Created Light;
    Enlighten them that I Guide them to do right.
Because they dishonored Me, because their priests practiced blasphemy
    Because their judges are unjust, because in Me they showed no trust
Their future will be bleak and filled with doom;
    In strange lands will they dig their tomb.

Hosea listened to God's angry spleen vented because Israel
    Made itself unclean.
In the hot sun gliding the pillowed hills Hosea spoke words
    That filled him with chills.

Hear my words fellow Israelites!
    Listen to me you who chase delights!

In gods of stone and wood have you trusted
    And after a golden bull have you lusted.

Like me you are wedded to a whore.
    My wife three children to me bore.
Jezreel, my first born, recalled the disgrace
    Of the murders done in that place
By Jehu founder of this present dynasty, cursed be its destiny.
    My next child, a daughter, was Unloved named
Because the Name of God was defamed.
    My next child, Not-My-People, a son,
Has been disowned by The Holy One.
    Your whore, Baal, leads you astray and from the true
God takes you away.
    Surely it should be clear that Israel was once held dear
By God whom you have forsaken when will you awaken?
    Unloved remain not; Not-My-People be not a blot.
Our God have you profaned; our God have you pained.
    Be not like my whoring wife exemplify fidelity in your life.
Be loyal to God above, who embraces you with merciful love.
    Must you be stubborn like mules? Must you ignore God's Sacred rules?
God does not ask you to slaughter your kine;
    God requires neither virgin oil nor wine.
God requires you by the covenant to abide and that the code given
    Moses to be your guide.

At that moment silence reigned
    Hosea's spirit was completely drained.
The people of Israel heard Hosea's pleas
    And immediately Fell upon their knees.
They pledged their love for God will be true
    And false gods will no longer pursue.
The people of Israel sincerely repented
    And the God of justice then relented.
God said to Hosea how angry was I but how can
    My beloved Israel I deny?
With all of their faults they still are Mine;
    They radiate with light for My Sun to shine.

Beloved-By-God be they renamed;
   My-People be they again proclaimed.

THE LEGEND OF JONAH

God spoke to Jonah, saying Nineveh is a city of sin.
    Go there and cleanse the wickedness therein.
But Jonah was afraid and ran the other way
    Who was he to tell the people that they went astray.
While on a boat headed for Spain
    There arose clouds bursting with rain.
The boat he was on rocked and rolled;
    Its steering the captain no longer controlled.
"Pray to your gods this tempest to stop
    As each sailor's stomach was going flip flop/ Jonah
who was hiding in the hold of the boat
    Said he was to blame for loss of the float."
He jumped into the water so the storm would subside
    And once again return to the normal tide.
A fish sent by God was there waiting
    As the raging waters were abating.
Jonah heard his heart thumping;
    Jonah felt his skin jumping.
The gigantic fish a safe haven provided
    For the prophet Jonah, who had been misguided.
"O Lord," he cried, in his distress to You my thanks do I profess
    For saving my life of so little worth among the righteous here on earth.
God surrounded Jonah with Heavenly Grace and Jonah's soul
    did warmly embrace. In three days, not one more,
The fish disgorged Jonah and sent him to shore.
    Immediately did he to Nineveh go with the Grace of God
Was he all aglow.
    God's message he gave with a silver tongue
And the penitent people around him clung.
    They went into mourning for the wrongs they had done

And raised themselves out of bleak oblivion.
    And God's heart was filled with sublime pity
For the wayward children of Nineveh city.
    But Jonah complained these people have a venal trait;
And should punishment not pity be their deserving fate?
    But Jonah learned that God forgives even the wayward
Who in this world lives.

MICAH

Micah looked about and saw
    Prodigal rich who are mockeries of humanity;
Priests who are parodies of piety;
    And judges who are travesties of justice.
Throbbing at the very heart of the people
    Are self-proclaimed prophets who personify sham ethics
And practice sacred rites for personal gain.
    Enlightened people had slumped into darkness.
Israel had gone astray; its foundation was in decay.
    Then the words of God came to Micah.
How anguished they were; how filled with hurt.
    Judah had abandoned the Divine concepts;
Israel had deserted God's precepts.
    Did they not remember who freed them from slavery?
Who decreed that their home will be in Zion?
    Who gave them the strength of the lion?
The words of God stirred Micah's soul
    And from his tongue there did unroll.

"O ye rich folk of Judah!" Micah railed.
    How God mournfully grieves, Micah flailed.
You defile the marrow of God's elect.
    From God's moral laws do you detect.
The tattered raiment of the poor you crave
    And their battered bodied then enslave.
From daily worries they seek release yet
    You give them no moment of peace.
How haughty are your airs; how selfish are your prayers.
    At the wretched destitute you sneer;
And your punishment will be severe.
    You who today are depraved will tomorrow be enslaved.

O ye priests, who are pledged to shun the personal
    Gift do from moral moorings drift.
Instead of disdaining the profane you *ordain* the profane.
    You who worship greed will find yourself in abject need.

O ye judges who are so easily bribed;
    The sense of fairness you proscribed.
By the Supreme Judge will you be tried;
    The severest decree will be applied.

O ye false prophets! Micah scolded.
    You have God's elect cuckolded.
If they give you no money or food
    you offer oracles that delude.
You false prophets are a moral blight;
    your days will be as black as night.

It came to pass that in war Zion was defeated.
    But God saw Zion was mistreated.
And when Zion's sinners repented
    from severe decrees god relented.
As God's anger abated Zion's foes were frustrated.
    Hope replaced despair and sacrifice, by prayer.

And like Isaiah Micah avowed
    That with God's Goodness all are endowed.
To all I say let your swords turn into ploughshares
    And your spears, into pruning hooks.
Let no nation lift up a weapon against another
    Neither a stranger nor a brother.
Never teach war again.
    There will soon come a day when
You will sit under your fig tree
    And you will savor serenity.

ISAIAH'S VISION

Isaiah strode up the hill; all was quiet, all was still.
    A crowd gathered in the midday light, under the sun,
Hot and bright.
    God drew a curtain across the sun,
A veil of darkness then was spun.
    Suddenly from the heavens high lightning sticks serrated the sky.
Peels of thunder shook the vale, raining down balls of icy hail.
    Wrapped in his fringed prayer shawl, obedient to God's urgent call,
Isaiah's voice trembled with fear proclaimed God's message to every ear.
    God needs not sacrifices to expiate your guilt;
God needs not sacrifices from alters you built.
    God needs not offerings of bloodied beasts;
God needs not service of patronizing priests.
    What God's Children are expected
To do is to obey Moses' laws anew.
    Renounce your evil ways! Denounce the one who slays!
Steal not from the rich nor from the poor!
    And the ways of false gods today abjure!
To the widow and orphan be kind and just!
    To the strangers give your trust!
Resolutely pursue the righteous path, lest you earn
    God's anger and wrath. Do now what God commands;
Mercy and justice God demands.
    If you do not this message carry out,
If you continue the Lord's words to flout,
    Know you that a merciless foe with sharpened sword
Will sweep down from the north, and you'll be gored.
    The crowd shrugged their shoulders and strolled away
And Isaiah left the hilltop in utter dismay.

ISAIAH ENTREATS ZION

A tempest rose from Babylon tossing fire balls across the fields,
    Turning Israel's homes to ashes and melting David's shields.
Our stomachs ached with hunger; our dreams and hopes were dashed.
    Our heroes fought with courage; their efforts, though, were smashed.
Hearken to me Zion, sapphire in God's sacred crown,
    God returns to comfort you, and you'll not walk alone.
Triumphantly march to Jerusalem! Triumphantly declare God's name!
    Triumphantly light Torah's torch and bless Its eternal flame.

ISAIAH'S PROPHESY

A prophet rose in Zion whose tears filled the Sea of Shame,
    Where he keened, "Judah's lion will soon be limping lame."
Isaiah saw storm clouds growing, spreading a fiery rage
    And winds without pity sowing pain that had no gauge.
There was yet time to alter its selfish, sinful ways,
    But Zion continued to falter and strayed into exile's blaze.

THESE WORDS CAME TO ISAIAH

O my people Israel, tempest tossed and uncomforted
    In compassion and justice I will build a temple for you
Filled with precious gems where your children,
    Disciples of My Heavenly Grace, will forge a future of peace.
Because Israel, burnished with righteousness,
    Whose covenant with Me was witnessed at Sinai,
Will spread My Goodness throughout the lands
    And glorify My Heavenly Kingdom. AMEN

JEREMIAH'S MISSION

How Lord can You send me on this mission?
    I am terrified of crowds. They'll stone me;
They'll mock me, they'll sneer,
    "Look who the Lord has sent to admonish us.
A child! Someone who cannot wipe his own nose."
    "Jeremiah! Jeremiah!" The Lord replied,
"I chose you when you lay in your mother's uterus.
    I sanctified you before you left your mother's womb.
I guided your growing up.
    I watched over your coming to manhood.
You are a holy man, a paragon to all. You are My prophet,
    A seer for all nations. I will lift your legs to climb high hills.
I will open your eyes to witness My Divinity.
    I will fill your mouth with My Words
That will echo throughout the generations."
    "Sinners: kings, priests, false prophets, and commoners.
Listen with your hearts to The Almighty, Lord of the Universe,"
    Without faltering Jeremiah continued God's sermon.
"Remember the words of the Lord Who led you out of Egypt,
    And gave you The Law,
More wholesome than milk and sweeter than honey,
    And willed this land in which you dwell.
I speak and the skies tremble with fear;
    I raise my arms and the seas swirl with rage.
You, once my faithful bride, are in awe of stone gods carved
    By man and placed 'neath palm trees.
Know you not that I carved the mountains?
    Know you not that I formed the birds that fly and the animals that roam?
In you My People I sowed honesty but reap deception;
    In you I sowed virtue but reap corruption;

In you My People I sowed love but reap vexation.
 You have sinned upon the hills; you have sinned by the shores of the seas;
You have sinned in the orchards; you have sinned by the rills.
 In sadness I rent My robe; in mourning I sit Myself low.
Abandon your evil ways; return to the paths of righteousness
 And I will grant you My Forgiveness and I will return
My love to you."
 Jeremiah's legs trembled as they walked down the mountain.
Before his eyes that moments earlier beheld God,
 He saw the gathered crowd
With rocks in their hands chanting,
 "Look who the Lord has sent to admonish us.
A child! Someone who cannot wipe his own nose."

JEREMIAH REVEALS GOD'S ANGUISH

The hopes of the Lord were betrayed;
    The words of the Lord were ignored.
Zion, an island of mercy surrounded
    On all sides by God's wisdom,
Was polluted by the sins of its kings and false priests.
    Girded in sackcloth, God lamented the demise of The Law;
Wallowing in ashes, God mourned Zion's every flaw.
    Again and again the words of the Lord came to Jeremiah
Whose voice spoke the bitterness of God;
    Whose message offered the comfort of God.
"Do justice unto the stranger;
    Protect the orphan; succor the widow.
Show caring to your brother; show kindness to your neighbor.
    That is My Law.
Mend your ways and you will dwell in this sacred land
    Pledged to Abraham, Isaac, Jacob, Moses.
I will protect you from every foe: and I will heal
    Your every wound inflicted by your enemy.
The disease that covers your souls will scab as it heals.
    Sing psalms of praise to God."
The people turned away from these pleas;
    They scorned God's greatness with the greatest of ease.
And their songs perjured God's glory;
    And their poems to God were derogatory.
Every brother was a scoundrel;
    And every neighbor, a slanderer.
The kings excelled in wickedness;
    And the priests were unsurpassed in deceit.
Israel was ensnared by its own conceit;
    Judah was trapped by its own greed.

Only the poor find comfort in the ways of God;
    Only the persecuted, peace in the paths they trod.
And the sun cast no shadows in Jerusalem;
    And the moon hid its face from Zion.
But the disease covering the souls gushed
    With pus and did not heal.
No one asked for forgiveness;
    No one repented; and God,
Now silent, was tormented.

EZEKIEL'S VISION

In Babylon's hills, Zion's children would fear
    That their history would end and they'd disappear.
I, Ezekiel shivered in fright that soon would
    Be quenched Israel's glowing light.
Then the spirit of God revealing itself to me,
    Said, child of Adam, I am in great agony.
Israel has strayed and is not contrite and amongst
    My people is spreading a blight.
You, Ezekiel, strength of the Lord, have always
    Their unclean ways abhorred.
Faithful you have been to Moses' Law your God
    You have revered and held in awe.
Therefore, I have chosen you to exhort the exiles
    To abandon the gods that they court.
Then I looked down from the top of the hill;
    The sight I saw gave me a chill.
Piles of bones were baked by the sun sentenced
    By Death to oblivion.
These bones will live, the Lord God to me said,
    It is hopeless, said I, they are all quite dead.
But out of a dream filled with mystery, skeletons
    Walked into hallowed history.

ZEPHANIA

The Words of the Lord roared in Zephania's ears. "Judah!
    I will punish your sins and destroy
The marrow of your nation: your homes, your orchards, your fields.
    You will lie desolate for many years.
Your dead will be unburied in the streets;
    Maggots will feed on their remains;
Wolves shall devour your bleating sheep.
    Thus will be the punishment for your deceit.

Soldiers will quiver with fear in their armor.
    Storms of fire will melt your temples;
Darkness and gloom will cover the hills.
    No punishment is more severe."
The voice softened, "I will repeal your sentence
    If you learn modesty from the humble
And virtue from the righteous.
    Then will My Ears hear your penance.

Once you have your sins confessed, cling to the One True God
    Who shelters the poor and protects the oppressed."
God's voice thundered, "But your foes, wanton weavers of lust,
    Those licentious embroiderers of lechery,
Swiftly and decisively will they be destroyed
    Because God is mighty and God is just."

Again the voice softened, "A day is coming soon
    When all nations will worship Me alone
And when Israel, My child, will do no more wrong
    And no person will another impugn.
On that day Judah will instill My heart with a song
    And there will be joyful dancing.

And My children will chant psalms of thanksgiving and will My hope for a just world fulfill."

NAHUM'S PROCLAMATIONS

Assyria! Curse'd be your name! Bathed be you in a hot, red flame.
    Besieged by locusts be all your regions defeat and death
Reward your legions.
    Erased from history be your viper face;
Forgotten be your every trace.
    Gloom and doom be your fate; hemorrhages will burst
From your river gate.
    Israel in glory will be homeward returning joyously
In song with ardor burning.
    Killers will rampage and will Nineveh loot liquidating
The rich mercantile route;
    Mountains will tremble and hills will quake; narrows
Will crumble and bridges will break.
    Oblivious you've been to the those in need; models
You've been of lust and greed.
    Quaking hearts their flows will dry, ravaging brains until you die.
Scarlet bodies will blanket your wheat and turn the earth
    To a bloody street.
Unjustly have you nursed your grudges, villainy flowed
    In the minds of your judges.
Wanton wrongs went unabated, Xenophobic
    Hate you've consecrated.
Yesterday you basked in power and glory—zoom, now,
    To a death loathsome and gory.

NAHUM TALKS TO GOD

God of Zion Your people cry in pain; God of Zion hear them complain
    That You handed them to the Assyrian foe who threw them in rivers
And drowned them in woe.
    Is this the mercy of God, The Just, to such villains
Zion's souls to entrust?
    Life was better when we were in Egypt enslaved from which
Our bitterness You had saved.
    Yes we erred and followed false dreams but a Forgiving God
With kindness redeems.
    God answered pious Nahum in a lightning flash that turned Assyrian
Forests to a pile of ash.
    Zion had made a grave mistake when its God they did forsake.
But, God had made a mistake as well to thrust Zion's people
    Into the Assyrian hell. Tears from the heavens were overflowing
Filling rainbows with glistening and glowing.
    Nahum, numb from having spoken thus to God,
Knelt in humility The Just Judge to laud.

HISTORY IS WRITTEN ON THE TEMPLE WALL: A POEM FOR TWO VOICES*

*The second voice, in *italics*, is from Psalm 1.
Psalms are often read during memorial services

Now I am an aged wall, crumbling here and there, wailing,
    Crying true tears,
Remembering what once was. The last to see the rays of the sun each day
    I saw more of history then the other walls combined.
Back then I buttressed The Holy Temple.
    Supporting the other walls, sustaining Zion
As fats of thousands of splattering impure sacrifices
    Penetrated the pores of my stones and decorated them with decay
I started to deteriorate, not so much from a chemical reaction
    But from the weight of Zion's sins. First, it was Solomon himself.
The wise one. The pious one.
    He built an altar to a pagan god to please one of his all
Too many alien wives.
    Then his son, Rehoboam further defiled the Temple and sinned against
You Lord, Adonai. After repenting, You, God of compassion, forgave him.
    Still the stench of sin remained.
His son Abijah succeeded him and added his sin to those of his fathers.
    But his son, Asa, abolished pagan worship and purified the Temple.
Adonai! You looked favorably upon him.

    Blessed are they that walk not in the counsel of the sinners
        Nor stand in the way of the sinners.

But the seeds of cruelty sown by his father sprouted in his declining days
    And once again sin was added to sin. It drained my core of its essence.
When he was gathered to his ancestors Johoshafat, his son, was crowned king.
    He did what was good in Your eyes.

Blessed are they whose delight is in the Lord.

Then his son, Jehoram, was crowned king.
    Having killed his own brothers,
He married the daughter of Ahab, King of Israel,
    Your enemy and enemy of Judah.
He built pagan altars; worshipped idols;
    Removed priests from their sacred duties.

The wicked are like the chaff which the wind drives away.

No one lamented his death when it came; no one recited psalms.
    Ahaziah, his son, ruled, less than a year.
Like father, like son, another layer of sin darkened my face.
    His mother reigned next. She was no better.
After her passing, Joash, son of Ahaziah ruled.
    He smashed idols and cleansed the Temple.
But a skulking evil spirit showed its face
    And he killed the high priest, in the Temple courtyard.
In the courtyard no less!
    His hypocrite son, Amaziah, reluctantly continued the cleansing
But died in a war with Israel.
    Then, his son, Uzziah, acted righteously and You, Adonai,
Renewed the Temple.
    But toward the end of his days he became arrogant
And subordinated the priests to him.
    You gave him a skin disease, making him ritually unclean.
His son, Jotham, succeeded him.
    He walked in the ways of Moses, The Law giver.

Blessed are they who meditate day and night in the Law of the Lord.

But his son, Ahaz, did not. Ahaz even sacrificed his own sons
    On a metal altar to Baal.
His sins weigh heavy on me yet. But his son, Hezekiah,
    Purified the Temple and rededicated it.
Although the sins of his fathers had eroded my core,
    I felt renewed, ritually clean, standing proudly to honor You,

Author of the Universe.

> *The leaf of the righteous does not wither.*

But his son, Manasseh, rebuilt the places of pagan worship
    And sacrificed his own sons
As had his grandfather, Ahaz. My innards began to crumble.
    I watched him chained and manacled and dragged off to Babylon.

> *Sinners do not stand in the congregation of the righteous.*

He repented his sins and You, Font of Mercy, forgave him.
    Upon his return to Jerusalem he repaired Your alter.

> *The Lord knows the ways of the righteous.*

But his son, Amon, sinned against You and did not repent.
    I watched his advisors assassinate him.
Imagine a son of Zion taking the life of another son of Zion.
    It was not the first time I witnessed this
And is not to be the last.

> *The ways of the sinner shall perish.*

His son, Josiah, strictly obeyed the laws of Moses.
    I heard him read the Book of the Covenant.
His voice was penitent and sincere. His melodies
    So stirred me that I trembled with awe.

> *The righteous bring forth their fruit in the proper season.*

He died in battle, though, and Jeremiah composed a lament for him.
    Joahaz was next in the Davidic line.
But his brother Jehoyakim, favored by the king of Egypt, replaced him.
    More sin. More blot on the history of Zion.
More disease growing on my face.
    Nebuchadnezzar dragged him in chains to Babylon.

His son, Jehoyachin, ruled three months.
    In that time he defiled the Temple more than any of his predecessors.
His uncle Zedekiah ruled by the appointment of Nebuchadnezzar.
    When he allowed the Babylonian tyrants to slaughter
Zion's youth in the Temple,
    The upper layer of my stony face toppled
From the weight of such sin: the slaughter of the future.
    The soul of Zion hemorrhaged and was not stanched.

My cracks are filled with shame because he spoke ill of Jeremiah,
    The sainted prophet.
The other walls of the Temple were torched by the Babylonian
    Aggressors and fell. I, injured, an old wall,
Weakened here and there, heavy with tears,
    Charred with ashes of memory, still remain upright,
A reminder of Zion's wayward ways But also a hopeful model that spirits
    Can be cleansed and Zion can be reborn into righteousness.
On that day all creation will walk in Your path, bringing
    You joy and granting You peace.

TISH'A B'AV 586 B.C.E.

The sun was swallowed by a cloud of pink and disappeared
    Before the eye could blink.
Darkness reigned; shadows faded when concealed Chaldeans
    From hills invaded
The city of Zion slashing and burning Judah's lion.
    Skulking like jackals on the prowl at midnight
The Chaldeans began to yowl
    And rushed away from their makeshift camps
And sent up flares from lighted lamps.
    They sped down hills wantonly and fast and set forests on fire,
Thick and vast.
    Night skies blazed; houses were razed.
The fires spread and thousands were dead.
    Orphaned were children; widowed were wives.
Innocent babies lost their lives.
    Like fire ants the Chaldeans sprinted to The Temple gates.
The sleeping priests knew not what ruin awaits.
    Into the Temple in waves they rolled and stole its copper,
Bronze, silver, and gold.
    They Holy of Holies was willfully defaced
And God's dwelling place, defiantly disgraced.
    Beheaded priests were strewn in piles,
Victims of vicious Chaldean wiles.
    Holy men burned with patricians in pyres
And The Temple was consumed by angry fires.
    The stench of death was all about, felling the impious
As well as the devout. Valiant Judeans were trapped
    And enchained and the blood of freedom from each was drained.
Toward Babylon they began the trek,
    The yoke of captivity upon each neck,

Looking back The Temple they saw,
    Once hallowed ground and cloaked in awe,
Now smoldering in sanguine fiery ashes
    Capriciously sizzling in frightening flashes.
And when Babylon's waters were reached each sat
    And wept and God beseeched.
"Do not despair," was heard The Reply,
    "The dream of Zion will never die."

THE VISION OF OBADIAH

A vision came to Obadiah; a prophesy to God's servant.
    O exiles of Israel, remnants of Zion,
I will gather you from Bavel, and I will assemble you in Shepharad.
    I will reunite you to My people and I will reconnect
You to My community.
    Causeless enmity between nations will halt and
My children will show charity to one another;
    As it was once between Esau and Jacob
As it is between the persecuted and the rescued.
    Blessed are they who reclaim they legacy;
Happy are they who are restored to their heritage.
    But Edom you have saddened the Lord;
You have brought sorrow into God's kingdom.
    Edom. What kind of cousin were you to jeer
When your uncle Jacob's children were led off to Babylonia?
    Edom. What kind of cousin were you to cheer as your uncle
Jacob's holy city went up in flames?
    Edom. What kind of cousin were you to revel at their misfortune?
Edom. What kind of cousin were you to the murder to remnant and then gloat?
    Edom. What kind of cousin were you to scavenge
Among the ashes of the holy city?
    You have written your fate in history; you have chartered your future.
Your punishment is to drink of the bitter cup of misery;
    Your sentence is to vanish from the face of the earth!

JUDITH'S VICTORY OVER THE ASSYRIANS

As the returnees The Temple was rebuilding, a menace
    From the East innocent blood was spilling.
Nebuchadnezzar terrorized nations far and wide over
    The fertile crescent he sought to preside.
The exiles were weary; their prospects were eerie.
    Into Judah the Assyrians scattered; whomever they saw,
They cruelly battered.
    Many Judeans hid in the hills; sick with fever
They shivered with chills.
    The people moaned; the people groaned for our sins
Have we not already atoned?
    Why are we now in such dire straits;
Why is there no food upon our plates?
    Is it better to surrender and become Assyrian slaves
Or lie as carrion without benefit of graves?
    The people accosted Uzziah, the priest, saying you eat your feast
But we are without shelter and without food because of your attitude
    Toward the Assyrians to whom you would not condescend
And now we are a people who did Nebuchadnezzar offend.
    Wait my people. I will pray and prod and beg for mercy
From The One God.
    If in five days amnesty is not granted then to the Assyria
We'll be transplanted.
    Calmly she left the general's tent and back to her home
She contentedly went.
    When the Assyrians saw Holofernes' lifeless head they trembled
And from Zion they sped.
    From Jerusalem came the High Priest to honor Judith at a victory feast.
Before all assembled a blessing he gave to Judith, the widow,
    Who Zion did save.

Long life to you he said again and again and the people responded,
    "Amen, Amen."

It is better to live as slaves than to die in battle as weaklings and knaves,
    At that time there lived a widow devout who sent her servant to search
Out the town officials who she, Judith, did reprimand
    Because they would surrender the sacred land.
How dare you, she said, put yourselves in God's place;
    How dare you test God's Grace.
The human is too blind to see into God's mind.
    Our town must not surrender; our town needs a defender.
The officials were chastened by the widow devout
    From whose soul virtue did sprout.
Judith's eyes moved from man to man and she said I have a plan.
    Trust me to do it right ask me nothing just give me the night.
To eliminate those who are aggressing, Uzziah said,
    Daughter of Israel, I give you my blessing.
Judith retreated to the room where she'd pray
    And asked of God to show her the way
To use a sword as did Simon of old who avenged
    The raped Dinah with an action bold.
The Assyrians are boastful and proud and terrorize Zion
    Like a thundercloud.
Please Lord stand by my side as I, a woman, break their pride.
    Their general Holofernes may be wise in war but You,
God, are my Counselor.
    God sharpened her mind a strategy to find.
Her legs did not quail as she put on her veil
    And entered Holofernes tent.
By the God of Zion had she been sent.
    A table of cakes, figs and wine she spread
But it was Judith he wanted to lie in his bed.
    He drank and drank until he fell asleep then Judith
Toward him did stealthily creep.
    She unsheathed the sword hidden beneath her dress
And across his throat it did she impress.

SUSANAH

Her beauty was without compare! How comely was her face
How elegant was her grace never would she stroll about with an air.
    With deep devotion to God she would pray to send help to those
    In direst need, to heal the sick with utmost speed, and mourners'
    Anguish to tenderly allay.

Her husband, Joakim, in her had trust, but employed two judges,
Corrupt and depraved who swooned when they saw her and craved
Her body, so filled were they with lust.
    One day they did upon her spy, her servants having left her alone.
    A poisoned envy within them had grown, each begged for the chance
    With her to lie. But she refused. So that all would shun her they
    Proclaimed her a whore. They said they saw her kiss her amour
    Who had her chemise with his hand undone.

The people believe those judges foul who condemned Susanah to death.
With a gasp of her remaining breath she sent out a wailing howl,
    "Oh God Who watches over all that I do correct this injustice
    Of the judges uncouth. Send a messenger who will tell the truth
    And prevent justness from going askew."

God asked of Daniel who was brave and wise to defend Susanah, righteous
And devout, Whose name was smeared by judges who spout lies and
Against her the people mobilize.
    Then came David who proved to the lot that Susanah was faithful,
    Of this he was sure, she had always been virtuous, she had always
    Been pure, and that he in their lies the judges had caught.

O what misery they had wrought. So the two judged, tainted and depraved,
Their sentence to Susanah themselves received for having the people of
Israel deceived. And the virtuous Susanah by Daniel was saved.

JERUSALEM, THE NEW

Through your keen-sighted eyes, Daniel, I can now see Jerusalem
A newborn crawling out of an ancient womb
Bearing crosses, crescents, and stars of David up the sacred mounts
And beating them into plowshares.

RETURN FROM EXILE

The Judeans into exile went and had years to mourn and to lament
    Strangers took over their Jerusalem homes
And busily built colonies in honeycombs.
    The strangers' children, knowing nothing of the past,
Thought their ownership would always last.
    And the first Jews who from exile returned
Were by the strangers cursed and spurned.
    Although the strangers resisted the returnees insisted,
"We have permission from the Persian king to reclaim everything
    We lost when we were dragged into exile by the Assyrians,
Base and vile."
    The strangers said the Jews had no rights.
And scuffled with them in violent flights.
    But alas the Persian kings decreed that the Jews
Who from captivity had been freed were the rightful owners
    of the land given to them by God's command.
Stranger and Jew lived side by side, arguing their claims was justified.

CYRUS

Day after day the Judean exiles filled the waters of Babylon with their tears.
    "O God," they keened, "send us a redeemer.
We have suffered for so many years.
    Orphans are we and widows, too; in sackcloth we dress.
We smear our faces with ashes and our sins confess."

Although exile purified their souls and every sin did they repent,
    Angered over their iniquities, God did not relent.
"Our souls are no longer black; to the Torah we adhere."
    And, in time, God saw that their atonement was sincere.

In Persia there was a king who embodied all that was right
    And was inspired to conquer Babylon, civilization's blight.
*Koresh was his name *Cyrus
    And for purity was he known. (kosher, pure, an anagram of Koresh)
With his army of Persian soldiers the Babylonians were overthrown.

"Children of Israel," he wrote, "return home rededicated
    And rebuild your Holy House which to God was consecrated."
And he gave back the cattle, the silver and the gold,
    As well as the sacred relics the Babylonians stole.

And the Israelites learned a lesson: a righteous life to lead
    And were grateful to the Persian savior
Who from bondage had them freed.
    And God learned a lesson, too. Vengeful not to be;
But to accept human imperfections and to the repentant grant amnesty.

RENEWAL IN THE DAYS OF EZRA AND NEHEMIAH

Memory, in tatters, was swallowed by the abyss of Time
    Where the spark of Sinai, smothered by indifference,
Drifted into extinction.
    Then there gathered in Jerusalem the exiles who had returned:
Priests, gate keepers, singers, temple servants, persons of distinction
    Husbands and "wives and all their sons and daughters."
Nehemia, X, 28
    In God's eyes each one the same as another;
In thinking and wisdom, each equal to the other.
    All with one purpose: to hear the Levites read from the scroll of the Law
That God had given to Moses. At that moment of bonding,
    They rededicated themselves to God
At that moment they again became God's people.
    Then did the sun peering through history
Rekindle the lamp that guided their ancestors
    Through the bleakness of the past.
And they passed it on for untold generations to come.

EZRA

When Ezra, the priest, to Zion returned, his eyes wept when he learned
    That many bachelor Jews did foreign wives choose.
Assimilation corrodes the marrow of our souls and with pomp extols
    What is vile and does our God defile.
He gathered the people at The Temple gate
    And adjured the men to send back any mate
Whose false gods accepts and lives not by the precepts
    Of the Mosaic creed as God had decreed.
That day saddened brides cried in shame
    For each had lost her marriage name.
Ezra believed that rangers impure would be an overture
    To dissolution of the race and in time
Jews would disappear without trace.
    The people hailed Ezra, the wise;
Never would he his faith compromise.
    There was a Jew, though, who loved his wife
So that he did not agree to let her go.
    And the community threw stones at his head until life
Left his body and he fell down dead.

THE WORDS OF THE LORD TO JOEL

Hearken to the words of the Lord whose wrath upon you has been poured.
    You, every man, woman, and child of Judea.
Seek not a panacea for the locust swarms, rolling in like winter storms.
    They have your fig trees and vines devoured;
They have all new crops deflowered,
    The sheep have no grass for eating and roam about aimlessly bleating.
The animals of the wild wail and cry because the streams
    They drink from have all gone dry.
You people filled with woe loudly, loudly the shofar blow.
    As you hear the shofar blasting afflict your body with humble fasting.
Sincerely repent the wayward way; return to God Whom you betray.
    The people prayed with hearts sincere,
Neither in shallow words nor verbal veneer.
    And God made the land fertile once more as it had been in days of yore.
Zion again became righteous and chaste
    And its foes were trapped and laid waste.
None of the vicious guilty were spared and Zion's soul was again repaired.
    To its former glory was Jerusalem restored thanks
To the love of the merciful Lord.

HAGGAI

The Lord God inspired Haggai to give this message to the People of Israel.

"Your homes are luxuriously decorated
    But My Temple still lies desecrated.
You have planted much, but your harvest is spare.
    You have clothing but it is threadbare.
The working man has too little to live on;
    So many of the strong and the young have gone.
Now go to the woods and cut down trees
    Hew stones from the hills, the Lord decrees,
Get masons and carpenters who are skilled
    And My Holy Temple with haste rebuild!"
The people hearkened to the words of the Lord
    And a shrine splendid from the ashes soared.
No longer was The Temple in desolation,
    It had been restored with dedication.
The Lord blessed the soil with sun
    And rain and in its season came plentiful grain.

VISIONS OF ZECHARIAH

Zechariah wandered between the crags,
    Prancing like a goat when from his heart a vision
Came that formed words inside his throat.
    Horses galloped to and fro as if looking for a home
And Zechariah asked out loud why do these horses roam?
    An angel riding a steed of red said he had asked the Lord above
Why do you still rage at Judah? Show them, God, Your Love.
    And the Lord replied, their ancestors practiced sinful ways.
The angel politely countered but the seed of their seed
    Have not been strays.
The Almighty relented, seeing the angel's point
    And told him to rebuild The Temple
which the angels will anoint.

Another vision to Zechariah came in which a man held a measuring stick
    "What do you do?" the prophet asked.
"Surveying Jerusalem by arithmetic."
    Then angels spoke to the prophet to stop the man surveying
Because God will Jerusalem with a wall of fire be arraying.

STILL ANOTHER VISION

A silent voice called, "Zechariah" around the bend comes The Messiah
To redeem the people of Israel from its torment, from its travail.
    Lightning arrows will fly about: black clouds will thunder sprout.
    The mighty king will a donkey ride lowly, meekly, and dignified.
At that time wars will cease, and the king will bring lasting peace
To nations far and wide over which God alone will preside.
    And every man, woman and child who from their homelands were exiled
    Will wear a crown of gold which will God's merciful love enfold.

THE MISSION OF MALACHI

Malachi stood on the top of the hill announcing the words God had spoken,
"I have always shown my love for you, but you have the covenant broken.
    The priests light fires of offering, but empty is each word; shallow,
    each deed I seek prayers that are from the heart not from priestly greed.
There will come a day when evil will burn like straw,
But the righteous will rise like the golden sun because they obey My holy law."

JOB'S SUIT

Why me, Adonai? Why me? What have I done to deserve my fate?
    What sin have I committed to be so punished?
Yesterday I had ten children;
    Yesterday I had fertile land, sheep, and wealth.
Yesterday the poor begged alms of me;
    Yesterday the priests sought my counsel.
Yesterday my skin was clear and I was in good health.
    Did I not make proper sacrifices to You
In the name of my forgetful children?
    Did I not make proper sacrifices of thanks
To You for the bounty You gave me?
    Today all of my children are dead. My three daughters were raped.
Today the winds dried my fields; today the marauding
    Chaldeans burned them, stole my sheep, and destroyed my house.
Today my skin is sick and I am distressed.
    Today the poor scoff at me and the priests scorn me.
Where can I now find shelter? How can I now earn a living?
    What I have been taught and what I learned well
Is that the good sow kindness and reap righteousness;
    And the righteous plant piety and harvest grace.
Adonai does not punish the innocent; Elohim does not flog the virtuous.
    My wife says, "Denounce Adonai!" My wife says, "Curse Elohim."
Because I have lost all, my friends say, I have faltered;
    Because I have been so humbled, my comrades say, I have sinned.
My calamities, they say, grew from my iniquities;
    My wounds, they say, erupt from my sins.
But when have I committed an iniquity? But how have I sinned?
    Adonai, You have filled my dreams with terror. Elohim,
You blanket my soul with torment.
    Why have You dismissed me like a nobody?
Why have You robbed me of being a somebody?

Is sorrow to be my legacy? Is pain to be my heritage?
    My friends say do not doubt Adonai;
My comrades say do not question Elohim.
    What comfort have they given me? What consolation do they offer?
I am equal to them in wisdom: they speak clichés, folklore, ignorance.
    Did You Adonai appoint them prosecutors?
Did You Adonai name them to be my accusers?
    My friends have abandoned me! You have deserted me.
Who will now defend me? Who but myself will be my advocate?
    Can You Adonai explain my misery?
Can You Elohim unravel my torment?
    Do my angry words flow from my affliction?
Does my rage grow from my misfortune?
    Hear me voice, O Adonai! Listen to my words, Elohim.
Do not destroy my hope; do not demolish my faith.
    Have I condemned You for *Your* blunders?
Have I blamed You for *Your* mistakes?
    Then a voice was heard through the storm and mournful
Words sprung from the sea of sorrows.
    Job your pain is My pain, too.
Job your distress is Mine also.
    Survival means struggle; life is filled with trials.
Question Me! Doubt Me!
    But never give up the struggle. Never surrender!

ANTIOCHUS'S LAST WILL AND TESTAMENT

Into the looking glass Antiochus gazed;
    A curse on your soul his Self-appraised.
He wept as he of the wizen-face viewed his past before him race.
    He clung to the last strand of life, all alone without child or wife.
Waves of sadness pummeled his brain
    As memory brought him to the days of his reign
When he plundered The Temple and profaned each room
    And sent innocent children to their doom.
Oh what gloom now visits Antiochus's mind. How many lives were lost?
    And at what human cost?
How many lives were cut short in the frenzy of battle sport?
    How many bodies had been gored by the thirst of a careless sword?
And the pain of the wounded and the lame of all of these I carry the same
    Into the grave where I'll join the dead
And into the ignominy which I merited.
    How callous was I on the Sabbath to attack unarmed victims
who could not fight back.
    And Judah, the brave Maccabee, gathered troops to fight against me.
Outnumbered, They fought miraculously with resolve
    And defeated my army
In glorious battle that made widows and orphans on each side-
    Oh how kings so often misguide.
Now I understand how resolute was their stand
    To defend their land against foreign oppressors
Who defiled their temple.
    Curse aggressors who overwhelmed them in strife
And changed the Mosaic way of life.
    Of course, there were turncoats who helped my cause
But we exploited each other and neither of us deserve applause.
    Oh Yahweh! Oh Zeus! Bring balm to my soul; make my life whole

And from my guilt bring release and let me find peace.
    But not a word Antiochus thought was ever heard
Because more battles flared and no city was spared.
    More dead lay in streets, more wounded Death greets,
More ashes were smeared on faces sad
    More sackcloth was worn as the world went mad.

WHERE ARE THE PROPHETS?

"Ah" is an ending of many Hebrew names. It means "God." Isaiah means God's savior; Jeremiah, God's loftiness; Zechariah, God's remembering; and Zephania, God's mystery. "El" is also an ending of many Hebrew names. Samuel means God's name; Joel, YHWH is God; Ezekiel, God's strength; and Daniel, God's judgment. Perhaps, upon conversion, prophets were renamed with attributes of God.

In their graves the prophets silently lie;
    In their burial places are they mute.
But from Eternity their words thunder;
    From beyond Time their voices sizzle like lightning.
They are the consciences of morally-starved spirits;
    They are the scruples of ethnically-hungry souls.
Gathered in their holy places are Isaiah,
    Jeremiah, Zechariah, and Zephania;
Assembled in their celestial rewards are Samuel,
    Joel, Ezekiel, and Daniel.
These were among God's anointed;
    These were among God's appointed.
Simple shepherds and lowly priests;
    Humble craftsmen and modest smiths.
    One day they were ordinary citizens, no different from others.
Then a sudden summons from the Divine transformed them
    From reluctant appointees into God's willing messengers
And from hesitant speakers into God's eloquent spokesmen.
    To their eyes was revealed every scintilla
Of every flicker of every flame,
    Every faint edge of the clouds, every cell of pollen of a flower,
Every droplet of sweat between the hairs of a camel's mustache.
    In their ears was heard every whisper of the most distant zephyr,
Every sigh of the afflicted, every sprouting of every seed,
    Every wave of every heartbeat.

In their hands came balm for healing the destitute, the ill, the shackled;
    The oppressed, the afflicted, the wronged, and the sinners.
They were the reflections radiating the mystery of God;
    They were the mirrors reflecting the wonder of God,
And the retinae transmitting the awe of God.
    They spoke God's thoughts with cleansed tongues;
They revealed God's words with chaste souls.
    Hearken to the word of God, they would say;
Listen to God's commands, they would inveigh.
    Do good and not evil; act righteously and not out of malice.
God rewards the virtuous and punishes the transgressor.
    But they also contended with God to forgive the wayward
And they pleaded with God to show compassion to the sinner.
    Their words live in our hearts still;
Their voices echo in our minds yet.
    Their authority reprimands our misdeeds
But their caring comforts us in our struggles.

GOLDEN SAYINGS OF SOLOMON

Solomon gathered scholars of all generations: past, present, and future
    To teach them what he had learned from his life.
The scholars recast his teachings for their students.
    And their students refashioned them for their generations.
These are the golden words that glistened like dew drops
    upon Solomon's tongue;
These are the splendid thoughts that shone like sunlight upon Solomon's lips,
    Listen to my words with a keen ear;
Hearken to my thoughts with a discerning heart.
    Wisdom calls in the streets and in the marketplace,
Sapience summons all at the city gates. Wisdom speaks to all:
    The young, the old; the wise, the dolt; the sage, the oaf;
Sapience speaks to fathers, mothers; sisters and brothers;
    teachers and tyros; rulers and subjects.

Let these sayings be your guide; let these precepts be your beacon.
    At all times under all circumstances.
Scorn not knowledge, Flout not learning;
    Confess humbly what you know not,
Modesty, display what you understand;
    Be honest, just, and fair, Be loyal and faithful;
Scorn evil, Speak Truth;
    Plan carefully, Prepare diligently; Be calm, Conquer inner tumult;
Cherish your loved ones, Treasure your friends;
    Be ambitious; Shun indolence; Value virtue; Never cheat;
Learn from rebuke, Practice proficiency;
    Be strong in a crisis, Be steadfast to resolve a dilemma;
Hold your wrath, Radiate your delight;
    Revile no one's name, nor the undertakings of others.
Do not lament your failures, Do not rejoice when others stumble;
    Vex not at the insolence of others.

Be solemn in your grief, envy not;
    Correct children when they err; Never abandoned hope;
Love builds; Drain yourself of malice; Gloat not over your wealth,
    Pray with a pure heart; Remember these sayings, too.
Share your happiness with others; Let not gloom be your companion,
    Respect the knowledge of the elderly;
Favor not the rich because of their wealth deficits;
    Do not exploit the helpless; Hold all to the same standard of merit,
Praise even the smallest; shun deceit.
    Accept flaws, bring comfort to those who appreciate the courtesy of
others; Be happy in your mirth, Think before you speak;
    Plan carefully; Hate destroys;
Unhamper yourself of grudges, despise pride and arrogance;
    Brag not about your misfortune, Revere God.

Never forget these proverbs. Reveal your bitterness to no one.
    Serenity restores the soul.
Let not woe be your friend; honor the observations
    Of the poor because they do not pander to the rich.
Gauge all with the same yardstick.

THE WILL OF KOHELLET*

*A madras based on Ecclesiastes, 1–3.

Kohellet stood before The Supreme Judge who was considering his fate.

"Identify yourself, preacher," asked The Voice.
 "I am Kohellet of the Davidic line who reigned in Zion."
"Why mention your lineage?
 Does it qualify you for some special treatment?" asked The Voice.

As an arrogant, omniscient sovereign he believed it was his due;
 As a humble man of fleeting morality it was not he knew.
Torn between the two referenda, Kohellet was silent, evidence of his wisdom.
 "What, preacher, is your legacy to humanity?" asked The Voice.

Kohellet took a deep breath, knowing he was on the threshold of death.
 "To the future I will a North Star to guide it in the navigating
Of the repetitive rhythm of life, fruitless as it is."
 Know ye, children to come, that there is a cycle to life
Like the ebb and flow of the tides.
 Each event has its own phase; each period has its own moment.

A time to sow and a time to reap. A time to wound and a time to heal.
 A time to destroy and a time to build. A time to mourn and a time to laugh.
A time to lose and a time to find. A time to cast away and a time to gather.
 A time to be distant and a time to be close.
A time to tear and a time to mend. A time to speak and a time to be silent.
 A time to hate and a time to love. A time to make war
And a time to make peace.
 A time to enter this world and a time to leave.

But between the apogee and perigee lies a vast ocean of ambiguity.
    The cup of life is filled with emptiness.
The noble purposes in the heart are meaningless.
    The mind seeking knowledge gathers ignorance.
The soul filled with charity is self-serving.

Generations to come! Futile it is to fathom the Divine Design!
    Your mission is to prove me right or wrong!

The Supreme Judge contemplated the words of Kohellet
    And granted them immortality.

A CODICIL TO THE WILL OF KOHELLET*

*The book of Kohellet, Ecclesiastes, is read on the Sabbath of Succot, a pilgrimage festival, during which one Torah cycle ends and another begins. The text deals with cycles in Nature and in human society, a season for every phase of life. Ecclesiastes, 1–3 is the legacy of Kohellet This codicil augments that will.

Oh ye generations to come, Succot pilgrims in search of sacred knowledge,
    I have learned about life through much pain and abundant joy.
From my adventures I have culled wisdom which I will to you.
    Too much reflection invites imperfection;
The soul that is unduly scrutinized becomes unraveled.
    Still study the waxing and waning of the moon!
Know that all human endeavors, likewise, have recurrent phases:

A time to think, a time to feel; a time to vent emotions, a time to hold back;
    A time to be gregarious, a time to be alone; a time to take risks,
A time to be cautious;
    A time to win, a time to lose; a time to add, a time to decrease;
A time to unite, a time to separate; a time to wander, a time to return;

A time to be jovial, a time to be serious; a time to conform,
    A time to deviate;
A time to accept, a time to challenge; a time to remember, a time to forget;
    A time to perceive, a time to overlook; a time to speak,
A time to be silent.

With a stilled tongue, witnessed by all generations to come, I am

    Kohellet of the sovereign Davidic line.

TOBIT, A GOOD MAN, AS SEEN FROM THE EYES OF HIS BEST FRIEND

When I returned from the mission to Medea I jumped upon
    My master's lap and cuddled close to him.
He smelled me and tickled my spotted fur; I didn't stir even though
    I wanted to cry
Sympathetically as he sobbed, tears bursting from his eyes
    Like raindrops from the skies
Dropping upon my head mixing with road dust caking my skin.
    "Kelev*, it is you! You have returned!" I just whimpered. *dog
"Oh Kelev. You have returned." I snuggled closer to him.
    My paws were raw from having walked in the brambles;
My stomach ached from eating so many field mice.
    I limped; I could not digest my food; I needed a bath.
Still yapped with great glee when
    The young master, Tobias, like his father, a good man,
Came down the path.
    "Father! Father! I am here with Sarah, my bride."
"Oh that I could see her." Tobit swallowed his words.
    "Her beauty wants not to hide from your eyes," Tobias said.
"Father when we were journeying to Medea Kelev
    Ran into the water to refresh himself.
A large fish appeared. He chased it and I caught it. Rafael, our companion,
    A master of healing, truly an angel, told me
To cut out the fish's gall bladder
    And to apply it to your eyes when we returned."
My master said that only a miracle from God would restore his sight.
    And a miracle took place. My master regained his sight.
For the first time in many months he saw light.
    First it was like a flash of gold radiating from the sun
Scintillating, brilliant, dazzling, enchanting and beguiling.
    At that very moment he saw Rafael become one with the light

And mysteriously disappear. Then Tobit turned to Sarah.
　　The same grace that dazzled only a moment before burnished her face
And revealed the goodness of her soul nourish his anguished being.
　　I was with him when he was blinded. Assyrian soldiers made a game
Of murdering Jews And throwing their bodies into the marketplace;
　　Flies and maggots swarmed about the corpses
Then other soldiers would release wild wolves who would tear
　　The dead into pieces and chew their flesh.
Could there be a crueler outrage? I could tell when I heard
　　The sniggering of the soldiers
That there was another Jewish victim. My master would crawl
　　Into the market place at night.
As I stood guard he removed each body, Stinking with death,
　　And would give it a proper burial.
We returned from this merciful mission late one night.
　　Not wishing to waken Anna, my mistress,
Tobit and I slept side by side in the courtyard.
　　At dawn birds dropped warm dung upon his eyes
And blinded him. How he despaired. How anguished he felt
　　Not performing his acts of righteousness.
Blinded, he no longer worked to support his family;
　　He no longer sought the poor to aid them.
He no longer felt he was a man. He prayed to God for healing
　　But no cure had come.
Anna, a weaver, supported the family. Soon she became tired,
　　Haggard, and ill-tempered.
This saddened my master all the more.
　　Many years before he had left bags of silver with a kinsman.
Remembering this he sent Tobias to Medea to reclaim them.
　　His leaving saddened Tobit and Anna.
They feared that Tobias would meet a sad end.
　　No one could comfort them; they lay awake imagining horrible scenes.
Tobias assured them that I and the stranger, Rafael, would protect him.
　　They worried nevertheless. My master listened attentively
As I continued my tale
　　"We arrived in Ecbatana at the home of a kinsman, Raguel.
His daughter, Sarah, entered the room.
　　Tobias's face flushed and his legs waxed weak and melted into the floor.

His eyes sparkled and his ears heard songs that no one was singing.
    He was in love.
Sarah's heart humped with excitement; her face flushed, too.
    Her eyes sparkled, too, and her ears heard songs that no one
Was singing. She was in love.
    Tobias asked for Sarah's hand in marriage.
Sarah was frightened because she has been wed seven times before
    And each time the groom died before the marriage bed was reached.
The gossip in Ecbatana was that Sarah was a witch inhabited by a demon.
    Sarah was despondent. She felt uglier than garbage.
She was bad luck. She was afraid to wed Tobias:
    She loved him too much to let him die. Rafael told Tobias
To burn the heart and liver of the fish,
    The one that I had chased to the shore, the one whose gall bladder
Returned your sight.
    The aroma of the incense so changed Sarah that she felt
She was rid of the demon
    And saw her beauty as Tobias saw it. Handsome! She was cured.
They wed. The silver was retrieved.

We departed for Nineveh with sheep, camels, and goats.
    Often along the road Sarah would lift me on to her camel
And hold me close to her heart and would rock me to sleep.

The spirit of Rafael brought back the memory of how you hid me,
    A pup, inside your cloak when the Assyrians sacked Jerusalem and
Made us walk to Nineveh.
    You shared your rations with me, kept me warm, and clean.
I am the only dog to have been taken into the Diaspora.
    Master, the mistress Sarah is a righteous woman."

In the days that followed Tobit and Sarah walked through
    The streets of Nineveh feeding the hungry, clothing the poor,
Sheltering the needy,
    And burying the cruelty defiled. In the evening they gave thanks to God
For allowing them to perform their good works, each petting my fur
    As I snuggled close to them welled within them.
As they were healed so did they heal.

GOOD LIVING: A GUIDE MY GRANDFATHER WILLED TO ME: A MIDRASH ON ECCLESIASTICUS

1.

Grandfather, I would say, Let's take a coconut and play
    Or let's swim in the brook "Yes," he would answer
Handing me his book,
    Rocking back and forth in his chair, "Child, my treasure, my heir,
We have so much to learn and even more to unlearn.
    Help me examine what I wrote and review each and every note.
I want to be precise; I want to be understood;
    I want my lessons to make people reach a higher good.
I want them to be better than they now are. Much better by far.
    Who first these words did not speak: Was it a Babylonian,
A Jew, perhaps, a Greek?
    I do not know who spoke them originally, but they
have been remolded by me from fragments
    I amassed that our ancestors to us have passed.
Remember what the wise Solomon once wrote,
    And this is the exact quote,
"There is nothing new under the sun."

What I have done is taken the wisdom of all ages gathered
    By prophets and by sages
And recast them to unfold a philosophy of life more precious than gold
    That will bring inspired insight to life-travelers
Who walk the path of right.

Then his voice trailed off and came to a stop-
    So heavy was the silence I thought it would drop.
After pausing to meditate, his body began to undulate,
    And as he was swaying, I heard him praying.

"Lord of the universe from
    Whom all Good does flow teach us that we may
Wisdom know. You who are so generous grant understanding to us."
    Then Simeon ben Yehoshua ben Eleazar ben Sira,
My granddad, grew silent. He forbade any talking.
    Again it was time for meditating, Even outdoors the winds were abating.

2.

Grandfather now in Egypt I sit translating into Greek
    Your thoughts and wit.
I am doing what you once did ask but it has been no easy task
    Because even in translating into one's own tongue
From which a thought was originally sprung
    A part of the essence is lost.
There is an even great cost
    When translating into a foreign speech
The thoughts that one wants to teach.

A meaning in one's place and time changes in another era and clime.
    Still the thoughts you spoke I have tried to transmit and your
God-given wisdom to posterity will submit.
    It will not suffer stagnation but will grow in the minds
Of each new generation
    Who will adapt your messages to the lives they know.
Surely their souls with your splendent light will glow.
    And their grandchildren and their grandchildren's grandchildren
And every future generation will have your guide to improve civilization.

3.

As if from a dream, grandfather one day awoke
    And in golden whispers, inspired, he spoke,
"Wisdom was created before all. Wisdom was there before Adam's fall.
    Adam had God's command contradicted and from Paradise
Had been evicted. He paid a heavy price—and how.
    He had to labor by the sweat of his brow.

Eve, his wife, gave birth in pain, and keened when their Cain
    Had his brother slain. In those primeval days of which I speak, God's
First mortals were morally weak.
    They did not resist temptation and provoked God's consternation.
Oh how they did Wisdom shun, dispatching it to oblivion.
    They lacked respect for The Lord's Sacred Word
And scorned all God's guides that they ever heard.
    My child, Wisdom comes to those who worship God
With sincerity and who Creation's wonders daily laud.
    Wisdom grows from awe of the Lord;
Wisdom blossoms when God is adored.
    It was mortally wounded whenever people raged;
It convulsed and died when wars were waged.
    Child! Even when distressed be in no rush to speak
Control your passions and never shriek."

"Neither hypocritical nor arrogant be;
    Be humble even when you disagree."
Grandfather's energies now spent, he lay down to rest.
    We continued when he realized he lost his zest.

4.

The next day grandfather awoke with smiling eyes.
    His ideas were pleasing, there was nothing to revise.
"Child, we owe much to Abraham who founded our nation."
    He bought land in Canaan and gave fair compensation.
While others would at God laugh and sneer Abraham's love
    For God was sincere.
Stored in his heart was each Sacred Thought which to his children
    He diligently taught.
"Like the stars in the skies will your nation be."
    Moses, the teacher, was without a peer;
To this day we revere that seer.
    In this stuttering man the Lord God saw
The one to teach The Sacred Law.
    Up a mountain ascended a quavering clod;

Down a mountain descended the spokesman of God
    Beaming with light and filled with awe carrying the tablets
Where inscribed was the law:
    The laws he now read to all of Israel and insisted
That they be obeyed without fail.
    'At all times be aware that there is but one God found everywhere
Whose Name shall never be pronounced in vain
    Or ever spoken with an air of disdain.
Labor six days of every week but on the seventh rest do seek.
    Your parents you must always obey and you will never go astray.
Never kill another: not a stranger, nor a brother.

    Do not adultery commit or to passion wantonly submit.
Never steal another's things: whether of the poor or of kings.
    Never falsely accuse; never another abuse.
Respect another's property; lest there be anarchy.'

So many laws did they that day hear; so many laws to which to adhere.
    But there were even more to come,
Many our forebears found burdensome.
    But Moses gave each law the very same weight: none was open
To any debate. The message each contains that is embedded
    In our brains is to all people be merciful, just, "and fair
And of false gods and alien ways always beware."

5.

One day I heard grandfather cry, "My mind is squeezed out dry.
    My brain is an empty space; my words have fallen out of place."
Then swooping down from out of nowhere was a bird quite rare:
    Black with feathers shimmering in the sun
Sent to him by The Holy One.
    It spoke not a word yet grandfather every sound had heard.
Then spreading its feathers away it flew and grandfather discovered
    What he always knew. The secret of a good life from his mind
Then sprung and a simple message rolled down his tongue,
    "What Aaron, Joshua, and Samuel shared was a nature that showed
They cared for people no matter their estate.

What was important to them was to consecrate oneself
    To God immortal—in no way to be likened to any mortal.
This lesson teaches humility. Can the highest degree
    Mortals attain be little higher than an ant?
What cause do they have to be so arrogant to think that their views
    Must prevail when they measure themselves on a cosmic scale?

Can they mountains grow? Can they make rivers flow?
    Can they animals create? Can they life forms mutate?
Humble we must be in what we say. Are we not all just made of clay?
    Even with facts we know quite well there is an air
Of mystery we cannot expel.

The very act of cogitating about Wisdom is elevating.
    It is life's supreme mission; it is the mind's nutrition.
Do not relegate it to a lower caste; our ignorance and deviance
    Are unsurpassed. Those who gained Wisdom have joy unfurled
And are already making this a better world."

"So many of God's children are truly blessed, but there are others
    Who are distressed: The widow, the orphan, and the lame,
The victims of cruelty wallowing in shame.
    They all lack love, shelter, raiment, and food
Any one of which is a prelude
    To disease. And their degradation lowers love of self
In their own estimation

And is scored by those Good Fortune once kissed.
    We must plan our lives to give them an assist.
Sheltering, clothing, and feeding the poor
    While not being a cure will provide them comfort so they can rise
And their in-born talents maximize."

6.

And as for the victims of heinous deeds don't
    Cut them down as petty weeds

But show them all love sincere; everyone by God is held dear.
    What can we do for those depressed,
Those who feel they are unblessed?
    We should stretch out our arms in understanding
So their sense of worth will be expanding.
    What do acts of mercy do by showing we care?
We raise the hopes of those in despair.

For acts of kindness like these we change people's destinies.
    Such acts of charity will unfetter and makes this world so much better.
Will we receive The Almighty's embrace?
    Will we be crowned with heavenly grace?
When we a cup of mercy have poured the good deed
    That follows is its own reward.

"Listen to these thoughts that I compiled;
    Listen carefully my love, my child."
It was a sunny day in Spring when Grandfather began
    To sing in his resonant baritone, rocking back
And forth, oscillating each tone,
    'The righteous person is like a tree spreading its branches
Like a canopy "In season it brings forth tasty fruit."
    The righteous are so astute
That none of their branches have a withering leaf so strong
    Has been their belief In Almighty God and so righteous
Have been the paths they trod.
    The upright succeed in whatever they pursue.
But the wicked are like chaff that the wind blows askew.'

Those are the images of David,
    The king whose words will ever cling
To the soul whenever they are spoken.
    They can mend a heart that has been broken.
Those words are like the broomrape plant.
    They attach to your roots and enchant
With their spikes of gold wondrous to behold.

'The Lord is my shepherd I shall not want.
    He leadeth me beside still waters and restores my soul."

Mortals will always know grief and will always seek relief.
    David planted hope in our souls which in time of grief consoles.
It does not a loss replace—nor tears of sorrow chase-
    But each phrase in those lines is like the sun that shines,
Radiating warmth throughout the soul and making us again
    Feel complete, feel whole. The elegant way David would speak!
What mystique There is in the patter of his meter.
    Can the scent of any word-flower be sweeter?

'The Lord will give strength unto His people
    And will bless his people with peace."

After Winter's dreary days, these words are comforting
    Like the flowers that are reborn in the Spring.
"David, who to our souls like a gardener tended,
    Planted balm which the knives of anguish transcended."

8.

"Evil, child, is a disease; it's stench more vile than rotting cheese.
    It sickens; it afflicts; it turns good people into derelicts."

The wise Solomon assembled each saying to turn us away
    From asinine braying and bring us closer to the Divine
And lets us bask in God's sunshine.

"Listen to what your father and mother tell you.
    Their teaching will improve your character.
Resist the immoral person who seduces you with smooth talk.
    The Lord does not tolerate a proud look, a lying tongue,
Or one who stirs up trouble among friends of family.
    Do not be taken in by the charm of a flatterer;
You do not need another to gauge your worth.
    Honesty can save your life.
The sensible person gathers crops when they are ripe.
    Sensible people accept good advice.
Anyone who spreads gossip is a fool.
    Never ask a lazy person to do something for you.

Such a person is acid in your mouth and smoke in your eyes.
    The righteous speak Kindly; the wicked hurt others.
You do yourself a kindness when you yourself are kind"
    Each of these sayings of Solomon is a gem,
A sparkling jewel in the diadem
    Of righteous ways that goodness brings and fear allays.
The luster of each saying is brilliant.
    It is like a rock resilient
To scratching. It is always catching
    Light reflecting it for all to see.
Each is a legacy
    From the great minds of the past who
For us have these jewels amassed.

9.

"Grandfather you are so wise. How well you harmonize
    Present-day knowledge which is so vast
With that of generations past."
    "Child, the fragments that have come down through
The ages from scholars, priests, prophets, and sages
    Have by chance coalesced in my mind and have become intertwined
With the virtues taught by ethical titans whom people
    Like you and me enlightens.
My words would be empty without the seer, Elijah.
    My sentence, vacant without the prophet, Elisha.
Would I know about justice without the morality of Jeremiah?
    Would I know about mercy without the compassion of Isaiah?
Solomon's sons did not follow in their father's path
    And did such terrible deeds to incur God's wrath.

First each son tried to grab as his own the gilded throne
    Of Zion and split Judah's lion asunder. It is no wonder
That a glorious nation based on the foundation
    Of Torah brighter than the candles of a Menorah Was snuffed out?
Was thrown about? Solomon's Rehoboam! Solomon's Jeroboam!
    The greedy brothers hated one another. Each sought to wrest power

From the other. And thus did Israel's North from Judea's South secede.
    What a wretched deed! They weakened each side.
When two brothers collide
    In anger each is diminished.
When the fight continues both are finished.
    Mortals must learn to analyze and find ways to compromise
So that we all live in amity and harvest the fruit of harmony."

10.

"Grandfather!" I said. "I often hear Isaiah's voice inside of me."
    "Of course!" he replied.
"Isaiah's voice is even inside generations yet to be.
    Moses gave us laws. Amos recited our flaws.
But Isaiah who by God was sent taught us all that if we repent-
    And our ways are no longer depraved—we will be saved.
He is our conscience. He torments
    Only when we go astray. So every scheme we must weigh
In order to feel free of sin, of guilt, of shame, and of chagrin.
    I hear his sobbing voice proclaiming
From the mountain top we have a choice
    And pleading with us to scorn temptation.
God has placed us on probation.
    Abhor the Moloch, an idol, a fraud
And return to the ways of the Holy God.
    Isaiah reminds us of what is right and wrong.
Listen to him and become morally strong.
    Practice the virtues he advocated
And to God become reconsecrated.
    Then we will achieve the highest state:
Paradise on earth can be our fate.

We will be with God's glory graced
    And by the grandeur of God become embraced.
What is clear from what Isaiah has said our
    Destiny is what we have merited.
Never betray God by unseemly deeds and follow
    Only where virtue leads."

11.

"Grandfather. How can I ill fate not worsen?
   How can I become a better person?"
"Child, allow these rules within you to preside;
   Let these rules always be your guide.
Honor your father with all of your heart;
   Sincerely respect your mother who did impart
To you a map with the pathways of the wise.
   With the bereaved agonize;
With the poor their hunger taste;
   Distance yourself from the unchaste.
Do not think ill of those who are old;
   They are wiser than you a thousandfold.
Sin draws a curtain across the light and earns
   For the sinner the darkness of night.
An acquaintance is not a friend until mutual trust has ripened.
   Don't be another's protégé or agree with whatever others say if
their words hurt or if their actions pervert.
   God does not forgive the inveterate sinner
And in God's eyes you are no winner
   If your righteousness you flaunt.
You must never widows and orphans taunt.
   Give them a helping hand. Change the course that you have planned
If it failure brings.
   With your neighbors be friends; feuding siblings should make amends.
Filthy talk demeans and is no more beautiful then latrines.
   The rich cast a spell when they speak even when they folly wreak
But when the poor speaks a word too often listeners call it absurd.
   To defraud the poor is to oppress the oppressed
Who are already broke and sadly depressed.
   Analyze whatever words you hear not on the basis
Of how the speakers appear
   But on their quality and cogency.
Like God show all respect and the vulnerable do protect;
   Be merciful and just and righteous people always trust.
Never gossip or repeat a tale;
   Never falsely accuse or do blackmail.

It is often better to be silent be than to bite another's reputation like a flea.
    If it is not your business do not get involved
You will be considered at fault and not get absolved.
    Never lazy be but show the world your industry.
Do not flatter or give a compliment undeserved;
    Be not boastful but be reserved.
Wail and cry when loved ones die.
    But there is a time when you must withdraw
From gloom and your normal life you must resume.
    Instruct yourself to be of good cheer and, above all,
Almighty God revere. The prophets say,
    'Do you think God is willing to be honored by spilling
The blood of the first lamb born? Such a ritual does God scorn.
    Ritual slaughter is a human convention, a human invention.
God seeks a heart that is pure.
    Perfunctory displays of worship you must abjure.
The Lord takes delight in prayers of the upright;
    But sacrifices from those who sin and are putrid within.
Good deeds without thought of reward
    Is how we can best revere the Lord."

12.

After mulling over his last words, "Grandfather," I said
    "You were by spirits of the prophets visited."
"The flame of Sinai that burned within Ezekiel,
    within Nahum, Habbakuk, Joel, and Daniel
Sheds light on what is pure; and reveals a cure
    To the ailing human soul; righteous living is within our own control.
Enoch, a grandchild, too, though not a Jew,
    Taught that if people transgress they should confess
And ask that God forgive so that a life that is pure they will live.
    And who saved the mortals from the flood?
The gentile, Noah, whose soul also flows in our blood.
    So, my child, we can from everyone something learn;
Never another point of view spurn."

13.

"Grandfather," I asked while I was reconciling
    So many of the thoughts I was compiling,
"Can the many thoughts that you offer be reduced to one?"
    "That cannot be done," He replied.
"Every human has more than one trait.
    I would confiscate God-given individuality to engage in such brevity.
Humans are complex; there is no single index
    Which can be used to measure them.
Although complex each is a gem
    That has a sheen such that the world has never before seen.
The luster of People is here within you and me
    And it is everywhere and within generations yet to be."

14.

I asked "What message is there for generations to come
    So that one can achieve the optimum?
How wise was his reply, "At all times yourself dignify.
    Do not your talents ever debase or your merits ever abase.
These gifts God, The Holy One, has granted you.
    These faculties did God imbue in you through glorious creation.
Any negation brings vexation.
    So look in the glass and see how beautifully
You are blessed and in God's eyes are seen among the best.

Self-reprimands sting they do not teach you anything.
    Certainly not to do better. So self-distrust from yourself unfetter.
There is no excuse to run yourself down; upon self-abasement
    The Lord does frown. An insult to yourself
Is a reproach to God so upon yourself spare the rod.

Upon yourself at all times be just
    And in yourself always have trust."

EUGULOGY FOR ONIAS*

*Approximately 164 BCE

O Onias how Jerusalem grieves for you.
    Its houses are shrouded in black.
Its men wear sackcloth; its women weep day and night.
    We knew leave when you were High Priest;
We aimed for righteousness
    To emulate your example of piety. Now your body is lifeless
We will ever remember your love of kindness;
    And will never forget your hatred of wickedness.

You taught us justice. But how unjust was
    Your own brother Jason who stole the High Priesthood from you
And led our children away from YHWH to Zeus.
    The Torah was disdained; the Sabbath was profaned;
The Temple was polluted; our faithful were executed.
    And Simon, the Benjaminite captain, undermined your authority,
Mocked you in the market and jeered at you by the Temple gates.
    This same Simon sent his brother, Menelaus,
To complain about the high priesthood to the governor.

Menelaus outbid your brother, may his name rot in the grave,
    For the High Priesthood.
But you were revolted by how foul had become
    The sacred priestly office, first held by Aaron,
Brother of the saintly Moses.
    How brave you had been to speak against the unjust;
How daring were you to rail at priests that disgust.
    Then Menelaus stole the Temple vessels and presented
them to the king's deputy
    Who lured you out of your sanctuary and murdered you

And set brother against brother
    In a battle that daily shreds the fragile fabric of the Jewish people.
You are gone, Onias, man of peace, who sanctified the Temple;
    And Antiochus, man of war, has come and abominated it.

LAMENT OF ARISTOBULUS*

*Son of John Hyrcanus, king and high priest, 104–3 B.C.
After his death his brother Alexander Yannai assumed the high priesthood and kingship and married the widow of Antigonus.

Be quiet mother! Your ranting ruptures my repose.
    Disdain not your damp dungeon; it is your reward. A just reward.
Why whine? That meager stew you are fed crawls with maggots;
    It is a fitting diet.
Your shrieking disturbs my appetite. You scream as if you are in labor.
    You whimper that I was suckling but your royal teats.
They were filled with sour milk. Your sacrifices on my behalf?
    It was your duty. Your love for me? It was your illusion.
What do I, an accident of your passion, owe you?
    The seeds of my father's loins languish in your womb,
Now brood in prison except for my truly beloved brother, Antigonus,
    Who was too ambitious. He now languishes in his grave.
Magnified and glorified in God's Name!

Bow down to me, mother. I, Judea Aristobulus,
    High priest in Israel, am king
Anointed by God!!! And you rancid mother have not
    Even one sesterce to give Charon
To ferry you across the River Styx.
    May vultures peck out your innards.
Stay out of my dreams.

              Be quiet mother!!!

ALEXANDER YANNAI

O Antigonus, dearly departed brother,
    Your dear Salome released me from prison.
I being the oldest brother was bound by levirate law
    To marry your childless wife.
Now I seek your counsel. The Pharisees harass me,
    Their king and high priest.
They pelt me with ritual citrons; I am embarrassed
    To come home to Salome, your widow,
And tell her of my humiliation. You say crucify the foe?*
    What sage wisdom.
May you spend eternity in heaven at the feet of God.
    I will slaughter a lamb in your memory.

*He crucified 800 Pharisees on the advice of Diogenes, a Sadducee, executed later by Pharisees.

IN PRAISE OF SALOME ALEXANDRA*

*Salome Alexandra, Shalomtsiyon, widow of tyrannical Hasmonean kings, Aristobulus and his brother, Alexander Yannai, was sole monarch of Israel from 76 B.C.E. to 67 B.C.E.

Shalomtsiyon, beloved queen: pious, righteous,
    God-fearing, and sainted;
Unstained, unblemished, uncorrupted, untainted;
    Courageous, caring, confident; Humble, modest and reverent.
You brought peace and prosperity to Zion.
    You alone, sovereign of Israel, cleansed the Augean stables
And forgave both the belligerent Sadducee and the truculent Pharisee.
    You alone, sovereign of Israel, with a dimly lighted lamp
Led her people out of the abyss of despair into an Eden of hope
    Where the Spirit of God hovers. You alone, sovereign of Israel,

Were esteemed by neighboring kings for your wisdom and grace.
    You alone, sovereign of Israel, turned
The swords of our valiant soldiers into plowshares.
    Through treaty you stopped enemy kings from invading
Zion's sacred soil.
    And that soil flourished: palm trees bore succulent dates;
Meadows overflowing with golden grain swayed in the breeze;
    Lentils grew large under the smiling sun.
Beloved queen, sovereign of Israel, you were a voice not an echo;
    You were a presence not a shadow; you were a fortress not a footstool.
You, Shalomtsiyon, epitome of virtue, kindled our way
    To the future to be a light to all nations.

EULOGY FOR JULIUS CAESAR*

*Based on Josephus Antiquities, XIV, 185–267

Julius Caesar, consul, imperator, priest.
    We laud you in death as we did in life.
Your name will ever be a blessing to Jews.
    You ordered the kings of Syria and Phoenicia
To bestow upon the Jews as free gifts
    Their lands including villages countries, and towns.

You declared that the Jews shall possess Jerusalem,
    To be their religious epicenter,
And they may enclose that city with walls.
    You enjoined the people of Delos to permit Jews
To practice their own customs,
    Even though other religious societies may not.

You commanded the people of Halicarnassus
    To allow Jews to celebrate their Sabbath
And perform sacred rites according to Mosaic law.
    You enjoined the people of Sardis to grant Jews
The right to assemble on their holy days
    And to provide foods ritual law permit fit for eating.

You sent a rule to the people of Ephesus.
    That Jews may observe their Sabbath
According to their ancient laws without impediment.
    You hailed the Jewish soldier who heroically aided
The Romans in their causes.
    May the bond between Rome and Jerusalem grow stronger.

Julius Caesar, consul, imperator, priest.
 We laud you in death as we did in life.
Your name will ever be a blessing to Jews.

ASAAC BEN MAIER

Asaac ben Maier had been inclined to talk to God wherever he walked
    Whether in his home or along the way,
Whether he sat in the synagogue or at his workbench.
    When he lay down and when he rose up.
God was forever by his side, within his body and inside his mind.
    One day as he gazed upon the hills,
Those lovingly sculpted creations of rocks
    Of God's magnificent creation,
Meditating on Torah-taught mercy and justice
    His face reddened with outrage and his body shivered with chills.
Innocent masses without pedigree
    Were treated unjustly and mercilessly in the courts of the priests.
So he ran to the Temple in time for the afternoon offering
    And with a voice from God offered this plea
To the Sadducee holding a flame.
    Feed the poor who stole to eat, heal the sick whom poverty diseased
House the homeless who are out of work be merciful and just,
    No matter one's class,
And do all these deeds in God's Holy Name.
    The Sadducee priest sneered at the man
And tied him to a tree where people passed by and spat on his face
    And threw rocks at his head. And when his head bled
They whacked it with a stick. Asaac spoke, "I laugh at your actions.
    My father, Maier, enlightened me to human urgencies.
He taught me to crave social justice and eschew unfairness.
    God, he explained cares not for sacrifices but listens to hearts sincere.
We are all God's children: No one is any more cherished than another."
    The priest shrieked, "You! Tso-ake ben Afel; Wailing, son of Darkness,
Pharisee! Separatist! Revisionist! Sower of treason!!
    Turd whose stench defiles the Torah!!! You twist God's words

for your own purpose!! !!"
   "You accuse me of your own sin," Asaac calmly replied,
"I speak not treason; I speak truth that grows with the times."
   Fuming, the priest built a fire beneath Asaac's body,
Singeing his face, his fingers, his feet before it devoured him.

LEGACY OF THE SADDUCEES

> Zealots:
> Falsely righteous,
> Uncompromising, arrogant, insidious,
> Truly destructive
> Fanatics

JOHN, THE BAPTIST

Gentle were his unfeigned words wafting in the wind
    To every ear that listened to everyone who sinned.
There are two paths in life which one will be thine?
    To one paved with refuse, or the one that is divine?
His gospel was for all folks wherever they might dwell.
    Righteousness led to Heaven, evil led to Hell.
To live according to Moses' law was John's aim and highest goal
    Then wash from every sinner the filth upon his soul.
Herod, the Judean king, Moses' Torah had forsaken
    By putting himself above the law when his brother's wife had taken.

John told a crowd of listeners about Herod's sinning ways
    Which angers the God of the Jews and Moses' laws betrays.
One night as Herod tossed and turned in his royal bed
    He watched a Roman soldier cut off the Baptist's head.

No more would John's silver tongue
    Speak against Herod's reign.
To celebrate, Salome, danced
    About a plate of oozing brain.

JOHN, BAPTIST IMMORTAL: A DREAM

Each night tossing in his bed Herod watched the Baptist's head
    Rise from the grave when the light was dim
And roll its eyes and stare at him.
    My voice is louder now, spoke the hollow head.
You endowed me with life. I am not dead.
    Terror would strike at Herod's heart as he would knife the ghost apart.
But each time his knife would rise the head would increase its size.
    And around Herod's head it danced and spun
Just as Salome about *that* head had done.
    Herod, Herod, Pilate's cat's paw, never forget
That you broke Moses' law
    When you stole from your brother's side his very own wife
And made her your bride.
    Herod would shriek at the darkness of night but could not
Erase John's head from sight.
    And when Death its taut grip at last
Had spawn on Herod's lips was the name of John.

PILATE IN JERUSALEM-ALONE

On the eve that Pilate wed he had been banned from his marriage bed
    By the emperor Tiberius who dispatched him
Instead to Jerusalem-alone.
    There he quelled the rioting throng with sword
And whip of leather thong
    But how he pined for Claudia, his love, in Jerusalem-alone.
Without her he was frustrated although he has often with concubines mated
    But he was never truly sated in Jerusalem-alone.
Images of Caligula entered the city one night and aroused
    In the Jews a very great fright
Which Pilate greeted with great delight in Jerusalem-alone.
    Seeing the images the Jews fell to the ground
And to one another in chains were bound
    But Pilate sneered and merely frowned in Jerusalem-alone.
He whipped their backs a hundred whacks
    While violating Romani pax in Jerusalem-alone. Jesus,
Jewish teacher and guide, had Roman rule defied,
    For which Pilate had him crucified, in Jerusalem-alone.
Jesus and Claudia were one in his mind and the forgiveness
    Pilate sought he did not find
Until one night on arsenic he dined in Jerusalem-alone.

WHAT IS HATEFUL TO YOU DO NOT TO OTHERS DO

In the marketplace, in the gardens, in the Temple courtyard
    The latest aphorism was heard from the lips of the learned Hillel.
"By not increasing one's knowledge, one decreases it."
    Upon hearing this, youths scurried to their studies with greater resolve.
"By magnifying one's own name, one destroys it."

Upon hearing this, priests restrained from lauding themselves.
    "Do not say anything unintelligible
And hope that your words will be understood."
    Upon hearing this, politicians curbed their
tongues. "Do not separate yourself from the
congregation."

Upon hearing this those drifting into alien ways returned to the fold.
    "If I am not for myself who will be for me?
But if I am for myself alone what am I?"
    Upon hearing this, children sang the words as they played their games.

"The more wealth, the more worry;
The more worry, the more worms."

Upon hearing this, merchants followed Hillel's example of doing charity:
Visiting the sick,
    Feeding the poor,
        Comforting the oppressed,
            And counseling the mourners.

The Light of God's radiance dwelled within Hillel day and night
    And he sensed what was right and good but also
what was evil and hurtful.
    One day Hillel witnessed a stoning.

The man had been accused of violating the Sabbath.
    The Light flickering within Hillel's soul
Revealed that wanton disregard of human worth
    Was not in God's plan. "Halt," sobbed Hillel,

    "Ignorant piety is no virtue."

The people dropped their stones
    Not because Hillel's voice was so commanding
But because it was so soft and sincere.

    "Judge not another until you are in that person's place.
    Make not the law a burden but a joy to uphold."

The scholar in his gentle way
    Saved a man's life and the lives of many generations to come.
That day a heathen followed Hillel to the ritual bath
    Where he regularly washed his grime matted skin
And purified his soul
        Stained with the sins of his people.
            "Prince of Teachers!" called the heathen.
Hillel replied, "I eschew honorific titles. Just call me 'Hillel'".
    "Hillel," the heathen beckoned, "Your reputation is well known.
Your sayings are on everyone's tongues
    And are changing the uncivil ways of people.
I would like to become one of your disciples
    But I wish to do so quickly while standing on one foot.
What can I do?"
    Hillel stopped a moment and pondered the challenge.

      "What is hateful to you, do not do unto others.
          All of the rest is commentary."

The heathen hopped away singing,
    "What is hateful to you do not do unto others.
        All of the rest is commentary."
            And so it is!

LORD! SEND US A SAVIOR

In the beginning there was
    The Word from which radiated spreading Light
Which issued a bursting sound which transformed matter into a body
    Within which there was a beating heart and a brain governing
Thought and action. From deep within the cosmos
    Flew in a mercy-filled soul
To give color to thought and virtue to action.
    There were Your gifts to all of humanity.
"A blanket of darkness covers human souls.
    Soldiers oppress the innocent;
Kings burden the poor with taxes; priests hoard silver and gold.
    O Lord send us a savior who will lift the burdens of life."
The people prayed for a messenger from God who would
    Show them the pathways of light
Who would preserve creation, who would bring to humanity true justice,
    Who would embrace us all with Your loving kindness.

THE MESSENGER FROM THE NORTH

The Light of God's Radiance lifted Hillel as he entered
    Eternity to sit in God's Council still his thoughts
Echoed throughout Judea.
    Fathers heard children chanting the songs
That they themselves once sang.
    "If I am not for myself who will be for me?
But if I am for myself alone what am I?"
    Merchants continued Hillel's practice of daily study
And visited the sick, fed the hungry, comforted the oppressed,
    And consoled the mourners.
Some disciples received Hillel's mantle of humility;
    Others became arrogant and placed obstacles
In the way of joyful observance.
    They forgot the saying, "Make not the law a burden
But a joy to uphold."
    But throbbing, though, the heart of Judaism
Was the rhythm of "What is hateful to you, do not do unto others.
    All of the rest is commentary."

Traveling to Jerusalem from the North was a messenger
    Steeped in the Messages of Hillel.
Everywhere he went he delivered them.
    The light of Hillel's candle had brightened his soul.
He fed the poor and they flourished;
    He touched the sick and they were healed;
Upholding the oppressed, they were comforted;
    Comforting the mourners, they were consoled
Everywhere he went he told his followers: God loves you,
    Righteous and sinners, man and woman,
Rich and poor, priests and laity, king and commoner.
    He was the resurrection of the soul of Israel.

WHO IS THAT MAN OF NAZARETH?

So much Isaiah spoke is still a mystery.
    Daily meditation provides the key
To unlocking the secrets of the text.
    What we cannot today explain becomes clearer on the next.
Who is this SERVANT that Isaiah describes?
    According to the scribe
The servant is plain, lacking attractive features,
    Despised by all, especially preachers.
But suffering is the servant's fate; pain is the servant's state.
    The servant bears the punishment we all deserve
And serves the sentences we all should serve.
    Harsh treatment does the servant endure-
This servant who loved the rich and fed the poor
    Is this servant a woman or man? Is the servant from a noble clan?
Is the servant a scion of a priest? Is the servant alive or deceased?
    Is this servant the one God has sent? Is this servant
The deliverer Isaiah had meant?
    Does the servant bear pain and aggression
And every kind of cruel oppression?
    Is the servant an allegory, a device in oratory?
Perhaps this servant is you or me? The tale is still a mystery.
    What is clear from what Isaiah said our destiny is what we merited.
Never betray God by unseemly deeds and follow only where future leads.

THE MINISTRY OF JESUS

Those were sad times. Those were times of oppression.
    The falsely accused despaired of the judges.
The innocents like slaves were lashed;
    The sick were stabbed by knives of pain; the hungry begged for food;
The naked shivered; sinners pleaded for absolution.
    The righteous were mutilated; holy ones, decapitated.
The Children of Israel swam in a sea of suffering.
    Rome sneered at their distress; It knew no mercy.
The wretched sobbed in prayer,
    "Free us, Heal us, feed us, clothe us, be just unto us.
Be merciful. Forgive us. Save our bodies from violation. Help us.
    Deliver us. Change the ways of the Romans. Send us a miracle."
Their desperate pleas pierced the ears of God.
    Spasms of sorrow shook the Heavens;
Compassion flowed like a gentle spring.

A presence, radiant and pure, arose in Judea.
    The sadness of his people mauled his soul;
The torment of his people battered his body.
    Above the din of the wailing
His gentle voice unfolded like the petals of a flower.
    "Hear me, Oh Israel," he began.
"Jail me with your false judgements.
    Give wings to your shackles
And let them fly into my bosom where
    I will endure your imprisonment.
Invest me with your wounds, send me your sickness, give me your hunger,
    Chill me with your nakedness, plague me with your sins.
Let me be cut up in your place; let me be beheaded in your stead.
    No more will you suffer; no more will you languish in pain.
Your distress will be mine; your agony will be mine."

As if to magnets many were drawn to that sweet voice of hope.
    They heard its echoes day and night
And following it where it led, they were transformed.

The victims were free of the lash;
    The ill, healed; the hungry, fed; the naked, clothed;
The accused, judged fairly; the sinners forgiven and redeemed.
    They sang this song, "Israel will be saved; it will become whole again,
Uplifted by a miracle sent by The Compassionate of God."
    And in the distance was heard the bleating of a sacrificed lamb
Where a man was nailed to crossed branches and slumped over.

HELENA OF ADIABENE

C 30 A.D.

Helena, Queen of Adiabene, cleansed her heart of all indecency,
    Purged her soul of every unchaste thought,
Filled her mind with what the Torah taught:
    To be humble, just, kind and the good in others always to find.
Such virtues she exemplified during her reign;
    Such beauty in life she sought to attain.
Judaism beckoned her its tenets to embrace;
    That she did with joy and grace not for ambition
Or for fame but to attain the sacred was her aim.
    She'd enter The Temple her thanks to offer
And at the altar first fruits she would proffer.
    When she left to traverse Jerusalem's roads
She found dried up Jews in shabby abodes.
    They begged for food; there was none to be found—poverty
And famine was all around.
    She sent her servants far and wide to buy food
Which would sustenance provide.
    When they returned the hungry they fed with figs
And rice and grain for bread.
    All did Queen Helena their savior proclaim
And in her soul glowed God's Holy Flame.

PAUL: APPRENTICE, APOSTATE, APOSTLE, MARTYR

Saul, a young man of considerable decorum
    Was there to be counted for the synagogue quorum
Required to conduct the daily prayers, and to spy
    Upon the Jewish betrayers.
How he loved to study The Law, how he worshipped God
    And with so much awe.
The prophets had had so much to say about how to behave in a Godly way.
    From Aaron and Elijah his zealotry sprung; the words of Jeremiah
And Isaiah were on his tongue.
    "Go to Jerusalem to study with the wise;
With Gamaliel you will learn to critically analyze.
    Such a pilgrimage," he was by his teachers told,
"will increase your wisdom a thousand fold."

Outside the Temple Mount he sat at the feet of Rabban Gamaliel
    And sipped his knowledge sweet.

The date palm fronds clacked in the breeze as Saul
    Studied with scholars with focus and ease.
Tell me Gamaliel, who like Hillel his kin, eschewed honorific titles,
    "What exactly is sin?"
Saul peered at his teacher, saintly and pure.
    "It is human imperfection," Gamaliel replied.
"Is there no cure?" Saul like an old man sighed.
    Saul was tormented by spirits within
That robbed him of appetite and sallowed his skin.
    Gamaliel said, "We live to improve upon God's design
Then the light of The Holy Spirit will within us shine.
    Whatever we do is for the benefit of humanity
It is not bounded by race or nationality."
    "Oh wise Gamaliel let me study with you let me learn

Exactly what is true,"
    With all of his heart Saul had pleaded and with all of *his* heart Gamaliel acceded.

But soon Saul became uneasy; his stomach grew queasy;
    His heart was embittered his brain skittered.
He had found no panacea for the evil of Rome or the sins of Judea.
    Why does no one now find Hillel's words true,
"What is hateful do not unto others do"?
    These words he asked stabbed the priests
Who turned on him like a pack of beasts.
    Scalding insults were thrown; his skin burned as if by brimstone.
Then rocks were hurled, Saul was in dread and from Jerusalem,
    Bleeding, Saul then fled.

Bruised in body and bruised in mind he searched
    For answers few could find.
Bad memories about him sprawled as he recalled
    That he had flung insult upon insult at the newly formed cult
Of the Nazarene, to him unclean.
    How he oppressed anyone who transgressed
Or from the Torah strayed or insincerely prayed.
    What joy there was and yet so sad to denounce those who are bad
And to scold and to twit every hypocrite
    Pretending pious to be but living lives of falsity.
He had walked the path God had shown but now felt all alone
    And hollow as a reed a little no one in God's chosen breed.

Saul, suffering from bodily qualm,
    Was searching for an all-embracing balm.
Perhaps a charm; perhaps a welcoming arm.
    He had asked his teacher; he had asked the priest
Can the human throw off the part that is beast?
    Must imperfection inevitable be?
Is there no way from sin to flee?

Why are there so many laws to perform?
    Why do the priests accept no reform?

Why is each law interpreted differently; why do the wise scholars disagree?
    Whose views should I accept and whose views should I reject?
It is also so confusing which path to be choosing.
    Why cannot life's options simple be? O, Lord, send me the key!

He touched the gashes where yesterday he bled from a stone
    That was thrown right at his head
While haranguing a throng in the Temple yard,
    Observed and ignored by a Roman guard.
But the deepest wound of all, drilling and stabbing like an awl
    Was being chased from the fold which from his youth he had extolled.
"Ignorant tent maker," he still heard the jeer and shivered
    With fever recalling the smear.
Thoughts like those stoked his rage which the God of Moses
    No more could assuage.
His fever sent his brain teeming with visions which God
    Toward him was beaming. "Don't you know Moses
that our people are straying?"
    Then he saw Jesus upon the cross swaying.
Saul lamented. His pain was greater than mine;
    My wounds compared to his are benign."
His days were anguish-filled; his nights, haunted;
    But he awoke each day undaunted
And pursued his dream of a flawless world, hoping
    That day it will be unfurled.
One sunny afternoon suddenly turned dark as coal.
    He felt a squeezing from his troubled soul.
Then brilliant lightning blinded his eyes
    And defeating thunder unmasked the disguise
Of the message from Jesus on the cross impaled
    Which now to Saul with love was unveiled
When he fell to the ground in a swirl and a swoon
    And bedded himself on a soft, sandy dune.
"Follow the words of I who died, a death like Mine will decide.
    And you will be saved. Mine is the simple way you have craved.
Sin has spread throughout the land. So reach out and touch
    My hand and your sins from you will be driven by
My grace. You will be forgiven.
    The Holy Spirit will within you dwell

And my message will upon you cast a spell
    And upon sinners of every race and every nation.
Through you it will reach everyone of every station
    Who yearn to live a noble life filled with love and devoid of strife.
Go out and teach; let your voice and pen the multitudes reach."
    The voice was gentle, the voice was kind.
The voice whose echo was with him entwined.
    Like a whirlwind he spun around and saw Gamaliel
And Jesus together bound.
    A new world was rising. A world filled with light.
A world that would deliver him from his plight.
    His mind reeled in ecstasy, and when he awoke it was to apostasy.
His mind was free of the shackles of Torah and filled
    With the light of a heavenly menorah.
There was no whip in the hand of God above
    But a red rose extended with sincerest love.
At that moment he dedicated his life to spread
    The good news of Jesus which within him was bred.
When he got up he was healthy and strong,
    No longer afraid of a rock-throwing throng.
All about him the words of Jesus were swarming;
    His mind and body were transforming.
"No longer will I go by the Hebrew name 'Saul';
    Henceforth call me by the Latin 'Paul.'
No longer will I in the old ways plod but devote my heart
    To the new Israel of God."

He traveled the world known to him,
    Sometimes weary and weak of limb.
Yet he continued his Jesus-given mission,
    Never diminished in his ambition,
He spoke to Jews and gentiles alike.
    At the heart of sin did he strike.
A circumcised penis does not a Jewish man make
    But an honest heart makes no mistake.
All people, gentile or Jew, can their faith in God renew
    Through Jesus, anointed, and by God appointed
To rid the world of sin and greed and fill it up with every good deed.

That was what Moses had intended
But his reign of teaching now has ended.
    Yes I have always been a Pharisee and was taught with certainty
That after death we are selected to become resurrected
    And to sit next to God, Almighty King,
While we listen to King David sing.
    This with all my heart I believe is a reward
Every mortal can achieve.
    This message is from Jesus, the eloquent,
Through Him to me for you was sent.
    With a zeal he once chastised the Christian
He now evangelized among the heathen.
    He had been transformed and around him there swarmed
Jew and gentile, Roman and Greek.
    They flocked to him to hear him speak.
From God's path they had gone astray;
    How they wished they could again find His way.
Through Jesus's mission to Paul they would become
    Moral one and all. Hear me, he would say,
You who are righteous and you who stray,
    There is but one guiding rule that we need: mercy.
That is the seed That into redemption will flower.
    Nothing can compare with God's loving power.
Once Paul had been unforgiving now he was a fountain of forgiving;
    Once Paul had been unmerciful now he was merciful;
Once Paul had been unloving now he was filled with loving.

But Paul's successes brought him foes who, in turn, caused him woes.
    While sitting in a Roman jail a zealot did him assail.
And as he lay dying he saw gentle Gamaliel crying,
    Saul, my son, my dear, dear one.
What a cruel end has come to you because
    You did your Jewish faith eschew.

May God have mercy upon your soul. Weeping,
    He chanted from the Torah scroll,
Held securely in Jesus's hands, the words of God the soul expands.

GRANDEUR IN ROME

Jews exiled to Rome brought with them their moral ideas and religious practice which the "God-fearing" Romans tolerated, admired, and engaged in as well.

Portia was a pagan maiden; Sarah was Judean bred.
    They were best of friends and virtuous lives they led.
On the sixth day of every week they would walk side by side
    To the sparkling Tiber to wash clothes in the ebbing tide.

Sarah would sing Sabbath hymns, Portia would harmonize
    To the paeans praising the merciful One:
The Just Healer and All Wise.
    The swelling tunes which did God extol reaching to Heaven above
Cleansed and sweetened their souls with God's Abundant Love.

Upon returning to Sarah's home the two with devotion
    prayed
And then inhaled the Shabbat scent that did each
Jewish home pervade.
    Before Portia returned to her house, she recited Bible verses in Greek
That she had been studying every day of that past week.

Sarah who read the Hebrew knew the text by heart
    And the two would discuss the messages that the Torah did impart.
Then as the suns set over glorious Rome, Sarah rekindled the Sabbath lights
    And Portia joined in the blessings that Sabbath peace invites.

Portia kissed Sarah and then returned home where her father toasted
    Caligula self-proclaimed god in Rome.
But her heart wept for the utopia
    That minutes before she had known upon welcoming the Sabbath
Queen, Font of spiritual joy, healing balm, and sacred time serene.

CIVIL WAR IN JERUSALEM: MURDER IN THE TEMPLE

The people were divided into many a faction.
    Some sought peace with Rome; others action
Against the invaders, the wealthy, and the priests
    Who thieved their meager harvest during major feasts.
While some Judeans retreated in languor others poured oil
    On their flaming anger.
The Zealots, poor and grievously oppressed,
    Believing their cause was Heaven blessed
Entered the temple with intent to kill some for cause; some for thrill.
    From beneath their shawls with fringes dangling
They yanked their daggers and with priests were tangling.
    Now the priests became the sacrifice; each was stabbed
Not once but twice.
    The sacred grounds were tinted red of priestly blood were they fed.
The Zealots then looted the Temple of its wealth.
    Hid their daggers and left in stealth.

MAYHEM IN CAESAREA. 66 C.E.

The sun rose, the cocks crowed, the Mediterranean flowed.
    The daily ritual resumed in Caesarea consumed
By hatred between the Greek and the Jew for whom each other was taboo.
    The Greeks sneered, "Circumcised swine";
The Jews retorted, "Alexander was asinine."
    The Greeks answered, "Oozing pubic sores";
The Jews replied, "Sons of whores."
    The Greeks yelled, "Turd"; the Jews snickered,
"Entrails of the Daeddalus bird".
    The Greeks chafed, "God's rejection"; the Jews jibed, "Anal infection."
The Greeks scoffed, "Cesspool of kidney juice."
    The Jews mocked, "Garbage! Offal!! Refuse!!!"
The Greeks jeered, "We'll nail you to a crucifix."
    The Jews warned, "We'll sail you down the River Styx."
The cursing match went on until the sun was gone
    While farmers quietly tended their crops
And smiths hammered away in their shops.
    Then a rumor shouted the news the judge had decided against the Jews.
The Greeks roaring like thunder, looted and broke Jewish homes asunder.
    They set fire to the Jewish Quarter, all that was left
Were chunks of mortar.
    A Torah was set ablaze, the mood of the Jews was deep malaise.
Rising high were curls of fire, but blazing deeper was Jewish ire.
    They had no time to bury their dead, the Jews in the skirmish
Toward Jerusalem now fled.
    They swam in guilt and wept in shame that the Greeks
Had defiled God's Holy Name.
    As they were leaving what had once been their home
The Greek-speaking soldiers, agents of Rome,
    Took pails of sand filled with flies and flung them at the refugees' eyes.

THE LION CHASES THE WOLF: JERUSALEM 66 C.E.

The diseased and the anguished entered the city
    Praying their kinsmen would comfort them with pity.
The people who had been of two minds about Rome
    Now took up arms to regain their home.
They stabbed the soldiers, they plundered their camps,
    They ignited the oils contained in their lamps
And hurled them at the Roman foe who retreated
    From Jerusalem incognito.
The victors cheered near The Temple gate,
    "We have decided the Roman fate."

THE LION BITES ITSELF: JERUSALEM 70 C.E.

Throughout Judea, Titus was leveling Jewish buildings;
    Refugees, seeking sanctuary, swarmed into the sacred city,
Jerusalem, a place of peace, according to the root meaning of the word.
    The Romans were yet to march upon the Temple,
Center of the civil conflict
Besieged by fringed-shawled fanatics camping on the Temple grounds.
    There Eleazar ben Simon was competing with John of Gischala
To head the campaign
    And both battled the upstart Simon bar Giora.
Their men were killing one another in the streets,
    Innocent Jewish blood flowed from the civil war.
In the marketplace rotting fruits were flung
    At passers by the young. Gold from The Temple treasury was looted
Corn stored for years of famine was torched,
    Brave warriors screamed in pain as their flesh seared.
The stench of Jewish flesh suffocated the newly widowed and orphaned
    Whose stomachs ached with hunger. There was despair!
There was madness!
    The ousted moderates grumbled who is the adversary?
And they mumbled, "Who else but us."

THE PACK OF WOLVES BITE THE LION HERE, THERE, AND EVERYWHERE: JERUSALEM 70 C.E.

The moon had vanished from view; the day was about to begin anew.
    The Roman legions which on Mount Scopus were camping.
Now toward the Holy Temple were tramping.

       As each foot stepped on the dry brush echoing was
       crush, crush, crush. From the Mount of Olives the
       Xth legion crept while the people in the city still slept.

From the north the Vth legion moved in and waited for the signal
    The attack to begin. By the time the morning shofar was sounded
The Temple was completely surrounded.

       The noose grew tighter. Hardly any Jewish fighter
       Could now escape. Romans were filling the landscape.

The Jewish warriors knowing they would die, having been cut off
    from the supply, drew lots to decide who should be eaten.
They knew they were beaten.

But they resolved to kill many a foe who would surely deliver upon them
    So much woe. Huge earthwork embankments were erected;
Many of Simon's forces had defected.

       The battle was helter skelter; no flank could
       Find shelter. Rocks and javelins were thrown
       By each side; here and there a soldier died.

Then the battering rams of the Xth came on the scene
    And the Temple ramparts began to careen
Piling rubble upon to resistance force killing each warrior without remorse.

    The Romans were galvanized by their superiority
    And plunged through the debris, like triumphant wolves
    Were yowling and through Temple chambers were prowling

Spearing everyone in sight with relish and delight.
    Spears were flung here and there not a living creature did they spare.
They cut off the heads of the escaping foe and smashed holy vessels
    Wherever they'd go.
The high priest kneeling down to pray was placed in chains
    And dragged away.
The Holy of Holies was overturned and the sacred scriptures
    To a crisp were burned.
The corpses in the sanctuary were smoking; the stench was choking.

    Those Jews who were saved were the castrated and put on
    display and humiliated. A chapter in Jewish history was
    closing as the moral giants lay decomposing. The last
    Shofar was blown from hallowed ground, but no one remained to
    hear the sound.

WE HAVE LOST HOPE

O Lord we the children that You once blessed
    Are by the Romans bitterly oppressed.
We have beseeched Your succor each day we pray.
    Please we beg You our misery allay.
But we Your people to whom You were once endeared
    Believe that now You have disappeared.
Dear God, once You were Light but are now opaque.
    Lamah azavtanu? Why did You us forsake?

MOURNING BUT NO CORPSES

Josephus, priest, historian, and general in the Galilee,
    Was trapped with other soldiers.
The will of the group was to kill one another
    And for the one remaining soldier to take his own life.
All of the soldiers complied. But Josephus refused to kill anyone,
    Including himself. But word spread throughout Judea
That Josephus was dead.
    In mourning, Jews everywhere wore sackcloth.
When Josephus appeared he was spat upon as a traitor.
    History remembers him as such.
Yet he was obeying the prohibitions against murder and suicide.

Yochanan ben Zakai was trapped in the siege of Jerusalem.
    Word spread throughout Judea that the learned sage was dead.
A thirty day period of mourning was declared.
    His students wore sackcloth and covered themselves with ashes
And moaned in mourning him.

They petitioned Vespasian, the Roman general,
    To bury ben Zakai outside of the city walls.
Permission was granted and when the outskirts were reached

Yochanan opened the coffin and surrendered to Vespasian
    Whom he augured would become Emperor of Rome.
The future emperor gave him land in Yavneh to build an academy,
    Which, though, sown in subterfuge, grew
To be the tree of Jewish scholarship
    For all to grasp and graft onto evolving generations.
Rabban Gamaliel II of scholarly line, who did in learning
    Ben Zakai offspring outshine,
Preempted the office that Yochanan once held
    And the founder's heirs in shame expelled.

ELEGY IN THE TEMPLE COURTYARD

A shofar blew a plaintive sound afar proclaiming
    The Holy Temple is no more.
No more in Springtime will a lamb unflawed on altar lie,
    As sacrifice to God.
No more will grain by pilgrims brought display
    The bounty the farmers besought.
Grieving priests smeared with ash dug for Temple treasures
    But only found trash.
Plodding down brambles path appealing for bread;
    They received no food—all the people were dead.
Darkness settled on their glorious past.
    What is the future for the highest caste? O God, they wailed,
Have you abandoned us? Have You handed us to the barbarous
    Romans who robbed and raped our sacred land
And turned our orchards into piles of sand?
    O God, merciful and compassionate,
How could You such a destruction permit?
    With downcast eyes and tear-filled faces the mournful priests
Walked in measured paces
    To magnify and sanctify God's Name and to rekindle,
With hope, God's Holy Flame.
    We will rebuild this sacred land of Yours ravaged by Romans
And internal wars.
    Then they dug deep pits to bury the dead, some without arms,
Some missing their head.
    They poured lime on the bodies once with life—here a daughter,
There a husband and wife.
    "O just and merciful God," the priests cried take good care
Of these innocents who died.
    Ten mourning doves perched on the Western Wall

Solemnly lamenting Judea's fall
    Cooed their dirge for generations to hear to listen
With heart while trickling a tear.
    "Oy v'avoy what we once had is gone.
But we promise You God that we'll carry on." Woe oh woe.

A LETTER FROM TITUS MY DEAREST BERENICE*,

*Berenice, daughter of Agrippa I, had married kings. She met Titus during the siege of Jerusalem. He took her to his palace in Rome where she lived until Vespasian, his father, demanded her expulsion.

My joy.
The only peace that I have ever known.
Because of you the sun shone upon me and upon Rome.
My palace was your home.
How we would loll about in bed as if we were already wed.
And at your behest I would kiss the nipples of your breast.
And when you found my treasure we would share the pleasure
It would give. To this day I relive
Those moments sublime and the heights of ecstasy we would climb.
When our fervor was spent and we were both content,
We would discuss Socrates and would discuss the works of Sophocles,
Upon that Greek I do not dote. He once wrote:

Women should be seen, but not heard. How absurd.

When I a truth did seek, your lips would wisdom speak.
How clearly I remember one chilly December
Afternoon when Rome knew only cries and I was seeking emotional relief
Through passion—as was my fashion.
We were embracing, oh how my heart was racing,
And while I was getting all excited, you this passage from Sophocles recited
"Why worship gods who do ill?" You explained it was not your God's will
That Vesuvius exploded or the plague eroded
The health of many a Roman or that the raging fire was an omen
Of the end of my reign. Your words were so plain:
The will of God is not understood, but evil days highlight those that are good.

Then rumors flew that the wily Jewess was establishing herself as empress.
Her inferior race will Rome's grandeur erase.
Infected by a circumcised penis, carrying the disease of Venus,

She spreads blindness through her bodily kindness.
How she disdains our Roman food. It is utterly rude
That she refuses our salted ham and prefers, instead, a roasted lamb.
She is vile; she is perverse. She has sent upon us a curse.
And then someone spread the news that I chose the faith of the Jews
Rather than pray to Jupiter, god supreme, whose name I daily did blaspheme.
I knew they were all lies planted by my father's spies.
Then my father demanded, "send the woman away." And I didn't.
But I miss you every day.
I miss your wisdom; I miss your wit. I miss you more than I dare admit.
O that history will not inflict us, with deepest love, your emperor,

Titus

THE EPITAPH

Here lie victims who witnessed human rage.
They'll be remembered in every age
As sacrifices to wanton greed on the pretext
that they were of alien creed.
Oh God forgive us our stupidity:
That our aim in life is cupidity.

MASADA 73 C.E.

A thunderous silence resounded on the mesa.
    No bird chirped, no bee buzzed, no dog yapped.
All was still until an old grandmother and her daughter,
    Frightened, enraged, hungry from fasting,
Flesh torn from scratching themselves, climbed out of the cave
    With five children, confused, yowling,
And sobbing uncontrollably.
    The old woman unburdened a shrill scream,
"Oh foolish eccentrics, fanatics, lunatics.
    You wallowed in the slough of your own despair
And murdered generations to come." Her daughter, though,
    Flailed at the sky,
Every sound she uttered was stuffed with sarcasm,
    "God of miracles! Oh powerful One,
Resurrect my husband, my children's father! Where is *Your* outrage??
    O mighty unleash Your fury! Foes fight us but against
Your Torah is the war they wage!!!"
    Their brains echoed, "O Lord why did You forsake us?"
The last tearful words of the 960 martyrs
    Who now lay in pools of their own blood which spurted
From their throats
    As the husband slashed the necks of his wife and children.
Then draping himself over them, prayer shawl spread haphazardly,
    Applied the dagger to his heart.
No more would their eyes smile; no more would their ears
    Hear the whisper of the wind;
No more would their noses smell the sweet scent of Spring;
    No more would their mouths taste the juicy fruits of Autumn;
No more would their hands feel the tenderness of another's touch.
    All but the seven surviving candles of the menorah were snuffed out.
To what end? No prisoner was shacked or shamed; no man, crucified.

No child was fed to the lions.
    No woman was subjected to the basest outrage.
Flavius Silva and the Tenth Legion came
    To conquer but were themselves vanquished.
And the voices of the Grandmother, the mother and the children
    Retell the story of Masada to this very day whenever
Seven candles are kindled.

FIRST THE LION BIT THE WOLF THEN THE WOLF TAMED THE LION

The wolves set up their dens throughout Judea.
    To satisfy their fancies, they trapped lions.
But the sovereigns of the jungle resolved not to be intimidated.
    They preened their manes, shaggy like the fringes of prayer shawls,
And with their pride sought lupine dens and crushed them.
    Wherever there had been a den the lions built a synagogue-and a fort.
Although the wolves lost many of their pack, the lions suffered as well.
    A canny king of the sovereigns was needed to save and reclaim Judea.

From the Judean Hills rose the smartest and bravest lion,
    Simon bar Kozevah, born of a star.
He had a plan to outwit the wolves. He organized the lions.
    He curbed their in-fighting over dress, food recipes, and prayer styles.
To lift them from their despair the lions crowned him
    Messiah sent by God, scepter in hand.
Under his command, bands of lions bit the tails of the wolves
    Whose yelps were even heard in Rome.
A gleaming gibbet of sun rekindled the path of the Jews who shouted,
    "For the Liberation of Jerusalem."
Their tragedy was transformed into triumph.

Hadrian, Emperor of the Wolves, ordered his soldiers to raze Judea.
    Legions came from Britain, from Rome, from Egypt, and from Syria
To stanch the flow of Roman blood. Their strategy was methodical.
    Slowly but ruthlessly they set aflame Jewish enclaves and leveled them.
The Jews whom they did not kill-there were 580,000 dead-
    Were taken as slaves sold in the marketplace for less
Than the price of a horse.
    The Judean desert turned red with Jewish blood and is stained to this day,

The wolves cornered Simon bar Kozevah who ripped his flesh
    With an iron comb until life left him.

The pride of the lions was crushed.
    A dark cloud blocked the sun which had earlier
Rekindled the path of the Jews.
    Their triumph was transformed to tragedy.
The roar was gone. There was only soft feline purring.
    Those lions who were free turned away
From warfare toward The Law.
    Rededicating themselves to God, they chanted with moist eyes,
"In the beginning God created heaven and earth
    And the earth was empty and void."
In these words they found new meanings
    And discovered new paths that lead to a better world.
On the very grounds where the Holy Temple once
    stood Hadrian built to Jupiter a temple
Where Yood-Hay-Vav-Hay was pronounced Jove.

IV
POST BIBLICAL HISTORY

THE JEW IS REDEFINED

To put a stop to the rebellious Judeans, Rome exiled them to the far corners of the empire. Wherever Jews settled they drew benefits from their hosts. However, they did not waver from their Mosaic roots. Priests and Levites were assigned honorary positions in each community. The religious leadership was in the hands of the rabbis some of whom were trained in Palestine; others in Babylonia. The rabbis gave essentially the same message wherever Jews were found. Early in this period, Rome was a pagan nation. With a few exceptions its emperors accorded religious tolerance to any group that made no effort to undermine the empire. Christians were gaining in numbers and competing with Jews for adherents. There were skirmishes between the groups; there were anti-Semitic sermons. Not until Constantine converted to Christianity, though, had there been political support for the children of Jesus. Despite Christian efforts to proselytize and apostasy by some Jews, most children of Abraham remained faithful to their roots. The Jews avoided confrontation whenever possible. In the seventh century another force arose which challenged both Christianity and Judaism. Islam! For centuries there were schisms among both Christians and Muslims. At times there were peaceful relations; at other times, the two forces clashed over Palestine and the land holy to Jews, Christians, and Muslims was drenched in blood. From the Muslims Jews learned sciences and literature. It adapted Muslim poetry to Jewish themes. Muslims conquered Spain where many Jews were living. Jews flourished in Muslim Spain. Not only did they overachieve in economics but enriched their own heritage through literature, especially rabbinic thought. Once Christians reconquered Spain, conditions deteriorated for both Muslims and Jews. By the end of the fifteenth century both minorities, resisting forced conversion to Christianity, were expelled from Spain. Jews were again dispersed. Some made their way to Muslim countries; others, to western European havens; some, to the Americas. Hopes rose within the Jewish community for a messiah. In the century that followed many false messiahs arose. Still the Jewish community was not saved. Some scholars turned their efforts to unlocking secret messages in The Torah. And a special form of Kabbalah-Jewish mysticism developed. This form challenged mainstream Judaism and set the scene for movements that offered hope and happiness and not merely amassing the knowledge of the sacred texts. One such popular movement was Chasidism which spread like wildfire across Eastern Europe. About the same time that this was happening, Western Europe played host to scientific innovators. One mark of the scientist is a disposition to question. Some challenged the very existence of God; others questioned traditional practices. This occurred among Christians as well as among Jews. Not only were there revolutions in ideas but also against political systems. The French Revolution spread ideas about liberty; the American Revolution, about freedom. As America was expanding westward, its gates opened to immigrants who helped build the barren land. Among them were Jews who first settled in the eastern seaboard and then made their way west. The freedom found in America became a challenge to the immigrants steeped in Jewish lore and practice. Soon the Jews experienced conflicts with other ethnic groups as well as an internal conflict about what it means to be a Jew. The twentieth century was to inflict a new meaning to the place of the Jew in history.

ONE ERA ENDS AND ANOTHER BEGINS

Daggers that take lives away melt into pointers
For the Torah that gives life.

YESTERDAY, TODAY, TOMORROW

Judaism plants hope and fear in an endless braid
Stretching from first to last days.

BEDROCK OF JUDAISM

The righteous Simon has said, the world's foundation
Is learning, prayer, and kind deeds.

AFTER THE DESTRUCTION OF THE SECOND TEMPLE

The centurions arrived from everywhere tiny Judea attacked,
    Razed The Temple to the ground and the Holy City sacked.
With raised swords the Jewish valiant fought the Roman foe
    But were utterly defeated. Freely did blood flow.

The remnant of Israel in Torah themselves then did enfold
    Replacing the sword with a pen and reshaped the Jewish mold.
Exegesis of Mosaic law became its goal and end
    Led by rabbis, not generals, they did Jewish culture amend.

Prayer replaced the battle cry; study was the main pursuit.
    The search for wisdom was preeminent, Torah was its root.
To the many anguished questions about their miserable plight
    In every nation of the world who would them indict

As God-killers or infidels wallowing in sin
    Was faith in God, the Holy Paladin.
Attacked by every sect, despised by every nation
    They were called "scum of the earth" because they refused renunciation
Of their faith or adoption of another creed.
    Although threatened with martyrdom, from
Judaism they would not secede.

Theirs was an inspired purpose in God's eternal plan
    To help redeem the faltering world and dethrone the charlatan.
This mission angered the strangers, filling them with ire.
    So they robbed and raped the innocents and punished them by fire.

But every attack only magnified the Jewish resolve to survive
    And from their ashes ascended, a people united and alive.
In the ebb and flow of history through good times and through woes
    The Jew has been ready to adapt to whatever history bestows.

THE HEROES OF YESTERDAY

The heroes of yesterday are but gnats today in a sea of irony.

WISDOM OF BEN ZOMA

To be wise learn from others. To be strong tame your passions.
To be happy be content with your lot. To be honored honor others.

LEGACY OF BEN SIRACH

Deep in the dark, quiet womb of the cosmos in ore that sparkles with gold
    Abides Wisdom set there by God, a heritage for all to gather,
Refine and polish.
    But only the faithful, quiet of tongue, devout, reverent,
And righteous in thought and deed
    Have the vision to find it and the grit to shine it.

ETHICS OF THE FATHERS: A MIDRASH

Chaos begets chaos and decency begets decency.
    Our sages knew human deceits and conceits,
Human flaws and disregard for God's sacred laws.
    But they also knew that humans sought what is good
And their efforts were to do what they should.
    They developed guides for bringing order out of chaos
Through ethical living.
    Saintly sages in eternal abode labored to explain the Mosaic code
Sat together under God's canopy to unravel abstruse Torah in amity.
    When they were alive, they searched for answers to what caused
And cured ethical cancers.
    Now they can examine in sublime peace the code of conduct
In God's Masterpiece.
    The Torah holds the key to noble ways
for every era throughout the days.
    A voice from beyond began the exchange,
"How can humans their conduct rearrange?"
    A rabbi from the distant past maintained
That the meaning of FOUR must be explained.

ETHICS OF THE FATHERS: THE MEANINGS OF FOUR

For a canopy to protect us it has FOUR arms.
For a civilization to protect us it has four standards.

Judah ben Tema said to do the will of God FOUR stands for
    The boldness of a leopard, the lightness of an eagle,
The swiftness of a deer, and the strength of a lion.
    Another sage said there are FOUR kinds of people
The sinner who neither studies nor practices the law,
    The dolt who attends classes but does not practice the law,
The parrot who does not attend classes but recites the law,
    And the saint who studies the law and practices it.
Another sage said there are FOUR kinds of students
    The sponge soaks up everything;
The funnel takes information in one end and pours it out the other;
    The strainer retains the dregs while pouring out the wine;
The sieve discards the dust while keeping the fine flour.
    Another scholar gave his meaning to FOUR.
There are four kinds of people.
    The scoundrel says what is mine is mine and what is yours is mine.
The bumpkin says what is yours is mine and what is mine is yours.
    The sinner says what is mine is mine and what is yours is mine.
The saint says what is mine is yours and what is yours is yours.
    Another scholar desired FOUR kinds of students:
The hare learns quickly and forgets quickly;
    The tortoise learns slowly and forgets slowly;
The sloth learns slowly and forgets quickly; the scholar learns quickly
    And forgets slowly.
Another scholar described FOUR types of charity givers.
    The braggart gives but wants no one else to give.
The hog wants everyone to give though not he.
    The saint gives and sets an example of charity.
The sinner gives not and sets an example of callousness for others.

Ben Zoma said The wise learn from everyone.

    The mighty control their impulses.

The rich are content with their fate. The honored honor others.

    Rabbi Shimon said there is the crown of royalty,

The crown of priesthood,

    The crown of royalty, but the crown of a good name

Is the greatest of all.

    The canopy of Heaven protects us when we retain what we learn, we practice what we learn,

    We are charitable, and set a good example for others.

If the canopy loses an arm it wobbles.

    If a civilization loses even one principle it totters.

ETHICS OF THE FATHERS: THE MEANINGS OF THREE

A rabbi from the distant past maintained that
the meaning of THREE must be explained.

He had said THREE are the pillars upon which the world
    Is founded Three are the principles upon which life is grounded.
His THREE pillars were principles: caution in judgment, education
    for all, sanctuary of our heritage.
Simon the Just thought of THREE as learning, service, and kindness.
    According to Joshua ben Perahyah THREE is learning,
Friendship, and fairness in judgement.
    According to Netai of Arbel THREE
Is avoiding evil, shunning bad company,
    And being aware of God's retribution.
Shmayah and his partner Antalyon regarded THREE
    As loving work, disdaining abuse of power,
And being cautious of rulers. According the Hillel THREE
    Is love of peace, respect for others, and sowing the seeds
of the Sacred Law.
    Akavyah deemed THREE as knowing one's humble origin,
Accepting one's mortality, and being accountable to God.
    One sage said that the THREE virtues of the Children of Abraham
Are generosity, modesty, and humility, whereas the traits
    Of the Children of the wicked Balaam
Are selfishness, conceit, and arrogance.
    Performing charitable deeds stems from true Torah learning,
Humbly making judgements implies out paltry biological origins,
    Accountability means shunning the conceited
And befriending persons of virtue.
    Without three pillars the world falters.
Without three principles humanity founders.

ETHICS OF THE FATHERS: THE MEANINGS OF TWO

A rabbi from the distant past maintained
that the meaning of TWO* must be explained.

*TWO refers to legs we stand on.
TWO refers to the rules that guide us.

Rabbi Yishmael said no enmity comes to one who restrains
    From making judgments;
One who judges pompously is an arrogant fool.
    Rabbi Yonatan said when the poor fulfill the Torah
They do so when rich.
    The rich who neglect the Torah neglect is when they become poor.
Rabbi Azzai said the consequences of violating a commandment are sin;
    The reward of fulfilling the commandments is a commandment.
Rabbi Tsadik said, Take not the words of the Torah
    To aggrandize yourself nor as an adze to dig with.
We have two choices: to walk in the path of righteousness
    Or to walk in the path of sin.
Both choices require two legs.
    But the path of righteousness improves the world.
We cannot walk on one leg nor can we live with one rule.

ETHICS OF THE FATHERS: THE MEANING OF ONE

A rabbi from the distant past maintained that
the meaning of ONE must be explained.

ONE refers to the One God Whom we know through study of the Torah.
    Rabbi Meir said engage in the work of the Torah with humility
God rewards those who labor with the Torah.
    Without Torah study one cannot find God;
Without God there is no civilization.

BRURIA BAT HANANIA

A daughter arose in Israel whose wisdom did prevail
    Over that of the learned men who gathered in groups
Of ten to discuss the law.
    She was quick to find a flaw in an argument and would augment
What they knew by giving them a clue
    Through her explanations which were biblical quotations,
Succinct and clear, at which she had no peer.
    And when there was a confusing passage Bruria would dredge
Meaning hitherto obscure that was transmitted in the literature
    As the way the law should go.
To you, Bruria, we owe thanks for explaining the code
    from which enlightened Judaism has since flowed.

ENOCH

Enoch meditated day and night; bathing in ritual waters,
    He purged every unchaste thought;
He dedicated himself to God with his heart, soul, and mind.
    He flagellated himself and went without food, water,
And sleep gathering the woes of the world in his bosom
    With sincerity he enwrapped himself in the Divinity of God.
Then the Heavens opened.
    Winged angels in alabaster cloaks descended embracing
Him with such warmth that his body yielded in surrender.
    In an instant they raised him high and together they flew
In solar orbits to the Celestial Abode of the Sacred.
    There were heavens within heavens.

In the First Heaven were 200 angels guarding stars
    And the chambers containing snow, ice, dew, and clouds.
In the Second Heaven were fallen angels suffering for their sins.
    Love them for they are still holy; forgive them for even angels falter.
The Third Heaven was divided into South and North.
    In the South was Paradise: its four rivers and the Tree of Life
Where the righteous dwell.
    Trees bearing fruit of the most exquisite tastes and exotic rainbow
Flowers of beauteous patterns.
    In the North was a prison where the wicked dwell in torment,
Darkness, and mist Surrounded by a dark fire and ice and fierce angels
    Inflicting torment with pain-giving weapons.
The alabaster angels rose higher to the Fourth Heaven
    Where the mysteries of the sun, moon, tides,
And season were disentangled.

How great is God, Creator of the cosmos, who arranged the heavenly hosts,
    Sources of light and warmth, and memorials of Time.

Beyond this was the Fifth Heaven, abode of the fallen angels,
    Trapped in their own sinfulness, their wrongs slide
From precipice to chasm
    Bouncing without remorse in wildly crashing waters
Before they climb back to the precipice to repeat the cycle.
    The angelic guides then revealed the Sixth Heaven
Where seven angels supervise the world order, ushering in sun
    When there is darkness,
Rains where there is drought, food where there is hunger,
    Healing where there is illness
And order where there is turbulence.

Then the guiding angels paused to rest as did God
    On the seventh day of creation.
When all purified themselves the Lord God was revealed
    Seated on a throne surrounded by angels.
It was the Heaven of Heavens.
    Enoch hears the tender but robust voice of God
Explain the mysteries of the universe
    So that he will share them upon his return to Earth:
Where the sun gets its sparks; where holiness is born;
    Where life gets its essence and its limits;
How justice is attained; where is consecrated love.
    God's message is: People who undo the chambers of their hearts
Discover all that is good and then they will know God.

BATTLE OF THE PROOF TEXTS

Judah, an Ammonite proselyte, knees like jelly and with racing heart,
    Whispered to the assembled rabbis, may I take the love of my life,
A daughter of Israel as wife.
    Rabban Gamaliel, the Second, said, "No."
Half of the assembled rabbis repeated, "No."
    Rabbi Joshua, as was his wont, disagreed
And half of the assembled rabbis repeated, "Yes."
    Then Rabban Gamaliel unsheathed his sword
And holding its hilt firmly,
    Vehemently thrust his sharp-edged tongue,
"An Ammonite may not enter the congregation of the Lord."
    Rabbi Joshua, in a riposte, jabbed,
"Sennacharib exiled the mighty Ammonites."
    Rabban Gamaliel, his honor at stake, parried.
"I will return the captivity of Ammon." Rabbi Joshua lunged,
    "I will return the captivity of Israel, (Amos 9:14)
But they have not yet returned."
    Half of the assembled rabbis repeated,
"But they have not yet returned."
    Rabbi Joshua sheathed his argument
And Judah married his loved one.
    After sixty generations the Deuteronomy prohibition is voided.

THE TRINITY: EUSEBIUS, AUGUSTINE, JOHN CHRYSOSTOM*

*Third and fourth century Christian theologians

Eusebius of Caesarea said, the proper view of religion
    Was founded by the Jew.
But myopia blinded Jews from conceding Judaism as preceding
    The true religion, that of the Christ, and into sinful ways are enticed.
Oh had they the four gospels accepted, they would not now be rejected.
    They are scum and are despised not God's chosen people to be prized.

And Augustine of Hippo said we should not wish the Jew to be dead.
    They live by God's design. These descendants of the ancient line,
Are here for good Christians to humiliate, to scold, to sneer at, and to berate
    Because the Church has vanquished the Synagogue
which repudiates its own decalogue.
    They are scum and are despised not God's chosen to be prized.

And John Chrysostom of Syria said Christ arose from the dead,
    A fact we know to be true, but one rejected by the Jew.
Jews hold their view to cover their guilt. Had they not been
    The ones who the Lord's Blood split?
They are pagans. Nothing more. Against a false god they daily whore.
    They are scum and are despised and are not God's chosen to be prized.
The words of the trinity cling to the ears of every Christian
    Filled with fears
That their own miserable fate was caused by the Jew
    And it was the Christian mission to subdue Jews
and to inflict pain on them who hold the Son of God in disdain.
    They are scum and to be despised not God's chosen to be prized.

And when these views are applied citizenship to the Jew was denied.
    Wherever there is evil the Jews are to blame permitting
The Church to rob, rape, and slay in God's name.

JULIAN, EMPEROR OF ROME 361 CE

The roar of the Judea's lion was reduced to a feeble yelp.
    How it longed to return to Zion but it could not without help.
Send us a savior they moaned. Send us a savior they groaned.

The Roman soldiers without reason accused the Jews of treason
    And hacked them with their swords to show them who were the lords.
Out of the inferno of history Christians had plotted
    To harm the Jews who rotted
The foundation of society with their Talmudic alchemy.

Then out of this abyss of despair, a living nightmare,
    Arose Julian, Emperor of Rome, Who said, Jewish brothers
I'll rebuild your home.
    He took from the Roman treasury money for the Temple's masonry
And to restore the sacrificial altar and for Levites
    To chant their psalter.

Artisans from many lands came to Zion with their talented hands
    And began the task of rebuilding and the ornaments regarding.
Then from the bowels of the earth so deep came a quaking
    Converting the Temple to a heap.
And the workers who had persisted from all labors now desisted
    Because they saw this as a sign that God opposed
Rebuilding the shrine
    And they crossed themselves in fear and then left the Jewish Sphere.

WHY ARE THESE TIMES DIFFERENT FROM ALL OTHER TIMES?

Why are these times different from all other times?
    Yesterday we lived in the country or in the town
In a village or in a hamlet.
    Today we are permitted to live on a narrow street
With iron gates closed at night
    Divorcing us from the rest of the community as in a "get."*
*Jewish divorce
    Yesterday we wore all manner of clothes with or without adornments.
Today we wear plain black suits and drab dresses, and a yellow badge.
    Yesterday we worked as tradesmen, in craftsmen, bankers, or doctors.
Today we are paupers permitted to perform only menial labor.
    Yesterday we paid taxes to the exilarch in Baghdad
And to the head of the Yeshiva in Eretz Yisrael.
    Today we pay taxes to the local rabbi, the priest, the bishop,
The prince, and the chief of police.
    Yesterday we sang, danced, studied Talmud, the stars, mathematics,
Greek tragedies, and Arabic poetry.
    Today, our Talmud books are in ashes and we, people of The Book,
Have no books to read.
    Yesterday we spoke to our gentile neighbors about our mutual
Oppression and our growing children.
    Today we speak only among ourselves and both we
And our gentile neighbors have developed suspicions about one another,
    Jealousies, and disdain.
Yesterday we traveled freely from one place to another
    And flee from our persecutors.
Today we may only walk within the confines of our ghetto.
    Yesterday we prayed to God for salvation.
Today we ask does He ignore our petitions?
    Does He favor another people? or does He exist?

We have been slaves to Pharaoh in Egypt;
    To the Davidic line of kings, priests, and rabbis;
To our gentile neighbors and their priests and princes.
    Dear God when will You set us free?

MAIMONIDEAN DEGREES OF CHARITY

If you give away some bread people eat it right away;
    But if you give them seed instead they'll feed themselves someday.
Yet if you teach the humane creed that no one must hunger know,
    Sub rosa give them bread and seed that they may eat
While seeds they sow.

THEOBOLD, THE APOSTATE

Theobold had a fancy for little Christian boys.
 To him they were like toys.
And when little William came his way on the grass with the boy he lay.
 But when his passion was spent he thrust a knife into the boy's heart.
Theobold heard voices in the wind telling him what to say:
 His mother was a whore; his father, a conspirator; his rabbi was a liar,
And his bride-to-be, unchaste.
 Theobold heard the gurgling brook telling him what to do:
Carry wood on the Sabbath; steal from the orphan's fund;
 Spread lies about your neighbor; and crave his beautiful wife.
Theobold thirsted for the nectar of love, but he brought pain
 To the people he pursued.
How can one give love at all to him so filled with gall.
 To prevent their ire from corroding themselves,
The Norwich Jews ignored the man.
 Then one day in the village square Theobold made the sign of the cross
And shouted The Torah is not the plinth of civilization. The true religion
 Is found in the death of Jesus, God's only son, Whom the Jews repudiate.
He tossed his phylacteries to the ground and stomped on them with his feet,
 Then read for all to hear from the parchment written in symbols queer:
Mix the blood of a Gentile youth with matzoh flour to honor Passover.
 The blood of the youth is The blood of Christ
Both of whom the Jews killed, their vengeance to fulfill.
 The Christians stormed the Jewish shops and burned everything in sight.
There was not a chink of hope that Jewish lives would be spared their plight.
 According to the monastic scribe a flame was set to the Jewish tribe
Jews became martyrs and Theobold, a hero was called;
 William was on that day as a saint installed.
On the orders of the Norwich priest the day was solemnized with a feast.

NICHOLAS DONIN, THE APOSTATE

Louis IXth gave Brother Nicholas his sword and said,
    "Plunge this into the Jew
That is the only way to debate him." No, he replied. If I kill the rabbi
    One Jew will be dead. But if I destroy his Talmud generations
Will die Or turn to Christ for guidance.
    And so the trial began. The Talmud, Brother Nicholas said,
States Jesus is dying in Hell in boiling excrement.
    The people lunged for the Rabbi guarded by his students.
The Talmud, he continued, said that the Messiah,
    Both human and divine, had already come to save humanity.
But the learned rabbi denies this. The crowd grew even more restless.
    The Talmud, he went on, says Christianity is a scourge.
The mob howled and threw rocks.
    The people were blinded by their rage
The rabbi frantically raised his arms and shrieked,
    Peace be on both our peoples.
We have always lived side by side, sharing joys and griefs,
    Bounties and hardships.
Then some yelled in the court, there has been more violence and injustice
    Since the time of Christ than before.
The crowd could not be contained and tractate after tractate
    Of the Talmud was torched.
The burning books smoldered for six days and six nights.
    Endure the Jewish stench, proclaimed the apostate,
And we will be rid of the Jew forever.
    But the Talmud did not die nor did any of its students.

A KARAITE K'TUBAH*

*Based on a k'tubah cited in Goiten, S.D. A Mediterranean Society. California, 1971

I, Hezekiah, descendant of Aaron's tribe,
    Do in this marriage deed hereby inscribe
That by Mosaic Law will I abide and will provide Sarna, my bride,
    With her every wish and need. Her will I clothe, house, and feed.
I will satisfy her sexual longing by prolonging
    Joy according to the custom of the Jew. Never will I subdue her.
She will never be oppressed by me. Nor by me ever distressed.
    Nor will I ever deceive her. But with tender love
Will I interweave with her.
    And I say this for all Jews to know that this is so.
This is so! Amen.

REB MENDEL'S AMULETS

The amulets, the beadle, Reb Mendel, sold were more precious,
    He said, than rubies or gold.
He would inscribe on parchment deep within incantations
    To stave off sickness and ward off sin.
Ritually pure, he guaranteed, his amulets held a deed
    To a good life now filled with sin and in the next world
An even better one.
    Still the plague did not subside; in every household someone died.
"Liar, wretch, fake," the villagers yelled,
    And with a jagged rock the beadle was felled.
Standing over him they shrieked in despair,
    "For our humble souls did you *ever* care?
You preyed on the fears of the superstitious
    And robbed the poor. You are malicious."
They dragged him to the cemetery and dug a grave
    Where they would bury
The plundering cur. The entire village would be the happier
    But first they swaddled him to a tree,
Ignoring the bleeding beadle's plea.
    "I'll return your money," he insisted. The villagers, though, all resisted.
Then his arms like eagle wings were spread
    And he was pelted with rocks until he was dead.
Into the grave he was allocated but their appetite for revenge
    Was not placated until their amulets at the corpse they flung
And filled the hole with horse's dung.
    "May worms eat your penis! May rats give you the disease of Venus!
May moles disperse your every bone! May your grave be unmarked
    And without a stone.
The villagers cursed and laughed and cried, they were so terrified
    That reason from them had fled and left them shivering in frozen dread.

Their frenzy made them numb and they trudged
    From the grave in delirium.
They had lost their souls in a moment of rage and locked
    Their humanity in an animal cage.
Lilith and Asrael came out to play and helped Reb Mendel
    Begin his decay.
They separated his body from his soul then read from the scroll
    Welcoming Mendel to eternal fire, the basic element of their empire.
Into 613 worms their essence they inspired to turn to dust
    He who expired.
They danced and larked in wild abandon and dragged
    Mendel's soul into Oblivion.
His amulets and incantations were of no worth to him
    Whose flesh was decaying in the earth.
And at the villagers they laughed with raucous glee because
    Their souls own would never be free.

THE LAW OF RETURN

They drove me from York; in France they chased me with pitchfork.
    They banished me from Linz and Vienna; they drove me out of Sienna.
From Cologne and Vicenza was I sent away; in Milan and Florence
    Heavy ransoms did I pay
Then I was ejected like someone infected with diseases
    Of the Devil. How they did revel
In my despair shouting, "Jew! Heir
    Of the sow whom you embrace like man does his frau.
Excrement and garbage is your fare; your soul is threadbare.
    But if you were no longer Jesus to spurn, to your homes
you may return."
    The Jewish souls who had been banned
Wandered heartbroken from land to land.
    They were by highwaymen waylaid and after they their ransoms paid
Were castrated; their children mutilated.
    Their women were mauled in a manner that appalled.
They mourned with plaintive cries for the corpses covered with flies.
    They appealed to God for a sign that they should return to Palestine.
No rainbow appeared; there was no Call.
    Only a new calamity that would them befall.

NATHAN, THE MUTE

The crusaders marched into town, King Richard leading the way.
    They chanted to Mother Mary, Ave Maria help us the heathen slay.
The shops of the Jews were shut, the doors of their homes were bolted.
    No one on Jew Street walked about although by cannons
all were jolted
    Except for Nathan, deaf and mute, smiling all of the time.
He was by a Prior arrested for committing the crime of being Jewish.
    He was shown the Torah and the cross
And signaled to choose only one.
    He embraced the Torah and gave a toss to Jesus.
This angered the bishop and his men
    So they bound him to the back of a wagon
And asked him to choose again.
    But he heard not a word and the driver took off with speed,
Dragging the silent Nathan struggling to be freed.
    In vain did Nathan struggle, in a moment he was dead
And the crusaders toasted the Prior who held up Nathan's head.
    Thank you Mother Mary for victory over the heathen Jew
Who refused to be converted to the one faith that is true.

BUT YOUR HOLINESS THE JEWS ALREADY CONFESSED: THE BLACK DEATH

Yersinia pestis, a bacillus wee, attached itself to the common flea
    Which infected rats gathered in masses in the Russian
Steppe among the grasses.
    The infected rodents then boarded ships and here and there took nips
Of the crew who grew very ill, with coughs, groin buboes, fevers, and chills.
    The agitated sailors who fell into fits became confused
And were losing their wits.
    Their sputum was foamy and colored pink, all about them
Was a wretched stink.
    The buboes broke in a week or two and the disease spread
When breezes blew.
    The bacillus floated through the air and sickly sailors
Fell into despair
    Before Kind Death took them away from a misery
No known herb could allay.
    When the ships at last landed some ailing sailors disbanded
And moved in among the city's obscure, spreading the disease
    To the gypsies and the poor
Who wandered with sailors from place to place
    Infecting people of every race.
Alarming grew the number of dead, among the uninfected
    There was a dread
That they would be the next to die.
    They spent sleepless nights asking why is this affliction rampaging?
Why oh why is the epidemic raging?
    The self-righteous condemned those who were ill
As licentious and lacking in will.
    Others denounced the monks and grandees as the ones
Who had spread the dreaded disease.
    But monks and grandees died in misery—seized by the epidemic malady.

Someone had to be the cause, everyone knew;
    The habit of hate pointed to the Jew
Bred, it was said, of subhuman species with stench more revolting
    Than bloody feces.
He spread the poison who aim was to kill Christians
    With the disease that began with a chill.
Jews were rounded up and interrogated; they were prodded,
    Beaten, and castrated.
In some towns Jews accepted their fate and martyred themselves
    Rather than wait
To be tortured. Linked arm-in-arm they strode and leaped
    In song to their final abode.
In a Swiss castle a Savoy Jew was stripped bare, a burning stick
    Was singeing his hair,
He was prodded repeatedly with pointed darts, shamefully violating
    His private parts.
Reasoning with the torturers was to no avail, they too much enjoyed
    The Jewish travail.
Israel's wiles they were sure he was to blame! Are Jews
    Not the ones who defame
God's only Son? Did they not sentence Him to oblivion?
    So the Jew of Savoy confessed that it was his rabbi who possessed
Poison that he, John of Savoy, dropped in wells which
    The dreaded disease everywhere expels.
Quod omnes Judaei a septem he said proves that a universal plot
    The Jews promote.
The confession was sent to every land and Jews were tried
    And then were banned.
But the clement Pope Clement VI in a Bull sent to all bishoprics
    Declared that the disease invades every race and nation every creed,
Calling, and every station.
    It kills the rich and it kills the poor; it kills the White Man
And it kills the Moor.
    The Jew, he said, must not be blamed for the loss of lives
The plague has claimed.

The tormenting plague went askew and exploded in places
    Without even one Jew.

But your Holiness, the Jews already confessed, rose
    The angry mob to protest,
Let's destroy these snakes Satan conceives who Christians
    By guile daily deceives.
But the Pope replied, his soul in remorse, invalid
    Is a confession taken by force!
And entered the flesh of Israel's brave killed by madmen
    The Church later forgave.

PURIM IN CASTILLE, 1339

Many years ago in the kingdom of Castille,
    Lived a derelict knight aflame with zeal
To spread the power of the Holy See in the palace of Spain's majesty.
    Gonzalo Martinez de Oviedo was his name
And in barbarous savagery lay his flame.
    He sent to prison his protector, the Jew, Señor Don Joseph,
The tax collector.
    Torment was the thanks Don Joseph received
And was given the cruelest torture ever conceived.
    Then Gonzalo wrote a royal decree,
All Jews must convert to Christianity
    Or be killed at the baptismal font.
His power over Jews was his want to flaunt.
    Dona Leonora de Guzman had the ear of the king
And urged Alfonso not to bring
    Destruction upon the Jews of Castille who Gonzalo
Ordered before him to kneel.
    The king listened to Dona Guzman's ardent plea
And rescinded Gonzalo's decree
    Alfonso then exercises his royal power and ordered Gonzalo,
Of temperament sour,
    To explain the reason he accused Jews of treason.
But Gonzalo tried to kill the king instead so the king
    Had him burned until he was dead.
The knight was by Moses' abdiel replaced
    And was by the king warmly embraced.
This all happened in the month of Adar according to the Jewish calendar.
    Another Haman had tried the Jews to flay,
But was the one the king chose to slay.
    To celebrate their miraculous deliverance Toledo's Jews
Went to the streets to dance
    And added another festive day to the joyous Purim holiday.

CONVERSO LAMENT

Like so many S'fardim before us we bent like tree branches in the wind.
    And when we straightened our limbs to renew our integrity
We were cut down by marauding crowds in the name of God
    And either burned in a pyre or grafted on to an alien branch
Of the bough of Abraham.
    We sprouted here, there, and everywhere—*in secret.*
Our offshoots were a masquerade,
    A charade of our original stalk in the name of Pi-ku-ach nefesh.
But our souls were pillaged; our heritage was raped; our faith was defaced,
    Tears clung like dew drops to every leaf of every page
Of every chapter of our history.
    Although emptied of our vitae, we still kindled
A candle on Shabbat eve
    That our ancestors will see the path leading to Gan Aden.
We kindled another candle to recall our charred ancestors,
    Betrayed by their own kinsmen.
During the Inquisition we kindled another candle to renew our hope,
    That though our golden links are tarnished,
We will one day soon join hands
    With all members of the one family of Israel with dignity,
Self-respect, and love.

MASSACRE IN MASHAD, IRAN MARCH 1839

They hid in privies; they hid in carts awaiting their leader's signal.
    And when it came turbulence broke out,
Fury surging from their hearts.
    With sharpened sabers they sought to maim
Every Jew who came in sight.
    They looted every synagogue and set its books to flame.

"Pigs," they shouted to the dying crowd;
    "You are nothing but filthy swine"
And grabbed the women and raped them
    Until their faith they disavowed.
Many to Islam converted but secretly practiced the ancient rite
    And when freedom they found in other lands
To Judaism they reverted.

THE CENTURIES DARKENED OUR PATHS

The centuries darkened our paths, my child, while Israel the world did roam
   In search of a glimmer of light that would show the way back home.
Eleven months of every year have we mourned our tragic losses
   Wrapped in the tattered prayer shawls slashed by sabers
And by crosses.
   We wandered many a hostile desert seeking a place to rest,
An oasis to slake our parched mouths, determined has been our quest.
   The time is long past due for us to go back home,
We'll not be tossed asunder nor again be forced to roam.

OTHER FAITHS SEEN FROM THE EYES OF A BUDDHIST

Israel conquered Canaan by brandishing its sword
With the advice and guidance of the Mighty Lord.
Christians wielded theology to improve the quality of life
And Constantine said, choose Jesus or my sharpened knife.
Muhamed taught the pagan with the aid of the scimitar
And marauded, looted, and converted anyone perpendicular.

The Hindu with gods a plenty
Scorn the castes without a penny.
But the Buddhist through the power of mind
Finds a path through the undefined.
He needs no guns, no knives, no swords
To know Four Truths and spiritual rewards.

THE EXORCISM OF SARAH BAS PLONY

It was at Havdalah before the end of Sabbath day
    As for a good week all did pray.
The women were led by Isaac, The Blind,
    When was heard a voice, loud and undefined.
Was it that of a woman? a man? or, perhaps, a lion?
    Asked the worshippers who were faced toward Zion.
It came from behind the Women's curtain; everyone knew that for certain.
    Sarah lay on the floor, her eyes were growing wild,
All the women had cared for her since she was a child.
    The orphan Sarah of a father unknown had been adopted
By village women as their very own.
    But now fear seized their hearts. Sarah had been practicing
The black arts.
    She had invoked Satan to take her as his wife. Instead,
He stabbed her with his silver knife.
    Women tried to waken her, but she would not budge.
She was being tried by fire by the Heavenly Judge.
    "Guilty! Guilty! Guilty! am I" was heard her growling cry.

The evening prayers were interrupted; heart-felt words
    Were being corrupted.
Onto the pulpit Sarah then was carried and Rabbi Halawi
    Asked her if she had Satan married.
"Satan is my husband and lives inside of me and stabs me
    With his knife in the place where I pee.
The crowd was aghast to hear what she expressed then she shouted,
    "He is removing my breast."
Havdalah had been profaned, the rabbi then explained,
    This Sabbath has drifted astray, we must exorcise Satan right away.

The men grumbled and the women wept salt tears
    But no one could evaporate their fears.
As Sarah lay there ranting the rabbi began his chanting.

His stentorian voice was commanding;
    His words were demanding Satan to leave Sarah, his prey.
He summoned God to take Satan away.
    He explained, "Each person is truly four,
And often some of the four are at war.
    A self, a complement, a twin, a negative.
May the negative be neutralized by the positive.

Amen. Amen. Amen. Amen.

May the strength of the twin enter Sarah within
    And make her strong as well; may Satan return to Hell.

Amen. Amen. Amen. Amen.

May the complement give her what she lacks
    May Metatron give Satan a thousand whacks.
May Satan ooze out of Sarah's being;
    May we stomp upon him as he is fleeing.

Amen!   Amen!! Amen!!! Amen!!!!

The men circled Sarah seventy times and whispered
    Words in cryptic rhymes.
Moths skittered toward the light and the beadle announced
    It was past midnight.
Then from the hills came a shofar call;
    And from Sarah's voice, a thunder squall.
Her face was contorted and twisted with pain as the presence
    Of Satan began to wane.
She no longer felt Satan's embrace and opened
    Her eyes and saw the rabbi's face.
He cantillated, "Blessed is God, holy and true
    Who created Sarah, then made her anew."

"Amen! Amen!" came the worshippers' reply
    And as they looked at Sarah, no longer awry,
They heard God say, "I have Sarah's soul refilled."
    Again they prayed as the Lord God had willed.
Now that Satan was completely banned the women
    Took Sarah by the hand
And prayed with a fervor as never before that peace
    Will be Sarah's forevermore.

MARTIN LUTHER: FRIEND AND FOE

Luther practicing his scowl in the mirror watched his eyes turn red with rage.
    "Ach. Das ist gut," he whispered. Then he modulated his voice.
First a murmur, a shade of a sound, then a rise in pitch, finally, a blaring scream.
    "Ach. Das ist ganz besser," he sneered.
In measured steps he walked toward the Lord's Table
    Bowed, closed his eyes, and crossed himself. Slowly he ascended the pulpit.
Dramatically he caressed the binding of The Bible, the very Bible he had
    Translated into his native tongue.
Coughs rebounded against the thick granite walls.
    Looking out at his parishioners who worshipped him more than God,
Words tumbling forth from his lips echoing throughout the nave.
    Each word spoke pain; each sound was filled with distress;
Each thought unveiled humiliation.
    "Butchers! My beloved butchers!!
History will not forget nor must the future fail to remember
    That I courted the Jews and those subhumans despised me.
I told the entire world that Jesus was born a Jew.
    But they, the userers, would not embrace Him.
I showed them that their Talmud is obsolete.
    Read the inspired gospel not rabbinic prattle, I beseeched them.
I reminded them that popes had condoned their persecution."
    He now spoke barely above a whisper; the assembly strained to hear him.
"Accept the New Covenant and you will be saved, I urged.
    And they scoffed, 'We live by the original covenant. Accept ours.'
Are they not a stiff-necked people?"

The stored hatred for every kind of indignity life deals burst forth "Ja! Ja! Ja!"
    With each assenting voice the flames of their anger grew redder
Than a cow's blood.
    Pulses thumped wildly; hands filled with energy begged to cleave

And slash. Luther raised his hand exultant but aghast.
    His voice cracked as it lunged for a screech,
Rolling with rage he thundered,

"Jew, double-dyed thief, murderer, rapist of the German soul! Jew,
    Bloated with conceit and reeking with deceit.
O progeny of the hooked nosed albatross!
    Ye sowers of chaos! Ye reapers of sin!
You will not corrode German valor or curdle German resolve."

Long was the pause that followed.
    Broken was the dam that had suppressed anger against the Jew,
Offenders of the pious Luther.

Squeezing his Bible, he continued,
    "Are they not the werewolves who spread the plague?
Are they not the dogs who steal food from our starving
    German children?
Are these not the bastard offspring of the Satan who mocks our ways?
    Are these not the swine who snorted at Jesus, Son of God?

Shall we hunger while they eat?
    Shall we be silent while they trample upon our souls?
Shall we be meek while they turn our pain into profit?
    Shall we bend while they shatter our pride?"

His voice again pitched towards the rafters.
    Enunciating each syllable he concluded,
"Do we not hang thieves on the gallows?
    Do we not break heads of high-way-men on the wheel?
        Do we not cut off the heads of kill-ers?

Curse with me this race of evil-do-ers!
    Damn the Christ-killers who disdain our German heritage.
        Jesus is Love. Amen."

Butchers by the hundred ran out of the church chanting
    "Jesus is Love! Jesus is Love!"

Unleashing their power, they clawed Jews and dragged
    Them from their homes to gallows.
After looting their possessions, they put to flame "sidurim", "torot",
    And homes.
Luther smiled a knowing smile. His repudiation of the Jews was avenged.
    And when the seeder of German pride passed into eternity,
He became an inert moon
    Ever pulling surly waves of vengeance to inundate
The unbaptized Jews.
    Cresting waves of violence fell and dashed Jewish souls
Against the rocks.
    Never again did Jew or German know contentment.

FOUL CALLED THE RABBIS

The scholars of the Talmud twisted the plaits of The Law until
    The split hairs were snarled, knotted and tangled.
Halachah* was heaped with piles of confusion.
    *traditional doctrine Rabbis from France and Germany
Decided the law one way; those from Spain and Italy, another.
    Century crisscrossed century with responsa after responsa.
"God! We have no clear guide to Your Law."
    Joseph Karo pleaded "Show me how to cleanse the Halachah
Of its impurities.
    Bewildering is the weight of local custom;
Disconcerting is the welter of opinion.
    Halachic rulings ignoring opposing views has produced chaos.
There are so many codes and they do not always agree.
    Teach me how to clear up the inconsistencies.
Show me how to reconcile the disparities.
    Bring us out of the fog."
Inspired by the Light of God Joseph disentangled the snarled braids
    And cut the knotted hairs.
He meticulously arranged a table for the Halachah.
    Strong were its legs; nutritious was its fare.
Based on a majority opinion of other codifiers,
    A lucid code of laws shone with God's Light.
He announced, "We now have one Torah and one code."
    "Foul," cried the usually humble Isserles.
"Joseph, my friend, your code shines but through a Sephardic prism.
    You ignored the genius of the German and French rabbis.
You snubbed Italian and Polish scholars.
    The legs of your table are wobbly: the top of your table is naked.
I will cover it with a plain cloth
    That preserves the mysteries of the Talmud and would

Be acceptable here in Cracow,
    As well as in Germany, in France, even in your own Saphed."

"Foul" cried Hayyim ben Bezalel.
    "Your code, Isserles, is too lenient.
Ignoring the decisions of the German rabbinate,
    It has a Polish veneer.
The saintly dei Rossi, the doctor of Mantua, exorcised the Talmud
    of its raveled riddles and enigma.
Judaism ignored the Greek translations of the Tanach.
    Its calendric inconsistencies demanded reconciliation.
How ignorant we are of our own poetic and noncanonical exilic writings,"
    Insisted the frail dei Rossi who knew books better than he knew people.
"Foul," cried the rabbis of Rome, Ferrara, Padua, Verona.
    Cherem*, they said, awaits anyone reading
The works of dei Rossi. *excommunication
    Joseph Caro declared dei Rossi excommunicated.
Alas God intervened and withdrew life from the sainted Joseph.
    But what Joseph began his disciples completed.
Banished was the dei Rossi name; forgotten were his writings
    Until the Haskalah, like a rooster's crow when the sun rises,
Awoke the Jewish world from its unbridled dreams
    Spawned by shadows and ghosts.
Unbridled dreams based not on reason but on fantasies woven in ecstasy.
    His writings were disinterred, discussed, studied, and admired.
Dei Rossi's name was redeemed and reborn and the learned rabbis
    Sit around even today and scrutinize the arranged table,
Lifting the cloth to unveil Halachah:
    Navigator of Jewish conduct derived from practice, wisdom, mystery,
And fog. And peering at them are the piercing eyes of Dei Rossi.

THE EARTHQUAKE

First the earth guffawed, then it mumbled, then it grumbled;
    It quivered, swayed, and shook.
In an instant it turned homes into shacks piling them into random stacks,
    The cracking earth meandered like tree roots.
Into the breaches Ferrara tumbled:
    People howled, cows lowed, chickens screamed, horses neighed,
Sheep bleated, dogs barked, and jackasses brayed.
    For ten days the earth quaked and chaos pervaded

As stones from the hills into the city cascaded.
    Houses fell apart; pathways were pocked;
And tree branches lay without limbs.
    On the last day as the priest sang their hymns
And groined vaults of the cathedral ruptured and the roof fell in.
    The dyspeptic earth retched one last time,
And the clefts in the cathedral cellar was filled with slime.

Curious, the bookish Azariah Dei Rossi strolled among that debris.
    He halted his prayers to examine Nature's spree.
Peeking through the rock crumbs was a tattered leather parchment
    Begging to be saved.
Ornate calligraphic letters in Greek smudged by the centuries speak
    Of a Letter of Aristeas to his brother Philocrates.

Tell me who you are Aristeas buried for centuries in the graveyard of ideas!
    Azariah read. His voice faltering by centuries of disuse:
"The intention of Ptolemy Philadelphus, Egypt's king,
    Is to translate the Book of Moses, Prophets,
and Writings from Hebrew to Greek and discover their mystique.
    Ptolemy wrote to Eleazar, The High priest,

To invite scholars from every tribe to a royal feast
    In Alexandria where a library held books of every faith.
There they would translate the Jewish canon into Greek.

He sent Arestes, a Jewish advisor, he called him the best,
    To Jerusalem on the quest
To return with the scholars so wise that they could graft
    Jewish knowledge on to the Greek.
The hybrid would be a better breed than any creed it did succeed.
    Arestes agreed, seeing little difference between the Greek and the Jew,
Each worshipping one God accepted as True.
    Seventy-two scholars assembled and before they began
their task the king had many questions to ask
    In the manner of Socrates, according to Aristeas.

Q. What is the highest good in life?

> A. *To know that God is Lord of the Universe, And our finest achievement is not our success But God's who brings all things to fulfillment.*

Azariah studied on.
    To better define the ideal paragon.
The Laws of Nature have not been drawn up at random
Or by whim but with a view to
Truth unembellished and without trim.

Menedemus, the philosopher of Eritrea asserts
    That the universe is managed by providence.
Since man is a creation of God, all power and beauty
    Of speech proceed from The Deity.

The questioning went on to better establish the ideal paragon.

Q. What is the true mark of piety?

> A. *To accept that God is all knowing and constantly at work in the Universe. No man who acts unjustly and works wickedness escapes His notice. God is our benefactor. And, we must imitate Him and be free of offense to claim our innocence.*

Q. Can we be spared disturbing thoughts in sleep?

A. Reason does not reign when we are asleep.
We only imagine that we fly through air.
In waking life, though, reason reigns in thought's lair.
As you, Ptolemy, master and king Govern your words
and to the rule of piety cling. Never abuse your power.
Be steadfast in self-discipline and to all a beacon-tower.

Q. What is it that is most beneficial to health?

A. Temperance, and it would not be possible to achieve fruition
Without God having created such a disposition.
Ptolemy was impressed with every reply.

He had faith that the seventy-two scholars would clarify
The famed Jewish writing that so many would daily be reciting."

Azariah Dei Rossi translated the lost text in a manner true and fair
And sent it to Jewish scholars everywhere.

First they guffawed, then they mumbled, then they grumbled.
    Then they quivered in anxiety, swayed in prayer, and shook in rage.
He had made random cracks in the history of Judaism
    And insulted every sage
And from the tree of knowledge unfurled branches meandering
    Throughout the world.
Points in Halachah in one country were not always the same in another.
    Although they were all fed by the same mother,
The milk of the Torah. "Azariah", they indicted
    "You have snuffed out the light of our menorah."
How the rabbis howled, lowed, screamed, neighed, bleated,
    Barked, and brayed.

They inveighed against him who had Israel's House detached.
    Pocked its pathways and its limbs had been snatched.
Finally, its lofty ideas supported by the groined vaults ruptured
    Because of their faults.

They dyspeptic rabbis retched one last time and indicted
    Azariah for the crime
Of being too knowing of the vile, even of possessing Gentile
    Translations of the Holy Book and developing a Christian outlook.
History has inscribed that he was
    excommunicated, and his works proscribed.
May his memory be a blessing for coalescing
    Scholarship from many a source with courage and without remorse.

Hymns were often written based on the text provided by a scholar.
    The gem "Yigdal" is one such based as it is on the 13 principles
Of faith propounded by Reb Moshe ben Maimon, the Rambam.
    The rendering below is of those principles.

SO GRAND IS GOD

So grand is ELOHIM, GOD we praise
    Who prevailed before Time's primeval days.
God is ONE, unique, and without peer, unseen,
    Endless, yet always near.
None compares with ONE so holy, praised by wealthy and by the lowly.
    Existing before the day of creation, the very first cause of causation.
Without body without frame eternal is the Divine Flame.
    Behold OUR Creator: Majestic, timeless, none is greater.
Those chosen prophets wreathed in glory transmitted
    To all the Sacred Story.

The lawgiver, Moses, discerned GOD's reality
    And first to teach 'bout GOD's regality.
To him was given the Torah true, a servant to teach what God foreknew.
    The Torah is firm, without flaw; its truths are the bedrock of human law.

Mysteries to us that are concealed from the very start
    Were by GOD revealed.
Righteous deeds earn reward; evil acts merit rebuke from the LORD.

We await the day of millennium when salvation at last will come
    Then voices of now and of past Time will sing
Their praises to God Sublime.

EULOGY FOR THE RAMBAM, REB MOSHE BEN MAIMON

We have gathered together here today to honor
    The Rambam whom the Lord God has taken away
To offer his counsel for making corrections to Creation's
    Unplanned imperfections.
Until ben Maimon, no sage without flaw, interpreted so clearly
    The sacred Law
Which Moses, our teacher, from Sinai brought,
    The very laws which God to him had taught.
Where did the Rambam find the time to do tasks
    Accomplished by so very few?
He healed the sick, no matter their wealth,
    He studied herbs and balms, to improve human health.
He served as judge on his one day of rest, and though he was tired,
    He did this with zest.
And when he had time to spare, time, to him a commodity rare,
    He interpreted the Holy Books with uncommon zeal
To discover new meanings those books would reveal.
    Did scholars agree with all that he wrote?
Many differed with him on what Scriptures connote
    Because he pursued Truth based upon reason
Unblemished by superstition.
    This was treason to them and they burned his books,
Claiming that he forsook the ancestral faith.
    Over him they suspended a wraith
Of apostasy. But he saw what no one else could see
    A Judaism in which all are free to choose how to live their lives
As righteous Jews yet based on the soundness of law.
    That Judaism the Rambam foresaw
Would teach the world that God's spirit swirled
    About each of us, righteous or flawed
Because we all are children in the family of God.

RABBI NACHMANIDES AND THE APOSTATE PABLO CHRISTIANI

The fabric of Judaism was fraying
While most of the Jews were praying
Others were damning Maimonides, a saint,
And smearing his sacred memory with taint.
He was too logical and wrote for the elite;
Not for the man in the street.
Order of the rational was subdued by fervor of the mystical.
As this inner struggle went on for the Jewish soul
Arose an apostate with a heinous goal:
To plot a sordid sedition
And besmirch in debate Jewish erudition.
The Talmud allowed, Pablo Christiani contended
That Jesus, son of God, suffered and ascended,
After the temporal world He did bless
To Heaven with his father to coalesce
Nachmanides, a rabbi of renown, this claim disputed.
One from a human womb cannot be thus transmuted.
Further, he argued, Pablo the Talmud misread.
The lies of the church had become holy bread.
If peace and justice is to come upon the Messiah's birth
How come there is war and corruption every place on earth?
King James of Aragon heard the rabbi's position
And was well convinced of his erudition.
Three hundred solids was the rabbi's reward,
A decision that the Dominican Inquisition abhorred.
A price was put on Nachmanides head
The church leaders clearly wanted him dead.
So he left Spain to begin life anew
And entered Jerusalem where there was hardly one Jew.
There he founded a yeshiva for praying and learning
And from afar to Zion students were returning.

During the Middle Ages Judaic poetry flourished. Some like Psalm 1 below recast the verse into contemporary medium. Others like the ones following are in the style of the "Davidic" psalms but are original outpourings of the human heart.

HAPPY ARE THEY WHO LISTEN NOT TO THE WICKED

Happy are they who listen not to the wicked;
    Glad are they who are deaf to the words of sinners.
The wicked are like chaff blown away by the winds;
    The sinners like the flower devoured by slugs.
But they who listen to God's wisdom;
    They who heed the words of the Lord
Are like the blossoms which enrich us all.
    They are like the fruit who seeds endure forever.

DEAR LORD, I MUST CONFESS A GRIEVOUS FAULT

A psalm for all. Sanctified is Your name. Everlasting is Your flame.

Dear Lord, I must confess a grievous fault;
    Too often my tongue my friends assault.
Even though my lips show smiles all too often they're planning guiles.
    So many evil words I know and from my angry heart they flow.
On bended knee I kneel and pray: show me how to live Your way.
    Tomorrow when my tongue will speak let me be Your servant meek,
Only expressing words of praise only voicing the respectful phrase.

MY PAIN OVERFLOWS LIKE A RIVER

My pain overflows like a river; my anguish is deeper than the sea.
    Shelter me from my foes; rescue me from my enemies.
But, Lord, Your anguish is greater than mine
    And Your pain stabs sharper than a knife.
Where will You find shelter? Where's Your rescue from human strife?

At night I hear You weep; in the morning I am wet with Your tears.
    Like the mourner who cries for a loved one Your laments fill my ears.
Yet Your heart pours out mercy; Your soul overflows with love not pride.
    And with You I'll walk in righteousness, my teacher and My guide.
                  Amen.

ALMIGHTY GOD, MERCIFUL AND TRUE

Almighty God. Merciful, mighty and true
    For Your loving blessings I thank You. Hallelujah.

ALMIGHTY GOD, BLESSED BE YOUR NAME

Almighty God, Blessed be Your Name. Beacon of wisdom.
Counsel and guide us to become
Friendly amid alienation, dignified among arrogance,
Merciful amid cruelty, truthful amid deceit,
Builders amid destruction, able amid helplessness,
Forgiving amid insult, modest amid pretension,
Generous amid selfishness, striving amid struggle,
Considerate amid carelessness, calm amid turmoil,
Fair amid injustice, believing amid faithlessness,
Hopeful amid despair, and loving amid hatred.

IN SILENT PAUSES

In silent pauses we hear Your voice rising
    To paint drab banality in silver and gold;
Rising to grant peace and serenity to every heart raging from every-day life;
    Rising to fill with sublimity our ears muddled
with the cacophony of the commonplace.
    Oh Lord, open our eyes to see Your glory;
Oh Lord, open our ears to hear Your truths.
    Oh Lord, open our hearts to receive Your love.

The reality was that oppression abounded and to escape
    It many Jews left the faith.

FROM CHIEF RABBI TO BISHOP: THE CONVERSION OF HA LEVI TO PABLO DE SANTA MARIA, BISHOP OF BURGOS

Convert or die! Convert or die!
    Spoke Shlomo Ha-Levi, Chief rabbi Of Burgos.
Pi-ku-ach nefesh* was his cry. *Preservation of the soul
    As he prostrated himself before the cross
He embraced the gloss of Christianity, an albatross
    Hovering over K'hal Yis-ra-el* protesting without avail
And anguishing with travail. *The Jewish people
    So many were spellbound by their rabbi profound
That their phylacteries they unwound
    And left the faith of their ancestors and crept
Along the corridors of The Church, conquerors
    Of their souls like moles and Rabbi Shlomo
Enrolls them in the church of Christ
    Which enticed them with life priced beyond pots of gold
Aglow behind the rainbow. A life without woe.
    Being dubbed Bishop of Burgos with Christ's own sword
By Pope Benedict XIII, his lord,
    Was to be the rabbi's reward.

THE SPANISH INQUISITION: SEED, ROOT, STEM, AND FLOWER: AN ESSAY*

1.

Every people of every nation regards its civilization
    As the very best—better than all the rest.
And to show that it is superior it requires a foe it deems inferior.
    Who? Who should so be named? The Jew.
The clannish Jew, Manetho proclaimed.
    The priest of the Nile, his quill in caustic poison
Dipped indictments on papyrus caustically dripped,
    Condemn the Jews for cruelty to the ancient Egyptians
Who banished the purveyors of savagery and polluters of Egyptian ancestry.

2.

Apion received tuition from Manetho.
    His quill soaked in snake venom denounced
Zion's Children as disparagers of Greek superiority
    And charged them with sacrifice of gentiles, eaten slice by slice.

3.

The Greek received tuition from Apion and introduced
    A chapter in Anti-Jew history by burning Jews of Alexandria,
A hitherto unknown cruelty, divinely inspired by entail augury.

4.

The Roman rhetorician, Apollonius Molon,
    Received tuition from the Greeks
And, in fits of rage, dipped his barb in vitriol,
    And condemned the Jews as brazen, brash,
Reckless, atheistic, and of faint heart whose imageless
    God was a silent, reeking fart.

5.

St. John Chrysostom received tuition from Apollonius,
    Who under the standard of the cross,
Initiated stabbings, knifings, and stoning of the sanctimonious Jews.
    Convert in Antioch, he insisted, or be banished
And so the Jews of Antioch vanished.

6.

Sisebut, the Visigoth kings Spain, received tuition from St. John.
    Jews, he ordered, convert or die.
And thousands hid their prayer shawls inside a lie.

7.

Agobard fanned the flames Sisebut kindled and further spread the word
    To massacre the superstitious, insolent Jews in the name of the Son.
Jews were stoned, knifed, and set on fire one by one.

8.

Church council after church council receiving tuition from
    Agobard condemned the Jew and permitted
Appropriating their property.
    Then they banished some and converting others by force.
Emigration for many was the only recourse.

9.

The crusaders received tuition from the Council
    Who drove Jews into caves like sheep
And when they were fast asleep burned them.
    In this manner Jews were massacred in Castrojeriz, Toledo,
Escalona, Leon by the sword wielding crusader.
    Those who escaped were sold to the slave trader.

10.

Ferrand Martinez, priest of the masses,
    Defying orders from the crown, the nobles,
And the cardinals, received tuition from the crusaders.
    With a thumping heart and a frenzied brain,
Inciting his worshippers, he frenetically shouted from the pulpit,
    Raise the sword, scepter of Christ's Castilian church,
And with zeal slash Jews to bits and pieces then raze
    Their foul synagogues with fiery blazes
And God will reward you by forgiving your debts
    Which will vanish in flames.
Rage! Rise up in revenge against the repugnant Jews,
    Detritus of Satan, stench of vomitus,
Who spurn Jesus, Son of God, and scoff at His teachings.
    And Jews, rich and poor, old and young, men and women,
Victims of the caprices of evil minds,
    Were grabbed in the streets and beaten, their bloodied
Heads were bashed against one another.
    The plaited hair of dead Jewesses was cut
And gathered in piles to stuff pillows.
    With delight they ripped open the guts of the still convulsing bodies
And watched life depart from the once joy-filled Jews.
    With unremitting ardor they torched the synagogues
And watched the holy parchment perish in smoke
    Filling their noses with the stench of sacred Jewish history.
Blood of the Juderia of Seville bubbled from culverts
    Where cadavers, agony fixed on their faces, were flung.
The devastation was contagious.
    Alcala de Guadaira, Carmona, and Ecija received tuition from Seville

And their Jewish Quarters were leveled and Jews,
    "Christianity's" irritants were crushed like crawling ants.

11.

Receiving tuition from them, CorDov Baera heaped two thousand corpses
    In mounds on the synagogue steps where swords
Were run through babies
    As their mothers shrieked while being raped
To the tumultuous applause of the witnesses awaiting their turns.
    Shackled fathers watched as their families
Were violated and dismembered.
    Jailers anointed the faces of the anguished husbands
With olive oil and then set them on fire.
    Such was the fate of the Chosen of God. Word
Reached Valencia of the success of the Castilians
    Where *hombres de poca y pobre condicion* rimmed
Through the gates of the Juderia,
    Crushing the heads of infants, looting houses,
Raping, maiming, and killing.
    Here, too, corpses were strewn upon the synagogue steps.]
The remnants of the community carried crosses. Agonized,
    They were forcibly baptized.

12.

Palma, Lerida, Majorca, Perpignan, Barcelona,
    And Gerona received tuition from CorDor Baera.
No mercy was shown to the Jews; the survivors had not time for grief.
    They fled the cities without burying their dead whose organs
Were picked apart by vultures.
    And the pages of history indicted the martyrs as the belligerents.
Jew convert! Jew convert! Jew convert!
    Conversos* filled the empty spaces of the Jewish community.
*Jews outwardly Christian
    They flourished. 'Though loyal, they were shunned.
But there were lessons lurking from Spain's bestiality
    That would forever stain human history

13.

Bishop Don Juan de Tordesillas receiving tuition from history,
    Sentenced conversos to death;
Marcos Garcia planned to destroy them;
    Sarmiento unleashed the beasts lurking inside the mob in Toledo.
After converso homes were looted and their daughters
    Were raped again and again, Old Christians grabbed
The hilt of the cross and bashed the skulls of the New Christians
    Of the "perverse lineage of the Jews."
Lying on the ground senseless and trembling in Death's hold,
    They were dismembered by the barbarians
On a holy mission carried out with loathing
    To murder the wretched conversos.
The thirst for killing was unquenchable.
    Toledo was a desert of compassion;
Toledo was a wasteland of humanity where enmity inhabited the soul
    And cleansing the land of the pestilent Jew, the goal.

14.

Pero Galvez, Vicar of the Cathedral of Toledo,
    Received tuition from history.
He set up a Commission of Inquiry and condemned
    To death conversos, "Jews masquerading as Christians."
Conversos who escaped the mob suckling
    The teats of treachery were burned at the stake.
Jubilation spread throughout Toledo
    And there was drunkenness and debauchery in every alley.
Converso deaths was beyond tally.

15.

Tomas de Torquemada received tuition from the Inquisitors,
    Not from his uncle, Cardinal Juan descended
From the ancient tribes of Israel.
    Tomas planted prayer shawls, Jewish prayer books, and Torah scrolls

In the homes of conversos who were then tried in his court
    For surreptitiously practicing Judaism.
False witnesses by the score gave evidence against their neighbors
    Who were sent to prison.
The rat-bitten conversos were dragged out of dungeons,
    Forced to wear the badge of a double yellow crucifix
And the sanbenito imprinted with demonic images.
    Then were they placed on racks and squeezed
On the turning wheel until their guts burst.
    Under torture, they confessed to being secret Jews.
They died anyway.
    The Grand Arsonist of The Inquisition
Condemned them to the flames.
    The mob taunted the burning skin finding ecstatic joy
In hating and exhilaration in abhorring
    They laughed with glee and howled as writhing converso
Flesh crinkled in the flames.
    Melancholia seized the Jewish community
As they departed from Spain.
    Could a Spaniard be found who is sane?

16.

Deza, Archbishop of Seville, received office and tuition from Tomas.
    With his hangman, Diego Lucero,
He bled The Holy Mother of her compassion.
    They shouted, "Give me Jews that I may burn them."
The pillaged, raped, dismembered before an encouraging mob.
    Infants ripped from their mothers,
Were choked to death to stifle their cried.
    Their mothers fell victim to barbarous appetites for sex and murder.
Together Deza and Lucero butchered Jews, knights priests,
    And nuns who denounced their unchristian ways.
Dead conversos were tried and convicted in his court
    And set on fire in a pyre with other corpses.
Spain was a desert of compassion,
    A wilderness of base wiles where carnage reigned
Among consenting smiles.

17.

Ximenes de Cisneros, third Inquisitor-General,
  Commander-in-Chief of a loyal army,
Received tuition from Archbishop Deza.
  He relented the torture of priests and nuns accused of heresy.
But vibrating with viciousness, he drew upon malice
  Lurking in the crevices of his mind
And flung it proudly as he murdered the conversos.
  Wretched were his victims helplessly reduced to trash
Rising to the clouds in smoke and ash.

18.

An ensemble of Inquisitor-Generals who reaped tuition
  From the past sowed to generations to come
"Solutions" to the Jewish problem:
  Intimidation, expropriation, deportation, humiliation and immolation.
They taught "exterminate the Jewish taint with zeal."
  Hell, once a figment of imagination, became real.
Genuflecting to Avarice, they metastasized the cancer of hate in their breasts
  To other parts of the Catholic body in Portugal and Italy.
Extracting grace from Christian kindness,
  They redefined mania as morality,
And cruelty as charity.

The Talmudic text, Ethics of the Fathers contains moral aphorisms. Many a section begins with "so and so received torah (learning or tuition) from so and so". This parallelism is observed in this poem. Manetho, an Egyptian priest, c 270 BC; Alexandria pogrom, c 38 AD; Apion, c 38 CE; Apollonius c first century CE; St. John Chrysostom 387 CE; Sisebut 612 CE; Agobard, c 9th century CE; Castojeriz 1035 CE; Toledo and Escalona 1109 CE; Leon 1230 CE; Crusader crematoria in Alsace and Colmar, 1338 CE; Father Ferrand Martinez, 1378 CE and triggered a chain of pogroms that killed thousands of Jews; pogrom in Seville, 1391 CE; hombres de poca y pobre condicion, men of low status; Bishop Don Juan de Tordesillas c 1420; Peri Galvez c 1449; Tomas de Tourquemada, First Grand Inquisitor, c 1490; Deza c 1499; Ximenes de Cisneros c 1510. In 1808 Joseph Bonaparte suppressed the Inquisition; it was restored by Ferdinand VII in 1814; it was suppressed again in 1829; re-stored in 1823; suppressed in 1834 in Europe but continued in Mexico. This poem had "chai" sections. *Hebrew word for life. Its numerical value is 18.

CONVERSO REAFFIRMATION

And when we straightened our limbs we were cut down
    By marauding crowds
In the name of God and either burned in a pyre
    Or grafted on to an alien offshoot
Of the tree of Abraham, watered and pruned,
    To blossom here, there, and everywhere—in stealth,
In secret, in subterfuge.

And our souls were pillaged; our heritage was raped;
    Our faith was defaced, tears cling like dew drops
To every leaf   of every page   of every chapter of our history.

Ostracized, we are fugitives, refugees, and wanderers without a birthright.
    Still we kindled a candle on Shabbat eve
So that our ancestors will not stumble in Gan-Aden*
    *Paradise, Garden of Eden
We kindled another candle to recall our charred ancestors
    Sacrificed on the alters of evangelism.
And now the fog is lifting, the sun shines through our veins
    And chases the gloom from our seed
And we kindle another candle to celebrate ha-tik-vah, the hope,
    That our scions will be restored to our roots, the ancient tree of Israel,
With worth, respect, acceptance for ourselves and by klal Yisrael.*
    *The Jewish Community

    Like so many S'fardim* before we bent like saplings in the wind. *Jews of Spanish heritage

DO WE HAVE MESSIAHS?*

The righteous Rabbi Elijah, stern of face,
    Handed each of the assembled a braided candle,
And mournfully intoned, before this Holy Ark on this hallowed ground
    We recall the names of messiahs false,
Eternal pariahs shunned by saintly Jewish souls.
    His hands shook as he read the names of the scoundrels
None were called to lead by Adonai, Our Lord,
    But were dragged into history by a braying hoard
Who exploited the despair of their persecuted brother and sisters.
    'They aspired to write their names in the pages of fame;
May their names be inscribed in in in infamy;' he was stuttering.
    'Howl, s-s-stamp your feet, and s-s-s spit at every name I am uttering.'

Moses of Crete. He and his followers were swallowed
    By the sea Whose waves did not part upon his command.
Severus, mutilator of the law, met his end by the executioner's claw.
    Abu-Isa was slain by the Caliph.
Yudgham, his follower, profaned the Holy Text, was executed next.
    Mushka, his disciple, followed and was consumed by Death's maw.
The Linon messiah said he could fly, K'hal Yisrael watched him die.
    Ibn Aryeh mutilated the decalogue and was flogged in the synagogue.
David Alroy, of royal seed, announced "Fly with me to Zion
    And you will be freed."
The body of the Yemenite messiah was separated from his head.

Abraham Abulafia had proclaimed redemption would come soon
    But was scorned as a clown and a buffoon.
'Come to the synagogue dressed in white and we will take flight To Israel.
    'The congregation waited and waited.
In the end the Avilla and Ayllon messiahs were repudiated
    Ascher Lamlein prophesied, 'Messiah will be here in six months.

Jews repent.' His failure fomented apostasy.
    Redemption draws nigh Don Isaac Abravenel predicted.
Disillusioned and penniless, his followers repudiated him
    Then nullified their Jewish roots.
David Reubeni and Solomon Molcho had papal connections.
    But were cited for sowing discord; Death was their reward.

Prophets, there were many. Inez heard the voices of souls
    Pronouncing God's name.
The fools of Herrara stopped work, fasted and all in vain.
    Maria Gomez claimed to have ascended to heaven to talk with God;
The rabbis shook their heads and proclaimed her odd.
    Isaac Luria Ashkenazi and Hayyim Vital found sparks
In God's broken vessels being cleansed of evil.
    But salvation was not near-at-hand; thousands were burned in Portugal.
Luis Dias and his followers were entombed in fire
    For circumcising Jewish children,
Preparing them for the coming of the Messiah.
    Sabbatai Sevi, flew into ecstasy then dropped into melancholia,
Birth pangs of the Mother of The Messiah, it was said.
    But he was not an effulgent of Heaven nor an emanation of God's Light,
But an effluent of human sewage who charmed the masses,
    Purged no evil from the cosmos,
Violated Jewish law and found refuge in Islam
    Because Nehemia Hazedek reported him to the authorities.
Then Nehemia returned to Lvov and converted back to
    Judaism but was despised by Polish and German Jewry
And wandered into obscurity.
    And now the most vile, loathsome, and reprehensible of them all:
Jacob Frank, King of Sabbatai Sevi's ignorant scum,
Proclaimed himself God, the true messiah.

A sadist who beat his disobedient followers.
    A schemer was incarnated his wife as the Virgin Shechinah.
An organizer who named twelve disciples and called them "brothers."
    A sorcerer who charmed twelve concubines and called them "sisters."
A pied piper who led his flock into sin and then into the abyss, baptism.
    Rabbi Elijah wept copious tears; Rabbi Elijah ripped his caftan.

These scoundrels led Jewish souls into fire.
 These scoundrels led Jewish souls into dire poverty.
These scoundrels led Jewish souls, already in pain, into despair.
 These scoundrels led Jewish souls to Christ and to Mohammed.
These scoundrels sowed false hope and we harvest despondency.
 May they forever be cursed.
There was a long silence.
 With a "whoosh" all assembled blew out their candles
Then wiped the spittle from their faces and glumly left the sanctuary.

---

*Moses of Crete, c. 475; Severus, c 729; Abu-Isa, c 755; Linon, messiah c. 1060; Ibn Aryeh, c 1100; David Alroy. c 1120; Yemenite, c 1171; Abraham Abulafia, c 1271; Avilla and Ayllon, 1295; Ascher Lamlein, 1502; Don Isaac Abravenel, 1503; David Rehbein and Solomon Molche, 1524; Inez of Herrra c 1500; Maria Gomez of Chillon, c 1500; Isaac Luria and Hayyim Vital, c 1560; Luis Dias, Lisbon 1542; Sabbatai Sevi, 1648 whose messianic status was proclaimed in a dream by Nathan Ashkenazi of Gaza; Jacob Frank, a Sabbatian, c 1760. But instead he met a ghastly death.

CHEREM*

The vibrato voice of Nehemiah Cohen quivered in the Hereafter.
    His words were Hebrew; his chant filled with joy and laughter;
But how he blended the tempo-varying sonata, operatic lilt,
    And Doric scale with a mournful Kol Nidre wail!
His kavanah! Ah his ta-am*, his kavanah, his intent.
    *Savor The aroma of the sacrament,
Bleeding with years of oppression and pleading with pangs of confession
    Retold the history of the Jews of slow welcoming and quick adieus.
"Hazzan*, you are an enchanter of souls," *cantor Spoke,
    Azariah Rossi, a paisan, "our people your voice consoles."
"How long has it been that we have enjoyed our herem?"
    "Decades? Centuries? Minutes? Seconds? Our Eternity we have earned."
The Hereafter was filled with music and thought.
    All they ever sought was the presence of God wherein
To dwell as specks in a pod.
    Then a hacking tubercular cough resounded
And rebounded throughout limitless Time Curling about solace sublime.
    Azariah's spirit was filled with delight.
"Baruch atah Spinoza*," he welcomed the new sight.
    *Blessed art thou, Spinoza. Spinoza's Hebrew name was
He laughed at his own pun, Baruch, enjoying a moment of fun.
    Spinoza and Uriel Da Costa entered hand in hand
Neither could their exile understand.
Or why they had been from the Jewry evicted.
    Both of them of heresy had been convicted.
"Aha Uriel," taunted Azariah with a slight chortle
    "Now you will discover that the soul is immortal.
As long as history keeps it alive a soul will survive."
    Uriel humiliated by the stomping of feet on his back
And saddened by his rabbi's attack was now gladdened
    By this new society that would forever be his destiny.

"Baruch. Here there are no natural laws to defy;
    Natural laws do not go awry.
But we do not have miracles from January to December
    As long as there is someone to remember
That we sowed the seeds that grew into their deeds.
    Uriel! God is omnipresent and heals our torment.
Spinoza spoke through an ethereal haze, "Azariah",
    God's Name did I ever praise.
God is eternal life and creation, Author of the universe and its foundation.
    God codified the laws of Nature but did not Adam create,
Nor is there a messiah for us to await
    To usher in a reign of sanity. God is the moral compass of humanity
But did not cover upon Moses the mantle of laws.
    Every society has them as well as scofflaws.
God, Source of love, does not from mercy recess
    The innocent to torture, maim, and distress.
The lens I have ground through a glass clear I have found That God,
    Master of reason, is just as did to us entrust
To preserve creation but no one person or faith whatever the station
    Is chosen to know God revealed;
God is ever present but always concealed."

And the four spirits who suffered excommunication
    Praised God with adulation.
And looked about but never found the expelling rabbis
    Who made them renowned.
The volleys of curses that had their living beings lacerated
    Were now by God's mercy completely negated.

*Nehemiah Cohen, a cantor in Ferrara in the fifteenth century was placed in Cherem, excommunication, for singing a nontraditional tune for the priestly blessing. Azariah de Rossi, sixteenth century scholar in Mantua, was excommunicated for his critique of the traditional calendrical calculations of the coming of the Messiah, as well as for using Christian references in his writings. Uriel de Costa, seventeenth century, a Sephardic emigre to Holland, was excommunicated for denying the immortality of the soul and for claiming that religion is man made. To reenter the Jewish community he recanted his views, received 39 lashes of the whip, prostrated himself before the community who then stomped on his back after which he committed suicide. Benedict Spinoza also of the seventeenth century and also a Sephardic emigre to Holland was excommunicated for rejecting supernatural interpretations of Biblical events, questioning the immortality of the soul, and holding the view that individuals have a right to interpret Bible according their own experience and need no illumination by Rabbinic authority

LESSER PURIM HOLIDAYS

B'rachot 54 a

When we Jews are saved from a calamity,
when we Jews escape a ruler's tyranny,
When we Jews achieve a victory over overwhelming forces
The rabbis bid us to celebrate the anniversary
Of our rescue and deliverance.
So when a catastrophe is abated
A local Purim holiday is celebrated.

NATURAL CALAMITIES

In Provence a Purim holiday was declared
When the plague ended and Jews were spared.
      25th Iyar 1631

Konvi's Jewry celebrated
When the plague there abated.
      25th Tevet 1810

In Ancora when the quaking earth
Stopped and hearts were filled with mirth
      21st of Tevet 1690

People in the streets did dance
Having been delivered from their circumstance.
      12th Sh'vat 1742

In Leghorn they danced as well
When an earthquake on them befell.
      25th Tammuz 1809

And when the earth in Sermide trembled
All of the Jews in the synagogue assembled
For a Purim feast after burying the deceased.
In Tunisia Purim shaynee was declared
When the Jewish quarter was spared
      24 Tevet 1891

From a natural catastrophe thereby, recharging the Jew's esprit.
For bringing us miracles like these which redeemed us
And added more days to our lives and more life to our days
And more seed to our generations. We give thanks to You O God!

WAR

Jews were saved from wars in Algeria and celebrate Purim Edom.
    4th Cheshvan 1540

Jews of Chios Purim of the good lady.
    8th Iyar 1595

Because they were saved from Franco-Turkish war
How the spirits of the Jews of Lepanto soared.

    11th Tevet 1699
When they were saved from during another Turkish war.
And every Posener Jew celebrated their Purim.
    1st of Heshvon, 1704

After the war between the Poles and Swedes
Komotini had a Purim as well.
    22nd Elul 1768

When saved from a Turkish hell.
In 1797 Purim was declared in Chieri, In Ivrea, and in Turino.
    1st of Av: 1st Shevat;

During the war with France
And in Belgrade the Jews were saved
From destruction during the Turko-Serbian War.
    19th Sivan 1822

REB YANKEL'S SON, MENDEL, THE SCHNORRER

When all is said and done Reb Yankel's sons, almost every one,
    Went into commerce, except for Mendel, the "simpleton".
He had heard the "call" to serve others not in the ways of his brothers
    But as a mitzvah facilitator for elderly, lonely mothers.

When he came of age he was advised by a sage
    To allow others to do good and he would earn his wage
In heaven above. So he cultivated a gimp and walked like a chimp
    And knocked on any door. Invited in he entered with an "oy" and a limp.

"Pious Missus," he would say "today is your day
    To earn credit in Heaven so for your own sake a little kindness display.
A piece of bread is all I ask. For you, virtuous missus, a simple task
    To perform out of the goodness of your heart
And you will in Heaven's glory bask."

She would slice from her choicest bread, a blessing he then said.
    "Perhaps, a wedge of cheese?" he solicited.
Cheese, herring and potatoes she would spread on her best china.
    "Please, generous missus, a glass of wine."
He then blessed the fruit of the vine.
    Again, and again, and again.
She received ever more recognition in the Eyes of The Divine.

He succeeded in his ambition of securing daily nutrition
    By allowing others to earn mitzvot and improving
their spiritual condition
    In Heaven and his on earth. "You will add to your treasured worth
In God's Eyes, unselfish missus, if you a ruble give to eliminate my dearth.
    A ruble give to improve my estate.

I have a dog to feed and also a wife whose insults jab me like a knife."
    A ruble Reb Mendel would receive and be sent away.
"May you, kind-hearted missus, have eighteen blessings in the afterlife,"
    He would say.
The wine having gone to his feet numbed his senses when they met concrete
    And he completely forgot which leg to limp on.
Mothers watched as he ran down the street.
    They were delighted with the miracle wrought
By doing good deeds as they had been taught.
    Behold, they healed a wretch who,
Through their kindness, a malady fate had brought.

WITNESS TO CREATION: KABBALAT SHAMAYIM

The diminutive Rabbi Maier, pale, old, and bent,
    Was honored with the first aliya, reserved for the most eminent.
No one was purer in heart nor more pious in deed.
    No one was more righteous nor in charity did exceed.
But he felt unworthy of the honor. The beleaguering of the innocent
    Ripped the vestment of his faith
for he was angered by God's abandonment!
    Ya-amod Ha-Rav Maier B'Reb Aharon, cohane
tsadik,* The rabbi was invited to recite
    The first Torah blessings of the new year.
His smile was a mix of shame and delight

As he gathered his Tallis about his finger and reverently touched the scrolls.
    With moist eyes closed he kissed the crumpled cloth.
Draping his head and face with his tallis**
    He extols, "Borchu es adonoi, ham'vorach."***
The congregation answers with pride,
    "Boruch adonoi ham'vorach l'olom vaw-ed."****
Then swept up by an awesome tide
    He chanted the remaining benediction, chagrin reddening his face.
Enthralled by a force within the Torah he was encircled by God's embrace.
    He abandoned his doubts, he evicted every fear;
He bid God give balm to his soul and into his life to reappear.

Cantillating the first word of the Torah, "B'rayshis"*****,
    The rabbi watches the first and last letters falling.
Staring at him was "Reshi"******. It was the Head of God calling.
    Drawn Into the word he beholds spiraling staircases

Intertwining with each other and angels dwelling in the empty spaces
    Where they were singing the Names of YHVH, The Ineffable:*******

Adonai, El, Elohim, Shadai, Shamayim, Tsvaot, Ehye, Chanun, V'rachum,
    Names that terrify and mystify.
Rav Maier is electrified by the angelic voices.
    Repeating the sounds he hears in God's Abode he rejoices.

As he ascends the ladder of the double helix whose rungs
    Are stronger than flint
Yet smoother than silk. He reaches for and finds the secrets of the print
    Divine Glory, yesod—foundation, and malkut—Divine Realm.
As he climbs rung by rung through double rings: guanine and adenine;
    Across the bridges of sweetness through cytosine and thymine.

Into the most recondite of mysteries through spindles of light
    He rises spinning and curling and is embraced
By Sephirot******** bright.
    His mind crowned with a glittering diadem casting a splendid spray
Of everlasting bewildering reality, the absolute Unity
    And Infinity of God's sway.

Maier! he hears a voice say, Maier! You are watching history
    From formless beginning evolving to now
In all of its awesome mystery.
    Behold Keter, the nothingness of what is not;
Behold Keter, pure infinity,
    Behold Keter, all being and non-being; behold Keter,
Every possibility.
    Keter, the cause of causes, plucked and squeezed
The essence of Divine Thought from oblivion
    And is spreading the Perfect and Intelligible
About the Cosmos and all Infinity is merging into One.
    Then Chochma pours out of Keter
And releases Binah Dwelling within it, a luminescent nebula.
    Light and dark projects and reflects Oneness of God,
All knowledge interconnects.
    Keter, Chochma, and Binah wrap themselves
In the veil of immanence,
    The small face with eyes of grace, the Sacred Happiness of Providence.
Rav Maier, cohane tsadik, bathes himself in luminous grace
    Cascading out of the darkness, Creation's birthplace

Where God creator of Din, Rigor, establishes the Light of Right
    And the Dark of Wrong.

They who walk in wrongness are weak;
    They who walk in rightness are strong.
Lest humans exploit God's leniency standards of behavior are being set
    That are spawned from Grace, the gem in the divine coronet.

Rigor and Grace join as partners as give balance to creation's debut.
    And then the Beauty of God is revealed: a prism of every hue
And a treasury of every form sculpted to the finest degree
    Penetrating and penetrated by other emanations
According to the Divine decree.

Behold how it dazzles with knowledge;
    Behold how it radiates with God's shine
And is the Netsach, Victory, over forces dark,
    Gilding the road to Glory divine.
From his inner voice came "Baw-raw"*********,
    The second word in the Torah.
How excited he is to be a witness to Creation as he stares
    At the flickering lights of the menorah.

There before him is The Foundation of the cosmos.
    All emptiness is filled with God's Glory.
And all steps lead to the Kingdom of God where Sephirot
    Orbit God's dormitory.
From empty spaces in the cosmos, the next word, "Elohim"**********
    Is sung by angels beyond count.
Giving praise to The Creator, Judge, Beauty,
    Foundation Whose Grace is paramount.
Ecstasy fills the rabbi. Returning from his pilgrimage,
    He stands erect, tall, radiant with color,
No longer old but a youth immersed in his heritage.

Facing his flock he announces,
    "From Nothing emerged the seed of Creation.
It grew, blossomed, and, then, flowered.
    All possibilities come from Mutation

And become realities when God's radiance upon us is showered."
    He had been a witness to the Glory of God
And was freed of his torment.
    And with God-given compassion he forged forgiveness
For all the ill that befalls the innocent.

****

*Rise honorable Rabbi Maier, Son of Aaron, of the priestly clan.
    "Maier" means he who shed light
Tallis, a fringed prayer shawl. ; * Blessed art Thou O God,
    The Sanctified. ****Blessed art Thou O, sanctified, forever.;
***** The first word of Genesis. In the beginning.
    ******My head; *******The Ineffable:
There are said to be 72 names for God.

********Divine spheres or emanations: The Great Face: Keter-crown,
    Chochma-God's Thoughts, Binah—intelligence; the small face:
Chesed—grace, Din-setting rigorous standards, Tiferet-God's beauty,
    Netsach—victory, hod—Divine Glory, yesod—foundation,
And malkut—Divine Realm.
    *********"Baw-raw"—created, the second word
In the Book of Genesis. **********
    "Elohim"—God, the third word in the Book of Genesis

Many tales from the 18th and 19th century
    East European Jewish lore contain lesson,
Among them is the broad category of Chasidic tales,
    Some of which follow.

SEVEN CHASIDIC STORIES

BAAL SHEM TOV

Israel Ben Eliezar gazed at layers of schist sparkling in the midday sun
    Stretching their fingers to the cobalt blue glacier capping the mountain.
Sheep bleated psalms on the hillside. He heard them talking with God
    As they swallowed the emerald green grass.
Oak trees swayed in the breeze revealing clusters of acorns
    That would sow a forest-to be. He filled his pipe with tobacco and puffed.
He was finding God. Like a tallit, God's brilliance enveloped him:
    Dazzling, scintillating, beguiling, enthralling, spellbinding.
It was pure white, cleaner than cream with more glow than snow
    And more innocent than pearls, alabaster and ivory combined.
Radiant, refulgent, and lucent proclaiming the Divine Presence.
    As he watched he began to twist, turn, and gyrate into the Pure White.

The Pure White separated into Red, Yellow, and Blue.
    The band of red was copper absorbed by ruby;
The band of blue was cobalt melded to sapphire.
    And the band of yellow was gold fused with topaz.
These then coalesced forming purple, green, and orange.
    These separated and mingled with distant cousins of the wheel
And merged into cyan, magenta, burnt sienna, vermillion, umber.
    By whim they migrated toward one another and all was black.
But several shades oozed out of the blackness of entropy
    And he saw new hues forming shapes, symbols, letters-
Hebrew letters-Words of the Torah revealing their secrets:
    God's gift to the Jews to be taught to humanity:
Laws to follow; holidays to observe; joys to partake in; sufferings to endure;

Prayers to recite; praises to offer, history to glory in; and defeats to mourn.
    The entire history of his people, past and future,

Were divulged and transmitted.
    In ecstasy he gyrated, reeled, whirled, twirled, rotated, pivoted,
Raised his leg in syn-co-pa-ted dance and spun
    About a granite hillock like the earth circles about the sun.
Without willing it he heard wordless tunes sung by angels.
    Without planning it these same tunes left his lips.

The Shechinah, God's luminous presence, wrapped around him.
    And he radiated like flickering sparks of sunshine.
He was bounded by God and bonded to God.
    God was within him in everything he did:
His prayers, his eating, his work, his walking,
    His talking, his dealings with family.
God was merciful and kind to everyone no matter the rank.
    It was that knowledge of God residing within that brought him joy
And that joy, raised his soul to God to return the joy
    To be dispatched to other souls.
He had no need to flagellate himself or to fast.
    God wants all creatures to emote joy and that was happiness
for all Creation.

"Israel Ben Eliezar" he heard the Shechinah whisper
"You, My chosen one, are worthy to be called,
    'Baal Shem Tov', Lord of A Good Name."

AT THE SYNAGOGUE GATES

The Baal Shem Tov stands at the synagogue gates and there he waits.
    Students pause questions to ask and in his light to bask,
"Is it for the Messiah that you tarry? Do you await some other dignitary?"
    "No," he replied, "In this House of Worship
There is a stench emanating from every bench
    Where each worshipper drops prayers like leaves
And themselves and the community deceives
    Into believing that the prayers offered
With locomotion arise out of true devotion.
    But perfunctory are their prayers and they fall to the ground in layers.
As worshippers sway their prayers decay.

The room is filled with swill; the haughty worshippers spread ill will."
    He turned and left the gates then gyrates
Singing songs without words to the nesting birds.
    And when he paused, his students, awed,
Saw the true meaning of avodah*: acts of kindness blossoming
    From kavanah**. *worship; **intention
Prayer, they learned, is feeding those lacking food; freeing those
    In servitude; Clothing the poor and treating no one as inferior.
First his protegees copied his ways,
    But then they made his avodah theirs and step by step their prayers
Flew to rejoin The Divine where prayers were polished
    With a radiant shine. "Now," said The Lord of A Good Name,
"I can enter the synagogue and be warmed by the flame
    Of God's Holy word and sip Torah's nectar like a hummingbird."

BASED ON TWO TALES OF Dov BAER OF MEZERITCH

Out of a void God created Time and Space unfolded
    And there was Heaven, earth, and life.
The tsadik, emancipated from the worldly,
    Melts Time and folds back the warps of Space
As they were before the moment of creation.
    That is a miracle.
Immerse yourself in the words of the Torah,
    Every word, every space between the words, every cantillation.
Be an ear to the voice of God: every sound, every pause, every vibration,
    And you will hear what Moses hearkened to on Mount Sinai.
But if you hear your own voice
    You no longer are discovering the wisdom of God.

OBITUARY FOR THE GREAT MAGGID

The Book of Splendor says: Mercy is the right arm; rigor is the left.
    The magic of Mezeritch dragged his left foot
In this world so that mercy will always be awake and rigor be dormant.
    Through God's mercy and wisdom was the Maggid created
And Dov Baer was merciful and wise.

THERE IS ROOM HERE FOR BUT ONE TSADIK

Based on the introduction by Reb Nathan to Nahman's
    Book Sippuray HaMaasiyot.
At the top of his lungs Nahman screamed, Aryeh Leib,
    The Old Man, is a sham.
He is not as ascetic as I am; he is not as pious as I am;
    He cannot explain the mysteries of Torah like I do.
He does not deserve a portion in the world to come like I do.
    Excommunicate him! And the people of Zlatopol replied
There is room here for but one Tsadik.
    Gay Avek* Nahman. *Go away
And Nahman left the Ukraine for Bratslav where he was revered
    As the perfection of mankind,
Equal in wisdom to King Solomon, Honorable lord, teacher, and master,
    Glorious and mighty pride, holy and awesome rabbi,
The Great Light, The Supernal Light,
    The Precious and Holy Light, Blessed be his name.

ANECDOTES IN THE MANNER OF RABBI LEVI YITSCHAK OF BERDITCHEV

1.

The beloved rabbi was deep in prayer when out of the corner of his eye
    He spied several men whose lips were moving indifferently
And whose bodies rotated from side to side,
    Knees bent and straightened in repetitive rhythm.
The beloved rabbi approached each, their hearts to reach.
    Extending his hand he said, 'Shalom alaychem.'
Absently each returned his greeting as if they were attending
    A synagogue meeting.
Why, they asked, do you interrupt your prayers so and your greetings

Upon us bestow? Reb Yid, he replied to the first,
    "You are far away in your granary."
"You," Reb Yid said to the next, "are at the docks catching fish."
    And to the third he said, with a wink,

"You are at the tavern having a drink."
    Seeing you had been elsewhere,
I merely welcomed you back to the House of Study.

2.

The beloved rabbi was strolling to the marketplace
    When he noticed a man known for his bad temper and flaws.
He ran toward him, and giving him a warm embrace
    In a manner permitted by the sacred laws,
Said, "Sir Noble, how I envy you.
    Each of your shortcomings has become translated into a golden hue
And radiates to all seekers of Truth."
    The noble blushed for he was ashamed.
And he who was often uncouth the rabbi's wisdom proclaimed.

3. EIZIK TAUB, THE KALIVER REBBE, THE TSADIK OF NAGYKALLA, HUNGARY

Every morning when he'd awake and heard the cock a crowing
    The Kaliver would his prayers make
To the tune of hungry cows lowing.
    He'd don his chemise and his pants like other Magyars did each day
And strolled to the village mendicants and invited them to pray.

How many there in a stupor were from too much whiskey drinking?
    Reb Eizik came to minister to them whose bodies
Were from vomit stinking.
    The tsadik would wash them clean and then their prayers enlisted;
Ten outcasts would about him convene to thank God that they existed.
    Then the saintly tsadik would serve them bread and cheese
And offer potions to the sick to free them of disease.
    I beg you yellow bird with wings of blue
Has there been a tune you've heard that will our souls renew?

The tsadik would then start to dance with the beggars and the ill
    Who would absorb his radiance and to the wordless tune would thrill.

"Wait, my rose, wait" he'd sing Zion will be ours tomorrow
    And flashes of brilliance on the wing dried his tears of sorrow.

The Magyar rebbe, an unpretentious man, worked
    Side by side with lumberjacks,
Taught Torah to a gypsy caravan, and helped the poor rebuild their shacks.
    In the evening the tune of rustling trees
He played on the shepherd's flute.
    And before bedtime sh'ma he would declare amnesty
For all of ill-repute.

"I laud the Lord in Heaven above Whose Glory we daily praise
    And who embraces all with Devoted Love and our troubles
allays." Every day God Made the sun to smile and its blessings bring
    To the tsadik who practiced no guile but taught the world to sing.

The Ill are crying,
    Their pain squeezes the brain
Spare them their grief; give them relief;
    On You they are relying.

EULOGY FOR MOSES MENDELSSOHN: THE GREAT EMANCIPATOR

Moses ben Menachem, Savant of Dessau,
    Heir to the rationalist Maimonides,
Successor to the God-intoxicated Spinoza,
    Friend of the keen-sighted Lessing, colleague of the skeptic Kant,
Devout, defender of the faith, paragon of humanism:
    Patient, modest, humble; raiser of probing questions
Who, through reason, found poignant answers
    To the dilemmas faced by Jews trapped inside
The mind of the Ghetto. He unhitched the hasp of the Ghetto gate
    And, limping with them, led them out of Egypt
Into a desert roiling in turmoil.
    Can Jews become a part of a free society yet
Separate themselves from it
    To be governed by their Halachah?
Can Halachah change as it did in the days of sages
    Of the Mishnah and Gemorrah?
Can Jews rise from an inferior civic status to an emancipated social status
    Without surrendering their Judaism?
Without compromising their freedom?
    Without denying their God? Without disavowing the Torah?

Not an echo of the past but a voice for the future
    Who begged his people to reconsider their seed,
Their roots, their branches.
    Are Jews only to learn Torah?
Can they not tear down the fences of ignorance
    And explore new paths to tread and discover Latin, Greek,
Mathematics, Anatomy, Astronomy, Natural Philosophy, Civil Law?
    Can they not, like freed Christians, bask in the sunshine

Of the modern era of Locke, Voltaire, Rousseau, and Leibniz?
   Judaism, neither fossil nor relic of the ancient past
Is an evolving religion with a destiny
   To bring God's teachings to all no matter their creed.
Teacher, silk merchant, charismatic spokesman for the Jewish cause,
   Persuasive writer
Who rid the synagogue of government inspectors
   Placed there to prevent calumny
Of Christians by Jews during the chanting of Aleynu;
   Denounced of practices that would excommunicate
Those who questioned rabbinic authority!
   His words echo throughout the generations,
"Compel no one to belong to a faith; expel none against their will."
   This hunchback of Herculean moral strength,
Ever in physical pain and always hopeful of a cure,
   Unchained the future of ancient superstitions
And rescued them from drowning in the stagnant waters or irrationality.

Courageously did he lead his people out of a dark tunnel
   Where they slaved under the whips of tyrannical rabbis,
Persecuting priests and oppressive emperors
   Who slithered and spread their venom
To paralyze the frightened people into behaving
   Not out of pursuit of virtue but out of fear of punishment.

And to the future he bequeathed his legacy: sharpen the lens to sense,
   Evaluate experience and find meaning within the prism of the times.
Then will Mount Sinai rise through the clouds,
   Its peak glimmering in the sunshine,
And the God of Nature will be revealed as part of Human Consciousness.
   And with love will you perform the Divine Commandments
And with justice will you treat your neighbor and the stranger.

MR. AND MRS. MORTARA. THIS JEW IS A CATHOLIC*

*On the night of June 23, 1858 Edgardo Mortara was taken from his home by the papal police and brought to the House of Catechumens. Despite pleas of Napoleon III and Moses Montefiore, Pope Pius IX did not return the child to his parents. Even when papal secular power ended, Edgardo, now called Pius, remained a Catholic. Given the title "apostolic missionary", he became a canon of the Church. This was not an isolated case. Earlier, the daughter of Angelo Ancona, a Jew, had been baptized without his knowledge and was seized by archbishop of Ferrara in 1817. She, too, lived as a Catholic.

The maid was ashamed and afraid she would be blamed
    That the babe in her charge, Edgardo, his forehead aglow
With fever. His cheeks pale and wan, would lose his life in a marathon
    With Death. Smelling his foul breath,
For her crucifix she then did reach, and the Lord Jesus did beseech
    Help me save this baby boy so that a long life he will enjoy.
From the cross came the reply that they boy will not die
    There is so much good the boy will do-
Baptize him and he'll be born anew.
    To the local priest the maid then sped
Assured the boy would by dawn not be dead.
    Edgardo in the baptismal font was placed
And by the Church was there embraced.
    The Mortaras were never told the story of the nursemaid bold.
But many years later-late in the night—in the waning of the lunar light,
    There came a pounding upon their door.
"Papal police," the Montaras heard the roar.
    Ha-bayn Ya-kir-lee* This child grew inside of me,
*prayer beginning "my dear son"
    The mother begged to keep her son but the policeman pointing his gun
    Took the child still asleep to the Vatican, there to keep.

Your Holiness, the Mortaras implored, return our son to us.
 But the Pius pope ignored their pleas.
And by his decree Edgardo was of his Jewishness dispossessed
 and the injustice was never redressed.

SHTETL LIFE

A Wedding

The Bride's Worries

Mama, Mama hold me tight I'm afraid of what will happen tonight.
    I am so very scared that I am unprepared
For the marriage bed; How violent is my dread.
    I worry about the look on my face; I tremble that he'll my dress unlace.
Will he judge me a beauty? Will I know my duty?
    Will he want me to be smart? Will he touch me on my lower part?
Will what he will do hurt? Will I bleed from my "You-know-what"
    Would it be like when I have the curse or will it be even worse?

The Mother's Comfort

Soroh, Soroh my innocent. From Heaven was your Dov Baer sent.
    Didn't the shad-chen* in his papers find a match for you
With a man who's kind? *a matchmaker
    Sorrolle, Sorrelle God is your guide. He will always be by your side.
Your husband to be was granted artistry
    And will behave like a man as God ordained when the world began.
Some women dutifully accept a man's fire;
    Others have in themselves deep-felt desire.
The important thing to know is that love is not instant. It must grow.
    Through their every sensation a bride and a groom
Recreate God's creation.

The Bride's Readiness

Soroh gathered her satin gown and placed on her head the wedding crown.
    At that moment she was a queen without qualm
But whispered to herself the Twenty-Third Psalm.

Community "Acceptance"

The rabbi was stroking his graying beard as the
    groom from his door shyly appeared.
His anxiety was growing as his cows were lowing.
    His mother gave a nod to friends
And kin upon whose lips there gathered a grin,
    As if to say in sotto voce "Who would such a schlemiel wed?
Only Soroh, the dunderhead."
    But instead of speaking such a thought
They only said what they ought,
    "Mazel tov! Mazel tov! They sang out in joy,
"May the first of your children be a healthy boy."
    Amen, chanted the crowd. Amen, Amen they cheered out loud.
The clarinetist licked his reed and from a puff of air he freed
    Sounds that could make you cry—not a person's eye was dry.
The fiddler's bow crossed the strings and released
    A tune like spreading wings.
The accordionist's fingers flew across the keys
    And heavenly music sprung from every squeeze.
Their song filled the air and everyone there
    Began to sing just like the birds of early Spring.

The Marriage Contract

Regally the orphan Soroh sat upon her throne as Dov Baer,
    Her betrothed, contemplated his heir.
What must he do for an heir to come about he had more
    On his mind than a little doubt.
His mother, an agunah*, prodded, "Rabbi proceed.
    Read the contract with speed." *abandoned wife
She needed to milk her lowing cows.
    (Dov Baer and his mother were not highbrows.)
"Dov Baer promises to give the widow, Esther,
    Whom God with Soroh blessed her,
Milk and cheese as long as she lives, a cemetery plot also he gives-
    And a new Tsenoh U'r-enoh* From the printer in Vilnoh.
*a Yiddish prayer book

Amen, Dov Baer wrote his name to agree.
Soroh will be his for eternity and upon him will a silken talis*
    bestow and for his mother a new dress will sew.
*a prayer shawl Amen Amen.
    The contract was signed, and God's grace about them was enshrined.
Marriages like this only in heaven are made;
    may torrents of joy from the couple cascade.
Then a hush fell upon the crowd and the bride's mother, in a moment proud,
    Nodded to all those assembled—even to the groom who trembled
Before the rabbi's winking eye and to the witnesses who came to testify
    That the marriage is true—and nothing will ever undo
The marriage bond now or in time beyond.

VI. The Marriage Ceremony

Dov Baer marched with the greatest of pride around
    His Soroh, his lovely bride,
Six or seven times. He had lost count.
    It was a march that Soroh would later recount
To her children because Dov Baer did not hesitate
    To march not six or seven times but eight.
Mazel tov! Mazel tov! Everyone gave a cheer
    As Dov Baer embraced Soroh his forever dear.
Then in rapture galore, more beautiful than ever before,
    Rose Soroh, the bride, the Spirit of God by her side.
Next to the groom she stood-
    Serene as a bride under the circumstances could.
"Harau art m'kudeshes lee" You are consecrated unto me.
    All heard the rabbi pronounce the blessing over the couple
That was professing their love for one another;
    Forever would they be friends to each other.
The bride took a sip of wine and told her groom, "I am thine."

The groom with the strongest of forces,
More than that of a thousand horses,
    Shattered a glass the ancient Temple to recall,
Standing today is but a crumbling wall,
    Announced to the entire world which around the sun daily twirled,

There is no adversity we can't overcome!
    And then broke out pandemonium.

VII. Meals and Grace

The guests ate of the finest of the fine and drank
    The very best of imported wine.
The men were kissing, singing, and dancing—the women
    Were reminiscing, clinging and prancing.
When the meal was finished grace was said
    And the bride and groom rushed off to bed.
And the spirit of God hovered over their lives from
    Which all worldly joy and rapture derives.

MONDAY MARKET

The Sabbath glow was still in their eyes as the merchants
    Went to the Monday market
A meager parnawsaw* for them to eke as they did on Monday
    Every week. *livelihood, a goal of life
Friday's unsold spinach, peppers, potatoes, apples, melons, and grapes
    Rotted in piles near the market wall next
To Mirele Wasserstein's herring stall.
    The suffocating aroma of decaying produce collected
In the herring lady's nostrils.
    "Epstein, where are you hiding?" The frantic Mirele was crying.

The wizened old man sauntering down the muddy path,
    Fringed tallis dancing in the breeze,
Was followed by a family of oinking swine making pilgrimage
    To the edible shrine.
When they beheld the Sabbath leftovers they slammed
    Their snouts into the pile
And gobbled the "delicacies" at will.
    Within minutes they had devoured all of the swill.
Without one word of grace after meals, they waddled back to Epstein's pen.
    Their mitzvah was done for the day,
Much to the scrawniest piglet's deep dismay.
    "Veiber! Veiber!*" the merchants called, in a cacophoncus chorus.
*Ladies, ladies
    "A bargain like this you can't pass by.
My merchandise is a first class buy."
    The wild-bearded Feldman sold butter and cheese lovingly
Prepared by his wife Rivkoh-who also filled the cans with milk.
    Nearby the dapper A-ron Cohen dealt in imported silk.
Dov Baer, my father, peddled produce; Rohchel Greenberg sold flour.
    Her voice cackled like a hen, but she made more money

Than any of the men.
    Clothes, produce, tsatskes* galore were on sale
For just a few kopeks *tsatskes-frills Tradesmen stopped at the
    "kiddusch"* stall where the peasants were ready to brawl. *tavern
Chickens clucked as they pecked at corn droppings;
    Cats and dogs chased the frightened chickens.
Children teased one another and got boxed
In the ear by some passing mother.
    And in the great hall of the synagogue juvenile scholars
Were singing a page of Talmud.
    Their voices wafted into the shtetl atmosphere
delivering Sacred knowledge for all to revere.
    And redolent in every village home was the aroma of baking bread.
The shtetl was ready to struggle another week
    As it did each Monday since time antique.

MY BRIS* CIRCUMCISION

The Birth

The women were returning from the cemetery
    Where they had prayed to The Dead
To intercede with God for the mother-to-be.
    In prayers, men rocked back and forth in dread
Before the toyriz* in the opened Ark pleading
    For a merciful intervention. *Holy scrolls
To the Divine Monarch for my mother's protection.
    Mammeh lay in her bed in spastic labor,
A cold, wet rag upon her head, pain jabbing her like a saber.

"Scream, scream, Sorrele", the midwife comforted.
    Mammeh screeched and, exhausted, heaved a groan.
Then, she, released hiding energy and transported me, her son,
    Her very own into this world. Mammeh's face
Was a mix of sweat, smiles, and tears.
    Anxiety and happiness swirled about axes of exuberance and fears.
A zawcher*, a kaddischel*, a baby boy, radiating parental respect
    *A male child to recite a doxology
To be inducted in eight days with joy into the sacred sect.

The midwife opened the door with a shout,
    "Sorrele just delivered a kaddischel! for Dov Baer."
In the shtetl cheers of joy spread throughout;
    Happiness was everywhere.
Unlike my brothers who died at birth I was alive and full of breath.
    I was a source of mirth, not a bundle of death.
"Dov Baer, Dov Baer!" Calls echoed down the river
    To bring back my father who was hiding
So as not to tempt the Evil Spirit lurking about when mammeh
    Was about to deliver.

Although mammeh and tatteh planned to call me "E-li-a-hu,"
    No one dared pronounce my name
But spoke of me only as "You-Know-Who"
    So that the Evil Spirit would lay no claim on me.

The midwife bathed me in olive oil and wrapped me in swaddling bands
    Then covered me like a prince royal with her loving hands.
Gently was I laid on a pillow soft next to my tired mother
    Where we both slept until I coughed and woke up each other.

Amulets from the ceiling were strung; on the curtains prayers were pinned.
    Then dribble from my mouth had sprung, and I passed a little wind.
I had never performed such acts before but in this new world there was
    Much to learn like the sibilance of my mother's snore
and hunger making my stomach churn.
    And while God was sending me a brand new soul
The shtetl women brought diapers and clothes,
    To cover me in comfort, their goal, from my head right to my toes.

And everyone suppressed the thought of what kind of man
    I would become.
Perhaps, I would be the deliverer sought and usher in the millennium.
    My parents received the gifts with thanks
And the visitors all took a peek
    And left my room without any angst, enthralled by my mystique.

You-Know-Who's First Sabbath

Returning from their Sabbath prayers were shtetl women and men
    All of them weighers, comparing my mass to back when
I was born. My special day was observed with almond cakes
    And boiled chick-peas.
Enough schnapps was served to ward off every disease.
    Each greeted my parents, while glancing at me,
"May You-Know-Who excel in Toyrah*, *Book of the law
    Marry into the wealthiest family,
And become a master of the gemoyrrah.* *a rabbinic text of law
    May all of his children be well and live a long and prosperous life.

And may he always as if in paradise dwell with a rich and beautiful wife."
    "Amen, Amen," Mammeh and tatteh said.
And the departing guests couldn't resist
    Pinching my cheeks, quite red, and the mezuzah* then kissed.
*Prayer parchment on the door post

The Night Before the Bris

A minyan* gathered in mammeh's room and read
    From the Book of Psalms *a quorum of adult Jewish men
To ward off any chance of doom and quash her many qualms.
    They shawckled* and prayed throughout the night,
Not one abandoned his mission *rocked and swayed
    And stopped only at the morning light to take a little nutrition.
And beneath mammeh's pillow lay the tool the Mohel*
    Would use on the morrow *the circumciser
Protected from the Spirit cruel that causes so much sorrow.

But the Evil Spirit dared not lurk where the Name of God is spoken.
    Its wicked spells did not work, through prayer each was broken.
That night Mammeh had no rest yet smiled when I awoke and nursed,
    Sucking at her milky breast and with her nipples conversed.
My stomach filled I returned to sleep guarded by God above
    Who my soul in His did keep and imbued us both with love.

The Bris

The guests arrived in their Sabbath best and quietly sat themselves down.
    They came to witness me get blessed and receive a penile crown.
In walked the famous Mohel, known from Warsaw to Budapest,
    In whose expert hands God's skill did dwell-
To which every parent would attest.
    To his bedroom Tatteh* returned and the mohel's
Knife retrieved, *father
    Happy the Evil Spirit was spurned and successfully deceived.

The Mohel's knife tatteh placed inside a prayer shawl And
    all impurities were erased with hospital alcohol.

The Mohel then rubbed his hands with disinfectant mighty strong And
    began the ritual God commands with a blessing and a song.

In spirits then he some cotton dipped and on to my lips had pressed
    Which I reflexively slowly sipped and to a stupor acquiesced.
On the sandak*'s pillow grandmother placed me;
    From there to the mayhem was I transmitted remember *godfather
A shield was placed on my member—I was later told because I don't

During the ceremony where I remained in custody
    With one swipe of the sharpest blade the mohel a crown had made
No pain did I feel during the incision;
    My contract with God was sealed through ritual circumcision.

The mohel's voice was filled with trills when he blessed the cup of wine
    He sent shivery chills down everyone's spine.
God of Abraham, his voice rang out, accept the son of Dov Baer

Let him live a life devout, and crown him an heir
    To a history Your kingdom beautifies. May he act in such a way
To bring na-chis* in Your eyes. Never will he go astray! contentment

Let his name in Israel be known like the prophet, E-li-ah-u*.
    And like David sit upon the throne and our faith renew.
The sandak sipped a drop of blood that from my penis dripped.
    Then stamping their feet with a thud every witness yipped,
  *Elijah
    "Mazel tov, Mazel tov." A clamor filled the room.
Bless the fruit of Dov Baer's loins!
    Bless the fruit of Sorrele's womb who his ancient people now joins!
"Sh'ma Yisrael," they prayed under their breath let this little Dov Baer
    Be saved from death by The Lord God above.
Everyone no matter the rank nor quality of voice,
    Danced and sang and ate and drank my bris to rejoice.

After The Bris

Lurking in the Shtetl mist there was the Spirit Evil
    And once your soul by it was kissed, there would
Be sorrow and upheaval.
    Because my parents two sons had lost they resolved
The Spirit to deceive
    And so I was sold to the Sandak at cost, a foggy duplicity to weave.
The Sandak gave me a different name. He called me "Little Moses".
    No Evil Spirit would dare lay claim in whom the sh-chi-nah* reposes.
*The Divine Presence

Let me tell you I was mighty scared that I had lost my mother
    Who had become quite despaired, losing one son after another.
Well it was all guise to chase the Evil Spirit away
    I had no reason to agonize nor to feel dismay
Because the Evil Spirit was cheated, and I was to mammeh returned.
    Sulking, the Spirit felt defeated and its evil ways was spurned.
And I grew into the son mammeh and tatteh had longed to see
    A very special someone to grace the family tree.

A DEATH

1. VIGIL FOR A DYING MAN

The tide of Reb Yitschak's life was ebbing, as it must in all living creatures.
    The gosase* burbled Psalm 23 his former students were chanting.
*The dying person
    In the twilight of his last day he was recanting, with jerking spasms,
His sins against God, his parents, his wife, and his friends.
    Quickly his thoughts turned to his good deeds which sowed
The seeds of righteousness in others.
    The smile in his eyes softened the dread exploding
In his students' hearts.

By tradition, they guarded the gosase until his soul departs.
    His heartbeat slowed; his lungs labored for breath.
A feather was placed upon his lips.
    The stench of death oozed from him as his life dwindled.
Tapers in the candelabrum we kindled.
    And when the feather no longer flickered reb Yitschak's
Soul slipped into God's waiting embrace.
    Eyes of those around swelled with tears as they recited
The sh'ma in that hour dim.
    Love God; teach the law to the children
Who are duty bound to transmit the legacy to their own
    And so on throughout the generations.

Then they began the deathwatch preparations.
    Wrapping his body in a sheet of white,
They closed his eyelids and extended his arms and hands
    Alongside his body lowered by the toes to the floor,
He lay there growling rigid, feet toward the door.
    They asked his forgiveness for wrongs, imagined or real,

They had done him and begged that he intercede on their behalf
    With the Almighty.
Together they wept, "May The True Judge be blessed."

The Chevreh Kadisha* came to wash Reb Yitschak.
    They dressed him in a kittel*
And draped a prayer shawl about his shoulders.
    *Burial society members *a shroud
They remained with the tamay* until the very next day *unclean (corpse)
    When he was placed in a coffin which was placed
On a wagon drawn by an old mare
    And taken to The House of Prayer where the community gathered
To honor the man who had dispatched the terror of their lives into oblivion
    And ushered into halcyon days of a golden era filled
With love for God with which their every prayer was spun.

2. EULOGY BEGUN

The rabbi began, "two decades ago, on erev Rosh Ha-shanah **New
    Year a wizened old man wandered into our village,
A pillaged shtetl, still smoldering from the arson committed
    By the bored police.
That man, with a scraggly gray beard, carried a valise holding
    Some clothes and holy books.
The sun illuminated his smiling, emerald eyes; the gentle breeze
    Carried his golden voice chanting,
"Rejoice, Rejoice a new beginning is nigh it is a time
    To change our ungodly ways."

"It will be done if each obeys the commandments of the Lord."
    And then he danced and laughed. Laughed!"
"Stranger," the then rabbi asked, "What are you doing here?"
    "I have come to teach all who adhere to the Laws of Moses."
"And your name, honored stranger?' "Yitschak,
    The son of Sarah and Avraham."
"He's a false messiah, a sham," shouted someone in the crowd.
    "Perhaps he has a son, Jacob," another gibed

"And a grandson, Joseph, in a multicolored coat clad."
    Then spoke an elder, "This man is surely mad.
Who needs another crazy coming to our village sowing discord?
    Is this some kind of joke, Lord?"
"I am no messiah," the stranger replied,
    "I seek only to release the joy concealed in our texts.
I ask no recompense other than student excellence."

"Aha!" shouted an onlooker. "We have a Kabbalist in our midst."
    "No," Reb Yitschak replied, "No Kabbaslist am I."

"I seek only to free the meanings Torah words imply."
    "Not even one kopek?" checked Moshe, the miser.
"Not even one," was Yitschak's reply.
    The then rabbi, may the righteous one rest in peace,
Said to give him a trial.

The doubters asked, though,
    "Would a man without guile teach the shtetl urchins for no pay?"
Reb Yitschak replied with kindness "I have savings enough
    To cover my needs. I am a pilgrim called to God's service.
To ignore God's summons I would be remiss."
    Several demanded, "Show us how you will teach
Show us how you will young minds reach."
    And Reb Yitschak obliged with a lesson from Genesis.

3. REB YITSCHAK'S LESSON

"The Book of Genesis begins with the word "b'rayshis."
    He paused as listeners filled with their own ideas
The empty shells of the familiar letters:
    *Bayz, Raysh, Aleph, Shin, Youd, Sawff.
He continued, 'We translate "B'rayshis" "in the beginning".
    But examine the letters. What do they spell?
The letters in the middle are Raysh, Aleph, Shin.*
    Whose head was in the beginning?
Hashem*. *An ordinary word for God
    Hashem is in the midst of The Beginning, The Creation.

What is also a part of rosh?
    Aleph, Shin which spells Aysh* Fire. Fervor.
In the beginning Hashem created the universe
    From His head filled with passion.
And the ash, the fire, became the sun. But the aysh was alive and growing.
    It split into countless klipot, tiny eternal sparks,
Luminous wisps of heaven,
    A gift from Hashem to every living creature providing
Their marrow with the vigor of life.
    Who is the very first? Hashem. The last letter of B'rayshis
Aleph and Sawff together spell "as"
    So "Brayshis" contains the Head of Hashem from which
Emanates the fiery light of the sun
    And the fulgent splendor guiding us toward a righteous life.
Its center is Aleph, Hashem, the very first.
    The last letter of Brayshis is Off which sounds like "soaf" the End,
The end of Time.
    And what is in the middle of "Rosh"?
Aleph. And who is Aleph, the very first.

Hashem is the Beginning, the Center, and The End of Time.
    Amen!   Amen!   Amen!

4. EULOGY COMPLETED

The spectators felt themselves rising to the sublime
    And agreed with the rabbi
To give Reb Yitschak a trial, acknowledging that he was by called by God.
    Whatever he taught, the children were enthralled.
They were wrapped in the spirit of the sh'chinah.* *God's presence
    They laughed and sang as they memorized the sayings
Of the venerated teachers of the Mishnah
    Whom they quoted without flaw.
And despite his age, Yitschak ben Avraham v'Sarah
    Was appointed the teacher to the young.
With a tone soft and sweet, he ignited the flame of mishnah learning.
    The rabbi paused to acclaim the devotion and inspiration of the teacher.

Wiping tears from his eyes he asked who better could have
    Plumbed the mystery
Of Judaism then this man who stepped out of the pages of history.
    Who better related the story of Moses, Joshua, and Deborah
As if he had known these heroes of history personally?

He wept when he recalled King Saul, a soul, troubled,
    Jealous and filled with gall.
And little David, the speck in Goliath's eye, who felled the giant
    And defeated many a surrounding nation.
The same David composed poems of elation to God Almighty.
    Yet he was morally weak; this famed King of Israel sent a man to war,
The Hittite Uriah,
    Knowing the battle would take his life.

Then he married the slain soldier's wife.
    Our Reb Yitschak's face became red with shame.
But quickly his mood changed. He danced with the Torah
    To commemorate Solomon's installing the menorah
In the ancient Temple. But that king was a distracted father
    And his children fought with one another.
In time Solomon's Temple blazed and was razed to the ground.
    Reb Yitschak rent his jacket and recited the kaddish for eleven months.

And when he shed a tear, his students did, too.
    And when he sang praises to The Lord, his students did as well.
He spun a mystical spell that transformed the people of the shtetl.
    The carpers stopped finding fault and the gossipers no longer evil spoke.
The blasphemers God's name did not invoke.
    Those who wronged another begged forgiveness;
Those who scoffed at the poor, gave charitably.
    He reinvigorated the marrow of our piety and rescued us from our ennui.
"He chased the cloud of gloom that hovers over us into she-ole*
    Where it belongs *the place of the dead
And we performed the mitsvot* with zest." *commandments

"And now beat your breast in grief and sorrow.
    Remember his pious life was with purpose;

Remember his was a life that touched us all.
    Cry! Weep! Howl! Bawl!
He planted in our hearts a love of learning God's
    Ways which bore wisdom's fruit.
It was his sacred pursuit to sow in our souls the seeds of righteousness.
    When they ripened into good deeds devotion to God
Became our daily quest. And now he will be laid to rest.
    His legacy will always be a part of us. Love learning,
Do good, speak well of others.
    May the name of Yitschak, son of Sarah and Avraham, be blessed."

5. THE FUNERAL

The rabbi in the lead set the solemn pace;
    The cantor's gait slowly did the rabbi's steps trace.
Then did the old mare on its journey start;
    Mournfully the drayman drove his rickety cart.
Students followed in the cortege reading psalms;
    Grief-absorbed, they lavished those begging for alms.
Each to himself sobbing men gamboled behind in sorrow
    Was one with the other entwined.
Holding hands women dressed in black followed next,
    Wailing dolefully and in spirit perplexed.
Children struggling with what does a death truly mean
    Were in the rear pondering the unforeseen.
They felt his presence as his grave was reached
    And for their wrongs his pardon beseeched.
Slowly, the pine coffin was set in the pit,
    The freshly dug cell did dankness emit.
Shovelful after shovelful fell with a thud
    Until the pine box was enveloped in mud.
The cantor chanted the ancient dirge 'Ayl Moleh rachamim,'*
    Despair to purge. *Lord filled with compassion
From the mourners gathered as one in sorrow
    Who will an emptiness feel on the morrow.
Squeezing his eyes the rabbi subdued his tears,
    Saying the kaddish* to the God he reveres. *doxology

And when the last sentence had been completed
    All who were present that sentence repeated.
With a knife the rabbi rent everyone's cloak,
    Making a tear quickly with only one stroke
To be a memento of the goodness lost which
    In the minds of all forever embossed.

6. THE LIFE AFTER DEATH

Many a secret Reb Yitschak took to his grave as many
    A human in wisdom is prone to do.
Like who was Reb Yitschak. Who was he, who?
    Merely a banker who made loans to desperate folks?
The interest he charged were usurious
    And he called in the loans when not paid in time?
What he did was not called a crime
    But there came a point when his conscience
rebelled and Reb Yitschak regretted his greedy ways
    And went to a rabbi to confess his sin
He no longer could live with such deep-rooted chagrin.
    The rabbi asked why should a gentile seek forgiveness from him.
Reb Yitschak answered I hereby my past eschew
    I want to live righteously as a Jew.
And so Reb Yitschak studied Torah and Talmud, too.
    When he was proficient enough to teach,
His rabbi took him to the ritual bath
    Where he was consecrated to follow a new path,
The one that Jews have been given to walk.
    When he told family and friends of his decision,
His wife laughed at his folly,
    His friends heaved a volley of saliva upon his face.
His parents unwilling to understand declared this man
    They had bred Dead! Forever Dead!
And never again mentioned his name.

So when the rabbi asked him what he will be called.
    He said, "Yitschak" to recall his wife's mocking laughter.

And adopted Avraham and Sarah as parents ever after.
    Then Reb Yitschak journeyed many a mile to find eager ears to teach.
On his way he dedicated his heart to reach the young
    To whom he would impart
The righteousness Torah teaches to those inspired to learn.
    Now once every year when his virtue
Is discussed the Kaddish is recited to recall his worth.
    But his secret molders down deep in the earth
Where it mingles with others decaying to dust.

THE AMERICAN EXPERIENCE

The First "Jew" in the Americas

An edict etched in mordant malice,
    Which by the Church was validated,
Was dispatched from the royal palace and to the Jews communicated,
    "Convert or leave this Catholic land.
If the former, it must be sincere lest you burn. You are banned."
Many a Jew left with a trunk and a tear.
    Luis de Torres, in Semitic languages skilled, accepted
Catholicism before a priest-
    After being in Church tenets carefully drilled,
Joined Columbus on his voyage to the "East".
    The venture met hot sun and wind lashed sea;
Whispers of "Sh'ma Israel" could be heard
    As the ships moved on to its destiny.
No one suspected that Columbus had erred.

Land was spotted and Luis was sent to explore,
    Columbus believing that an Asiatic tongue
Was spoken by the natives on the shore.
    So Luis climbed down the ship's ladder rung by rung
And was met by the natives with the broadest smiles.
    Luis was of a friendly disposition, and the natives,
Perceived by him as Temple exiles, aided the Spaniard in his mission.

Gold there was none only tobacco and maize
    Which he brought back to Spain as food and to delight.
Soon throughout Europe there arose the craze
    The smoke tobacco leaves as a sociable rite.
The king was so impressed with all that Luis achieved
    That he gave him the island of Cuba as reward.

Although it was not India as Columbus once believed, Cuba
    Was conquered without the sword.

THE FIRST MINYAN IN NEW AMSTERDAM*

*September, 1654

Jews! You are unwanted here in Brazil. Convert or leave!

The twenty-three men argued in sing songs
Talmudic style; if we convert it will show our guilt
And we will always be suspected, and always be rejected!
How can we convert to placate
A faith whose words are love and actions are hate?
Why should we convert when a spiritual aura is
daily reinvigorated by our living Torah?
So the twenty-three left Brazil with meager possession,
Escaping to freedom being a burning obsession.
But their ship was by Spanish pirates taken
Would they by God again be forsaken?
Then a French warship arrived and they were freed
And toward New Amsterdam did they speed.
There Governor Stuyvesant did then proclaim
You enemies and blasphemers of Christ's name
You hateful pariah
Who disdain our messiah
Go back to where you lived before.
There they were tempest tossed unwanted on any shore.
They gathered together and whispered sh'ma yis-ra-el
Oh God give us guidance in our travail.
Despite their hostile reception,
Without engaging in any deception,
They planted diversity's seed
By daily reciting the Jewish creed.

THE FIRST PROFESSOR OF HEBREW AT HARVARD USED TO BE A JEW*

*Taught at Harvard in the early eighteenth century. His Hebrew Grammar book was published in 1735.

Judah Monis*, a wandering
Jew arrived in Boston in 1722.
A scholar of some renown,
He aspired to wearing cap and gown.
But before beginning his teaching career,
In Harvard's hallowed atmosphere,
He was required to abjure his Jewish roots.
He did so and began his teaching pursuits.
However, his soul was soaked with trepidation
Because of his abdication
From the faith of his birth.
And from their graves deep down in the earth
He heard his ancestors glorifying
God with "Yisgadal" while renting their shrouds crying.

THE FIRST HEBREW TEACHER IN PHILADELPHIA

*circa February, 1769

Learnéd Jewish men were busy eking out a living;
    At home their wives were their care to children giving.
Jewish youth of that day wore growing
    Uneducated and little knowing
Much about their Mosaic roots
    Or of traditional Judaic pursuits.

The community leaders had been praying
    For someone who would be erudition displaying.
Oy Gottenoo, O God, send us a scholar who
    will our children in Hebrew grammar drill.
Someone whose fee is set to be fair
    And who himself is immersed in prayer.

Could it have been that God heard their plight
    And sent an angel to teach siddur to recite?
Emanuel Lyon who from England had sailed,
    Presented teaching credentials he himself had hailed.*
*An advertisement in the Pennsylvania Gazette
    of February 16, 1769 read that Emanuel Lyon
"Intends to teach the Hebrew Language, in its Purity . . ."

However! However! In undertaking his endeavor
    It was discovered he knew less
Hebrew than Christian preachers
    And even less still than itinerant teachers.
Pupils stopped attending his boring class
    Not one at a time but en masse.

So he pawned his belongings his debts to pay
    And was rescued by Rachel Moses who helped the stray
Redeem his clothes and find a new path
    That would give him direction and avoid the wrath
Of the tiny Jewish community that was now growing.
    But Lyons was a rogue and was tiptoeing
Around the law. How many he defrauded is beyond count
    How much money he owed was a stupendous amount.
He was a lout and often turned for solace to drink
    And became a master of the bluff and the hoodwink.

So the first Hebrew teacher, a devil, was wanted for trial
    For infamous deeds and activities vile.
How mistaken the community had been, how very naive
    To think Heaven sent a guide with tricks up his sleeve.
What they had, instead, is clearly no mystery:
    A blot on Philadelphia's Jewish history.

PHILIP MINIS OF SAVANNAH*

*Quotes are from the official record. 1832

Luddington's Bar reeked with drink; its patrons were filled with talk;
No one had come there to think, few legs were steady to walk.
In an atmosphere such as that, Philip Minis, a merchant of renown,
Came in to eat and drink and chat with other merchants of the town.

That was the day in '32 when a patron was itching to fight
And called Minis a "rotten Jew", descended from the "damned Israelite".
Minis ignored the man at first but when he said you're "to be pissed upon"
Minis forgot all about his thirst. James Stark had crossed the Rubicon.

He was an official of the state, filled with hate inside.
As his trunk began to gyrate, he shouted a duel is justified.
So he pulled out his gun and pointed it right at Minis's heart.
The patrons saw a bullet jettison toward the menu chart.

Minis then took aim and sped a bullet toward his foe.
He had intended only Stark to maim but upon him did death bestow.
A trial was held as the law required Minis to the charge admitted
That he had done in a vilifier, and the jury him acquitted.

BECOMING AN AMERICAN IN 1837

With scant command of the English tongue
Hugh née Chayim Steiner drifted westward,
From Philadelphia to Pittsburgh, never to be heard from again
As was then the wont of too many Jewish men.

Hannah, his agunah*, undertook then *abandoned wife
To become a dressmaker to make ends meet.
At ten, her son, Avner, learned the baker's trade
His sister, Zelda, nine, was in service as a maid.

All three were hard working but poorly paid.
One evening there appeared at their door
A bearded, smelly, disheveled man
Wearing phylacteries, he said he was of the Steiner clan.

He, Bawrooch, proclaimed he was a holy man
And that he walked across Germany to Holland
Then sailed on the Atlantic's merciless seas
Where he was a victim of many gastric agonies.

He needed a place to rest his arthritic knees
Worsened by the cold and the rain.
Hannah prepared a hot vegetable soup
So that the stranger could recoup

His energies. Avner and Zeldah in bed with the croup
Went without supper that night
After all, Hannah pleaded, this man is our brother.
And we Jews are trustees of one another.

When fatigue seized her bones, mother
Steiner prepared the beds:
Newspapers for blankets and mattresses
Zelda dreamed of brooms; Avner, of cakes; Hannah, of dresses.

So deeply did they sleep they did not hear the messes
Being made in the kitchen
By the stranger, outwardly devout,
As he was rummaging about

For the cache he sought being down-and out.
Where did the Steiners hide their money?
He asked out loud. Yet no one awoke
Even when a teacup broke.

He fished beneath Hannah's cloak
And found four dollars.
She stirred and saw a pair of eyes that lusted
In the immigrant whom she had trusted.

She awoke with a start, disgusted,
And smacked the man's face.
Faster than a lightning flash
He ran out with the cash.

After him she made a dash
But gone was the money for food and rent.
She applied to the association*   *Female Hebrew Benevolent Society,
For a small donation.   founded 1819

Miss Gratz reviewed the application
And found the indigent Steiners were industrious and frugal
And victims of the cousin's misdeeds.
They were given six dollars to cover their needs.

How grateful were they that the community heeds
The destitution of the poor.
They thanked the good ladies who kindness had shown
When fate a snare in their path had thrown.

Before Hannah was placed beneath her eternal stone
She taught Zeldah her craft at which she excelled as well.
Avner flourished in his trade, too.
And Miss Gratz's seeds of charity within them grew.

IN HONOR OF REBECCA GRATZ

When first he gazed upon Rebecca Gratz
His heart skipped beat after beat, his mind was awed.
Thomas Sully addressed his easel
And the portrait he painted was unflawed

Because Becky, herself, was in virtue pure
And with all of her soul a devout servant of God.
To educate the poor and heal the sick were duties and missions
And to fulfill her duty she needed no prod.

When there was no school to teach the Israelite young
She founded one and was its guide.
She started a Jewish orphanage
For children whose parents died.

"There are many kinds of trials in this life,
But an unsubdued spirit," she once wrote
"May overcome them all." Such was her profound belief
And the optimistic spirit she sought to promote.

Seraphic in spirit, worldly in mind
She had compassion for the distressed.
A candle in darkness, reason her bent,
And with God's love she had been blessed.

A TRIBUTE TO GRACE AGUILAR 1816-1847*

*An Anglo-Jewish writer admired by Rebecca Gratz

A nightingale sang rhapsodies to raise Jewish worth
To the heights of all righteous dwellers on Earth;
Her gentle words, balm to the ear,
To this day within our souls inhere:
That Israel's tradition is not merchant crass
But moral beauty that will never pass.
And that the tradition etched in our lore
Was by, was of, and, meant to be for
Men and Women the very same
To delight in the splendor of the eternal flame
Which first sparkled in the desert days gone by
Upon the craggy tors of Mount Sinai
And this beacon, far and wide,
Is still our lodestar and is still our guide.

ELLIS ISLAND

Itzik sewed for a living since he of age was ten;
He sewed for the soldiers along with the older men.
He'd cut out the cloth from a pattern of his own,
And proudly stitched the garment like a king upon his throne.
A-don o-lam* he sang while blasting along; *the hymn,
Lord of the universe iambic tetrameter was the rhythm of his song.

Russian soldiers would open the door;
They cursed his "Zhid" and spat on the floor.
What he earned could hardly be called a living
Since to his father all his earnings he was
Giving. At night he would dream of land where
success replaces despair and shatters duress.

When he turned fifteen, his future seeming grim,
"America" to "Hope", though, was a synonym.
So he packed a satchel with tailoring tools
And walked toward the border where only corruption rules.
Robbers lay in waiting about to attack;
But Itzik's scissors held them back.

He boarded a train and headed west
With pangs of sadness in his breast.
He found a town where he worked day and night,
His aim to reach America was clearly in sight.
Strengthening his resolve and fortitude
Were self-denial and gratitude.

He embarked from Bremen and settled in the hold,
Where a new chapter in his history was about to unfold.
Squashed in quarters meant for a few

Were blaspheming Jews performing acts taboo.
But Itzik was armed with a conscience upright
And closing his eyes would the Psalms recite.

There *the tired, poor, huddled masses,**
    *These words of Emma Lazarus are etched on the Statue of Liberty
The homeless wretched refuse of the lowly classes
Tossed by the tempest of an Atlantic storm
To the ship's railing retching did swarm
And returning to steerage puking and shrieking
They listened to the ship swaying and creaking.

In the crowded cell a stench did grow,
Itzik yearned to breathe free and be without vertigo.
After fourteen days upon the sea
One misty morning he howled with ecstasy
When he saw the flame of the lamp
That beckoned him to alight at the Island ramp.

Free at last! The newly arrived raised their voices.
FREE. Free from fanatical piety, penury, and calumny.
Then a guard marked them with mysterious chalk
And shouted slurs and barked out "Walk."
Disappointed and disoriented and by tempest thrown
They were grilled with questions in a language unknown.

"Amerikihs" golden door had many locks
And once opened it unveiled a Pandora's Box.
No ordeal ever left Itzik undaunted,
And he walked "Amerikih's" streets wherever he wanted.
But at night when into bed he would creep,
Waves of nostalgia overwhelmed his sleep.

A LETTER HOME*

*This letter, written is Yiddish, is translated into English. Some Hebrew and Yiddish words remain for their poignancy as does the mixture of sentence structures of the several languages.

XXX Cherry Street New York, N.Y. 21 Kislev, 5642 (Almost Chanukah)

Dear Mammeh,

In Amerikih I have been almost a year.
At first I did piece work at Cohen Tailor shop
But the shop got closed—by Cohen-
And I was paid never. But fear

Have not because German ladies from uptown,
Jewish of course, a job found for me
And money gave food to buy and rent to pay
For a room with a cot where I lay my head down

At night. Of course, I shared it.
With three other men for two dollars a week
Including breakfast: bread and tea
And cheese. In the kitchen sleep two women: one, a misfit

Who wants to go back to Hungary, her home,
As soon as enough money she raises
And one an observant woman is,
A proper woman about whom I could write a tome.

But don't worry. I am not ready to wed-
Yet. She, Frumeh, the pious one, in a candy factory
Works. Regrettably is, a RUSSISHE,**of Russian Jewish stock
Only nineteen—but with a good head

On her shoulders. Of course the kitchen door
Is locked. Still, a CHAYIM YANKEL, **an uncouth fellow
A roommate, from Odessa,
Thought every greenhorn woman was a whore

And tried to break the door down.
He made such a racket that
He woke me up. I kicked his TOOCHES* *buttocks
And punched him downtown.

I cuffed his groin. He left that night.
I still go to synagogue
But not every day, of course.
And, mammeh, I am contrite

About missing daily prayers.
But don't worry. I belong
To the CHEVRAH KADDISHA* *burial society
So I am not entirely a strayer
From my obligations. But I did shave my beard
Like so many modern Jewish men do.
There were man GOYIM and YIDDEN,* too, *Gentiles and JEWS
Who taunted me saying I looked weird

Like someone just off the boat.
Which, in truth, I was
Frumeh says I should not have shaved off
My YIDDISHKEIT*. A beard is an antidote *Judaism
To assimilation. But I did it anyway.
We go to night school together.
She already good English speaks
Like a native. My tongue, though, is made of clay.

But don't worry. I know how to make a living.
Some weeks I have nothing left from my wages
Except the hole of a bagel
Most weeks I have extra for charity giving.
I also found a way to make a little extra.
On Sundays several mens
Get together and play cards—for money-
I won fifteen dollars and took Frumeh to the opera,

In the balcony we sat and listened to YOSSELE* Verdi,
A TALLENISHCE * composer.
Don't worry, mammeh, *Giusseppi *Italian
I stop playing when enough GELT* *money
I have made to give some to the Free Loan Society

For the needy to borrow,
Without interest, to pay rent or buy furniture
Or have a bar mitzvah party
Or to pay the debts of a widow.

With some earnings I invited Frumeh to dine
At Weiner's Delicatessen with me.
The chicken broth was clear like amber
And the knishes, opaline.

But don't worry. She refused, this time, to be my guest
And she paid for her own dinner. We're too poor
To be serious, she said. Walking home—I had a little stomach
gas. She studies Bible in Hebrew and with zest.

The money I send is for you Amerikih to come.
On what I earn we could both live.
Amerikih is a great country
Sure here is swindler, there is a bum

But also there are decent folks
Struggling to become some bodies
Without fear of pogroms
That hated of Jews in Poland provokes.

Here you will find
Many who keep the traditions.
They sing Z'MIROT* on SHABBOS. *Hymns sung after the Sabbath meal
Of course, others toward traditions are disinclined.

People struggle like they do everywhere:
There is hunger and sickness
And loneliness. Such yearning for home
Because some times are good; other times, despair.

There are horse drawn steel-wheeled cars
That take you from street to street.
The wheels screech and people rush and push,
Bump and thump until you see stars.

In my building there live
Maybe two hundred peoples.
Most are Jews from Poland and Russia.
But, I spit three times,
There are also GOYIM* from Germany. Expletive!!! *Gentiles

From the hodgepodge rises a rainbow
Of people melded together by oppression:
Thrown out of their former homes
Now they are liberated of their woe.

Here there is freedom. Freedom from fear.
Freedom to work.
Freedom to pray if and the way one wishes.
Freedom to get ahead in a career.

But freedom is like the summer sun.
The gloomy night it melts
And our every path shines upon,
But it can burn you before the day is done.

I want you to know that I feel well-
today. No cough or running nose.

Colds I catch because the shop is damp, dark and dusty
And has a bad smell.

Understand the windows are always closed.
But to the doctor I have only been to
Once this month. So don't worry.
The doctor says I am exposed
To germs that live off the poor.
Of course, what else can a poor person have to give anyone?
Anyhow, next week for fifty cents
A coat I will buy at a secondhand store.

My sweater has a few holes.
And the cold winds of Winter
Blow needles in the damp night
And it's time to buy coals
For the little stove in my bedroom.
From says I can supplement my income
By becoming a MELAMED* *A teacher A MAVEN*
I am not. But to become her groom* an expert

I would even TOYRAH* teach the urchins who just want to play
*Bible Ball. Come to Amerikih mammeh come!
The customs here are foreign, but don't worry.
Come to Amerikih, and we will find our way.

Of course, your loving son, Itzik.

LAST WILL AND TESTAMENT OF IRVING NÉE ITZIK

(This poem symbolically represents a freedom which death bestowed on the hero. Almost entirely free of meter and rhyme it is a history of the hero's sojourning in America as an immigrant as well as his gratitude for that privilege. What he leaves to his family are moral guides not a contention for worldly goods.)

Irving, born Itzik, is dead. The will he wrote fifteen years ago
    Was read to a gathering of his family.
Nostalgia spread to his loved ones.
    With dread they reminisced his last few years in a wheelchair,
Later his confinement in bed.

They felt the knots in their legs when a limp invited itself into his;
    Their hands trembled when a palsy planted itself in his;
Their ears fell silent when deafness swelled in his;
    Their eyes were blurred when dimness spread throughout his;
Their mouths lost taste when demons dulled his tongue.
    But age did not stifle his taste for freedom;
Nor did daily travail blunt theirs.

Itzik, a nobody, came to America and was a stranger in a strange land.*
    *Adapted from Exodus, 2:22

And The Liberty Lady, beacon held high,
    Beckoned him to enter the promised land
To enjoy its treasures and pass them on to others.
    Her treasured lambent light we, his children, inherited.
When we gathered to witness his will he said this to us,
    "Frightened, alone, weak from the voyage
I sucked at the teats of the Liberty Lady
    And their nectar drizzled in my mouth;

Unbounded joy made my eyes drop tear after tear.
    My heart quivered with the thrill of freedom.
Freedom in the morning! Freedom at night!
    Gifted am I with freedom whose blessings chased
The foul air of the city from my mind.
    Whose blessings undid the humiliation of sweat shop,
Cramped sleeping quarters, meager diet,
And ridicule because of my beard and my Yiddish accent,
    both of which I quickly shed.

Freedom opened school doors to me where
    I absorbed like a sponge what education had to offer.
Freedom punctured the pain of being thrown to the ground by a hoodlum
    And robbed of my only two dollars—my rent money.
Freedom softened the sorrow
    Of losing my true love, your sweet mother, in the Triangle fire.
She was my heroine, my angel.
    To this day she guides me to wrestle with the masters
to improve the workers' lot.
    Morning and night I hear her charred voice speak to me
before I recite the SH'MA.
    Like a pledge of allegiance to God she directs me neither
to mourn nor to laud her
    But to dedicate my might to wrest injustice from frail mortals.
Let TSEDAKAH* reign! *Benevolence
    This legacy I pass on to you."

When deceivers spew their counterfeit slime-Be genuine;
    When extremists masquerade as righteous-Be sincere;
When moral eunuchs blight this world with bombast-Be upright;
    When sadness seizes the souls of those shackled to death-Be condoling;
When deputies of destruction damage God's world-Be builders;
    When the splendor of heaven cascades prosperity
upon your houses—be generous.

Our destiny is not to molder in the earth but to power each day with life.

With love Your father.
ITZIK IRVING

Witnessed on this day August 26, 1929 20 Ab 5689
by his children
Herman G, Deana G, Benjamin G

GENEALOGY OF AN AMERICAN JEWISH FAMILY

Avrahom and Sorohlih begat Seymour;
Seymour and Sandra begat Sean;
Sean and Theresa begat Patrick and Cecilia;
Patrick and Thomas adopted Huang Lee;
Cecilia and Deborah adopted Inger;
Huang Lee and Inger begat Avrahom and Soroh.

THE FIRST GRADUATION OF THE REFORM JEWISH SEMINARY IN CINCINNATI

At the graduation of the first Reform rabbis in America
    The seminary president did not skimp.
His guests were given a sumptuous meal, the first course being shrimp.
    And each distinguished guest from near and far got up and left his table
And felt as if Cain had once again murdered Abel.

THE LITTLE YID AND SANTA CLAUS

Santa put on his robe of red and fixed the wig upon his head
    Then seated himself among Macy's toys
To grant the wishes of girls and boys
    Who would sit upon his lap to ask for dolls
And trains that were in the store.
    "Have you been good the whole year round?"
He'd ask the children who were spellbound.

"Oh yes, Santa," each replied—a few misdeeds they had to hide
    To garner favor with the man in the beard
Whose suit of red with mollies they smeared.
    Santa would smile and give a gift or two,
And they would demurely say, "Santa, Santa than-thank you."
    Off the lap the children would slide,
Clutching their gifts quite satisfied.
    Then one day a boy wearing a ritual cap,
Arranging himself on Santa's lap,

Said, "Ich gloybe nicht in deer Senta Klutz"
    And refused Santa's souvenir derision
"Nem dawss," begged the man in red Take this.
    Handing the boy a gingerbread
Don't believe in you Klutz, a term of "Ich daft machen" a living.
    Santa explained, I need to make a living,
But the boy only ate Kosher and the cookie disdained.

Still the little boy understood this Santa's plight
    And with the bearded one did the Sh'ma recite
Sh'ma, (Hear O Israel the Lord is our God, The Lord is One)
    The first word of a Hebrew prayer to which the oft whispered

Reply is "Baruch shaym k'vod"-blessed is (God's) name.
    And gathering children quietly sang "Baruch shmo"
As Santa's bell rang. Blessed is His name.

KISHINEV'S HOUSE OF ETERNITY

Useless is the Jewish Cemetery unless there are dead to bury. To gratify the graveyard's greed in the newspaper a canard appeared: A LITTLE RUSSIAN BOY HAS BEEN SLAIN. The story said, BY JEWS—IT WAS PLAIN.

Seminarians rushed to Kishinev to avenge the boy
In actions for which they would find great joy.

In place there had been government plan the flames
    Of hatred to ignite and fan.
Like wild dogs the priests-to-be madly growled, crossed themselves,
    And like hyenas howled.
They looted the houses of the sleeping Jews and dragged
    Them out and did them abuse.
The women were raped; the man to trees nailed and the priests
    Cackled as their victims wailed.

Tolstoy and Gorki objected; Theodore Roosevelt was appalled
    Still in the streets of Kishinev Jewish corpses were sprawled.
And the grave greedily awaited to state its hunger
    For the old Jews as well as for those who were younger.

That Easter Day's blood had been washed by the rain
    And garbage is thrown where the Jews once had lain.
Later Kishinev was to the Rumanians ceded
    The pogrom of august three was again repeated.

In forty-one back to the Russians Kishinev came
    And once again did they the Jews defame.
Oh how the Jewish Cemetery howled to be fed
    It had not gorged enough on Jewish dead.

The Nazis, though, that hunger sated
    And Jews of all ages in trenches were collated.
Martyrs of Kishinev we remember you yet;
    Martyrs of Kishinev we will never forget.

A BOXING LESSON FOR BARNEY ROSOFSKY*

*Based on stories told about the professional boxer Barney Ross, who won many championships. He retired with 74 wins, three draws, four losses, and one no decision. He was wounded in Guadalcanal. He crusaded against illegal drugs. He never forgot the beatings he received from young Irish thugs or the priest who taught him how to box.

Pat and Mike went on a hunt as night was melting day
    For a religious Jewish runt on his way to pray.
Suddenly Barney was spotted; he was the rabbi's son.
    Behind the bushes they plotted to terrorize him for fun.

They grabbed his wrists, they slapped his head,
    They rammed his eyes with their fists and punched them
Until they trickled red.
    "Yid! Yid! Sheenie! Kike!" They snarled with every punch.
Pat hit hard; so did Mike until Barney plunged with a crunch.

His testicles ached where they met with a kick.
    White with rage into a church he staggered
And at a stained glass window threw a brick.
    Feeling avenged, toward home he swaggered.
"Boy, come here", shouted a priest. Barney's feet froze, he couldn't run.
    Barney growled like some wild beast. "What have you done my son?"

Blood and tears mixed on his face as he sobbed the boys
    Pounded him on a whim.
Then a sweet Irish brogue spoke, "Tis surely a disgrace
    To be beaten up held by each limb."
"Their sin is mine," said the priest contrite then gave
    Barney a warm embrace.

"I'll teach you son how to fight," he said cleaning
    The blood from Barney's face.

Every day out of school he flew and toward the gym Barney ran
    Where he was taught what to do by the Catholic clergyman.
One day Barney was sitting on a stoop, when Pat and Mike
    Spat on him as a joke
And called him, "Christ Killer. You pile of poop"
    Then grabbed his neck until he started to choke.
Barney got loose and like a tiger he paced, he twisted,
    And twitched then tossed a right,
A blow to Mike's eye with precision he placed.
    Hunching his shoulders he punched with delight.
Mike was down and Pat ran away but Barney chased him until
    He was caught.
Swaddled in hate, with reason astray, Barney boxed him
    Like the priest had taught.

OWED TO MORT LEVINE

In his bed about to die while eating corned beef on seeded rye
    Was the garment king, Levine,
Tended by his careful nurse, Claudine.
    Gurgling, "Sacré bleu", she grabbed Mort's tray.
Defiantly, he chewed on, the ulcered stray.
    "I'll call to get ze fu-nair-a; 'earrse,"
Sputtered the frightened Parisian nurse.

Grabbing the phone, Levine called Reb Cohn
    Who heard Mort cough and gasp and groan.
Mort hung up, choking with laugher-
    He was not ready for the ever after.
Through busy traffic the rabbi sped hoping
    To get to Mort before he was dead.
But when the rabbi asked Claudine for report.
    Drawing the sheet, she sobbed, "Il est mort."

Smiling contentedly, alas and alack,
    Mort passed on when he finished his snack.

GASTRONOMIC LOGIC

Georg Wilhelm Friedrich Hegel taught a class on Lox and Bagel.
"How does it get its gourmet taste?" He asked the students with palates chaste.
The cheese is what he hypothesized; the bits of lox they antithesized.
References galore Hegel traced; but student taste tests his proofs displaced.
Slabs of cheese, he persisted; bits of lox is what they insisted.
Into the night they argued and fought; proofs sublime mattered
not a jot. At dawn arose a Kant eclectic: "Mix lox with cheese."
Hail the dialectic!

JEWISH SENSE OF HUMOR

The Jews can laugh at themselves
But take a dim view
Of others laughing at them.

IT TAKES A SHTETL: A REMINISCENCE

Mendel, masquerading as a fiddler, donned his tattered tuxedo.
    Tails flapping like wings, and his bow squeaking across the strings
As he flew through the door of his shack. Hearing the scratchy tune
    And seeing Mendel's silhouette by the light of the moon,
Yoshke joined him tooting a flute which he had won
    In a dispute with the Warsaw Symphony.

The Lev, the misfit, the cacophony sounded like exquisite harmony
    And lured him and his clarinet which he held like a bayonet
Into the synagogue courtyard.

Itchik zipped up his harlequin suit, the one he bought from a circus recruit
    And joined them plunking on his guitar under
The eye of a twinkling star. How sweet was the spirit of shtetl!

Filled with happiness to the brim out came the villagers to celebrate Purim
    Clapping their hands and stamping their feet, singing
with abandon to the musical beat
    Were Mordecai, Esther, Ahasueros, and Vashti.

Children arrived by the score singing victory songs of yore,
    Clapping a pot and banging a pan and shouting,
"Hang the tyrant, Haman The barbarian."

Cats meowed; dogs bayed; sheep bleated; horses neighed;
    No one at all was complaining.
The mood of Purim was reigning.
    The sound was raucous; the mood was gay.

JEWISH ANTISEMITES OF THE NINETEENTH CENTURY

It was a mere tick in Time. Tyranny of the rabbinate had been overthrown.
    Jews were free to think, to feel, to love, and to hate.
And how some hated! How some raged!
    How little they knew of their past; yet how they despised its treasure.
How little concern was there for their kin;
    Yet how they ridiculed it beyond measure.
They sat in libraries and devoured every anti-semitic volume; They
    sat in taverns and drank in ever anti-semitic aphorism;
They sat in intellectual circles and outdid one another
    In assailing Jews for the sorry conditions of society-
Though none fed the poor, bathed them, housed them, or even knew them.
    These were Jewish intellectuals of the nineteenth century:
Adler, Bauer, Braun, Borne, Heine, Hochberg, Labsale, and Marx.
    Like Macbeth's witches they stirred a portion in a cauldron
To destroy Judaism and chanted, "Fair is foul, and foul is fair."*
    *Shakespeare, MACBETH. Act 1, Scene 1, line 12
How they reveled in their chutzpah; how they celebrated their revolt;
    How they exaggerated their own knowledge;
How they influenced the discontented.
    They detested Judaism, hated themselves, railed against one's apostles,
And bequeathed Jewish Self-Hatred to the yet unborn.
    To blame Judaism for their own miserable fates
Was avant-garde, fashionable, modish.
    They flailed wildly at their compatriots
Whose mere existence was a virus
    That quarantined them from the prestige of association
With the Christian intelligentsia.
    Rejected by state philosophic societies,
They were applauded by some Jewish intellectuals.
    And that approval revolted them.

No Christian love did these apostates have for others;
    There was no compassion for oppressed sisters and brothers.
They ate hate, drank hate, thought hate, spoke hate, and dreamed hate.
    They spread hate: black hate, hot hate, searing hate, molten hate.
Setting of a maelstrom of malice toward Jews,
    They drove torrents of racism reeling into the twentieth century,
Baptizing innocent Jewish babes with odium.
    They said that the exodus from Egypt was the expulsion of lepers;
They said that the Torah was a neolithic tribal relic;
    They said that the Talmud was a debaucher of the mind;
They said that the Siddur* reeked of perfumed turd;
    *Prayer book They said that the customs
Were founded on superstition;
    They said that the rabbi was a seducing illusionist;
And they said that the laity was a horde of brainless, bleating sheep.
    Capitalists are, in disguise, circumcised Jews
Whose usury drives the wheels of industry
    And pollutes society with its acrid stench.
Expunge the Jew from civilization
    And mankind if free of the Jew and all that is debasing,
So thundered, Karl Marx, Thor of the rabid radicals.

Only Heine relented his apostasy and then only on his death bed
    Where he lay the prisoner of a spirochete. He wept,
I am a mortally ill Jew, an emaciated image of misery.
    Sickened by atheistic philosophy, I return to the humble faith
Of the ordinary man.
    In my youth Chayim* departed from Judaism; Now chayim*
Departs from Heine. *Heine's Hebrew name *life

HAYYIM HEINE ON HEINRICH HEINE

Hitler ordered Heine's grave in the Montmartre destroyed.

I cannot fathom why so very sad am I.
    My tale was inscribed in some ancient lore:
That I be despised from the day I was born.

Despised merely because a Jew was I. A Jew?
    What did that imply? I, myself, loathed Jews of every flavor,
Everyone slithering in scorn.

'Twas easy my Jewishness to deny.
    Eins, zwei, drei, a Protestant was I*
*He said his baptism was the "entrance-ticket to European culture."
    To complete my degree requirements
With a few drops of water my heritage was forsworn.

But can anyone to another faith a Jew dye?
    Nay, nay came the cry
From the pack of yelping bigots
    Who dragged me clawed and torn.

Aye-aye-aye, then, did daily I sigh
    How can I my mistakes rectify?
Until to the humble faith of my people was I,
    As an ordinary man, reborn.

HEINE AND MARX

Religion is opium of the sad spirit
Said Heine—and Marx aped him.

WHO IS THE REBEL?

Father please listen to me,
"I am a Jewess"* *words of Karl Marx's daughter
No matter what *you* believe.

MONTAGU, THE ANTI-ZIONIST JEW

The Indian Secretary, Montagu, an anti-zionist Jew
    Examined Lord Balfour's Declaration, based
On Baron Rothschild's dictation,
    And deleted the part, its very heart,
That Palestine, a National Homeland will be
    For every branch of the Jewish tree.

LIKE A GIMEL

Like a gimel* my mother, face worn by grief, * ג
    Is stooped over in prayer whispering the Holy Name
With awe, sincerity, and devotion.
    In a trice of wide silence her heart pulses,
Expelling dybbuks defiantly hiding in cardiac caves.
    She gathers them and pushes them through vessels
Of holiness dispatching them to oblivion
    Where disappointed loves, squandered moments of happiness,
Curdled joy, bitter tastes of hardships, and unmerited self-reproach
    Meander aimlessly in search of a purpose.
Then she unshackles the memories, curse'd memories
    Of a starving stomach, confining sickness, unbred brain,
Scarred pride, self-doubts, envy, and despair.
    No longer their hostage, she sets them on fire and the ashes
Return as a golem that protects her from the errors of creation.
    And she says Amen.

EMMA LAZARUS AND THE IMMIGRANTS*

*The words in quotes are from her poem inscribed on the Statue of Liberty

Emma Lazarus implored, send to the Liberty Lady
    The "tired" and the "poor."
And they arrived seasick battered by "tempest" swells
    "Huddled" in ship holds that reeked of "wretched refuse."
But the "lamp" of hope revealed "the golden door"
    Where all could "breathe free."

THERE AND HERE: AN IMMIGRANT'S DILEMMA

Where do I belong? No one claims me as his own.
    One foot is in a land that chased me out; the other foot,
In a land that ignores me.
    Expatriated without a fatherland; ostracized in a land that took me in.
Outcast there; orphan here; a pariah there; a nobody here.
    Tossed out like garbage there; shunned like the plague here.
Pillaged by marauding looters there; swindled by shop owners here.
    Wrestling with the past there; struggling with tomorrow here.
Yet how I long for there—but how I love it here.

NO ONE FROM MY TRIBE

No one from my tribe would fondle my breasts
    And, laughing, say there are lots of women who need a job
Sewing blouses at five cents a piece in a smelly bedroom where twelve
    Sewing machines whir and buzz all day long and in my dreams.

No one from my tribe would reek of schnapps
    And erotically kiss the fringes of his little tallis soiled
From wiping his hands
    On it after slurping up a plate of borscht bought with the profit
Of my sewing a blouse at five cents a piece in a smelly bedroom
    Where twelve sewing machines
Whir and buzz all day long and in my dreams.

No one from my tribe would paint the windows black
    So that inspectors would not suspect
That a dozen immigrant women are shivering in a cold room
    In the middle of winter
Sewing blouses at five cents a piece and cannot stop to-
    You should excuse me-
Go to the bathroom without him spying on us in a smelly bedroom
    Where twelve sewing machines whir
And buzz all day long and in my dreams.

But one of the twelve from *my* tribe took a scissors
    And thrust it into the foreman's back
And let him lie there covered by blouses sewn at five cents a piece
    Without anyone reporting the mitzvah in a smelly bedroom
Where twelve sewing machines
    Whir and buzz all day long and in my dreams.

TATTEH* I WON'T SAY KADDISH** FOR YOU.

*Father **Memorial prayer

Tatteh. I won't say kaddish for you.
    'Though your bones lie in cold darkness
Deep in the ground you are alive inside of me still teaching me Torah.

What a mensch you were; what a teacher.
    When I was a child you never told me that with a pack on your back
You chugged to remote towns like a human freight train
    In the hot sun and in the cold rain
Selling shirts to people who spoke with a drawl and a twang.

Jew, how much is this shirt? One dollar, you'd say,
    And they said, Jew! that's too much.
One dollar, you'd say. How about eighty cents?
    One dollar, you'd say. O.K. ninety-five cents! One dollar,
You'd say, and that's what they paid.

Never did your sense of worth shrivel;
    Never did you curse those who cursed you;
Never did you cheat those who cheated you;
    And you shared your meager earnings with the less fortunate.
Embarrassed by the shape of your back, I used to call you lahmed——-> ל
    And I'd make fun of you with my friends, calling you lahmed back.
I even pretended I didn't know you. How little children understand.

I won't say kaddish for you because you are alive in my every word,
    In my every thought, in my every aspiration,
And in my every achievement.
    As I play with my own children on my day off from the office

I see you sweating in the hot sun, shivering in the cold rain,
    Bent back chugging from place to place, like a human freight train
Whispering, "son, seed of my loins, you will never
    Have to earn a living the way I did."

THE EXCOMMUNICATION OF RABBI MORDECAI*

*Inspired by the excommunications of Rabbis Mordecai Kaplan and Eliezer ben Hyrcanus.

Tall rabbis were there; short rabbis were there;
    Portly rabbis were there; gaunt rabbis were there.
Some rabbis wept; some, sneered; some chuckled; others, frowned.
    Some rabbis stood; others, sat; some, swayed; others, sat spread-eagled.
Some prayed; others read The Times;
    Some rabbis had long scraggly beards;
One sported a Vandyke. Some smoothed their silk jackets;
    Others, their threadbare sweaters.
Every mind had but one thought, Rabban Gamaliel riding
    The crest of a wave
As the venerated Rabbi Eliezer ben Hyrcanus, his brother-in-law,
    Was cast out of Klal Yisrael.

The lights of the hotel ballroom were dimmed;
    Tall black tapers were lighted.
A keening shriek escaped from an ancient mouth
    And sympathetic shrieks echoed throughout the room.
All rabbis covered their faces with their prayer shawls.
    "Oh God," the eldest rabbi implored,
"Wrench the dybbuk from this misguided ignoramus;
    Lift the Satan from his diseased soul; destroy the evil that he has done."
Those gathered assented, "Amen, amen." and the ghost of Rabban Gamaliel
    Scowled at the ghost of Rabbi Eliezer.
Piles of books written by the condemned rabbi were torched.
    Prayer books in which the name of God lovingly appeared on every page
Were transformed to ashes.
    Not siddurim* are these but offal the rabbis barked. *prayer books

Judaism as a civilization was in shambles.
    Deafening blast after blast of shofar
Sent shivers down the spines of the hotel guests
    And Rabbi Eliezer again rent his garments,
And his eyes tearing, again draped himself in black;
    And a plague again visited the world,
Destroying one third of the olive crop, one third of the wheat crop;
    One third of the barley crop;
And the eyes of the world were swollen with grief.

V

THE HOLOCAUST PERIOD

JEWISH ASHES CLOUD THE FIRMAMENT

Germany was licking its wounds after World War I, its injured pride as well as economic hardships fathered a nationalist movement. It needed 1. to assign blame for their miseries and 2. to unify German sentiments to regain lost standing in their own eyes. The Nazi, a post WW I movement gained political power in local elections and, through riveting rhetoric won the hearts of countless Germans. It not only attracted rogues but intellectuals as well. As the Nazis strength many joined the movement to enhance their own fortunes. Some joined because of a need to affiliate with a group bustling with activity. Ideologies of Aryan superiority and the inferiority of Jews and gypsies drew many, especially the youth, into Nazi ranks. Soon the fylfot, the cross looking like running legs, decorated houses, places of business, and entertainment palaces. It could be seen in banners and on uniforms. Achievement of national pride was at the expense of Jews. Gradually Jews, even veterans of World War I, were deprived of voting rights, rights to education, and rights of property. Yet apostate Jews were regarded as Jews. Germans goose stepped their way into countries to the east and west. There they collected booty and gathered Jews to be sent off to labor camps as well as to their deaths. Jews could not even die in dignity. Nazis removed the gold from the mouths of the naked corpses, gassed them and then incinerated them. Remaining Jews, regarded as offal, were belittled and dehumanized while being persecuted in concentration camps. Although the Nazi presence was palpable from the early 1930's until 1945, the year the Germans surrendered, there were in every conquered nation righteous gentiles who risked their own lives to save a Jew. After the war there was more international sentiment favoring the Jews than ever before. It became clear to the allies that Jews needed a homeland, a safe haven, Palestine now Israel. Its residents were mostly Arab but there was an increasing Jewish presence from pioneers who came there to rebuild the land and from persons displaced by World War II. Although many Jewish and Arab families got along at first, enmity between them grew. To this day they spill each other's blood.

SPREADING DARKNESS

While the world was fast asleep, a force arose with fury deep.
    In Deutschland was this force so disguised that when the world awoke it was surprised.
    Here's the tale as I know it now—told to me by a German frau.* *Wife
World War One brought German defeat a blow to its diffuse conceit.
    But it also spawned hunger and many lacks,
Crowded dwellings and a heavy tax.

Germans who viewed themselves as the superior race coveted
    The inferior Jews living space.
German anger burst to stanch their disgrace and sought the root
    Of their problems to erase.
The root, of course, they said was the Jews. Like a fire spread the news.
    Then Nazis looted each Jewish home and defaced
In synagogues each holy tome.
    They punched bearded sages and trampled each ancient face.
"Tis just," said they, "to purge the evil race."
    The final solution was a careful plan.
It first began with the Jewish ban.
    Then segregate. Agglutinate. Denudate. Then depilate.
Asphyxiate. Incinerate.

Scream each order with scorn.
    Bellow each order through an ear-splitting horn.
Subject the Jews to every kind of affront, then shoot them down
    As in a vermin hunt.
They shoved women and children into cattle cars;
    Guards smacked them with rifles making lasting scars.
They ripped women's dresses pawing private places
    And smashed hymens instilling disgraces.

The victims were showered with Zyklon gas then burned
    To a crisp like brush en masse.
Children were shot in the heart and the face and then disappeared
    Without any trace.
After the world awoke, it waged a war and defeated the Nazis
    Right to the core.
"Oh God," Hans pleaded, 'our sins erase."
    But God was still smoldering, too weak to grant grace.

THE ASHES OF HISTORY

The ashes of history blind my eyes;
    The silent sobs of the tormented deafen my ears.
The acrid smell of flesh on fire burn my nostrils.
    The caustic taste of Zyklon B lacerates my tongue.
You, innocent, innocent you who have been martyred
    Will never be forgotten
Your distress is my suffering; your agony is my pain.
    I ask you God how can I rise above
The tragic helplessness of humanity?
    I ask you God when can I throw away my sackcloth
Ripped anew each day To commemorate another sorrow.
    I ask you God is my destiny to be surrounded by flies
Injecting me with their poisons, leaving me to be eaten
    By worms when I expire?
Disdain Zion not! Send us an angel of mercy
    To release us from our bondage.
Send us an angel of mercy to redeem us.
    Rescue us from the terror that surrounds us.

N'KA-MAH*

*This allegory is about an event that occurred August, 1943 when 200 Jewish partisans headed by Josef Glazman left Vilna and gathered in Naroch Forest where they trained to fight the Nazis. The group was called "N-KAMAH" (Revenge, was later dismissed and many Jewish roosters were "unritually" slaughtered).

Roosters strutted from side to side cocked-caps fixed upon their skulls,
    Orange beards rocking with every stride heads bobbing as if in prayer.
Hens blithely ate their ration of corn—for their sustenance
    And for offspring yet unborn.
Then out of nowhere came a storm of wolves,

Claws still stained with innocent blood. Falling upon the frightened fowl,
    They smashed their eggs with a thunderous thud
And ripped chanticleer apart,
    Lacquering the coop Prussian red. There was no time to protest
That fowl are especially bred, chosen by THE F-R-M-R,

To herald a new day; to nourish the nations;
    To show others the way; to a good life.

Their mission is to crow the wake-up call!
    But animals in the farm and nearby
At the lupine wrong protested not at all.
    Some even gloated over the suffering of the chickens

Who entreated, "OH MIGHTY F-R-M-R, "Where is our sanctuary?
    We merely want to wander about the farm
Cheeping our praises to Thee."
    To no avail was their wail.

Then two hundred cocks, fighters all, slipped out of the barn,
    With chutzpah, with gall, and gathered in the forest
To develop a skill alien to their natures. Kill!   Kill!   Kill!
    One dawn into the barnyard they crept
Animals everywhere their message heard
    "Oh King David, you had ten thousand slain;
We slew ten wolves making us each a peerless bird.
    With N'KAMAH we will kill again."

ODE TO HANNAH SENESH*

*A martyred Hebrew poet who spied for the British army. She was tortured and killed by the Nazis.

Sights had lost their pictures; sounds, their shades of tone.
Tastes had lost their flavor; scents dried up alone.
Words were without meaning; actions were insincere.
Dreams turned into nightmares; life was just veneer.

The Nazis swept through Europe, brining death amidst their hate,
And stomped on what was noble with their goose step gait.
Though her tongue was silenced, she did not have a choice,
The evil men who martyred her could not still her voice.

Hannah stirred our senses and gave us cause to hope,
And prayed with us, "Eternal God show us how to cope."
She sprinkled sounds of rustling leaves upon the rolling seas,
Then gathered light from sun-filled skies and spun sweet
Reveries.

THE RIGHTEOUS TEN BOOMS

Nazi soldiers clad in brown, goose
    Stepped through old Haarlem town,
Shrilly shrieked, "The Jews are slime.
    Harb'ring them's a heinous crime."
Rising during this dawn of madness when
    Good hearts filled with pain and sadness
Was the righteous family of Ten Boom,
    Who shone like sun 'midst a growing gloom.

Papa, Betsy, and pious Corrie,
    Who'll live forever in hallowed glory,
Disguised a room and there did hide escaping Jews
    Who might have died.
The downcast Jews in isolation squalled
    in dread of extermination
Until Papa read from the sacred text,
    Perpetual elixir to souls perplexed.

To feed the guests growing by the score,
    Ration cards were stolen by a coconspirator.
Corrie knew that she was suspected.
    Still risking all, her Jews protected.
In time the Ten Booms were sent to jail
    Where a reign of evil did prevail.
For many days they had not eaten.
    And, in fact, were often beaten.

Yet the Ten Booms never would reveal
    Where the Jews they did conceal.
Papa died. The sisters staggered to camp
    To be in cells dark and damp.

Although the guards showed them
    Only disdain and inflicted upon them shame and pain,

The sisters reached high for the mighty Lord
    Who ruled the world with love, not sword.

Corrie taught Bible and each day would
    Pray for the innocents the Nazis did slay
At Ravensbruck camp where grief was bred
    By wicked guards who defiled the dead.
Betsy died there like so many others:
    Defectives, babies, and nursing mothers.

Then within Corrie rose a solemn ambition
    To spread God's love, life's sacred mission.
And as the war was finally ending
    Broken souls were in need of mending Corrie
Did as Betsy had willed,
    She healed both victims and those who killed.

ROUMANIA, ROUMANIA, ROUMANIA, ROUMANIA, ROUMANIA

Forgive me Father for I have sinned!
    This is my last confession. My soul is sick.
It reeks with anguish; it oozes pus.
    I cannot eat; I cannot sleep; I cannot embrace a woman.
I see headless ghosts dripping blood
    In my food, in my bed, in my arms.
Lightning sizzles my brain; skulls bounce like hail in my mind.
    Steel nails stick out of my wrists and impale me to my past.

I was a callow youth of only sixteen. Callow. Green.
    In spirit and in dress
A gift of the Iron Guard to the powerless. I was a nobody
    But they made me a somebody. We drank each other's blood
Then scudded through the streets looking for Jews.
    How I tingled whenever I fired my pistol for amusement
Then watched bearded old men drop.
    My friends looked up to me. "Bravo" they shouted.
Together we looted Jewish homes*
    *Based on events that occurred in Bucharest in early WW II
The women shrieked; the babies puled as we dragged
    The men to the ritual slaughterhouse
And made them crawl on all fours. Naked.
    Completely naked and wreaking of urine.
We gored them with prods and called them pigs, offal, turd

Then herded them up the ramp where we stamped
    Their Jewish behinds "Kosher".
When they reached the top we'd slit their jugulars and lop off their heads.
    And our bodies shook with excitement watching

The spurting streams of blood meandering all over the corpses.
    Then we tossed their bodies on a hook.
Was it all a dream? Did I only imagine it? Who came?
    Who looked? Who saw as we conquered?
Forgive me, Father, for I knew not what I did. Kyrie Eleison.
    Have mercy on me.

Then a frenzied voice from within growled, "mea culpa. mea culpa"
    As death crawled inside his body.
When he was no longer of the living
    There was silence. Ghastly silence without peer
Save for the splattering of an Effulgent Tear.

RIGHTEOUS GENTILES

Inspired by the Babe who lay in the manger,
Righteous gentiles defied danger
To save the lives of the Jewish stranger.

TWO CONSULS AND AN "AMBASSADOR": A TRYPTICH ESSAY ON VISAS

1. DR. ARISTEDES DE SOUSA MENDES.*

*Dr. Mendes, Portuguese consul in Bordeaux, having learned of the plight of 10,000 refugees many of them Jews, signed their passports to freedom. Stripped of his pension, he lived in ignominy until he was honored in Yad Vashem (1966) and in Portugal (1986). He once said, "If thousands of Jews can suffer because of one Catholic (Hitler), then surely it is permitted for one Catholic to suffer for so many Jews."

Consul Dr. Sousa Mendes. Honored Sir. Write us a visa!
    We the desperate refugees from Hitler's slaughter were weeping
While the rest of the world was sleeping.

Dr. Mendes brought his message to Salazar, Portugal's avatar
    Who said no visa for Jews.
But your honor, Portugal will be known in the annals of compassion
    For providing a haven for the desperate.
No. No visa for the Jews.
    But your honor, the marking of Jews is unconstitutional.

Sousa Mendes took to his bed where he languished, where he anguished.
    How can he countermand his government's orders?
How can he send innocents to their extinction? His woes harassed his body;
    His torment set his brain on fire; his soul was filed with ire.
In his dreams were babies crying; in his dreams were groans of the dying;

Then like Jesus, he rose on the third day.
    He fed his fasting body;

He filled his brain with plans; he filled his soul with human suffering.
    Mercy entered every chamber of his heart.
Electrified he signed the visas.

2. SEMPO SUGIHARA*

*Japanese consul in Kovno was approached by Dr. Zorah Warhaftig who asked him to grant Japanese transit visas to Polish Jews in Kovno so that they could get Soviet visas. The plan was to allow them to travel to Curacao where an entry permit was not necessary. Japanese government rejected the proposal. Sugihara went ahead and issued 1600 visas. He was shunned by his countrymen and disgraced by his government. He was honored at Yad Vashem and decades later in Japan.

Consul Sugihara. Honored Sir.
    Please grant Polish Jews living in Kovno
        Transit visas so they can emigrate
    Lest they be immolated.
        We have martyrs enough!

For days the consul tossed and turned while righteous
    Anger within him burned.
He saw dread in every Jewish eye; he heard screams that terrify.
    In his dreams were Jews dressed in sadness;
In his dreams were eyes burning with madness.
    The Nazi weasel Jewish blood was drinking
As their propaganda was the world hoodwinking.

The consul's heart with mercy was beating
    While en masses Nazis were Jews deleting.
His decision was clear: be true to what I hold dear.
    Can I allow innocents to die in a world that has gone awry?
Whatever punishment I am to receive I cannot my own conscience deceive.

Each visa kindled a cosmic spark bringing light to a world too dark.
    Each visa permitted passage to tomorrow into a world
With a little less sorrow.

3. PERE MARIE BENOIT*

*Pere Maries Benoit, a Capuchin friar, self-proclaimed "Ambassador to the Jews," forged 4000 passports enabling Jews to leave Bordeaux.

Every morning when he awoke he donned his brownish Capuchin cloak.
    And to Jesus on the cross he'd pray, "how can I serve You,
Honored Sir, today?"
    Each day the answer he received was clear, "the Jews, my kin,
Live in fear of cancellation. Plan their liberation."
    For many months he "passports" wrote admitting Jews to countries,
Near and remote. "Abba," Father to the Jew,
    Stopped a world from going askew.

KAPO KEINRICH SCHULZ*

*Kapo is the term for the trustee that the Nazis appointed to oversee the efforts of the work detail. A kapo wore a green triangle if he had been sent to a concentration camp for committing a crime. Kapo Schulz is a composite. A kapo wore a red triangle if he was a political prisoner. Greens were often, but not always, cruel; Reds were often, but not always, caring.

Heinrich Schulz wore a grin. For pittance murdered his kin.
    Sent to Dachau for this ghastly crime felt
Right at home in that grizzly clime.
    Murder and thievery were his credentials.
To the Nazi commander he met their essentials.
    They appointed him kapo over the workers
With permission to deal fiercely with all of the shirkers.
    He proudly wore the triangle of green
And aspired to become the meanest of mean.
    Strutting in his britches shiny and new
He spat tobacco globs at the passing Jew.

"Worthless scum" he'd often quip
    And never hesitated to use his whip.
Schneller, schneller (faster), was his two word command.
    He was merely obeying orders from the Vatterland.

One night while out on a binge
    He sang a song that made SS guards cringe.
The next day he was sent to the work detail
    Among the Reds and Poles whom he caused such travail.

As they were tramping through the slush
    Schulz was felled by a crush

Of vengeance built up in those
    He had sadistically whipped with a rubber hose.
He was stomped then sliced into many a piece
    And was fouled by whatever caprice
Lurked in the minds of those he had prodded.
    No one flinched; no one applauded

As he lay lifeless in the mud covered with blood,
    An arm here, a leg there, a piece of Schulz lay everywhere.

A TRIBUTE TO MISHA VEKSLER*

*Misha Veksler, a victim of polio, was a popular musician and conductor of the Jewish Theater Orchestra in Vilna, He died at age 36 in 1943.

My voice is mute; my pen is dry.
My arms are limp, my eyes don't cry.
My gait is halt, my dreams, awry.
My scores are soiled; my players gasify.
My songs are gone, my kin in mass graves lie.
For crumbs of bread my soul I'd sell, but there's no one left to buy.

A TRIBUTE TO THE MEMORY OF ANTON SCHMIDT*

*A German army sergeant who gave help to the Jewish underground. He was executed in March 1942.

In a time of cowardice, you were heroic.
In a time of mob hysteria, you retained reason.
In a time of injustice, you were righteous.
In a time of intimidation, you were stalwart.
In a time of crippled morality, you were a saint.
Christ's blood surged through your soul,
And you paid the same price.
Your name is honored among the martyrs.

THE LORE OF CHELM: AMUSING AND TRAGIC

The tales of Chelm are hanging from branches of every tree
    Like clothes that's almost laundered for the entire world to see
That some with reputed wisdom are nothing more than fools
    Although they have been enlightened in the very best of schools.
Remember when the snow had fallen and was already four feet deep
    And the sun sparkled upon it as Chelm awoke from sleep?
The wise men wanted to preserve the white blanket on display,
    So they walked through the streets of Chelm telling the people,
"Stay indoors today!"
    Remember when they snared the moon to be the first to bless its face?
They brought a pail of water to capture its shining grace?
    All gathered at the synagogue and watched the pail 'till dawn,
But when the wise men finished inside, the moon had already gone.

That was the Chelm of fiction, it courses through our veins
    Bringing our lives some laughter to pacify our brains.
But there is a Chelm of fact where folks toiled every day,
    When a twist of history took their lives away.*
The moon is seen no more, because the wise men, fools and innocents
    Were slaughtered in Hitler's war.

At *that* Chelm the night is dark, the moon is seen no more,
    Because the wise men, fools, and innocents
Were slaughtered in Hitler's war.

---

*By November, 1942 the yeshiva orphanage, home for the aged, and its 700 year old synagogue were destroyed and all the Jews were liquidated at Sobibor.

FOON BRAWCHIZ TSU K'LAWLIZ*

*From Benedictions to Curses; (Brawchot [Brawchiz] is also the name of a Book of the Talmud)

The new moon was yet to be born. Vilna was dark and of wet ashes stank.
    The Street of the Jews was a cemetery: lifeless, rotting, dank.
Rising from fresh-dug graves brash youths clothed in blackish dress
    Skulked through alleys until they reached the address

Of the printers: THE WIDOW AND BROTHERS ROMM,
    Publishers of the Talmud.
Without a whisper they approached the plates
    Containing B'rachot, the first Mishnah they'd studied.
Shraga grabbed the leaden letters and mused over the sh'ma recitaltime;
    Itzig scrambled "Hillel" with "Shamai" and laid waste their paradigm.

Say it with "kavanah" spelled Hirsch's letters.
    Schloymeh with a turn of his wrist,
The exemptions for mourners and newlyweds
    From saying the Sh'ma filled his fist.
At their deconstruction of the Talmud the seminarians
    Worked deep into the night
And weighed themselves down with letters of words they used to recite.

Into the gloom of Vilna's streets the bearers of Talmudic bits and pieces
    Moved slowly back to their graves and emptied their valises.
They melted the leaden letters and made bullets that would kill
    Nazi soldiers on patrol with Yeshiva students' skill.
And so history will remember those who took the B'rachot's verses
    Melted them down in their graves and then made Jewish curses.

GENERAL PATTON: WE'VE BEEN TO CAMP

Unloved, worthless, displaced, shaved-head, a grotesque toothless smile,
    They wandered like delirious cadavers out of their heinous exile.
The death camp faded in a surreal mist but not from their memories
    Where forever locked, fated to be are death, degradation, and disease.

General Patton snarled, unmoved by their plight,
    Get this fecal subhuman species out of my sight.
The survivors were ordered with aplomb personified,
    Back to Poland where in pogroms once more they died.

JOSEPH, JOSEPH YOU'RE MY BROTHER*

*In Honor of Pope John XXIII

"Though You and I have different mothers Joseph, Joseph, we are brothers.
    When I reach out to touch your hand take it, take it and understand
That darkest nights bred deeds unjust but dawning,
    Dawning are days of trust.
Join with me to hear God's voice whisper, whisper,
    "Treasured heirs rejoice
In this world I've created in love. Mend it! Mend it!
    Send forth the dove!"

YOU ARE OUR BROTHERS*

*Pope John Paul II took turns with the Chief rabbi of Rome reading psalms in the synagogue of Rome Reference to brotherhood is seen also in the words of a previous pope, John XXII.

Reading from the Psalms Pope John Paul II
    looked into the tear-filled face of the Chief Rabbi of Rome
In the synagogue sanctuary in Rome, saying, *achaynu*,
    Dearly beloved brothers, our elder brothers.
Catholic and Jew embraced each other
    In peace that dissolved the enmity of the centuries.

DEAR LILLIAN*

*Lillian Hellman, the author, downplayed Anne Frank's *Jewish* character

How could you deny that the Frank girl who kept a diary suffered
    And died because she was a Jewess?
The holocaust was a travesty, against civilization;
    You are a tragedy for confiscation
Of your heritage and severing your lineage.

THE LIGHT OF ISRAEL BECKONS

I, lamp unto the nations, beckon all from near and far:
    From America, Asia, and Europe.
Come, be you contented or hard-up. Observant or secular.
    Come, no matter the color of your skin; come,
No matter the origin of your kin.
    Come be you rich or poor; well-known or obscure.
Come be you survivor with numbered wrist, pogrom victim of the iron-fist.
    Come no matter your work: merchant, teacher, artist, clerk.
Come to my shore and nevermore will you be strangers in a strange land.

I SURVIVED

I survived exile to Babylon I survived Roman destruction of the Temple
    "Though I'm dragged from place to place.
I survived the Spanish Inquisition
    Although I was made to leave the faith of my ancestors.
I survived the Haskalah, the enlightenment
    Which blackened my Jewish soul.
I survived the Nazi terror which set my body ablaze.
    I survived because my heart is with the God of Zion.
I dangle like an acrobat between reason and mystery."

HOW I YEARN TO RETURN

How I yearn to return to the land where I was born
    And stroll through the age-old scenery
And watch the limbs of the date palm trees
    Clacking in the breeze and listen to the birds sing their morning song.
How I yearn to return to the hills burnished bright
    By the sun shining through cobalt skies
Awakening the gleam asleep in my eyes to give the lily its golden smile;
    The grass its verdant green; and all of God's creature their sheen.
How I yearn to return to hills Amos climbed to admonish sinners,
    To the roads pilgrims strode bearing gifts for the priests,
To the blood-stained fields where the brave were felled
    In defense of the land,
To the haven on earth, a gift from God to redeem
    The martyrs of yesterdays,
To vaporous vineyards cascading sacred succulent grapes,
    And to kneel at the site of my mother's grave.
How I yearn to return with a heart filled with joy
    To streets where I played when I was a boy,
To the synagogue where I a bar mitzvah became
    To that utopian country which sets my yearning aflame.

        Israel! Israel! I return.

I SURVIVED AUSCHWITZ

They took away my houses, they shaved off my hair
    They poked at my circumcision and snickered.
They violated my vulva and sneered
    They stole the contours that define what I see.

They took my shoes, my dresses, my underwear;
    They yanked gold fillings from my teeth and made jewelry;
They turned my Torah into toilet paper.
    But they did not take away my dreams.

They filled my ears with shouting
    They filled my mind with debris
They filled my lungs with gas
    And then they ignited me.

Tongues of red-hot flame turned my body to ashes.
    My ashes fouled the air,
My cinders filled the clouds,
    And my blood drenched the earth.

Messengers of hate you failed to erase me;
    Soldiers of darkness you lost the battle of human dignity.
I survived to tell the story to my children
    And they will to theirs for all generations.

DEAR MR. EICHMANN*

*Based on a letter to the English edition of *The Jordanian Times* published in Jerusalem. "dhimmi" are the despised.

Dear Mr. Eichmann, venerable Adolf,
I congratulate you on conferring a blessing on humanity
By liquidating six million despised dhimmi of the ancestry of Satan.
I mean the curse'd Jews. (I spit three times). You, sir, are a saint.

A LETTER FROM LATRUN*

*A major battle to free Jerusalem prior to Israel's statehood

Dearest Mother,

I hope this letter I write will not be received;
If it is, you will surely be bereaved.
In case I <u>do</u> join my ancestors
Know that I fought like the bravest of warriors.
Scared I am. Even greater an emotion than fear
Is my determination to open the road to Jerusalem
Not only to feed and uncage the lion of Judah and feed the besieged
But to write a page in history
That we have returned to our homeland
To live here in this sacred land in dignity.
I have not slept for two nights and I do not know where I find my energy
But I am wide awake and vigilant.
All around me cannons roar by day; artillery flashes jab the night sky;
And I never know where a grenade will explode.
The horns blows its hot winds;
There is little water to quench my thirst;
At times I think my kidneys will burst.
Hamsin flies by the millions buzz in my nose, my ears, my eyes.
I feel immersed in a waterless mikveh and "purified" by flies.
Although many young brave freedom fighters have gone to their eternity,
Here in Latrun the morale among the survivors is high.
I do not wish to belittle our leaders-
And I ask God for forgiveness for doing so-
But our generals have underestimated the foe.
How skilled and canny are the Jordanians
And how much woe they have inflicted upon us.

We call the Intelligence people arrogant dumb-dumbs;
Intelligence in their case is an oxymoron.
They are haughty and their assessments are faulty.
Still we fight on literally and figuratively
And if I do not see you again in this world
I know we will meet and embrace in the world to come.

    Your loving son

JERUSALEM. THE NEW

Through your keen-sighted eyes, Daniel, I can now see Jerusalem
A newborn crawling out of an ancient womb
Bearing crosses, crescents, and stars of David up the sacred mounts
And beating them into plowshares.

BROTHERS FOREVER NOW

Ahmad killed and lies there dead;
    His blood was spilled; his foe, too, bled.
Unwanted since the day of birth;
    Haunted by denied self-worth,
He wrestled his brother to win some land,
    A lush oasis in the desert sand.
That soil no one from him can sever;
    It covers his coffin forever and ever.

His parents scream in dreadful grief;
    His children wail without relief.
Joseph killed and lies there dead;
    His blood was spilled; his foe, too, bled.
Ahmad and Joseph lay side by side
    At the place where both had died.
From their graves rise anguished cries,
    Their own deaths to eulogize.

Although their souls are pocked with tears
    Their absurd deaths have made them peers.
Hand in hand the corpses trod.
    Hiding their faces, they confronted God:
Must hostages to history be youth's promised fate
    Replaying a script of ancient hate?
Teach our children to abjure strife
    And more than land to cherish life.

MY BROTHER'S WEEPER

Ahmad and Joseph, each conceived in love,
    Entered this world on the wings of a dove,
But suckled on poison at the breasts of their mothers
    And learned lessons of hate in schools with their brothers.
They maimed, they killed, and brought on much woe
    To themselves, their kin, as well as their foe.
Then each took a bride, a wife to adore
    And repeated the cycle etched in his lore:
To fight the other for months and for years
    Then stand around graves shedding his tears.

LOST YOUTH. GAINED LIBERTÉ*

*Inspired by the experience of Rabbi Albert Gabbai now of Philadelphia imprisoned by Egyptian police in 1958.

Sergeant Ahmed Muhamet of the Cairo Barracks
With a sardonic smile and a glinting gold-capped tooth
Said three minutes, "It would take to fill out a form
'Allah Akbar,' and you can go home." Sly was he and uncouth.

Slipping 'neath the horizon was the westering sun.
Shabbat was approaching and I, an eighteen year old youth,
Longed to taste my mother's challah, sing Shabbat z'mirot,
And savor Sabbath's blessings of Beauty and Truth.

My papers? I had none. "Aha, my son
We'll get you some." He shoved me on to a lorry
With old men about to sin by riding on the Sabbath
Pleading with the merciful God "I'm sorry; I'm sorry."

I anguished about my mother; my stomach did flip flops
But protested not fearing the crematory.
Three minutes turned into three years of hard labor,
Incredible food, and daily worry.

No sanitation. Emaciation. Degradation. Humiliation.
Stagnation. Vexation. Agitation. Damnation.

Why, oh, why had I been robbed of my boyhood?
In 1958 Israel was at war
And I was to be a pawn in the redemption
Of the Egyptian generals captured by the score.

Then one day, without any warning,
I was prodded onto a lorry with seven others
And driven away. Where? to an abandoned field?
Why? To be killed with my brothers?

At dusk we stopped at an airport.
The westering sun was dropping below the horizon.
I was given a paper saying that I am a French national.
Clutching my passport I was jetted to freedom.

LAST NIGHT THE WORLD WAS FILLED WITH RAGE

Last night the world was filled with rage that Reason could not assuage.
    Bombs exploded; missiles scudded. Streets were flooded with debris.
Anarchy reigned. Law was suspended and the dead lay unattended.

Dead are the seekers of thrill; dead are the one who would kill
    To settle an ancient slight to show the world that only they are right.
Dead are the counselors that ruled the city dead
    Are the dullards and the witty.

And the children who were lucky to survive and the children
    Who were lucky to be alive
Said, this must never happen again if girls are to be women
    And boys to be men.
And they cleared the debris and pledged to live in amity.

A doctrine or rite; an insult or slight
    That diminishes anyone diminishes everyone.

AFTERMATH OF THE YOM KIPPUR WAR

Now the war is over; my brothers are no longer here.
They gave their lives to their country because they held it dear.
Still I can't help wondering if there is another way
To staunch the flow of hatred without a bloody fray.
I don't suppose there'll ever be. So heated were the raging powers
That budding plants are ripped apart before blossoming into flowers.
Arab neighbors you are my kin, each of us Abraham's scion.
Let's grow together in God's garden in the land of Zion.

REMEMBERING PRIME MINISTER RABIN

Rabin, the sun rose and the sun shone
    Hope for peace was again reborn.
A voice rose above the crowd saying let's cleanse the air of hate;
    Sing with me a song of peace.
Then shots rang out, and you were dead
    And the finest prayers will not bring you back.
But, Rabin, know you well that though your blood spilled on sacred ground
    Your song of peace in our hearts resound.

HEAVEN'S GIFT

In the sacred silence of the stillest night watched forever
    By stars glistening and bright,
I hear the hymns the angels sing and beckon to the peace they're offering.
    I add to theirs my voice muted carried by the zephyrs,
Mellow and fluted.
    It returns to me with God's gift to share.
"Peace for everyone, everywhere."

ISRAEL, LAND OF BEAUTY

There is a land where mountains high send out its arms to reach the sky
    And sheep graze upon hills of green and mountain goats climb
The rugged ravine.
    Birds of every hue fly to places new
And a sea rolls in the shimmering sun bringing peace to everyone.
    Where every Jew can have a home and on seven continents
No more need roam.

ONE KID MAY HE REST IN PEACE*

*This poem follows the model of the Passover counting song, "Chad Gadya"-One Kid is based on a true story.

One Kid, a Russian emigre, son of a Jewish father,
    A dear kid with a promising career as a scientist,
Was buying food with two zuzim at the Mehaneh Yehudah Market.
    And then came a terrorist who exploded himself
And mangled many bodies including One Kid, a Russian emigre,
    Son of a Jewish father.
Then came a geneticist who through DNA testing identified
    Grigory Pesahovic,
A Russian emigre, who was buying food in the Mahaneh Yehudah Market
    With two zuzim.
And then came a father who wanted to bury his son's body,
    Identified by the geneticist from the remains
Mangled by an exploding terrorist
    In the Mahaneh Yehudah Market where One Kid,
Son of a Jewish father, was buying food with two zuzim.
    And then came a cemetery guardian who refused
The father burial permission
    Of a non-Jewish mother's kid, identified
By a geneticist from mangled remains
    By a terrorist who exploded himself in the Mahaneh Yehudah Market
Where One Kid, son of a Jewish father,
    Was buying food with two zuzim.
And then came a compassionate Greek Orthodox priest who,
    With fifteen mourners,
Under a hot summer sun, brought to a Christian cemetery the coffin
    With the remains of One Kid whose Jewish father
Had been refused burial
    By its guardian in a Jewish cemetery after a geneticist identified them

Because the explosion of the terrorist mangled the body
    In the Mahaneh Yehudah Market where One Kid
Was buying food with two zuzim.
    And then came the gentile mother who did not allow her son
To be buried in a Christian cemetery

By a compassionate Greek Orthodox priest who offered such burial
    After the father had been refused by the guardian
Of a Jewish cemetery burial
    Of the geneticist—identified remains of a terrorist explosion
In the Mahaneh Yehudah Market where One Kid
    Was buying food with two zuzim.
And then came a hearse to return the coffin to the morgue
    Of the Hadassah Hospital
Stopped by the boy's mother from burial by a compassionate
    Greek Orthodox priest
After the father had been refused by the guardian
    Of a Jewish cemetery burial
Of his son's geneticist-identified terrorist exploded remains
    From the Mahaneh Yehudah Market where One Kid
Was buying food with two zuzim.
    And then, days later, at the fringes of Givat Shaul cemetery,
In a Bahai-owned lot, were lowered the remains of One Kid
    In the coffin taken from the morgue of the Hadassah Hospital
Because a gentile mother did not permit a compassionate
    Greek Orthodox priest
Under a hot summer sun to bury the geneticist-identified remains,
    Denied burial by the guardian of the Jewish cemetery,
From a terrorist explosion in the Mahaneh Yehudah Market
    Where One Kid, son of a Jewish father,
Was buying food for two zuzim.
    And then came the Blessed, the Holy One,
Weeping copious tears over the tragedies.

OMRI JADAH: ZA TS AL*

*Remember the righteous one for a blessing

The mood was jovial at the Sea of Galilee that day* *August 5, 2000
    Barbecues were cooking kebabs and teenagers
Played games teenagers play.
    Boats were lolling in the emerald waves
And people of many races and creeds
    Bathed in the cooling waters where politics never intercedes.

Little George Leftov happily swam until he started to drown.
    "Help me! Help me." he cried as he bobbed up and down.
There in the middle of the lake—no longer afloat.
    His little voice was lost in the middle of his throat.

Struggling, the fledgling flailed his arms.
    When Omri Jadah, a plain Arab man,
Who was eying the horizon its beauty to scan
    Beheld tiny arms slashing the water.
There was only one thing to do: Save the drowning
    child—Whether it be Muslim or Jew.

He swam out and grabbed the boy and towed him
    Though his body was sore
And handed him to a friend waiting at the shore.
    There then came a strong undertow and dragged Omri away.
He never regained consciousness in hospital where he lay.

And solemnly thousands marched to honor a brother,
    A saintly hero whose heart knew only love for another.
Omri, Omri, victim of an errant tide;
    Omri, Omri you are righteousness personified!

ISRAEL DESPITE YOUR FAULTS YOU HAVE MY LOVE

After almost two thousand years of exile I have returned to you.
Your arms are wide open to embrace me, an anonymous Jew.
You have given dignity to downtrodden of every land
And have warmly welcomed those who are banned.
I enjoy a house, good health, and a skill
And will pass these to my children, if that's God's will.
I have fought in the wars to protect the nation
And was there for the Wall's liberation.
There are times when I am dismayed
That Jews stone Jews when they prayed
And Jews of color are denied a chance to build up their pride.
But I never give up the hope for the land of Israel's kaleidoscope.

THE LEMBA PETITION*

*The Lemba is a group from South Africa whose customs and rites are similar to Jewish groups elsewhere. Like the Ashkenazim and S'fardim, approximately 54% of the males in the elite Buba group have the kohane modal haplotype.

We are your dark skinned sisters and brothers with Jewish genes
    From our fathers and mothers.
Make room for us at your table and call us Jew. That is our label.
    We eat only kosher, never mixing milk and meat;
We dance in the synagogue to an ancient beat.
    We circumcise our males; we recite Torah tales
Which in our conversations are quoted
    Because our souls to God are devoted.
Our elite Buba clan have the Kohan DNA and on Shabbat
    We gather at the synagogue to pray.
There a wall proudly displays David's shield. And our hearts
    Throb with God, to us revealed.
Toward the North do we bury our dead;
    Toward Jerusalem do we place each head.
Muslims and Christians have us, too, afflicted
    And many a wound have upon us inflicted.
We are David's children in joy and misery though
    Lost in the byways of Jewish history.
We are the ebony in God's sacred spectrum
    Extend your hands and bid us welcome.
Receive us in peace at your table and call us Jew.
    That is our label.

SARAJEVO, 1998

In Sarajevo where hate oozes from every blade of grass,
Where malice blows from every gust of wind,
Where loathing flows with every rivulet,
Where rancor overthrows the sun in the sky,
Where bombs burst and deafen the ears, where fires rage and blind the eyes,
Jews save Muslims from marauding hordes
As Muslims saved Jews from the Nazi abattoir.
And in a ramshackle Jewish community center*,
Jewish children huddle with their Muslim friends
To study, play, laugh, sing, hope, and pray that doves of peace
Will nest within their innocent beings and staunch the flood of blood
So emerald grass will glow with love,
Zephyrs will hover in peace, rivulets will flow with kindness,
The sun will glow with mercy, ears will fill with happy tunes,
And eyes will behold the flowers of June.

*The elders of Zion feed, clothe, and give medical aid to the needy, seven of every eight are Muslims. During a Purim celebration a Muslim girl played the role of Esther and implored Ahasuerus to prevent the evil Haman from performing genocide on her people.

A DROP OF OIL AM I: THE HOLOCAUST EXPERIENCE

A drop of oil am I afloat on a sea of sorrow
Ever searching to coalesce with a kindred globule
But crinkled by other disconnected dabs who submerge me.
Still I rise up ever more determined yet still alone
And seeking to be united in love.

INGATHERING OF THE REMNANTS OF ISRAEL

Thrown out was I from my home to wander here and there
    Seeking a haven to dwell in but found nothing but despair.
I wound around mountain passes; I crossed rushing rivers cold,
    I trudged across the desert sands for an oasis to unfold.

I, the dhimmi, skulked in culverts flooded; I, the zhid,
    Hid inside bramble dense;
I, the marrano*, masqueraded as a Christian,
    Ashamed at my pretense. *pig
Then I heard a shofar blowing from the distant past,
    It beckoned me to return with each redeeming blast.

Scattered and forlorn was I until a home I found
    In Israel's hallowed soil where milk and honey abound.
Here I have found a haven where hope heals every woe
    Here I found an oasis where healing waters flow.

THERE WAS NO HOLOCAUST. BUT THERE WAS!

Drunken louts were weaving their way down Nowolipki
Street shouting, the Holocaust is another Jewish deceit.
Someone kicked a milk can covered with rust
Scattering all about gusts of dust
That awoke the ghosts of the One Shabbat* folk
Whose bodies had years ago gone up in smoke.
Their eyes had seen rape, beheading, and fire;
Their ears had heard the crackling of babes on a pyre;
Their stomachs ached for food to eat;
Their spirits sagged in utter defeat;
Pitted skin itched having been bitten by lice;
Faces were pocked having been nibbled by mice.
Ashes rose from the minds once wise;
And incinerated lips smiled in satirical guise.
All the facts were there for the world to know
Held throughout the war in escrow.
And from their places in heaven above
Embraced with tears by the God of Love
Who from every predicament their souls was buffering.
"Blessed be those whom fate saved from Suffering."

*The Oneg Shabbat society were archivists of the Warsaw Ghetto. They noted all aspects of daily life, including atrocities. Their notes were placed in metal containers, one of which languished at 68 Nowolipki Street. Some members of the society joined the freedom fighters. Most, however, were sent to Chelmno and Treblinka and perished. The final line is from a note found in a milk can many years after World War II.

MY PEOPLE IS LIKE A KALEIDOSCOPE

My people is like a kaleidoscope
An aggregation of many shapes and colors
Wandering about in a cylinder,
As our ancestors did in Egypt's deserts.
Revolving and rotating in arrangements that captivate
The parts combine in patterns which fascinate,
Reflecting motifs geometric,
Harmonious and symmetric.
No matter the design one beholds,
A people of beauty poignantly unfolds.

ISRAEL SURVIVES

Swarms of moths spawned in hate
Gnawed with rage Israel's flag of state.
But its cloth was spun of cactus spines
And David's star still brightly shines.

MY PEOPLE IS EVOLVING

Like the stars in the skies above us that's how many
    We can be Shining since
Time began and will for eternity.
    How much we have changed since Moses gave the Law;
How much we have remained the same by revering God with awe.

Foes we have had in very age; friends we've had who championed our way
    Who shared their bounty with us and comforted in our dismay.
For two thousand years we wandered in deserts far and wide
    And now we have a homeland where in peace we seek to reside.

We are many people of every sort of race
    Who rejoice on every holiday wrapped
In the faith that we embrace. Perfect? No.
    We still Sinai's mount are ascending.
But with respect and love for neighbor folk toward God's love
    We are ever wending.

AS ISRAEL KEPT THE SABBATH SO HAS THE SABBATH KEPT ISRAEL

THE SABBATH: DIVINE ZENITH.

The Sabbath is a festival that has united the Jews for millennia. Study, prayer, and song are interwoven. The Bible is studied; psalms are read; prayers are chanted. The mood is festive. Joy prevails; there is to be no mourning. It is the pinnacle of the week. Labor ceases and the day is devoted to renewal. So many family traditions have grown up around the Friday evening meal. Candles are kindled. Wine and bread are sanctified. Smiles replace frowns; songs replace laments; forgiveness replaces anger. The setting sun paints the soul in festive hues, flavors the food with holiness, and imbues the people with hope. The Sabbath is a day when God and people reach for each other to create a mood of peace.

BLESSED ARE THE CANDLES

Blessed are the candles that we kindle Sabbath eve;
Blessed is God above whose kindness we receive.

SHABBAT AND THE EARTH HAS FINISHED ITS DAILY ROUND

Shabbat and the earth has finished its daily round
    And we sit at the table spellbound.
No longer is there a frantic pace; no longer is the talk of the common place.
    The house is quiet, mystically still. Shabbat has arrived and good will
Hovers about the family. The word rife with discord is subdued by amity.
    Before us is the challah with its stylistic twists
Kneaded with love by mother's wrists.
    Then mother, dressed in her finest lace,
With a tender smile upon her face,
    Blesses the candles in whispers warm and soft
And sends her sagging spirits to cleansing zephyrs aloft.
    God, Source of my strength, she prays, imbue us
With the will Your mitsvot to gladly do.
    She kisses each of us on the forehead and the Shabbat soul
About us is spread.
    Father's eyes begin to shine when he rises to bless the wine.
And we join in and sing that song to say that it's to God that we belong.
    In our own ways we all Shabbat adorn and to holiness are again reborn.

MOTHER WHISPERS HER PRAYERS

Mother whispers her prayers beckoning
    God's splendor to illuminate our lives.
The fading rays of the Sun fill the room;
    Candlelight flickers on our faces.
Our feeble voices rise to sing,
    "Welcome angels, enter. Bless you.
Bring peace this Sabbath" Seraphim stirring
    In the Garden of The Lord attune
To the heartfelt invitation dawdling in their ears.
    They gather about the golden flames
And sing in chords sublime,
    The ancient greeting from the Lord,
"Peace unto you, this Sabbath day."
    With outstretched wings they enrobe our souls
With calm before they fly away.

AS SHABBAT DRAWS NEAR

As Shabbat draws near and bright stars in the night sky start
    To appear the tempo of life is slowing.
Thoughts turn to amnesty from self-inflicted anguish
    And to probing the mystery in God's design.
We recall those whom we cherish: loved one of now
    And those long gone
Who by their virtue still nourish us
    When we are with them or all alone.
We beckon angels to surround us with rest
    And to revive our weary bodies.
Imbue us, we pray, with the zest to savor
    Divine pleasures with rapture.

THE SPARKLING CANDLES ILLUMINATE OUR WAY

The sparkling Sabbath candles illuminate our steps through
    The dark paths of life and chase despair away.

ON SABBATH WE PAUSE FROM DAILY ROUTINE

On Sabbath we pause from daily routine
    And marvel at the wonders of creation
And warmly welcome the Sabbath queen
    With song in celebration.

BLESSED ARE WE WITH SABBATH BEAUTY

Blessed are we with Sabbath beauty, spreading its splendor bright.
Blessed are we with Sabbath peace that will reign throughout this night.
Blessed are we with Sabbath balm that makes an afflicted body right.
Blessed are we with Sabbath joy that grants our souls delight.

NOT BY MYSTIC CHARIOT

Not by mystic chariot to heaven do I ascend
    To sit by God's sovereign throne;
Nor rung by rung up Jacob's ladder climb to reach
    The threshold of God's splendor
But held in the arms of Sabbath angels I rise
    And Divine portals divide
Amid the sounding of trumpets welcomed
    Am I to God's majestic sanctuary.

WELCOME SABBATH WE SING TOGETHER

Welcome Sabbath we sing together; welcome Sabbath we sing alone.
Welcome Sabbath we pray you bring the peace that God has sown.

HOW GOOD IT IS TO CELEBRATE THIS SABBATH

How good it is to celebrate this Sabbath day of rest.
When all words end and thoughts turn to how richly we are blessed.

SILENTLY SETS THE AURIC SUN

The moment before the Sabbath unfolds, silently sets the auric sun
Over the hallowed horizon where it meets the ceaseless sea of Time.
Work is stopped, and burdens are made light.
Our whispering souls invite God to rest with us today.

MIRIAM'S DAUGHTERS JOIN HANDS

Miriam's daughters throughout the world join hands with one another
To pray for peace as their mothers did while blessing the scintillating
flames. Circle hands, circle the candles as the earth circles the sun
And meets the hallowed horizon at the ageless sea of Time.

AS THE SABBATH DAY IS GROWING NIGH

As Sabbath day is growing nigh and the week's work is done,
We ascend the heights to the Most High to embrace The Holy One.
There in the midst of Sacred Space where a gentle zephyr blows
Cloaked are we in Heavenly grace and serenity within us glows.

SIX DAYS EACH WEEK WE TOIL

Six days each week we toil with zest
    And on Sabbath day we renew our quest
To discover God all around in every sight, in every sound;
    In every secret the seed discloses;
In every tune the songsmith composes;
    In every canvas the artist paints;
In every passion endured by saints;
    In every thought of the blessèd sages;
And in every battle the physician wages.
    But highest on the list we compile
We find You, God, in every smile.

WHEN WORK FOR THE WEEK IS DONE

When work for the week is done
    And the sea reaches up to wash the sun,
Mothers whisper the ancient prayer appealing
    For peace as candles glare.
In a moment of silence, soft and still,
    Holy Seraphim rendezvous to fill
The Garden of Heaven in a bouquet of white
    As they listen to the Sabbath rite
Inviting them to enter each home
    With the joyous song "To you shalom."
Then gates of Heaven open wide
    And Seraphim carry the Sabbath bride
To all those who earnestly pray
    For God's blessing on this day.
They hover about the candle lights
    And sing their anthem throughout the night
With voices soft, sweet, sublime stretched
    To the very ends of Time.
In the morning we awake renewed
    And with your Spirit are again imbued.

'ROUND THE SUN THE EARTH HAS SPUN

'Round and 'round the Earth has spun in endless trek about the sun.
    Now as evening shadows fall wrapping Earth in dusky shawl,
The remaining plumes of feathered light dissolve inside the ebon night.
    Welcome Shabbat which God has blessed
And ordained for all a day of rest.
    Six days we've toiled and we've languished;
At life we've roiled and we've anguished.
    But now candles are lighted, and all cares cease
And in our souls is Sabbath peace.

MY MOTHER'S SABBATH CANDLESTICKS

My mother's Sabbath candlesticks stood proudly side by side
Just as God, The King, had stood next to Sabbath Queen, his bride.
On Sabbath eve mother would fill the cups so worn
With candles chaste and simple which would our home adorn.
With fingers frail she'd straighten the wicks leaning here and there
And striking a match made them glow with a golden glare.
Wisps of flame would spiral as my mother hid her eyes
While whispering the ancient blessings Sabbath to solemnize.
Angels would their wings unfurl, bringing peace to our anguished souls
And cloaking us in Sabbath rest as set down in the holy scrolls.
Many Sabbaths have come and gone many candles have been blessed,
But the flame of peace that mother roused glows daily within my breast.

THE WEEKLY QUEST FOR SHABBAT

Shabbat, apogee of the week,
    Elevates Jews out of their daily trough
Ever higher toward a celestial crest.
    Throughout history have they,
Breccia of civilization, upheaval after upheaval,
    Scintillating like sun bathed stones
Bonded together by Torah attained Shabbat peace.
    Sometimes presto; sometimes agitato; seldom adagio.
This scattered collection wanders in the sea of Time
    Whose pelagic synchrony, at the pleasure of the merciful Moon,
Undulates gracefully seeking out the next Shabbat
    When their souls again will rise
In whorls and eddy toward the sublime.

FILL EVERY EMPTY SPACE

Fill every empty space
    With the peace the Shabbat angel wings;
Fill every grain of silence
    With the songs the Shabbat angel sings;
Fill every vacant moment
    With the love the Shabbat angel brings.

        AND LET US SAY AMEN!

VI

FIGMENTS

This is a volume of stories arising out of my fancy and fabricated to bring joy to readers who may have experienced some of these events. Please free to build on them or experience them as is.

SUNDRIES

WHERE THERE'S A WILL

1.

I pondered how to tell my story. There was a storm, a hurricane that devastated the Northeast. There was a funeral. There was a tour of the Jewish Home For The Aged. Guilt. Forgiveness. There were couples dancing to Frank Sinatra. There was a seeming nuisance woman wearing an SS pin. There was a partially blind retired pharmacist who had no luck in love until he met Miriam, a widow. Both fell in love with Shakespeare's sonnets. So there you have it. It unfolds page by page although it happened in a lifetime. Read on.

Well, one fall day a storm brewing in the Atlantic near the Carolinas whipped its way up the East Coast damaging houses and flooding roads. The next day the sun came out and beamed its rays on Max Greenberg. A smile formed on his lips. Even he did not believe he could be happy. Not that he was a grouch it was just that life had exhausted and eroded his ego, as it does to so many. Work! And now retirement and diabetes with diminished vision. Oy vay. He said he was getting blind but not yet. His cab drove up to Hebrew Home for the Aged. The driver yanked the knob of the heavy oaken door and Max shyly glanced inside. The Star of David artistically sculpted on the door etched hope in his lonely, drab life. He muttered, "Is this where I belong?" "Yes! Yes! " he emphatically called out to no one in particular. He watched some old men laughing, their shoulders rising and falling in rhythm. He sighed and his heart beat a rapid rhythm. DUM, DUM, DUM, DUM, DUM. Gene Krupa. "At last!" he exhaled. The cabbie dropped two suitcases on the floor with a thud and held out his hand. The short stooped man looked back as his taxi sped away dodging fallen limbs and leaving a trail of gray, dusty road debris. The driver ignored the patches of orange and red that autumn painted on the trees as well as the contours of the road and vanished into the horizon. "The driver?" Max grumbled that the driver was a feckless, ignorant, ungrateful Pakistani who spoke no English. No smile. No salem aleykem! No thank you for a 35% tip. Just an indifferent robot moving other robots from one place to another.

"Don't look back," Max chided himself, "The future is here." Ben Zoma, The Talmud scholar, stated in the Sayings of the Elders, "Who is wise? One who learns from others." But what could he learn from the cab driver? "Control your impatience Max; control your temper." He had developed the habit of talking to himself: "Max this; Max that." Then the voice of his conscience, Hillel, another Talmud scholar, spoke from his 2000 years ago abode, jabbing him, "If I'm only for myself what am I? Right before the Days of Awe you maligned a man, a stranger trying his utmost to support his wife and children here and his parents in the old country." Max felt utter shame and remorse. His soul grew scarlet with sin; his face, beet red with chagrin.

Miss Lily Riger, the Home manager, appeared. Max smelled the lavender scent of a woman. Miss Lily was a tall blonde woman with a ringlet coif. She wore long dangling earrings that dazzled the eye with scintilla in the light like liquid jewels sparkling and twinkling as if dancing the tango. Max Greenberg apologized to her. "How can I help you?" Without warning a shabbily dressed woman accosted him. Her russet hair was tangled. Her torn slippers grazed her tattered bathrobe which revealed an unraveling asymmetric buttoned woolen sweater embroidered SS fastened with a cameo broach. Grabbing his arm, she caterwauled "I'm Sarah Stein. Sarah, you know, means 'princess.' From the Bible. Abraham's wife. My father, may he rest in peace, was chief rabbi of Lawrence Point." Sarah had a face like a striated cantaloupe sitting on top of a chunky body. Stepping up her pace, Miss Lily scowled. She gave Sarah a stern, rebuking look to shoo her away. As was her wont after being rebuked, Sarah's screwed her lips into an apostrophe.

Just then. Several undertakers in slate uniforms rolled a boxed corpse toward the exit. "DON'T LOOK NOW," Miss Lily spat in alarm. "People enter here and exit." Max looked away, his heart throbbing. That will happen to him. "Mrs. Levine left behind a legacy of kindness. Not just kindness but a legacy of funds we can draw on for repairs to restrooms and gardens. But avert your eyes." She spat again. Max recovered his composure and tried to smile his approval, of what he was not sure. His heart beat again like Gene Krupa. He imagined a casket opened and dancing corpse inviting him to do a Gene Kelly with him.

"Be careful," Miss Lily warned as Max tripped on a parked rollator. The parked vehicle fell on a motorized wheelchair. She made a mental note to make a parking space for these conveyances. "Always be sure your blind cane can be seen. Wave it now and again to be sure. Max grabbed his cane and waved it in the air. Miss Lily smiled her approval. She and Greenberg strolled until they reached Max's unit. He asked, "Who IS that woman?" Why does she have an embroidered SS? Doesn't she realize what SS means to a Jew escaping Nazi crematoria?" Miss Lily groaned, her hairdo bouncing as they walked, "Oy! She iyuz a nebesh and we feel sorry for her. She's not ower typical resident. You all." The two shrugged their shoulders in disbelief.

Miss Lily showed him his deluxe unit equipped with refrigerator, TV, washing machine. Dishwasher, microwave, plus many more amenities. There was a telephone extension in every room, Including the lavatory. Helping him unpack his cases, he told her he would do it himself later. She invited him to have dinner "on the hawmlisse". She corrected herself "on The Hoe-wam". They strolled toward the Dining Hall. He expected a din. But there was no noise; no wild cafeteria clanging dishes. Was he surprised! The dining area was spacious. Spotless, and serene. The wallpaper was flecked with gold; a crystal chandelier hung from the ceiling, highlighting the ambience of the dining area. The napkins were linen and matched the wallpaper. Not that Max saw any of this. Miss Lily described the decor to him. The food was uncommonly tasty. Soft music wafted in the air. Tommy Dorsey, Glenn Miller, Sammy Kaye. An old couple bounced up and down doing the Lindy. A couple rolling their wheelchairs to the music laughed heartily. The man and the woman had misshapen faces, most likely from a stroke. Max sat at a table with several affable men. They told him that his remaining days will not be spent more happily than at The Home. Making this an ideal place to live were a caring medical staff, a good exercise room, an Olympic size swimming pool, weekly movies, monthly concerts, lectures, and a bus that goes to museums, theater, ball games, and markets. "Are they boasting? Max asked himself." Later he found that the claim was true. That's what the shiny brochure he had received also explained. Sarah Stein stopped by and grabbed Greenberg's arm, "I'm Sarah Stein. Sarah, you know, means 'princess'. My father, may he rest in peace, was chief rabbi of Lawrence Point." Chuckling, the men urged him to pay no attention to her. The poor woman, more witless than a loon was harmless. "She will needle you if you let her." Miss Lily glared at Sarah. "I live here!" Greenberg explained. They welcomed him into the community and he was glad he squirreled his savings for his old age. "Max!" he gloated "I'm home".

"Ess, ess! Eat, eat!" The auburn haired rabbi's daughter, prodded him in an olio of English and Yiddish. She sounded like his tante Mirele. As he was growing up his aunt would fuss, "All skin and bones Ethel" implying that Max's mother, her sister, was delinquent in feeding him. One day to placate Mirele he drank glass after glass of milk until he retched and vomited on his aunt's flowered dress.

Although now almost legally blind, his hearing, taste buds, and memory were sharp. Just as he was getting ready to move into The Home he was knocked down and mugged twice in broad daylight. Both days neighbors looked on. Instead of chasing the muggers or calling the police, they slapped their fat sides and cackled. "Greenboig take down de vahl-pay-pah and move to Brookville." The Home is his cocoon into which he is reborn.

As he packed he reflected on the past forty years. He had served as an army pharmacist technician in France during WWII. For one day he had been married. ONE DAY!!!. His wife, what's-her name, a muted voice from the trash bin of his past. Although a spine tingling beauty with raven tresses, she was a spoiled, rich girl from Wellesley. Not the college, he sneered, but the town. She didn't even have the brains to go to State Teachers College in Framingham let alone Wellesley College. BUT she was amply endowed physically. And he had been mesmerized by her looks. With the face and body of a movie star she knew how to wear makeup, especially eye liner. How popular Maybelline make-up was at his pharmacy! Boy could she wiggle her hips: she excelled in snuggling up to a man. A coquette, she saw herself as a fashion plate. She excited the ancient urges dormant in the male brain since the beginning of Time . . . He admitted to himself that he was beguiled. Although a tease, she aroused his manly ardor. She slept with him only once, on their wedding night. She packed his bags and left them outside the hotel room door. "Adios Greenberg". She was already with child fathered by a married Gentile she had met at a bar. She was in love with him but he was already married and was only interested in having sex. She was a one night fling for both men. The Greenberg marriage gave legitimacy to her unborn offspring. Max never once saw the child who carried his last name and his genes. Nor did the newborn's father. A crevice in Max's brain was cemented with melancholy, not so much for what he had lost but for the dirty trick that was played on him. All of the lonely nights he sentenced himself to bitterness. "What would the bard say?" he muttered to himself. "From fairest creatures we desire increase/That thereby beauty's rose might ever die." "Sorry Will," he apologized to the bard with great regret. I will never pass my genes to anybody." He was unaware that he had. Yet he felt old. Quite old. "When forty winters besiege thy brow/And dig deep trenches in thy beauty's field." "Will," he mumbled "my trenches are even older and huge." Miss Riger asked him what he said. Max answered that he was talking to his superego. From then on he was careful not to voice his thoughts.

When he was ejected from the marriage bed Max became deathly ill. Pneumonia. He stayed in bed for two weeks. His head throbbed; his scalp itched. His cough sounded like a barking dog. He pumped himself with penicillin, a relatively new medicine then, and chicken soup, his mother's recipe, three times each day. Max's mother had never spoken a word of English and never used salty language. Yet while caring for Max she muttered in a stage whisper "Velsley kurveh, shtick tinif, Wellesley whore. piece of shit." That brought a smile to Max's face and he dedicated himself to getting better if no other reason to palliate his mother. He wanted to give his mother peace of mind even if he had no peace. "Mama," he scolded, "She was not a whore. Just a woman in trouble, Have some pity." "Humph," mama grunted. "O.K. Max," he pondered. "No! Marriage would never again be for me. He gave up a few nanoseconds of exotic pleasure he'd have to endure a lifetime of pain. It's not worth it." Furthermore, to this day he can't stand the smell of chicken soup.

That was years ago. Today he was, except for diabetes, healthy and living in a haven of hope, the Hebrew Home for The Aged. There is food, lodging, safety, medical care, entertainment, and companionship. There will be clean linens every week as well as housekeeping staff to dust and vacuum his unit. He said to himself *some people go to the retirement home to die; I go to live. I'm in like Flynn,* He was mumbling again. Unpacking his set of Shakespeare tapes, tape recorder, and clothes, he took a deep breath and told himself "I'm home at The Home."

Those tapes were his closest friends. When he retired from Feldman's Pharmacy, his goal in life was to listen to and memorize the entire collection of 154 Shakespeare's sonnets before he died. He was now up to sonnet 36 (two times chai) He had quite a few years yet.

A few days after his arrival at The Home was Yom Kippur, a day of repentance. A spirit of forgiveness, caring and love prevailed in the hearts of so many. For one entire day angry creatures, and there were many from the CEO to the rabbi, laid aside their personal feuds, rages, jealousies, and self pities. Despite this spirit of soothing relief October's sun brought with it a sprinkling of sadness. A few puddles of light were reluctantly saying good bye to summer. The earth seemed to sip them, garner, and stockpile them for the next spring. So many people squandered the sun. Greenberg remembered that. He, too, had taken Old Sol for granted. Today, he could only recall the sweet memories of sunshine's past. Today, he wished that he had noticed the flowers and birds exquisitely colored by the sun, sitting on a park bench and kibbitzing and lying on a blanket at the beach playing whist. Today he wished he had noticed the shapes and hues of paintings at the museum. Today, it does not matter to him that the sun was dull or bright or if the birds' plumage was red, blue, or grey. He could only make out vague shadows. His soul was filled with forgiveness for sins committed and for others imagined from his keen sense of guilt. He felt he did not measure up to the standards people apply to an aging man or woman. Sarah Stein often reminded him of that. "You're skinny. Your posture is stooped. You stutter. Your face is homely, pock marked." "But God Gave me this face," he would protest. He was going to tell her that he had chicken pox when he was five and picked at the scabs until they got infected. There was no sense in defending himself at his age, especially since he was a newcomer at The Home. He tried to forgive her, but he could not understand why she picked on him.

During the closing N'eelah Torah service the rabbi summoned Max to the podium to honor the Torah, the holy scrolls. Some man, he didn't know his name, took his arm and walked with him. "Quite an honor," he whispered. "Glassberg," he confided. "I'm Motte Glassberg." Welcome to The Home. Greenberg clutched his white cane and walked with Motte. Max joined the congregation in singing "Sh'ma Yisrael." All were astounded by Greenberg's vibrant, resonant tenor voice. They were jolted, electrified by the voice soaring from the stooped old man. Awed. He gave the Day of Repentance a deep meaning of majesty and reverence. God May Have Made him skinny, stooped, speech hesitant, and homely, and now almost blind, but He Gave him a voice that clutched the very marrow of his soul and made the residents shiver and swoon with atonement. As his final confession he begged the Pakistani cab driver for forgiveness.

When the reading of The Scriptures ended, everyone stood and cheered for Jonah or maybe the close of the Fast Day, Motte Glassberg grasped Greenberg's arm and whispered, "Please join me at my pew. I would be honored." Max was dumbfounded by the attention. To himself he said, "It would be rude to turn Mr. Glassberg down." So the two sat and prayed together. Motte Glassberg felt spiritually uplifted by Greenberg's sincere devotions. He imagined Shakespeare talking to him. "So thou through windows of thine age halt see/Despite wrinkles, this is thy golden time." Imagine, he thought, this is the best time of my life.

With the trumpet sound of the shofar the service had come to a close, Motte Glassberg invited Max to join him at his table for the Break The Fast. Max was hesitant. He couldn't believe that anyone would want his company. Motte Glassberg appealed to him. Reluctantly Greenberg agreed. Seated next to Motte Glassberg was Miriam Glassberg. Her voice was soft, with a barely audible lilt. It was a sweet voice. Greenberg's sharp hearing heard her introduce herself. "Welcome to The Home," she said. She complimented him on his singing. "It comes from my n'shama, my soul, not my throat or diaphragm," he said. "May I serve you?" she asked. "Please don't trouble yourself," he remarked. "No trouble at all," she replied. She came back with a glass of orange juice, a plate of blintzes, some apple sauce, and a cup of tea. Motte whispered into Greenberg's ear, "she is founder, and president of the Home's Hadassah." Again feeling sorry for himself he thought he heard Will chastising him, "Thy unused beauty must be tombed with thee,/Which used lives th' executor be." "Get off your self pity and make something of God's gifts to you." The sound of the shofar cleansed him of his sin of self-deflating.

Sarah Stein wiggled on to the seat occupied by Motte. "Arumph!" he said. "Find another table." Sarah in her high pitched voice squealed, "I'm Sarah Stein. Sarah, you know, means 'princess'. My father, may he rest in peace, was chief rabbi of Lawrence Point." Dumfounded, Greenberg remembered that voice. "Blurred cantaloupe face," he thought to himself. He rose to find another place to sit. Motte clutched his arm and asked him to remain at the table. Greenberg left for another table. Sarah, adjusted her fraying sweater and smoothed her unkempt hair, insisted that Greenberg eat more as he was too skinny. Miriam shook her head in disbelief.

Miriam decided to flatter Sarah. She told Sarah that she wanted to eat with her brother, and it would be a mitzvah, a good deed, one her sainted father, the late chief rabbi of Lawrence Point, would approve of, if she would give up her seat to Motte. Family first. Sarah rose and Miriam embraced her with "God Bless you."

As they were eating, Miriam asked Max what does he do all day. He said that he listens to tapes of Shakespeare's sonnets. "Do you mean", she asked, like, "When I do count the clock that tells the time, / And see the brave day sunk in hideous night;" "That's Sonnet 12," he said. "I'm fixated on that one." "The hideous night reminds me of my blind-ness." "Blindness," she said, "but certainly not lack of vision." Max was moved by Miriam's words. And they discussed other Shakespeare works. She said that she would like to join him when he listened to his tapes. He was hesitant. "Wouldn't that cause your husband to be suspicious?" "I am not married," she said. "Motte is my brother. I am a widow, but I use my maiden name." Thus began the friendship between Max and Miriam. "I am honored, Madam President," Greenberg said. "Please," Miriam said, "just call me Miriam."

The next day there was a knock on Greenberg's door. Greenberg's heart was all aflutter. He had not expected to entertain a woman. Not just any woman but kind, sweet Miriam Glassberg. Madam President, excuse the expression. Miriam who knew Shakespeare. They had something in common. "Come in please," he said. The door opened and a gruff voice announced, "I am Rabbi Sandler." Greenberg's heart sank. He stuttered, "G-Greenberg." "Yes I know," spoke the rabbi brusquely. "I'll come right to the point. First, welcome to The Home. O.K. That's done. I really came here to ask you to conduct daily services. The cantor you heard yesterday cost a fortune and he sings off key. Also he's not a resident. But you have a fine voice. Of course, we can't pay you but it would be an honor for you to lead the service," and, he thought to himself, it's one less thing for me to do.

Greenberg said that he would think about it. "What's to think about?" challenged the rabbi. "You've been praying all of your life. Continue praying only do it for the congregation. You'll do a mitzvah. Praying is talking to God. Speak to God for the residents." "I'll let you know," said Greenberg hesitating. The rabbi left in a huff. "Some people." the rabbi muttered. Max returned to his melancholy. Why was sonnet 12 so important to him? Some unfinished business. He gave his genes to some unknown babe. That's what Will was talking about. Life decays with time, hence the clock. Only breeding impedes that process. Actually he was doing what Will urged in his verse. This just angered Max more. How he was used. Then again God works in ways not understood by humans. This appeased him for the moment. He was a messenger of God, if only a tool. How insightful he was and how blind Max had been.

Greenberg was baffled almost to the point of understanding. Another knock. "I'm still thinking," he shouted. "Thinking about what?" a woman's voice sweetly called. "This is me Miriam." His heart thumped. "Come in please." He told her about the rabbi, about his understanding of sonnet 12, his anger, his coming to terms with the dirty trick the Wellesley tart played on him. She said she understood his past but to set it aside. She urged him, perhaps pleaded with him to conduct services on a trial basis. Crestfallen, he agreed. Miriam was not one to disagree with.

"Let's listen to your tapes," she said. Max played sonnet 33.

> Full many a glorious morning have I seen
> Flatter the mountain-tops with sovereign eye,
> Kissing with golden face the meadows green,
> Gilding pale streams with heavenly alchemy;

"That sonnet clutches my very essence, my soul, my n'shamah," Miriam said, her eyes filling with tears. "It takes my breath away." She reached for Greenberg's face, caressed it, and said, "Thank you, Max." Tears filled Max Greenberg's eyes and streaked down his cheeks. His heart thumped and his knees grew weak. Then together, gasping for air, they recited the next lines

> Anon permit the basest clouds to ride
> With ugly rack on his celestial face.

They both laughed at their duet.

"Rack?" Asked Miriam. Max explained, that's a wind driven mass of broken clouds. "What an image," Marveled Miriam. Max agreed. He took it very personally. "Clouds" to him meant his hazy eyes; "celestial face" to Miriam was her young features she pined for and was now leathery and wrinkled, sun blemished forever. Then they listened to the rest of the sonnet.

> Yet him for this my love no whit disdaineth
> Yet love thinks no less of him for this;
> Suns of the world may stain when heaven's sun staineth.

They both sighed and fell silent. Somewhere in the tenth dimension, Will Shakespeare applauded and God Was Satisfied and hopeful.

Minutes later they both giggled and then laughed heartily. "That was exhilarating," Miriam said. Catching his breath, Greenberg agreed. Miriam caressed the back of Greenberg's head and said, "Thanks, Max. Shall we do this again?" Swallowing hard at the strangely amazing emotions that made him shiver, Greenberg agreed.

From his other dimension Shakespeare gloated.

The next morning was Greenberg's first day leading the congregation in prayer. A knot of residents, strangers to him, were in the chapel. Nine men and one woman. Someone counted "not one, not two . . . not nine." The woman? Miriam Glassberg. The rabbi banged the lectern and began to chant the morning blessings. A din broke out. Moshe Saffiiri hollered, "There is no minyan." "We have ten here," objected Shalom Stern "if you include Miriam." Saffiiri in tears fought back, "I have to say kaddish for my dear mother. "You can't count the woman." Stern rose and said he would go to the cafeteria and grab a man.

Abramovitz shouted he doesn't say Kaddish for his mother; he says it for his son who married a shigseh. "What kind of name is Saffiiri? Are you sure you're Jewish or an Italian sneaking into the Hebrew Home. "Wait!" urged the rabbi. "Calm yourself. Whoever he is saying Kaddish for and for whatever reason let him honor God and remember the deceased. Him or her. The Torah, our sacred law, may serve as a tenth." Having counted not nine, Moshe calmed down and the rabbi took Greenberg by the arm and led him to the lectern. As the rabbi did he looked at Miriam and whispered, "Torah is feminine."

At first Max murmured the words that he so often heard at morning services. "Louder, louder," shouted Moshe Saffiiri in Yiddish. Then when it came to "The Sh'ma" Max was inspired as deputy of the worshippers to speak directly to the people of Israel, "Sh'ma Yis-ra-el," he thundered. His voice trilled. Issuing from his throat, running the gamut of his vocal range, was an arpeggio like the cantors of old vocalized. His words swirled, whirled, and eddied directly to Heaven and encircled the worshippers. And that was just the beginning. Each prayer awoke a sleeping spirit of bliss in everyone at the service. Even the rabbi who too often prayed mechanically was alive with reverence and experienced a deep level of meaning. He relived the history of his people, their trials and their triumphs. Max prayed with passion. Miriam shivered with rapture. Her heart beat fast with a strange feeling she had not had since she had been with her husband at The Wall in Jerusalem. As he continued to pray, his soul filled with pride but was not bloated. He trembled, his knees shook, sweat rolled down his neck.

The rabbi concluded the service with his usual invocation:
Oh God! Calm the angry;
Strengthen the weary;
Give balm to the distressed;
Comfort to the bereaved;
And hallow every moment as if it were The Sabbath.
All worshippers then said, "Amen," rose and hurried to the
Dining area to breakfast.

Max gave a huge sigh when the service was over; he was spent, exhilarated, ecstatic. Motte took Greenberg by the arm and thanked him. "Miriam and I would like you to join us for breakfast." As the three ate, patting Max's shoulders, Miriam said, "You were Marvelous with a capital M".

Later the two of them met in Max's room and listened to Shakespeare's. Sonnet 30

> When to the sessions of sweet silent thought
> I summon up remembrances of things past

Miriam was again at The Wall. Instead of her late husband Isaac's face she saw herself placing a note in a crag for Max. "Please God," she imagined she wrote, "Give Max Greenberg good health." Her eyes grew wistful as she thought back on the people she once knew, now deceased.

Jake Rubin, the drunk, wandered into the sonnet meeting asking if this where AA meets. He knew it wasn't but he was lonesome for company. He sat himself down and listened to the words of The Bard of Avon. From Jake's whiskey mouth gossip spread throughout The Home. The talk that got around was about Max's voice and Shakespeare. The next day the prayer room was so overcrowded that the rabbi moved the service to the sanctuary. Max's voice jolted them out of their lethargy. How easy it was to get lost in one's lacunae at The Home. Now, even more confident, Max Greenberg rendered the prayers, even the selection from the Talmud, with such spirit that smiles and tears came to all those there, even to the rabbi, but especially to Miriam. "Thank you, Cantor Greenberg," said the rabbi. Max was flattered beyond his wildest dreams. Max was the epitome of modesty; he was pious, not in veneer but in ardor.

Max again joined Motte and Miriam for breakfast. Before leading the morning prayers his ego had been shriveling. But now he found his comfort zone. His new stature as Cantor for The Home was curing him of self-doubt. He spoke freely about his life as a pharmacist, especially the precision it required and the relief the medicines he compounded gave to so many. He found solace in two religions: Judaism and Shakespeare. Other people would have laughed or smirked but both Motte and Miriam listened attentively, accepting the deep feelings Max was expressing.

Just as on the previous day Miriam joined Max in his room to listen to Sonnet 7. Jake heard:

> Lo! In the orient when the gracious light
>   Lifts up his burning head, each under eye
>   Doth homage to his new-appearing sight,
>   Serving with looks his sacred majesty;

Max explained that this sonnet meant much to him. First, the sun rising and setting meant being born and rising to one's zenith then after admiring one's youthful beauty descending alone into old age. The setting sun, he added, made him think of his loss of sight. First floaters; next glaucoma; finally, what he had: blurred vision. Then Miriam offered that the poem also addresses carrying on one's own legacy by being a model to an offspring. This only made Max sadder. Who would there be to carry on his birthright? Some stranger had the gift of his genes. Miriam explained that it would be anyone touched by the spirit of his entreaties to God, the Divine Presence. They would share them with countless others. Max grew more hopeful. If he was not fated to be the progenitor of the legacy he would be its conduit. Miriam added that poems stir the heart more so than statues to past heroes. Max still entranced by Shakespeare's words continued to reflect on The Bard's words. The bard called out to him, "My glass shall not persuade me I am old/ So long as youth and thou are of one date." The same age the bard explained. "How right you are, Will," Max said to himself. Then he noticed Jake faking a snore. He laughed and Jake sat up straight. Max and Miriam laughed quietly.

From his perch in the tenth dimension Shakespeare smiled. At night as sleep eluded him Max lay in bed and "heard" Miriam's sweet voice. That voice melted many bad memories of his past. He wondered how the owner of that sweet, soft voice could be interested in him at all. Certainly she could not be interested in his money. He was living on a pension nor did he have movie star looks. He was shy, not at all outgoing. He was a slow thinker and often hours after a conversation he remembered an additional fact, though it was too late to bring meaning to bear on the conversation. Whatever it was he felt he was blessed that he could spend time with her. Miriam, however, knew exactly why Max was so appealing. He was humble and sincere. Looks mean something to the young. Older folks seek the serenity of the soul and the warmth of companionship. His gentleness and strength of character drew him to her. He was a mensch, in every sense of the word, and she felt comfortable with him. She did not have to pretend that she was other than the person she is, a caring friend. The next day after Morning Services Max became bolder. Later he played a couplet from Midsummer Nights' Dream.

Love looks not with the eyes, but with the mind,
    And therefore is winged Cupid painted blind.

Miriam asked why Max played that particular tape. He was trembling because he did not want to hurt her or lose her friendship. "I'll play a sonnet instead," he pardoned himself. "No, no," insisted Miriam. "I am curious why you played that couplet today." Max hemmed and hawed. He began to explain that he had never gotten over his failed marriage. "One night I was married. The next day she sent me on my way. Cupid blinded my eyes. She was very attractive, but I was young and so stupid. Just out of the army. I had been duped. She was with child and marrying me gave that child legitimacy. She stunted my manhood, though. There I was, a veteran of World War II. Was my mission in life only to make some unknown child legitimate? But it was not all that bad, I suppose. I gave a Jewish child a last name. That was a mitzvah. And my wife's mother gave me $10,000. I used that guilt money and the G.I. Bill to go Pharmacy school. And here I am. Some good came of something rotten in Wellesley. When I think about it, that money tamed the tempest of my rage. But the memory sticks in my craw. Does a surge of sexual delight of a nanosecond usurp nightly anguish of being swindled? Still it is hazardous to thrive on hatred, alive in my memory and surfacing every now and again. No matter how I try to suppress it. Now is a time of forgiveness and it is my onus to overlook.

And here I am." "Of course," Miriam, sensed his sadness, her eyes glistening in empathy patted Max's shoulder. "Do it now. You will feel cleansed. To brood on the past magnifies one's misery. Where there is injury, pardon." "Francis of Assisi," exclaimed Motte and fell silent. Miriam, moved by Max's story, coiled her arms about his neck, hugged him and planted a kiss on his forehead. "I am so sorry," she said sincerely. Overcome with emotion, Max hugged her back and kissed her cheek. She was thinking, "Love looks not with the eyes, but with the mind". He was thinking, "And therefore is wingéd Cupid painted blind." The next day Miriam was not at morning prayers nor was Motte. After the morning prayers Max sat and ate alone.

He made his way to the Glassberg apartment and knocked on the door. "Miriam, Motte. Can I come in?" Wheezing Miriam signaled to Motte to send Max away. Max, absorbed in a reverie, had not heard her cough. He was downcast. He had driven away the first friends he had at The Home. Not just acquaintances but soul mates. Surges of guilt sizzled his brain and penetrated his being. Max cursed himself for having been so forward. "But she hugged and kissed me first," he argued with himself. "should I not do the same?" He thought for a moment. "No! It's all right for a woman to embrace a man but returning the hug is mistaken for other than friendship." Then he saw Miss Lilly and he was catapulted to the home.

The next morning as he was about to officiate at the morning service the rabbi took him aside. "It's too bad what happened to Miriam Glassberg. You know she's in the hospital." His heart thumped. What had he done that made her sick?" "I would like to visit her," he told the rabbi. "She can have no visitors." Max's heart sunk and the prayers he offered to God on behalf of the congregation were half-hearted. All day he had such a deep longing for Miriam. He tried to be cheerful but there was a deep void in his life. He missed her and wanted to hear her sweet voice beam its radiance toward him. Crestfallen, he tossed and turned in his sleep.

He imagined being together with her. That gave him solace. The rabbi asked him what was the matter with him. So deep were his feelings that it was difficult to put into words. Instead he put his heart and soul into the prayers. "Now that's what I call praying with devotion," beamed the rabbi.

Still at the end of the service as he sat alone he could only think that the jewel of his friendship with Miriam had lost its luster. The Rubin's moved their chairs to join him. They complimented him on his voice. He smiled and thanked them. He had not listened to their words. It was noise to him. He was forlorn.

This went on for another week. "You need your strength Max," a familiar voice said to him one morning. "Max! Remember me? Miriam?" He thought he was dreaming. Her voice was like honey, sweet, golden, mellow and smooth. The way she said, "Max! Remember me?" her tone was clear as a bell. "Miriam?" He asked sheepishly. "I thought I made you sick?" He tried to restrain a sob. "No," she said. "I had a cough with a high fever, bronchitis, and Motte took me to the hospital. I sent you away because I did not want you to catch what I had. When I was lying in my bed attached to a nebulizer I thought of you and the candid talks we had. That made me want to get better fast. You did that for me. Max." She kissed his hand.

In another dimension, the bard was excusing himself from a tête a tête with Alighieri. "Give my regards to Bea-trri-shay," he sang as he approached Max and Miriam. He was writing a few choice words for the couple. Hey, nonny, nonny, nonny. Dante hated them. The bard sniggered. "Don't fret, Dante. 'tis Much Ado about nothing." Then he chortled. Max imagined a halo circling above Miriam's head. She was an angel. He smiled for the first time in more than a week. He thanked the Rubin's for joining him. He lifted his spoon. Even the oatmeal which he abhorred tasted good. Later that morning Miriam knocked on his door. His heart was beating fast. He played Sonnet 18 on his tape recorder.

> Shall I compare thee to a summer's day?
> Thou art more lovely and more temperate:
> Rough winds do shake the darling buds of May,
> And summer's lease hath too short a date.

"I am growing older, Miriam," he said. "My lease on life hath too short a date." Miriam took his hand and said, "So is mine." They sat together musing over the deeper layer of meaning of the sonnet. How they fit into it. Each knew that they wanted to be together; that they wished to be a help to the other.

Shakespeare nodded his approval.

The next day at morning services Max, transformed, prayed like the cantors of his youth. His words twirled, swirled and encircling him and Miriam eddied toward God.

2.

Sarah Stein was leaving the Dining Room dragging two sloppily dressed red headed men in a heated argument. "Hey Max! Max! Hey Max Greenberg" she shouted. "These are my cousins. Max meet Jesse Stein; he calls himself Jesse Stone. This other red headed schlemiel is Jesse Stein. He calls himself Jay. They are named after our grandfather Jesse. May he rest in peace?" Playfully, she pinched Jay and punched Jesse. They moved back. Miss Lily nodded in disapproval. Sarah grabbed them and pulled them toward her. They resisted. Before long an argument broke out between the two cousins. They were known at the Home as "princes of rhubarb." Both men loosened their grips and tried to escape from her down the corridor. "Max!" she squealed "Men! My cousins would argue about anything. Which came first the chicken or the egg; Did God really Create the world in six days; if the patriarch Abraham had a television set and would it be on the Sabbath; would he have allowed Isaac to watch cartoons? I am cursed with such cousins.! They would often switch sides in the middle of an argument. Both men were attorneys." Max turned around and remembered SS on her sweater and hastened away. 'WAIT!" She shouted. "Just listen to them."

Jay, irritable as always, insisted the name he was thinking of is Leo Katz. He's a folk singer from Canada. Jesse circled his head with his finger. "You're crazy," he told Jay. There is no folk singer from anywhere by that name. "Furthermore, he is pro-Arab." Jay insisted. "You're the crazy one," Jesse Stone insisted. Still chewing on his breakfast overheard the cousins. "Settle our argument, Kaplan.' the red heads said together. "I heard the two of you. Who wouldn't? You have your facts mixed up. It's not Leo Katz. It's Leonard Cohen. He is Canadian. The Arabs? They boycotted his concert. He had gone to Israel to fight against the Arab armies. In 1973, Jay turned to his cousin and said "What does Kaplan know? It's Leo Katz. Kaplan is a know-it-all New Yorker" To that he nodded his head in agreement.

Kaplan shook his head in disbelief. As the cousins left, Kaplan stage whispered "Leonard Cohen." Jay told his cousin, "that Kaplan doesn't know his Katz from his elbow." Kaplan raised his arms and looking up toward heaven whispered "Hallelujah." Max had a broad grin on his lips as he walked toward his room.

Max decided to avoid all three Steins when Aaron Kaplan bumped into him at his doorway. Kaplan was escaping the Stein-Stone clan on his way to Max's group on Shakespeare's sonnets. Aaron had sold insurance before retiring. He was tall and heavy set, boisterous and crass overweight but deep down smart, sweet, and kind. "Max," he bellowed, "we haven't met. I like your voice. You have far to go." He chortled wiggling into the chair next to Max, displacing Miriam. "Didya take voice lessons? Are you a reject from the Metropolitan?" "Quite nervy," thought Miriam. She found a seat next to Sarah Stein sitting alone. Sarah was swallowing her sobs. Her voice creaked like a rusty hinge. "You didn't come to ridicule me, too? Kaplan just called me a Medusa and said my hair was all snarls, full of snakes, and that I gave him the willies. I looked like a horse's mane." "That is terrible," consoled Miriam. Sarah rasped, "You and Greenberg are doing hanky panky here in this room?" "No," Miriam answered, "Firstly, No ridicule. I'd like to be your friend. Secondly, Max and I listen to and discuss Shakespeare's sonnets." Sarah guffawed in disbelief. "I am glad that you joined us," Miriam said. "Really, really? "I'm here to check out what's going on," Sarah said.

Sarah looked at Max. Miriam nodded "yes." Max said, "I am glad that you joined us today. Sarah was apologetic and sweet. Max was taken aback. He shrugged his shoulders. "Of course, you are welcome." Then he recited Sonnet 30:

> When to the sessions of sweet silent thought
> I summon up remembrance of things past,
> I sigh the lack of many a thing I sought
> And with old woes new wail my dear time's waste:
> Then can I drown an eye, unused to flow,
> For precious friends hid in death's dateless night.

Shakespeare thumped his chest with pride. Someone understood him.

"Miriam," he said. "I have wasted most of my life engulfed in worry about My lost love. But in you I have found someone sublime. I would say divine. I want to begin a new life with you. My feelings for you run deep, difficult to put into words. I wish to be closer to you more and more each day." He couldn't believe he said all that, especially in front of Sarah. Miriam was glowing. She felt loved again. Max added spice to her life; he filled her vacuum with warmth. He gave her life meaning. She was quiet. "Miriam." he asked, "are you still there?" "Yes," she sighed. "For something that is difficult to put into words your words were like a dollop of honey on Rosh Hashanah." She took his hand and put it to her lips. "Kiss me," she begged. His finger searched for them, then stroked her lips gently, sweetly.

"May I tell Motte?" she asked. "We'll tell him together," Max replied. The silence in the room was broken by Sarah saying what Shakespeare taught her
"How much have I my precious life wasted
Today I seek how good it once tasted."

Miriam gazed at her in disbelief. "What did you just say?" Max asked. Sarah repeated herself. "Those are sentences in the same five iambs Shakespeare wrote his sonnets." Sarah demanded Max play another sonnet. Max played Sonnet two: "Time is fleeting. Wait not for you to age." Sarah said, "Bring forth now your offspring your beauty's gauge." Max said, 'Yes that's what this sonnet's about." Sarah turned to Miriam. "I am not dumb. I am not a pest. I know a lot. I wish that people thought more of me." Miriam said, "they should and they will I want you to spend the day with me. If you *will* it, you WILL change and so will others."

After breakfast Jay called to his cousin. "Watch this!" He yells, "Hey Shapiro! Shapiro!" Saffiiri turned around. Jay punched his cousin in the shoulder. "I knew it. Shapiro fancied up his name. It's like Levine pronouncing his name to rhyme with wine. They laughed and punched each other's shoulders. Both calling out "Shapiro" until Sarah, the princess, gently slapped their faces. Then they sheepishly left the room.

Later that morning Miriam and Sarah took the bus into the city. Miriam said that she wanted to buy a pair of shoes for herself. At the shoe boutique she bought a pair of black suede shoes. Sarah tried on a similar pair. "It's my treat," Miriam said. Sarah was nonplussed and accepted Miriam's kindness. Then Miriam bought a black dress. She said that black makes a woman look slimmer. Sarah who always felt that she had a weight problem eyed a black dress. "Try it on," Miriam urged. It fit perfectly. "It's my treat," Miriam said. "We are like sisters." said Sarah. "We are," Miriam laughed. "family" they both thought. "That's enough shopping," Miriam smiled. "Let's have lunch."

Miriam ordered a salad. Although Sarah was fond of hamburger and French fries she also ordered a salad. Miriam could not contain herself, "Sometimes you seem abrupt, even picking on Max. He is so mild mannered I wondered what he had done to you." Sarah grimaced. She gave a shy grin. She was trapped. "Miriam you ARE a cagey one," Sarah spoke sharply. Miriam looked at her expectantly. Sarah sank into her chair. "Yes, I am bitter. You'd be, too if you had my looks, my hair, and my luck." Miriam rose and embraced Sarah. "I am deeply sorry you have those feelings," offered Miriam. Sarah began as she was chomping on a piece of celery, "I'm Sarah Stein. Sarah, you know, means 'princess'. My father, may he rest in peace, was chief rabbi of Lawrence Point." Miriam scrutinized Sarah's tearing eyes. "You're upset, Sarah. I'm sorry if I made you feel bad." Sarah tossed her celery on to her plate.

Sarah could not contain herself and purged the ghosts hurling their ghoulish epithets at her. She confessed that she has been upset most of her life. When she was sixteen her mother had hand sewn a taffeta dress for her to wear to a school dance. She had had a perm at the beauty salon. She saved up to buy nylon stockings, a precious commodity in war time. Her mother had given her a broach that had been in the family for many years. It was an exquisitely carved cameo of Queen Victoria surrounded by tiny pearls. She still wears it on her sweater. At the dance the girls huddled together, ignoring her. One by one boys asked a girl to dance. No one asked Sarah. She just sat there like a klotz. One boy approached her and as she rose to take his arms to dance, he just sneered and walked away grimacing. Rankled, she was totally deflated. Not only was she not asked to dance but boys looked her in the eyes and sneered. Hers was a deep pain. She was nearly dying in shame. She stormed out in fury dragging her coat and waited outside in the cold rain until her father picked her up. She looked haggard; her perm in shambles. Her father knew her mood and remained silent. All night she thrashed in bed. The next day she exclaimed that she was quitting school. Her father protested then, stroking his beard, relented, "after all why does a girl need to be educated?" Her mother spoke with her and understood her daughter's pain and like good mothers knew just what to do.

Her mother was some solace but Sarah began to eat to excess, at times getting sick to her stomach. She ignored her appearance and health habits. Although anguished, she enjoyed looking in the mirror bedraggled. She has been bitter ever since and struck out against all men. She cannot help herself. Her habits were so ingrained that she cannot change even if she wanted to.

She paraphrased Shakespeare, "I am a Jewess. Hath not I eyes, hands, organs, dimensions, senses, affections, passions; fed with the same food, hurt with the same weapons, subject to the same diseases, healed by the same means, warmed and cooled by the same winter and summer as any other woman? Wrong me, I suffer and seek revenge as would any other wounded duckling."

So moved by her story, Miriam's face turned ashen. "You seem to know your Shakespeare," Miriam wanted to change the subject. "When I quit school, my mother and I would read together," replied Sarah. There was silence for quite some time. Miriam examining Sarah's face said, "Yes you are wounded. No, you are not an ugly duckling but a beautiful swan." Sarah's hurt was healing; the icy anger that flowed through her veins began to thaw.

Miriam said that she had an appointment at a beauty parlor. "Would you wait There for me, Sarah?" A volt of excitement shot through her mind. She took a deep breath and agreed. While waiting, the salon owner stopped and smiled at her. "Yours is such a beautiful face," she said. "But your hair is wild. Let me tame it. No charge. It's a free sample." Sarah smiled and nodded "yes". She could not believe that there were people who would be kind to her. The hairdresser deftly permed Sarah's hair. Sarah looked in the mirror and beheld a swan. She would no longer be a victim of sturm und drang. Lincoln freed the slaves. She was being emancipated.

On the bus back to The Home Sarah dissolved in hot tears. Miriam put her arm around her in comfort. Sarah sobs dwindled into whimpers. She took Miriam's handkerchief and wiped her nose. "Why are you so good to me?" Sarah asked. "Because you are a fine human being," Miriam answered. "Hillel says in the Ethics of the Elders" (She translated "avot" as <u>Elders</u>): 'Judge not others until you have been in their place.'" Sarah looked up at Miriam and a smile formed on her lips. "I miss my mother. She used to recite a poem by Mary Latham who wrote

'Pray, don't find fault with the man that limps,
Or stumbles along the road.
Unless you have worn the moccasins he wears,
Or stumbled beneath the same load.

Take the time to walk a mile in his moccasins.'

Of course, the sage Hillel made the same point almost 2000 years ago. We all need to have empathy for others. We should not judge." To herself she whispered, "I only wish others were not so critical of my appearance." Miriam overheard the whisper and kissed Sarah's forehead. They both wept. Other passengers were caught up in that moment and had their own reasons to cry.

As soon as they returned to The Home Sarah began to see others through different eyes. She resolved to go on a diet, to exercise daily, and to change the way she looks at others. After each Shakespeare session, she and Miriam went to the exercise room. There they were given a program that included exercise bike, treadmill, tread climber, and swimming. It was an exhausting program but Sarah, looking at Miriam's efforts was determined to change the way she looked and what she saw.

In less than a month, residents flocked around her, including Aaron Kaplan, the boisterous insurance salesman. Sarah stopped wearing shabby clothes and took great pains in caring for her hair. She washed it with an egg based shampoo, used a conditioner, and brushed it 100 strokes each day. In a few days her hair began to shine. It was the sheen that Aaron Kaplan noticed. As they spoke at lunch she explained that she quit school. Aaron confessed that he did, too. He had to go to work to help support his widowed mother. Instead of a formal education Sarah and her mother read daily. Now she studies Shakespeare's sonnets with Miriam Glassberg and Max Greenberg. "You mean the blind cantor?" he guffawed. "The very one," she replied. "Say, I'd like to sit in on your class, Sarah." *He called me 'Sarah'* she thought to herself.

The next day Max's room was filled to capacity. He played a tape of Shakespeare's first sonnet to acquaint Aaron with the sessions.
From fairest creatures we desire increase,
That thereby beauty's rose might never die,
But as the riper should by time decease,
His tender heir might bear his memory:

Sarah said that this is about passing on one's heritage. That's what Shakespeare meant. This is what he said,

> "The child is heir to parental beauty
> To pass it on is a sacred duty."

"Also," she added, "the rose is a symbol of all that is beautiful in the world. But beware of the thorns. Also the rose is delicate and is prone to rust and other diseases. Notice the artful way The Bard phrased that thought."

Max exclaimed, "Sarah you are right on target again." She beamed with pride. Aaron was impressed as was Miriam. He staged whispered to her that Shakespeare was an anal character.

She looked at him in shock. He thought the look meant "tell us." So he went on to say, Friends, Romans, Countrymen, Lend me your rears." He almost fell off the chair in laughter. Sarah's face turned redder than a beet. Staring at Aaron, her eyes shot darts at him. She wanted to holler at him. He felt her hot anger. "What's the matter bubbleh?" he jibed with a sardonic grin. "I'll tell you what's the matter you crude grobyan. You lack gravitas." He knew he'd done something wrong but did not want to let go. She just shook her head in dismay. "What is grava whatever?" he asked sheepishly. "It is dignity," she fumed. "You are not funny. I am sure there is goodness in you. Show it!" Chastened, Aaron begged her apology and reached for her hand. She forgave him and took his hand and gave it a meaningful squeeze. She felt a strange electricity surging up her arm. As did he.

Aaron invited himself to sit with Sarah at lunch "You've changed," he said to her. "I had not realized how you have become slimmer. Or how smart you are." "You could use a change, too," she began. "You are fat, loud, un-couth, and uncaring. My father would call you, 'common.'" Aaron was crestfallen. He wanted to be well liked but his personality was stuck in first gear. Men might admire his bravado but women might find it obnoxious. "Look!" she touched his arm lightly "I don't want to insult you but you are kind of heavy. Why don't you work out with me in the gym. It has done wonders for me as you can see." "I'll do it," his voice resonated throughout the room. Sarah raised her hand to lower his voice. "I'll do it," he whispered.

Aaron made several decisions during lunch. He will diet, exercise, attend Max's sonnet sessions. and, most of all, get to know Sarah better and to tell her how impressed he was with her knowledge of Shakespeare. When dessert was served, they both declined. As Sarah was drinking her tea, she declared, "Max and Miriam are going to marry."

Although Aaron knew nothing of Shakespeare, he wanted to be part of the Sonnet group. The language, though English, was foreign to him. Still he listened attentively, watching Sarah in rapture elaborating on and translating the words of the bard into modern American. How he admired her. He was in awe of the depth and breadth of her mind.

Diet was not easy for him, but he was determined to restrict his calories. Exercise was the most difficult. Yet after each Shakespeare session he followed Sarah into the exercise room and would work up quite a sweat. First, he bench pressed for ten minutes. Then he swam 20 laps in the heated indoor pool. Following a shower, he ate a salad without bread and then napped.

The sonnet sessions went on five days a week. Max sang some of Shakespeare's lyrics, Sarah translated and paraphrased them, Miriam glowed with her ardor for Max. After much thought Max and Miriam set the date for their nuptials for Thanksgiving Day. Both felt that they had much to be thankful for. Aaron insisted on paying for the wedding. He had money that was gathering no interest in the bank. Reluctantly Miriam and Max agreed. Motte was to be Max's best man and indeed he was. Sarah was to be Miriam's maid of honor. Aaron declined to be in the wedding party. Increasingly he wanted less attention. He was pleased that Sarah stopped calling him a loud mouth fatso. He knew it was only friendly needling. "Really," she smirked, "you look svelte and quite appealing. No kidding," They were now, without any qualms, holding hands at the sonnet sessions. Aaron was reading Shakespeare's sonnets before he went to sleep at night. It put him in the mood of being part of Western Civilization culture. For the first time in many years they both laughed.

Getting dressed for their wedding, Max wore a black tuxedo with tails. He had his "ruptured duck" pin from his army discharge. Miriam admired how handsome he looked. Miriam wore silk chartreuse pants with a gold flecked emerald tunic. She gazed in the mirror and liked the way she looked. A big smile filled her face. Sarah glanced at her. "It is my wedding, and this is what I want to remember". Then Sarah put on her wedding attire: silk emerald pants with gold flecked chartreuse tunic. Miriam looked at her suspiciously. Sarah insisted that this was our wedding, sister Miriam, and this is how I want to look. Both women blushed. I chose Miss Lilly to be my maid of honor. Max turned serious. "I MUST confess. I am not a virgin." Then he repeated his history. "You saved another human being. That's a mitzvah. A good deed. You saved a soul." He was absolved and absolved the Wellesley woman. God Works in mysterious ways.

The ceremony took place on Thanksgiving evening, coinciding with first night of Chanukah, all in the wedding party held a lighted taper throughout the ceremony. Wait!!! What's this? A woman who looks almost like Miriam appeared. She was wearing the olive green uniform of the Israeli army. On her sleeve were several chevrons. This officer was carrying the Israeli flag. Miriam was nonplussed. Was she hallucinating? She rushed to hug her. She looked at her brother. He shrugged his shoulders with tears in his eyes. When the wedding guests saw the flag they screamed with delight.

She was not the only new guest. Word got around The Home that there was to be a wedding. Residents who knew neither bride nor groom began to swarm in. Some limped, some came in walkers, some in wheelchairs, one in a hospital bed. Free eats! As is often the case in a tumult. The bride's name was confused. Some thought it was the Rabbi getting married.

Rabbi Sandler banged on a prayer book demanding attention. He, too, smiled as did Will in the tenth dimension.

The rabbi then chanted the blessings for the candles. He sang the traditional wedding blessing. "ha-ray at m'kudeshet li. With this ring I thee wed according to the laws of Moses." "You, Max and Miriam see sunlight at night and stars during the day. That is love." Then he read from Sonnet 116.

> Let me not to the marriage of true minds
>   Admit impediments. Love is not love
>   Which alters when it alteration finds
>   Or bends with the remover to remove:
>   O, no! It is an ever fixe´d mark,
>   That looks on tempests and is never shaken.

Sarah was dressed in an orange taffeta dress. Covering her shoulders was a shawl pinned at the bow with her mother's broach. Clutching her bouquet, she raised her voice.

> Max! Miriam!
> True love has no limits; it is timeless
> No words may your sublime caring assess.

A trumpet player sounded the shofar, the ram's horn, so holy. The marriage Ceremony was about to begin. The ushers and bride's maids, some in wheelchairs chanted each of seven blessings to which the marrying couple replied, "AMEN."

The rabbi addressed the bride and groom. "You, Max and You, Miriam trailing the zig zag trek through life found what is divine in each of you. Your rarity is exemplary and hopefully will become the norm for all." The invited guests could not believe what their ears heard and what their eyes saw.

With mouth agape was Miss Lilly. She was stunned and lost her southern drawl. Sarah's hair was meticulously coifed. She shook her head wondering if this is the same Sarah who used to pester everyone. Aaron, debonair, not usually flustered, tried to command the pit of his stomach to calm down. Not known for his social graces, looked at Sarah with silent admiration. "You may kiss the bride," the rabbi urged. Trembling, Max looked for her lips with his fingers. Miriam grasped them and brought them to her lips. Max tasted her lipstick. He then stomped on the glass. Miriam embraced him warmly. And everyone shouted, "Mazel tov!" Max said, quoting Ben Zoma, "Who is happy?" Miriam answered, "They who are content with their fortune. That is me, quite contented. And who, according to the sage Ben Zoma, is honored" Max answered, "Those who honor others. And you dear Miriam are the one I most honor." They clasped one another's hands.

After the seven blessings were recited Jay and Jesse lunged toward each other. Max and Miriam were solemnly blessed by the Stein-Stone clan. Jay punched his cousin on the shoulder. Both laughed. All chatter stopped. What was heard was the rippling water of the brook outside of The Home Banquet Hall until a string trio played Hatikvah. Hope sprung in everyone's heart. Several women spontaneously rose and circled the bride and groom. Swaying, their voices filled the room with elegant harmony.

The rabbi turned to Max and asked if he had anything to say. Max recited a poem he wrote.

MIRIAM IS SUNSHINE

She is the sunshine that breaks through the clouds;
    She is the calm within the storm.
In the garden of life, she is a scented rose
    From which sweetness e'er flows

She is the calm that stills angry tones;
    She is the courage when we are scared.
She does not dwell on what the past has bred
    She looks to the future instead.

And Sarah. Princess. You are the epitome of struggle
to find goodness in herself and others.

From the tenth dimension Shakespeare nodded his approval.
Singing, "Hey, nonny, nonny."

    Thus ends one tale and the beginning of another.

WHEN SORRELE FOUND ITZIG: A TASTE OF HONEY

"Up!Up! Boker boh" the pilot's voice sang through the loudspeaker. "This is your pilot speaking. Everybody up. It is morning." "Up, Up. Wake up!" the staff sergeant stewardess ordered as the lights in the main cabin came on "Rise and shine. You men in the back," she was addressing the men swiveling and rocking as they arranged their phylacteries. "Take your seats. We are landing in thirty minutes." They ignored her until she, her arms akimbo, marched toward them. Their trunks circled back and forth. One more minute they were gesturing with their fingers.

Itzig had another night of fitful sleep. It was like every night for the past month since leaving Boro Park. He stretched his arms and blinked several times. "Was it true?" he asked himself. "Am I really landing in Palestine?" Although his thoughts were muddled and his emotions perplexed, he would write to Sorrele that elements of clarity were surfacing from his deep confusion. Still he could not fathom why his brother, Joshua, could be so cruel. It was he who stole from the meager earnings from AVROHOM'S GLATT KOSHER CONFECTIONAIRE. That store was no bigger than a jail cell yet carried all sorts of candies, some imported from Palestine. "You say anything," Joshua had said "And I'll kill you." Then he punched Itzig in the stomach. Itzig foundered. Then Joshua stood over his brother and recited the Mourner's Kaddish. It was he who said he would give his gambling winnings to Israel, Israel Cohen, his bookie and then gave a sinister laugh like THE SHADOW, a flawless imitation of Orson Welles. Although aching from head to foot, Itzig had stuffed some books and clothes in a Navy surplus duffel bag and left home.

After his beating, he stumbled like a drunkard toward the BMT station. He fixed his skull cap that slipped underneath his black fedora. "Goodbye Boro Park, Goodbye my young scholars" he chanted to the tune of Hatikvah, the national anthem song of hope. Before reaching the subway station, his thoughts heavier than his duffel bag, he saw Sarah Pincus, his Sorrele. "I'm making aliya," he tearfully shouted. He fixed the strands of blonde sneaking out of her student nurse's cap. Breaking all rules of modesty, she hugged him fiercely and kissed him firmly on the lips. Next door neighbors, they had been friends since she was in first grade and he, in second. When he was in fourth grade he brought his Talmud book home and would study with her many an afternoon. When he prepared his assignments he would share the ancient words of the rabbis with her. She absorbed their wisdom like a sponge. His homework done, they would sing Hebrew songs. Together they had tasted the elixir of The Bible; were warmed by the fervor of the sages; were elevated by the ecstasy of the kabbalah; were awed by the brilliance of the commentaries; and, above all, were exalted by their devotion to God. "I will never forget you," she sobbed. And with the sweet taste of young love and the lingering scent of Sarah's lavender water, Itzig left Brooklyn for a destiny awaiting him in, as the Gentiles say, the Holy Land. "May God Watch over you," she sobbed.

On the plane Itzig imagined the brown hills of Jerusalem baked in the sun for countless centuries and the great men who walked them: David, Jeremiah, and countless scholars. He longed to walk in their ways and in their path. Then he worried did I abandon my father. He admitted to himself that his students needed him. Then, again, so did the country he wanted to help rebuild. And most of all he yearned for Sarah.

He was torn. Then he remembered his father's stories of suffering in Poland. It was from Warsaw that Jewish youth not only sought a haven in Zion but chose to rebuild it into the vibrant nation that it once had been. His pilgrimage was a mission. Those were romantic stories of poignant times. He thought of the moment when a recruiter arrived at his yeshiva. Join the League for a Building Palestine. Emancipate our people; rebuild our land. It appealed to him. Like our teacher Moses he hearkened to The Call. "Hi-nay-nee" here I am. My father would understand, he comforted himself.

After a turbulent sixteen hour flight that taxed the limits of his brain and digestive system, Itzig arrived in Lydda. A web of British security guards eyed him suspiciously until Uri of the kibbutz secretariat hustled him on to a battered bus. "Ba-ruch ha-bah," blesse'd is the one who has arrived. Itzig felt immediately wanted. At the kibbutz Uri led Itz to member bunks. "This one is yours." He pointed to a cot covered by a thin mattress. Then he told him that the Afternoon and Evening Prayers were about to begin after which they would sit down for supper. There was nothing ornate about the prayer room. Each kibbutz member took a folding chair and placed it next to a "chaver." "Chaverim!" Uri announced in Hebrew this is a new oleh. We'll call him "Itz". "Ba-ruch ha-bah Itz", they chanted. They sang many of the afternoon prayers 'Ashray yoshvay vaytecha" Happy are they who dwell in Your House." The service over, the chaverim took their folding chairs and piled them in a corner. Itz wrote to Sarah that Uri speaks in a machine gun staccato rhythm. When piqued his voice rises in an arpeggio like a harp strummed from lowest C to highest C.

Itz apologized that he knew Biblical Hebrew rather than Conversational Hebrew. Uri just laughed. Words sputtered out of his mouth. "You'll learn quickly. You might even add some words to our vocabulary. Who knows?" Then frantically he skittered back and forth like a hummingbird. There was much to be done before his bedtime and he trusted no one to help him.

Itzig wrote long letters to Sarah telling her about his visit to many sites, the pure air of Palestine, the sun baked hills of Jerusalem. He even found his way to the Dead Sea. He dodged many an obstacle. He was buoyed by the water and even more so by his daring venture. Raising turkeys on the kibbutz was a mitsvah, something worthwhile. But he was sad when they were slaughtered. On the other hand, people needed protein. When exploring the land he would often have to sneak through brush and rubble to catch a glimpse of its wonders. Everyone at his kibbutz was Orthodox in some way or another, many of them liberated from the camps just two years earlier. Some of the men were beardless. The weather being so hot he shaved his beard. He was still Orthodox but also comfortable. Sarah would write him letters telling of her joy at his good fortune to serve and of her hope that some day she would join his cause as a pioneer. What a privilege that would be. What a delight! They had so much in common. Both loved learning. Each was the other's best friend.

He also wrote a long letter to his father explaining his decision to make aliyah, pilgrimage to Zion. It was a pull to the land of the patriarchs. That was a half-truth he would confess next Yom Kippur. His brother Joshua tore it up as well as many of the letters telling of his joy at serving in Palestine. Joshua filled with rancor and jealousy, with a smirk on his face, would trash them. In time, Avrohom believed Itzig was dead. After many a month Avrohom rent his jacket and mourned his son. The mere mention of his name led Avrohom to say, "May his memory be a blessing". Because he was so busy putting bread on the table there was much that Avrohom did not know about his two sons. Itzig was a superior student at the Beis Yaacov Yeshiva. Itzig was not one to show off his achievements. His teachers lauded his wisdom, dedication, and ardor. He was especially gifted in Aramaic for a 21 year old man. So talented was he that he was invited to tutor a class in Talmud.

Itzig's students adored him. He was kind to them. Never was he sarcastic; never did he embarrass a student who made a mistake. After school Itzig often worked side by side with his father at AVROHOM'S GLATT KOSHER CONFECTIONAIRE. On the other hand, Joshua was the only student at the Yeshiva to be asked to leave. He would sass his teachers and would rarely turn in written assignments. In an act of defiance he attended Brooklyn College where he found his niche. He also would help out at his father's store but would pocket some of the sales and bet on horses with an ultra orthodox bookie. Itzig knew about this and accused his brother of breaking two commandments, stealing and dishonoring their father.

"Shame on you, Joshua, shame, shame," Itzig admonished. That was when his brother beat him up. That had been the last straw. When Avrohom returned from the candy store, Joshua, crossing his fingers so his father did not see, said that Itzig dipped his hand in the till and fled.

In her lifetime, the Widow Pincus slapped her daughter's face only twice. Once, when she became a woman; the second time when one she chanted from the Biblical text. Sarah was never to perform those functions reserved for men her mother insisted. Sarah protested "Why can't a woman study the holy books like men do?" Her mother raised her hand again. Like that of the patriarch Abraham about to sacrifice Isaac, it halted midair. "Sarah," her mother pleaded, "don't rebel against the ways of our people." Sarah had a rage that could curdle her mother's milk. Rather than dip her tongue in venom, she forced her lips to smile as she formed a plan to escape to Zion, to her Itzig. She had three more months of schooling before she would graduate from Beis Rochel Hospital School of Nursing where she mastered Anatomy, Microbiology, Pediatrics, Chemistry, Nutrition, and Patient Care. She was an all A student. She had the brains and drive to become a doctor but she lacked the tuition money for medical school. At home, though, she was content to study the Talmudic tractate BLESSINGS which she hid in a satin pillow case under her mattress. She wanted to learn when and how to pray.

One day she went to the emissary's office and told him that she was planning to emigrate to Palestine. Since the local quota had not been filled, he made kibbutz life sound attractive. Milking cows, planting corn, harvesting corn, feeding corn to the chickens, teaching children health care. Free room and board and what is more a free plane ride to Palestine, the land of hope where dreams come true. And Itzig would be there.

Secretly, Sarah obtained her birth certificate and passport. She withdrew funds from her bank account. One night she composed a letter to her mother. It took weeks of editing. Finally, she wrote,

DEAREST MAMA,

Since I first heard stories about Palestine from my teachers, I have wanted to go there and be a part of it. I am twenty years old, a trained nurse. Old enough to know my own mind and to be responsible for myself. I am leaving in a few weeks. Let's make them the best weeks of our lives. Please understand that I yearn to be a part of our people's destiny.

Your loving daughter,
Sorrele

Much to Sarah's surprise, her mother said that she understood. She herself left Warsaw when she was sixteen. When she arrived in America she was suckled on sorrow. By the time she was Sarah's age she was weaned on woe. Still nothing could have stopped her from building a new life in America. Then her husband's light was snuffed out by a virulent pneumococcus. The same fate befell Itzig's mother. Times were not easy for her and they wouldn't be for her Sorrele.

When Itzig learned of her plans he called her. The phone connection was poor, crackling and fading in and out. "Shalom Sarah," Itz kept repeating. Do you hear me? Listen!" He then shouted, "Do you hear me? Wait a few months before you come here. Beware." Then the line went dead. She understood him to say "Don't wait a few months to come here. Mahair." There was not a more miserable time to make aliya Itzig was trying to tell her. There had been explosions in every major city. Food shortages spread as well as fear that shoppers would become victims of a grenade attack. His kibbutz was training for war.

Reluctantly, he wrote to her that he learned how to fire a rifle. He amazed himself that he shot accurately. He got a high each time he hit the target. For self protection, he wrote to Sarah, he carried his rifle with him each time he went anywhere. Sarah felt that there was all the more reason to make aliya. Before she left for Palestine she stopped by AVRHOM'S GLATT KOSHER CONFECTIONAIRE to say goodbye to Itzig's father. "Alive?" Avrohom shrieked. "Itzig phoned you? You heard his actual voice?" Sarah explained that she had received many letters from Itzig. He was settled in his new surroundings on a religious kibbutz raising turkeys.

"I am going to Palestine to join him." Avrohom dug into his pocket and gave her a hundred dollar bill for Itzig. Joshua overheard the conversation. "Give him something from me" he said flicking his fingers. "You gave him enough, mister" Sarah stabbed, her face beet red. "You scoundrel. Out of envy offal spews from the depths of your soul." Joshua's ego melted like the wicked witch in the Wizard of Oz. He kicked the candy case like a four year old. Sarah brought her hand to her lips and blew them a kiss. "L'hit-ra-oat" she said. "Until we meet again."

From Itzig's letters she learned that his name was shortened to Itz. The first thing he noticed upon his arrival in Palestine, he wrote, was the warmth of the weather. Next was the warmth of the people. How cordial they were. "Ba-ruch ha-bah" he heard them say. Not "welcome" nor "greetings" but "Ba-ruch ha-bah". Blessed are you who arrived. From letters Sarah learned that Uri introduced Itz to the chaverim who led him to the dining area. There Itz saw several long tables with some 50 chaverim waiting for the food brigade to begin serving. The din was deafening. Raucous laughter pierced his ears. The meal was hardly sumptuous: a few slices of cheese, pumpernickel bread, and tea. The chaver sitting next to Itz, Avi, explained that the big meal is breakfast after the morning prayers. "We will show our gratitude to God by singing the Grace After Meals." Then there were more songs and even more until 9 o'clock in the evening when all the chaverim retired to their bunks.

Avi was a soft spoken chaver from rural Vermont where few Jews were to be found. Raised on a farm he would have been called a yokel or a rube by a city slicker. Gentle in manner and genteel, in manners, he was the height of refinement. Courteous to a fault, his demeanor was flawless. He would have been an anomaly in Boro Park. Like Itz he went to Palestine to build the land. A farmer's son, he intimately knew about agriculture. In his spare time he had schooled himself in Bible and Talmud.

Days later Itz and several new chaverim got into the battered bus and drove north to visit Haifa. The bus driver entered the Dining Room to locate his passengers. On the plane Sarah was reading Itz's letter about that trip. She was laughing out loud much to the dismay of the sleeping passengers. But she was too excited to sleep. Itz wrote that the driver was shouting, "Mahare, Mahare. I don't have all day." "Savlanut," shouted a chaver impatiently. Itz would soon get used to brusqueness. Itz wrote that he was enthralled by the rolling hills, the coast, but especially the date palm trees. He had never seen a palm tree in his life. The clacking of the fronds was a symphony of timpani. To take up the time the new members broke into song. Avi led the others in all of the hymns the kibbutz members sing on the Sabbath. How could a country boy know so many tunes Itz thought to himself. The members sang with all of their hearts and souls as the prayer says.

Once in Haifa, Itz wrote, that they got off the bus and walked around the city. There were British troops patrolling the streets. They looked mean, angry, and tired. Their days were numbered, though. The streets were filled with Arabs doing their food shopping. They gave friendly greetings to the kibbutzniks with Salaam aleykem. Itz repeated their greetings. Those were the first Arabic words he learned and they were so much like Hebrew. And there was a warmth to them. Yet Avi said to keep a watchful eye. He knew of the killing of Jewish workers by Arab militants in this very city and their chanting "Allahu Akbar." God is the Greatest. The two of them stopped at a food kiosk. He could not resist the tempting falafel sandwich. "Take a bite, b'vakashah," he urged Itz. "It is kosher, all vegetables. A homemade tahini sauce blankets a ball of fried chickpeas, onion, parsley. A pocket in pita bread keeps the balls and chopped vegetables in place." Itz hesitated. Not to hurt Avi's feelings he bit into the sandwich overflowing with a white sauce. Itz went on to describe the bus trip to farms growing bananas, olives, corn, watermelons, figs, and lentils. Then, he wrote, the bus circled Mount Carmel stopping at an edifice surrounded by magnificent gardens. There in plain sight was the golden domed Bahai temple where Abdul Baha, the founder of the Bahai religion was buried. The driver then took the group past many churches, mosques, and synagogues. He said that Haifa is a city of coexistence. Haifa, known as "the white dove", accommodates both Christian and Muslim Arabs as well as Greek Orthodox, Russian Orthodox, Roman Catholics, Maronites, and Jews. On the way back to the home kibbutz there was another intensive class in Modern Hebrew. Then the bus passed Roman ruins lying on the ground near the aqueducts at Caesarea.

Bladder tensions forced the group to holler for a rest stop. "Mahair, ma-hair," someone urgently shouted. Shouting, Itz wrote, is the only way to get the attention of an indifferent driver. The driver stopped at the dunes of Caesarea. "O.K. chaverim, this is a public bathroom." There was no building in sight. The men got off the bus and relieved themselves standing in the sand. "Mahair, Mahair," the driver demanded. The members barely had time to zip up their pants. Itz and Avi had severe stomach cramps and rid themselves of the undigested falafel sandwiches. Food would lose its allure for them for many days to come. Later they joked that their falafel was a powerful form of Arab revenge. As her plane lurched toward a landing, Sarah laughed until tears rolled down her cheek and wet Itz's letter.

When Sarah arrived in Palestine she was taken by taxi to her kibbutz. When she arrived the secretary bid her "Bruchah ha-ba-ah". Blessed is she who arrived. She felt wanted and instantly knew she would love Palestine. After a good night's rest Ruti, Secretary For Women, sat down with her to map out a plan for her stay at the kibbutz. Sarah could not help noticing the numbers on Ruti's wrist. Ruti was all business. "You are a trained nurse. We have many trained nurses from the camps. What we need is a m'tapel-let, a care giver, for the children, most of them orphans. Can you love them?" Sarah was nonplussed. How could she in good conscience turn down this request? What happened to all of the years of nurse's training. Sarah looked at Ruti's wrists and said, "of course". She tried to hide her disappointment.

But the tears in her eyes told a different story. Ruti put her arm around Sarah and said, "yi-hi-yeh tov Sorrele. It will be all right. We need you and you need us." That embrace dissolved her inner turmoil; it softened her. Not only did she feel wanted, she felt needed. "Show me the children," she begged Ruti. And there in the Children's Room she thought she heard the clarion call of the shofar summoning her to mission. And with gusto that was asleep in her soul for so long she embraced the little girls. Their smiles were her reward.

After she was settled and her brain cleaned of jet lag, she asked Ruti if she could phone Itz. Her answer frightened Sarah. The phone lines were down. There had been attacks on civilians throughout the land. Itz's kibbutz was burned to the ground. The turkeys were scorched; the palm trees, in ashes; the dead kibbutzniks, buried. No one knows who survived. "Please God," Sarah prayed, "Watch over my Itzchak." Sarah's kibbutz bordered the Mediterranean. At twilight she would walk to the edge and watch the reflection of the setting sun in the swelling waves. She thought if only the whole world would embrace the beauty and peace of that moment. Then she would trudge through the sand and pick up shells and ancient blue glass fragments left by the sea. She'd finger the shells and enjoy their smooth backs. "Children," she would say when she returned to the kibbutz "look at the present that God Gave us today."

The first Shabbat was both exhilarating and frightening. Shabbat, the Heart of Creation, was the source of Light, Peace, and Joy to the world. It was God's Gift to humanity. Sarah had never experienced such conviviality. The rabbi began his blessing, "This week crests toward its apogee and coalesces with eons of history. Heavenly Harps Strum And Celestial Voices Hum Their Welcome to the Shabbat Queen: Hallowed Presence, Beauty Pristine." He then recited the blessing over the wine and then the blessing over the bread, the reminder of the cake that the people gave to the priests in the days of The Temple.

All chanted Amen. Members sipped their wine and snapped a pillow from their golden glazed challah and repeated the blessing over bread. A large tureen of chicken soup filled with knaydlach balls appeared. As with most kibbutz foods the soup had more than a hint of garlic. The members smacked their lips. Following the soup were platters of sliced brisket, broiled chicken, and roasted potatoes. A rare treat. But it was Shabbat after all. The main course finished, watermelon chunks arrived as dessert. There was such friendliness among the members. Smiles and laughter were on every face at the long table even on a knot of gaunt faces whispering in Yiddish. Flower vases were everywhere to be seen on the clean linen tablecloths. Before the Grace After the Meal the members sang "tsur mishelo" from You my Rock O God have I eaten.

After Grace was sung, women rose and clacking their tongues ululated with gusto while doing the patch tanz. First, they joined hands and formed a single circle. Next, they turned eight steps to the right. Then, eight steps to the left. They then took two steps forward toward the middle and clapped their hands three times. Next, they took two steps backward, stamped their heels three times and rejoined their hands. They twirled and found a new partner. So many members wanted to be Sarah's partner. She had never been a good dancer, but the women showed her the steps and, fumbling at first, before she knew it she was dancing like a pro. Never had she known such joy, such Sabbath joy. She was a vital link in the history and preservation of her people.

At 3:00 A.M. shots rang out and several of the children awoke in tears. Frightened, the sheep bleated raucously and ran helter-skelter toward the gates. Rushing into Sarah's arms were two toddlers struggling for comfort. Who was to comfort Sarah, though? She herself was alarmed. Forgetting her own fright, with a racing heart she gathered the children to her bosom and said, "yihyeh tov. All will be well. God is our Guardian."

The watchmen fixed their rifle sights and shot. Then there were shots from elsewhere. After fifteen minutes quiet settled over the kibbutz. The next day three dead marauding Arabs, blood stained checkered kaffiyeh hanging from their heads, were found lying near the main building. One of the watchmen choked up and recited a passage from the Merchant of Venice in Hebrew.

I am a Jew. Hath not a Jew eyes? Hath not a Jew hands, organs, dimensions, senses, affections, passions; fed with the same food, hurt with the same weapons, subject to the same diseases, heal'd by the same means, warm'd and cool'd by the same winter and summer.

He continued, "And you were an Arab with eyes like mine, hands, and organs. And like me a mother's son."

At dawn the crowing of a strutting rooster awoke the members drowsy from little sleep. The rooster's call was like a shofar summoning members to prayer. The groggy members assembled in the Prayer Room, already humming with rumors of the early morning events. The rabbi banged the lectern and announced there was a quorum of men. All chanted the morning prayers with the ancient lilt.

Sarah bundled her little charges still shivering and sniffling spasms of fright and told them that God Watches over them. This was only slight comfort to them. As the morning service came to a close, the rabbi welcomed and praised the men still carrying rifles. The very one who killed the Arabs and recited Shakespeare hoarsely shrieked, "I slew my cousin Esau" and, sobbing, chanted the lament of the Mourner's Kaddish, doxology glorifying God. Sarah, shaken by those words, churned with emotion. On the one hand she was alive. On the other hand, there was something disturbing about the voice she heard. Was it a voice she recognized from the past or one of a heroic stranger she imbued with melancholy? Tears glinted in her eyes. How mixed were her emotions. They vacillated between alarm, dismay, and relief.

After lunch all of the members went to their cabins for a nap. Sarah's charges did not leave her side and whimpered in their sleep. When they awoke Sarah took them in her arms and said, "Let's all go for a Shabbat stroll and thank God we have the strength to overcome our fright." The two little girls held tightly to Sarah's hands. They were dressed in bright white blouses and blue skirts in honor of the Sabbath. The sun shone in the sky reflecting swaying palm trees; birds sang; and the air was filled with fragrance of orange blossoms. One little girl, Miriam, picked up a stray rock and watched it skitter across the water, rising five times. How her heart gladdened. Sheerah, the other girl, picked another stone and skittered *it* across the waters. How they all laughed: they forgot for a moment how scared they had been. When they returned to the kibbutz it was time for the afternoon and evening prayers. The sun was lowering in the west and tinges of pink streaked in the sky. Toward the conclusion of the service three bright stars appeared in the sky as the rabbi intoned the blessings over the wine. The ornate spice box was jiggled sending its clove and cinnamon fragrances into the air. The double-wicked twisted havdalah candle flared and blessed. The rabbi held curved fingers up to the flames. The shadow of his fingers reflected on to his palms. A few drops of wine doused the flames. He drank the wine and the kibbutz members sang out "Hamavdil", the separation of the sacred from the ordinary. Everyone wished each other a good week. A cluster of Yiddish speaking women sang with almost mystical fervor, "Ani ma-a-min." Even though The Messiah Tarries I still believe. All assembled shared that profound spiritual moment.

Sarah noticed the beardless man with the rifle, the one who shouted during the Mourner's Kaddish. A stabbing pain pierced her heart. She tapped him on the shoulder. "Do you know a kibbutznik called "Itz"? Aware of her lavender fragrance he turned around. He looked at her. His heart fluttered and spiraled upwards. "I am Itz". "From Brooklyn?," she pressed. "From Brooklyn," he replied. "Your father Avrohom owns a candy story?" she persisted. "He IS my father." he acknowledged. "But you are beardless," she was befuddled. "I am still Jewish, very Jewish," Itzig replied. Sarah pushed the rifle aside and without any shame embraced him. "You are my Itzig," she wept. "I have found you, my polestar, at last. He wiped her tear and kissed her cheek. He swooned, "Sorrele." They were holding hands as they left the Prayer Room. They headed toward the sea. Sarah rested her head on Itzig's shoulder as together they watched the reflection of the moon rippling in the waves.

After some time Itz began to kiss Sarah's hair. A glimmer of sadness wormed its way into his soul. "I must confess," he began, "There are some days I have misgivings about moving to Palestine." Sarah said, "So do I. It's one thing to read about the hardships, it's another to live it." "That's how I feel also," Itz said. "I wanted to teach Talmud but instead I took care of turkeys- until the Arabs torched my kibbutz." "I wanted to do nursing here," Sarah chimed in, "instead I am a m'tapellet." Both regretted what they had said. "Despite the gossip, the in-fighting, the career disappointment, and the fear of Arab raids, I belong here waiting for the procrastinating Messiah," Sarah proclaimed. "Me too," Itz agreed. "Would it be all right if I kissed you?" Itz asked. "All right? I would welcome it," Sarah blushed.

Together they walked hand in hand to their respective cabins. Neither slept well that night. Each felt they had fallen into an abyss of uncertainty. The next morning the rooster woke everyone. The little children gathered around Sarah. They needed her attention. She had much to think about. As did Itz. There was an announcement at the women's "luach modaot." The sign on the bulletin board read "Talmud lessons tonight." Itz didn't sign his name. That night Sarah brought her well-worn copy of the tractate Brachot, Blessings. The one she brought with her from America. Eighteen women showed up for class. When Itz walked in smiles appeared on everyone's face. Sarah's heart thumped with joy. Itz began "When is the proper time to recite the sh'ma in the evening?" There followed the varied views of the sages. Opinions ranged from nightfall to midnight to the light of dawn. There were differences of opinion in the class, too. The members enjoyed the disputation claiming it sharpened their minds. When class was over Sarah approached Itz. "Let's walk to the sea again." As they walked Sarah asked do you have any regrets? About last night?" Itz was tongue tied. He turned to her and stuttered, "N-N-None" as they watched the branches of the orange orchard, a patch of paradise, mirrored in the placid Mediterranean waters.

Sarah who was forward, a habit she learned in Brooklyn, said, "Let's marry." Itz was taken aback. A tempest brewed in his brain. Lightening surged; thunder crashed. He was unhinged. He argued with himself, "I'm too young, how can I support her, the times are unsettled, but I want no one else to be my wife." "Let's be realistic," he argued "I have no money, no job, no prospects." "I am realistic, too," Sarah disagreed. "I want no one else to go through life with. We can live on the kibbutz as husband and wife." Both listened to the waves gently rolling in and took it as a quiet affirmation from God. Then Sarah told Itz that before she came to Palestine his father gave her $100. She said that we can use the money to pay for a kibbutz wedding. "A ring?" he asked. "Who needs it?" she challenged.

Sarah and Itz called home. Despite the poor telephone reception, Avrohom and Mrs. Pincus understood. Sarah's mother said that she was not in good enough health to travel. Itz's father said that he was delighted with the news and will attend the wedding. Months passed as Sarah and Itz planned their future. "How many children?" Itz asked. Smiling, Sarah replied, "God Will Decide".

May 14, 1948 was the Day of Independence for the Jews and a Day of Catastrophe for the Arabs. Jewish guns blasted to celebrate; Arab guns, to avenge. It had also been the day that Sarah and Itzig had planned to be joined in holy matrimony. Amid the tumult, Sarah, dazzling in her ocean blue skirt and arabesque gilded brocaded white blouse, walked down the aisle of the kibbutz prayer room carrying her copy of Brachot encased in her satin pillowcase. She joined Itzig under the chuppah, the canopy, symbol of the home the couple will build together. Avi was his best man; Ruti was Sarah's matron of honor. The rabbi entered and raised his voice defying the racket of gunfire. "Mee adir?" "Who is the Most Mighty?"

The four open sides of the chuppah said, as in the days of yore, all are welcome into our home. How poignant was this moment as Itz's father's tallit, prayer shawl stretched across the canopy poles. At the bride's side were Miriam and Sheera, two flower girls. The two orphans would never leave her side as Sarah and Itz later adopted them. The wedding couple knew what it was like to grow up deprived of a parent. Sarah wore her mother's veil which Avrohom brought from Brooklyn. By Itz's side were his father and brother. The rabbi recited the blessing over the wine. Itz lifted the veil and gave Sarah a sip. Sarah smiled knowing that Itzig would always be with her. His father gave Itz Sarah's mother's wedding band. Itzig recited the ancient words "Ha-ray at m-ku-de-shet li b'ta-ba-at zu k'dat Moshe Yis-ra-el." With this ring I do thee wed according to the faith of Moses and Israel." Sarah looked at the ring, and remembering her mother, her knees grew weak. Her mother would always be a part of rather than apart from her.

At the conclusion of the ceremony Itz stomped on the the glass. At the sound of the shattered glass, his brother shouted "Am Yisrael chai. Long live Israel." "Forgive me." he begged Itz. "I was jealous of you. I was immature. Now I just look up to you, my dear brother." He turned to Sorrele and said, "Thank you, my sister, for nudging me to grow up." Itz shook his brother's hands, then he hugged his father. With loving eyes he looked at his Sorrele, embraced her and gave her a lingering kiss on her lips. Then Miriam scrambled up onto Sarah and grasped her shoulder. "Eema," she whispered; Sheera climbed onto Itz and clung to *his* shoulders and whispered "Abba". The kibbutz members then shouted, "Mazal tov. Am Yisrael chai." Long live Israel. This was a day for celebrations.

A TALE OF JAIL

Jake left the bar
Turned the key and started his car.
He drove the car real careful like
When along comes a cop. Everyone knew Sargent Mike.

"You drove through a light already red,"
That's what the angry cop had said.
Jake replied, "That's not what I'd seen.
When I drove by the light was green.

Mike, the cop, was getting mad, red beet angry mad
Then took out his pen and wrote on his pad.
Then he hauled meek Jake before the judge
Sitting on the bench chewing fudge.

The fudge judge sent Jake straight to jail
'Cause cashless Jake couldn't pay the bail.
Jake's gal, Sue, baked a chocolate cake
With a knife in the middle to saw a steak.

A cake that has a knife like a saw
Is just a bit outside the law.
So Sue joined Jake in the old jail cell
And there they stayed for quite a spell.

The day they both got their release,
They vowed to stay clear of police.
Neither stray not one iota;
They'll not be a part of any cop's quota.
Cops like Mike are always stalking
So the two don't drive they are only walking.

ONE FOR HERE AND ONE MORE TO GO

All was quiet at the Smarm and Treacle saloon
Except for the piano playing some old movie
tune. When in walks Jake O'Shea, tall and lean,
No critter alive was ever so mean.
He hitched up his pants and moseyed up to the
bar; Anyone could see that his face had a big red
scar. He barked at Old Dan, "Draw me an ale
And a mug to go for O'Neill who's sittin' in jail."

Old Dan drew an ale and then another.
Then Jake muttered something about Old Dan's mother.
Old Dan took the ale meant for O'Neill
And poured it on Jake with vindictive zeal.

Then Jake tossed his drink in the bartender's face
And all hell broke loose inside the place.
Jake flung his dukes straight up in the air
And accidentally smacked Seamus McNair

Who kicked Paddy Higgins smack in the knee
Then fell on top of Jimmy McGee.
To settle an old score Ryan punched Shea in the nose
And Shea spilled beer on Kelly's new clothes.

Chair legs flew and windows broke
And the sleeping Joe Higgins quickly awoke.
He punched O'Brien nearby on the floor,
Who stayed asleep and continued to snore.

About then the sheriff passed by
And a flying mug barely missed his eye.

"Who's the guy what threw the mug?"
The sheriff asked to arrest the thug.

Everyone at the Treacle pointed to Jake
Who said it was all a big mistake.
The sheriff cuffed him and dragged him to jail
Where he joined O'Neill athirst for a pint of ale.

O'Neill of the very parched throat,
Drank only on days he'd vote
In those days he wore a smile
That one could see for at least a mile.

Well he drank himself so silly
He fell into a bowl of chili.
He looked at himself and laughed so loud
He was entertaining the entire crowd.

So as not to waste the kidney beans
You'd have to stop him with squad of marines.
He ate and ate till he could eat no more
It took three men to git him off the floor.

A CONTEMPORARY SONG OF LOVE

Inspired and adapted from The Old Testament
    Song of Songs of Solomon
        With a Greek Chorus

CHORUS:
Beloved, dear ones! We sing to you the Song of Songs
Whose words from The Good Book are odes of love;
Before you, we scroll the mystic tunes that dwell in the soul.
These words devoted to the wise King Solomon confer long life.
He knew a thousand damsels and a thousand ways to love.
These verses are the story of an enthralled swain and his charmed maiden.
It begins with the scent of her body eddying from the boudoir:
Nard, saffron, cinnamon, cloves, myrrh, and ginger.
Then he kissed her ambrosial neck and they both shivered.
Then his touch anchors upon the curves of her thighs and they both tingle.
Then she gazes upon his face so full of grace and they swoon.
They are enchanted.
All praise their love more than a sip of most exotic of wines.
Some call it kismet, fate, destiny. We call it love.

MAIDEN: My beloved! More delicate are you than Chantilly lace.
When your lips meet mine I grow light headed.
How your scent electrifies me to rapture.
I am swarthy but my allure is deeper than my skin color
Kiss me. Warmly embrace me for I am yours forever.
I pray that you do not stare at me because my skin is dark, darkened by the sun.
My brothers were angry with me;
They forced me to take care of their vines in the hot, hot sun;
My own vines I neglected.
Who but you respected me for my brain not my body.

Answer me, my love, where do you graze your flock
And where do your sheep rest midday?
I will slip away then and we'll embrace.
I gaze upon your face, a face that stirs my heart, and enchants me.
I confess I am shunned like a veiled woman.
I don't understand why. I'll avoid those who mock and sneer.
Tell me where do your friends tend their sheep?
Let's meet elsewhere.

CHORUS:
If you do not know, most beautiful of women,
Follow the tracks of the sheep and graze your kids.
Seclude yourself beneath the fronds of a royal palm tree.
There you will meet your beloved; trembling, you will find bliss and surrender.

SWAIN:
I inhale your lily of the valley scent and my knees grow weak.
I kiss your cheek and swoon.
Beloved! Come into my chamber tonight and we will warmly embrace.
Then we will soar in love.
It will not be a wild, torrid, frenzied amour but it will be sweet, gentle, and tender.
Beloved! When you sing a melody of desire
Cherubs surround each note.

MAIDEN:
How sweet is the aroma of your blossoms.
It arouses more hope than a rose, flower of desire;
It is more comely than a sprig of an orchid plant whose beauty has no peer.
More melodious is your music than a cherub chant.
Tastier it is than the first bite of a juicy apple.
My mouth drools at the thought of sipping your nectar.
I am swarthy, it is true, but my allure is from deep within;
My charm delights hundreds, no thousands,

CHORUS:
Shun her not. Black is beautiful.
Her allure is mysterious and attractive

As is her skin color.
Making love to her is no sin if you are true to her.
Capitulate and embrace her.

SWAIN:
Hearken my beloved! Daughters of my realm adore me.
My coronet is more regal than any royal steed;
My flank is more lithesome than any of my own breed.
Kiss me with your warmest embrace;
Hold me close to your royal face.
Let me suck in your hot breath.
For yours is a love true and chaste;
Yours is a love divinely graced.
How delicate is your touch;
Your Yin is more adorned than a warm embrace.
Yours is a filagree of gilded dreams and silvery hopes.
I can't wait to wed. Let's elope!
The cleft of your breasts invites me to rest my head there.
But I will just admire your curves instead.
Your hair is reddish brown and shines;
It is exhilarating like the strongest wine.

How pungent the earth
   How cheerful your mirth
   Like a hibiscus whose firm stamen
   Readies to greet pollen.
   How delicate your scent like lily of the valley.
   You steal my kisses in the darkest alley
   And then your mouth drools from tasting my fruit .

CHORUS:
No wonder the youth of Jerusalem adore you. Your beauty is legend.

MAIDEN:
Oh Yang of mine. I pine to hear the sound of your voice. It is
sweet and tender. Sing to me chanson d'amour.

SWAIN:
Kiss me with the kisses of your mouth—
For your love is more delightful than wine
And your lips, sweeter than honey.
Shivers tingle my spine.

CHORUS:
The thought of her name tingles his spine. Kiss her and you will both swell in love. Embrace her and she will surrender.

SWAIN:
Pleasing is the fragrance of your perfumes;
Your name is like perfume splashing your ear lobes.
    No wonder the young women adore you!
    No wonder the older women admire you.
Their hearts skip a beat when they gaze upon your profile.
Take me away with you—let us make haste!
My royal highness, my princess, nay, my queen whisk me to your chamber.

CHORUS:
Hurry. Hasten to bed, Oh Yang! Whom she adores. Make love.
Make beautiful love and cleanse this polluted world.

MAIDEN:
How right they are to adore you!
Dark am I, yet lovely, a daughter of Israel.
Dark like the tents of my cousins, scions of Ismael.
Do not stare at me because I am dark, tell me again, you whom I love,
In my eagerness I confused myself.
Answer me. I adore your tender voice.
Where do you graze your flock and where do you rest your sheep at midday.
Should I don a veil to conceal myself from your friends?

CHORUS:
If you do not know, most beautiful of women, follow the tracks of the sheep.
Graze your young goats by the tents of the shepherds.

SWAIN:

I woo you, my darling. How lovely are you. My heart skips a beat.
How stunning you look wearing golden earrings studded with silver.

CHORUS:
Not only do your cheeks sparkle like reddest rubies but your lithe neck dazzles
with strings of pearls. Stunning are you in golden earrings studded with silver.

MAIDEN:
While the king was at his table,
My perfume spread its fragrance and wafted up his nostrils.
My beloved is to me a sachet of myrrh resting between my breasts.
My beloved is like a cluster of henna blossoms from the vines of Carmel.

SWAIN:
How beautiful you are, my darling!
   Oh, how beautiful!
   Your eyes are like emeralds. One glance and the future is free of worry.

CHORUS:
Kiss the emerald eye and yours will be a happy future, free of worry.

MAIDEN:
How handsome you are, my beloved!
   Oh, how charming!
   And our bed is verdant.

SWAIN:
Our love is as strong as a house built of cedar whose rafters are fir trees.

MAIDEN:
I am a rose of Sharon, a lily of the valley.

SWAIN:
Like a lily among thorns is my darling among ordinary women.

MAIDEN:
Like an apple tree among the trees of the forest is my beloved
Among the young men. I delight to sit in your shade.

Take me to the banquet hall and let your banner drape over me with love.
Strengthen me with raisins, refresh me with apples, for I am faint with love.

Then we kiss and I swim in a river of passion.

CHORUS:
Then they kiss and reminisce the bliss of each kiss and swim in a river
Of passion where they will be blessed by the Divine. Oh God!
Thank you for bringing her into his life. She will be his,
And he will be hers forever.

MAIDEN:
My beloved is like a young stag, full of energy, leaping from hill to hill.
Maidens! Maidens! When true love awakens enfold it in your bosom
And smile. Beguiled are you by such a wholesome love and sincere ardor;
A love without guile.

CHORUS:
O maidens! Leap like a gazelle and kindle desire in your hearts.

SWAIN:
O maidens! He leaps toward you like a gazelle to kindle desire in your heart.
Submit! Surrender! You will reap a bounty of rewards.
Daughters of Jerusalem, I charge you every gazelle and every doe of the field:
Do not arouse or awaken joy until it so desires.

MAIDEN:
Listen! My beloved! My prince!
    Look! He comes, leaping across the mountains, bounding over the hills.
My beloved is like a young stag.
Look! There he dashes toward me.
    Hurry! Hurry! I call. I can hardly wait to envelop him.
He runs and I will follow him to the ends of the earth.

CHORUS:
Oh young stag, don't stop to smell the roses. Hasten to the one who loves you.
She awaits the taste of your lips. She can taste the sweat forming beneath your
nostrils. Sample it and savor the salty skin.

SWAIN:
My beloved! You are a delicate lily among the brambles of life. A woman among women. A breath of fresh air that cleanses toxins. Your sweet voice fills my ears with rapture. My knees grow weak; my heart pulses. My beloved speak to me and say,
   "Arise, my darling,
   My beautiful one, come with me.
And we will watch the last vestige of winter.
Soon it will be over, and flowers will appear.
It is a miracle of Nature. You, too, are a miracle of Nature.

MAIDEN:
You know that you are mine, and I am yours. Envelop me in your loins. We are two and we will become one.

CHORUS:
They merged into one another; where there were two there now is one. They embody the rhythm of Nature and are blessed by God. We sang to you the song of songs from The Old Testament canon. Fragrant scents filled the boudoir: nard, saffron, cinnamon, cloves, myrrh, and ginger. Then a kiss moored on each ambrosial neck and their trembling bodies Grew weak.

LONG PAUSE. EXHALE

Together you enchant all. Yours is a love that cannot be quenched by time or place. You are lionized for your charm inspires every soul. Your love for each other is as strong as gold and as enduring as the stars in the sky.

PUT WINGS ON IT

My father was a fisherman. Like many fishermen he was more than fond of drink. Of course, when he had too much I had to watch out. Even if I had done no wrong he would take after me and slam me against the wall because I was the nearest object. Out of his mouth came the saltiest epithets a young child could hear. Saltiest? Yes, mixed with hot chili peppers. The names he'd call me are not in my speaking vocabulary, and I am a navy veteran. His outbursts did not happen too often because he'd only be home for a few days every few months. Nevertheless, they were memorable, and they hurt. Many a night I would go to sleep and plan my revenge, a redress that would never be realized. How can a little boy take on a big muscular man, especially a father? When I was four years old my mother either died or ran away. Aunt Flora, not a blood relative, came to take care of me. Why she came to live with me, I was not sure at the time, but she was kind, helpful, and when she would smile she made me feel ten feet tall. I just melted like butter sitting on a table on a hot summer's day. She made me feel I could do anything I set my mind to. I watched her and saw that *she* could do anything she set her mind to. I'd talk to her about my innermost feelings, many of them dark. For you see I was sure by the time that I was five that my mother was no longer with us because of some sinful thing I did. My father told me so. After his tirade about my behavior he'd grab me by the scruff of the neck and tell me that I had better ask the Loving Jesus for forgiveness. I tried to restrain myself but my eyes smarted and tears trickled down my face. Then he'd call me a baby, and I would go to Aunt Flora who would hug me warmly and say, "hard as it is, put wings on it and let it fly away." Mentally I had trouble doing that but then my father would go back to sea, and I would be free of his rage and the revenge it stirred in me, until the next time.

To this day I remember one incident clearly. I used to recite my evening prayers down by the waterfront. The ebb and flow of the waves had a cleansing effect on me, like a daily baptism. I was hypnotized by the milky waters lapping the rocks swirling shells and pebbles slapping the rocky shore until the moon called them back to the depths of the sea. I returned home and was so glad to see my father. He had not been home for several months. "Ya didn't say your prayers yet," he bellowed. His words were slurred. "I did father," I protested. "I never see *you* praying," I sassed. "It's your soul what's damned," he said and pushed me against the iron picket fence. I winced and then passed out. The next thing I knew I was in the Emergency Room of the hospital being sewed up. Aunt Flora took me home to an empty house. The herring bone stitches on my right shoulder faded but never cleared. Aunt Flora took me down to the water to bathe and heal. Brr it was cold; how it smarted. She said salt water was therapeutic and I should take the sting like a grown up—which I did. Still I learned to swim in it. Fast -very fast. When I got out of the water she would rub me with a warm towel. Then she'd massage my shoulder with an ointment made from an old Navajo recipe her grandmother had given her. She told me later that it was made of petroleum jelly and calendula mixed with althea, the true marshmallow. I was free of any pain after several months. Her fat little hands were soothing and probably as effective as the ointment.

To this day I wince in the mirror at the blackened scars on my back. Aunt Flora started me on an exercise rehabilitation program. First we'd play catch. We both had catcher's mitts. Then she'd pitch to me and I'd hit the ball. Even when I was fully recovered we practiced hit and catch. When my school mate Martha joined us the three of us would practice together. By the time I was in high school not only had I made the school swimming team, but I made the senior squad of the baseball team as well. Martha was a skilled pitcher but there was neither a Girl's baseball nor swimming class at City High.

Aunt Flora was not only a good cook but she kept the house neat and clean. "Cleanliness is next to Godliness," she'd say. In her spare time she'd pattern jewelry for sale to vacationers. She'd use silver tubes connecting variously shaped turquoise beads. She told me that her grandmother, a full blooded Navajo, had taught her. Aunt Flora taught me as well. During the summer months, we could clear at least a hundred dollars a month. A lot of money at that time. Not that we needed the money. My father, as irresponsible as he was as a parent, provided us with more than enough money to live on. Jewelry making was one of the things Aunt Flora and I did together in the long winter nights just for fun. It was not the only thing. She taught me to read and many a night she'd read Shakespeare's sonnets to me. I was reading:

Shall I compare thee to a summer's day?
Thou art more lovely and more temperate:

Rough winds do shake the darling buds of May,
And summer's lease hath all too short a date:
Sometime too hot the eye of heaven shines
And often is his gold complexion dimm'd;
And every fair from fair sometime declines,

She told me to look for little words in big words. I found "sum" in summer "love" in lovely; "some" in sometime. I sounded out temperate as "tem-per-'t". The "'t" she said was a half vowel called a schwa, a Hebrew word that made its way into the English language. Aunt Flora said look at that word and just say tem-per-'t. What does "temperate" mean I asked her. She said it means "Calm or gentle." Why, I asked her, would Shakespeare use such a long word and one that may have more than one meaning. She'd tell me that poets often do that not to confuse the listener but to invite listeners to find their own meanings in the poem. The eye of heaven, she said, was a way to picture the sun. Poets would use devices like that to paint a feeling with words. A poem is a portrait of an emotion made of words, sound, rhythm, and mental impressions. Another thing about Aunt Flora she never told me I was wrong. She'd always tell me what was the right way to say or do things.

Every day of every year we tended to the chickens we raised. She'd never slaughter any. To this day I cannot eat chicken in any form. I grew to love my birds. Red bantams would follow me around bobbing their tiny heads and clucking without a care in the world. I do eat eggs and have never had a problem with cholesterol. Near the chicken coop was an apple orchard. In the autumn I'd collect the apples and place them in baskets. Aunt Flora and I would bring them to the Saturday Farmer's Market and sell them. Then we'd drive home and sit on our lawn chairs, count our earnings and admire the grove of crepe myrtle trees with their satiny barks and frilly florets, some white, some pink, some red. The limbs grew lazily and without design. If I could be a tree, it'd be a crepe myrtle.

Although there were no neighbors nearby, I was not a lonely child. I never felt isolated. I kept busy watching clouds drift by and looking at the pelicans and gulls diving for food at the shore. Our land reached to the water's edge where the Atlantic met the bay. I'd watch the waves rise in distinct arcs and loll lazily toward the shore almost silently except during storms. Then the waves would crash against the rocks and rising waters would flood my yard. The sound of winds soughing and rustling trees is still music to me ears. Where I lived there was plenty of wind. During a gale windows would rattle. Aunt Flora would laugh and say, "God, Didn't know what to do with Gene Krupa and sent him to earth to keep him from making such a ruckus in Heaven." Then we'd both laugh. Many a clear wintry night I'd sit on the rocking chair on my porch and gaze at the moon. But it was Venus that caught my eye. How bright and glistening it was. If I knew what season of the year it was I'd never get lost at sea because Venus was my guide.

The natural world around me schooled me in a leisurely, languid rhythm. The earth was in no rush to revolve around the sun. It took twenty-four hours. The tulips were in no rush to open their buds and reveal their cup filled with dazzling splendor. The hens were in no rush to lay their eggs. Victorborge, my dog, a Great Dane, was the laziest dog in the world. He'd stretch out on his paws and lie around all day outside the chicken coop and guard the chickens. Although he was lazy he was very loyal. He made sure no hen escaped and no person came to steal them or their eggs. One bark would deter the fleeing chicken and frighten any intruder. Pity the poacher who tried to steal our chicks. Still Victorborge was in no rush to do anything. Even when we went for a walk I had to bribe him with a doggie biscuit just to get started.

Our house was comfortable but not elegant. It was surrounded by woods on three sides and the sea on the fourth. When my father came home from his trips he'd anchor his ship near the house and row his boat toward our own pier. I learned to row a boat when I was four. He gave me my own row boat. I not only developed strong muscles but a perspective of horizon and an understanding of how stars are helpful in navigation and how moon controls the tides. This was useful information when storms brewed. When Aunt Flora was busy cleaning or preparing meals I'd walk along the shore, listen to the seas gently roll in, and study the shapeless froth of the waves. Thus began the habit of attentiveness. But if you are attentive to one thing you can't be to others. Often Aunt Flora would ring the bell for dinner, but I did not hear her. I was too fascinated by the sea birds in flight, soaring and then diving for food. She'd walk to the shore and tap me on the shoulder. "I have a wonderful supper waiting just for you—and your favorite apple pie from the apples you yourself picked." She enunciated her words like a movie actress not like an Indian as portrayed on a movie screen.

Her words just made me melt. Never did I hear a complaint on her lips. We'd sit at the hand carved wooden table my father brought back from Kenya, and we'd talk about faraway places and customs of peoples in other lands. Then I would wash the dishes and we would sit by the fireplace and she would read to me. When we were not reading Shakespeare she read from Robinson Crusoe. She would read:

The pointed houses lean so you would swear
That they were falling. Tangled vessel masts

Like lifeless branches lean against the sky amid a mass of green,
and red, and rust, Red herrings, sheepskins, coal along the quays.

Aunt Flora read about Amsterdam with such passion that I yearned to go there and see the tangled vessel masts and fish for herring along the piers. I eventually did and saw Amsterdam through the eyes of Robinson Crusoe.

When I was six I was bussed to first grade in public school. Aunt Flora walked me up the path that led to the county road. My teacher, Miss Meaney, that's what I called her, was constantly scolding the pupils. I never did figure out what infractions merited her strident tone of voice. Too often when she called on me to recite my mind was on our pier watching the gulls diving for food. She would take a stick and whack me on my legs until I awoke with stinging pain. "Dummy," said she, "how much is 5+3?" I knew the answer but for the moment I was too nervous to say anything. On nights after a caning I would wake up in a wet bed. I told Aunt Flora that I was ashamed of wetting my bed. I also told her that Miss Meaney called me dummy and whacked me with a cane. Aunt Flora went to school and spoke to the teacher about how she treated me. "He can't read," Miss Meany said. "Of course, he can," Aunt Flora refuted her." He read Shakespeare when he was five." "Yes," Miss Meany said in a rage "but we are reading Dick and Jane and when I call on him to read he just stares at me. I would have chaos if every child did what they wanted."

When my father came home from a fishing trip before Thanksgiving, Aunt Flora told him of my travail. That next Monday, ashamed of me, he pulled me by my ear and dragged me to school and spoke to my teacher. She said that I was a dreamer and retarded. My father went into a rage and beat me in front of Miss Meaney and pushed me hard into the car, I can still feel the pain in my back from his anger. He drove off to St. Mary's By The Sea, a nearby Catholic parochial school. "My son is a dreamer," my father was scolding. "Teach him how to pay attention," he demanded. He left me there amid a sea of curious, gawking, chiding strangers. I had no idea why they stared at me the way they did. But I was a stranger to them, and they were strangers to me. Moreover, I was not Catholic. And my shirt, pants, and tie were colorful—Aunt Flora chose Southwest colors. I noticed that the boys and girls wore school uniforms. Sister Agatha said to me, "There is only one seat left in our class, dearie. It is the last seat in the last row. I heard the boys snicker, "Here's another dummy from public school." Did my reputation follow me? But no, that's how strangers were welcomed by the neighborhood children in that first grade. "Now I want you all to be kind to this poor unfortunate who came to us from public school." The pupils covered their mouths and giggled. "No laughing," said Sister Agatha with a big smile on her lips.

The classroom was arranged in rows. Girl, Boy, Girl, Boy and so forth. My seat was next to Martha who I learned was also a reject from public school and also Christian but not Catholic. She had golden blond hair and wore pig tails. Her ruffled dress was neatly ironed. The flowers looked so real I wanted to smell them. When I wasn't "watching" the gulls on the pier I was studying the flowers on Martha's dress. The class was rendering a catechism in unison. Then everyone was reciting the arithmetic lesson: 5 plus 1 equals 6, 5+2=7, 5 plus 3 equals 8, 5 plus 4 equals 9, and so forth.

Out of a clear blue sky, Sister Agatha called out to Martha, "Recite the 5 tables." Martha rose and recited without a mistake. "You get a star Martha." Sister Agatha wrote Martha's name on the blackboard and placed a star next to it. I could not help but notice that Martha was as tall as I and had the same build except she was a girl. Then Sister Agatha called on me to recite the six tables. I had no trouble with that. She wrote my name on the blackboard and placed a star next to it. I glowed. "Smarty Pants," the boys jeered. When the lesson was over, Sister Agatha took us to the playground for recess. "Dress warmly," she warned in a sweet Irish lilt "Tis the end of November." One monitor escorted the boys to the Boys' Room; another monitor escorted the girls to the Girls' Room. Sister Agatha stood watch to make sure that no one went to the wrong bathroom. There were exit doors to the playground when the children finished their business.

When I went to the playground I noticed Martha sitting alone under a tree while the girls jumped rope or just ran around. I sauntered over to her and asked how come she did not join the girls at their games. She answered sharply, "I don't see you playing with anyone neither." "I am new here," I said. "That don't make no difference," she answered back. "I'm no Catholic," she said, "what's more I ain't gut no father, and me mother works as a maid at ad hotel. I'm trash." "Not to me," I said, "but you do have a sharp tongue. That won't make you many friends." "Leave then," she said. "No. I like someone who stands up for his rights." "Her rights," she shot back. And we just sat under the tree looking at the passing clouds absorbed in our respective miseries but enjoying each other's company. Thus began our friendship. "How come you aren't wearing the school uniform?" "Can't afford it and won't take charity." I studied her neck and guessed what size it is from having made so many lady chokers.

Martha had a keen mind and a sharp tongue to go with it. "I seen you afore," she said as the school bell rang, and we were heading back to class. "Youz was selling apples at the Saturday Farmer's Market. "Youz was wid some short, squat lady. Waz dat yo ma?" "No I told her that the woman was Aunt Flora and she was like a mother to me. My birth mother was either dead or ran away. Martha said that she had no father. He was either dead or ran away, too. She had some trouble keeping the saints straight. I told the most important one was Simon who was called Peter, the first pope of Rome. He was not Catholic, not even Christian. He was born a Jew. She found that funny. Later when we studied the saints together we linked each saint with a funny story. "I like this way to study religion," she laughed. Her reading improved, too. Sounding out words worked for most words. The ones that she could not sound out, just like I did, she memorized the word form. Then she began to write words in interesting sentences. Sister Agatha called upon her each Friday afternoon, that was free time for us, to read one of her stories. The girls who had ignored her would listen intently as her stories were about poor, fatherless girls who fight all odds and became rich. Sister Agatha would place three stars after Martha's name.

When I got back home I told Aunt Flora about my day at school and that I had met Martha. I also told her that all of the boys wore school uniforms and I needed one so that I would look like the other boys. I also told her that Martha did not have a uniform and she had no money to buy one and refused the charity of the sisters of St. Mary's By the Sea.

Aunt Flora drove me to the uniform store where I was fitted for jackets, shirt, tie, and pants. I jumped when the salesman measured my inseam. Boy was I surprised. He sold us two sets of uniforms, "case one gits soiled". I asked Aunt Flora to buy sets for Martha. I described her size and build similar to mine as well as her neck size. When we got home, Aunt Flora washed Martha's uniform and I pounded it with a log to give it a used look. The next day I gave Martha the uniforms. She refused at first. I explained that they were not new and Aunt Flora wanted her to have them. No one better refuse Aunt Flora because she was a real Indian giver. Martha laughed and wore a school uniform after that day. "Now you both are one of us," Sister Agatha said looking at us and asked the class to rise and greet us.

One Friday when Sister Agatha was not looking, Georgie Walsh came over to Martha and said, "Nice story" and gave her a kiss. She pushed him away. He grabbed her pigtails and pulled them. She muffled a sob, but I really felt her scalp pain in mine. I got out of my seat and pushed him away. "I'll fix you," he said. "Meet me after school beyond the school yard. Come alone." "You puny Baptist," he said to me, "I'll pull yur hair until you are bald." We met after school. Martha held my books while I pummeled Georgie. When he was down on the ground, I had one foot on his stomach and Martha pulled his hair until his pain was unbearable. His voice screeched and he wet his pants. Martha walked home to her hotel and I, having missed my bus, walked all the way home greatly satisfied. Georgie left St. Mary's By The Sea and entered public school the next week. Aunt Flora asked why I was not on the bus. I told her the whole story. She said that she was proud of me. "No mother could be prouder to have a son like you." I turned to jelly and sat at the table making necklaces that we would sell in the summer.

After the incident with Georgie Walsh the boys included me in their games. It was March, still chilly out. Recess was indoors. The boys played basketball; the girls, volleyball. By this time Martha had a circle of friends who would rather listen to her stories than bang a ball over the net. When the month of May rolled in Sister Agatha started to quiz us on all that she taught us during the year. Martha excelled among the girls and I surpassed all of the boys. Martha no longer said "Youz" or "dah." Her pronunciation was faultless. In June we "graduated" to the second grade. I asked her what her summer plans were. She said she would hang around the hotel and clean rooms. "Why don't you come and visit on your day off. We could swim, fish, collect shells. You could even learn to row a boat." She was not sure her mother would allow her to do it. Aunt Flora drove into town and stopped at the hotel. Not only would Martha's mother allow a day visit now and then but said Martha could come for the whole summer. Martha could earn her keep by doing chores around the house. "Jist keep after her," Martha's mother said. Aunt Flora nodded her head. She never saw the point in arguing with anyone. And keeping after anyone was not her way. Martha moved in with us for the summer. We boated, I taught her how to row; we made jewelry, I taught her how to string beads; we went on Nature hikes, I taught her the names of trees, insects, and birds. When we visited the hen house she would pet Victorborge who took to her right away. At the end of each day, Aunt Flora took out her Robinson Crusoe or Shakespeare and read to us. In time, Martha would finish the stories or the poems.

Toward the end of the summer Aunt Flora took us on a fishing expedition in one of those tourist boats. She paid for tackle and bait. We were out to sea a bit. Martha baited her hook as did I. Of course, Aunt Flora told us how to do it. Within minutes Martha was fighting with a bluefish. The delight on Martha's face is etched in my memory. Aunt Flora helped reel in the catch. The other passengers offered Martha $15 to let them have her catch. "No way," she said. The boat captain snapped her picture showing her with her bluefish. When the boat landed we were dizzy with excitement. "For you little lady, I'll clean the fish for nuttin," said one of the sailors. We took the fish home and Aunt Flora cooked it over a charcoal fire along with some potatoes wrapped in aluminum foil.

It was Labor Day and Martha went home laden with shells, rocks, and memories of a wonderful summer of jewelry making, nature hikes, crabbing, fishing, feeding chickens, and, most of all, catching a bluefish. With tears in her eyes she hugged Aunt Flora and asked if she could visit again. Of course, Aunt Flora answered. As she left for Aunt Flora's car Martha petted Victorborge. That night Victorborge yowled and kept us all awake. By the end of the week he was whimpering so loudly we could not stand it.

Sister Agatha was our teacher again. The classes were so small that grades one and two were combined. "Welcome back last year's first graders," she said. Both Martha and I were glad to have our teacher back. "This is the first day of a new year. The most fitting way to begin this year is at the very, very beginning. We'll study the Creation story in Genesis. Remember boys and girls God Created the world in six days and on the seventh He rested. Were it not for Him and his Son we would not be here."

That afternoon Martha visited us, and we talked about what we learned in school. Aunt Flora said that Navajo, the people, her people, had a different story about how the world began. This is what she said. The Creator had an idea that became Light in the East. That thought went south and created Water, it went west and created Air, then it went north and created Pollen from emptiness. Pollen became the Earth.

When all the elements blended, the Holy People, the Navajo, were Created. After they were given the first laws, they created the earth and human beings. Together the Creator and the Holy People worked to create the Natural World. This Natural World was put in Hozho (BALANCE). Hozho is the harmony and peace when all of the Natural world depend on one another.

Martha said she was confused. "How can there be two explanations for how the world began?" Aunt Flora said, "there are many, many explanations. We don't know for sure how the world came into being. The important thing is that we should respect one another and keep the world in balance. Then we live with one another in peace."

That was a lot for both of us to understand, but we watched Aunt Flora and she brought Hozho to all of us. That was the Navajo way.

My father came home Columbus Day. He was not wearing his captain's suit and cap but a Brooks Brothers tweed and a hat like Spencer Tracy wore in several of his films. "I have something to tell you," he said to Aunt Flora and me. "I have to go away and I don't know when I will be back. Mr. Epstein takes care of my affairs. He will be here soon for me to sign some papers so take Victorborge for a walk else he will bite Epstein in the behind." As I was leaving to get Victorborge my father came over to me and held me in his arms and told me that he loved me, and the times he misbehaved he was sorry and would I please forgive him. It's the drink that makes him do crazy things. The scars on my shoulder tensed in anger. He held me tightly and I tasted tears, his and mine. "I forgive you father." I was hurting but Aunt Flora said that there is no point in bearing a grudge. "Put wings on it."

I called Victorborge and enticed him with a dog biscuit to join me. When we returned my father was gone as was Mr. Epstein. Aunt Flora was holding some papers in her hands. She said it was legal stuff. I was all emotional, dumbfounded. I did not know what was happening. Was it my fault again? I wondered. Aunt Flora noticed that I was upset. She said, "Put wings on it and let it fly away."

At the end of October I was given another jolt. Aunt Flora said that she got a call from Martha's mother who lost her job at the hotel and needed a place for Martha until she could get settled elsewhere. There would be more opportunities in a big city for unskilled people "like herself." She wanted Martha to have a better life than she had. Aunt Flora picked up tearful Martha at the hotel. When the two saw one another they melted into each others' arms, both weeping for joy and out of love. When Martha arrived at our house I was awaiting my surprise. Martha got out of the car and ran toward the chicken house and lay down beside Victorborge and clung to him. He howled for joy.

Martha had her old room. Aunt Flora ordered a desk for her, a dictionary, and writing tablets. It was hard for Martha to settle down. She followed Aunt Flora around like some of the bantams followed me. Imprinting they call it. After a few weeks Martha began to call Aunt Flora "Mother Flora". Aunt Flora was thrilled as she had no children of her own. On Halloween Aunt Flora drove us into town. We wore costumes she sewed. Both of us were dressed as Navajos. "I wouldn't give a plug nickel to an Indian," one woman said. "But we are collecting for UNICEF," I protested. "For dem I would give even less." She slammed the door in our faces. I was ready to pound on the door, but Martha whispered in my ear "Put wings on it." I smiled and we went to the next house and Martha put on her charm at the next house. She rang the bell and started an Indian Rain Dance. She leaped here and there and looked like the Hindu goddess Kali flailing her arms. The man gave her a dollar. I did the dance, too, and the man gave me fifty cents. We went from house to house, entertaining ourselves more than the homeowners. We raised about a hundred dollars before Aunt Flora picked us up and drove us home. Awaiting us were ruby red candy apples.

Martha and I had heard rumors about our respective parents. One rumor was that my father went to jail for robbery; another, that he became a spy for the CIA; another, that he eloped with Martha's mother. A week before Thanksgiving, we got the truth, at least in part. Aunt Flora told us to take Victorborge for a walk. Mr. Epstein had some papers for her to sign. Victorborge romped in the woods, chasing squirrels. After about an hour the three of us returned home. "Sit down, please," Aunt Flora asked us. "I'm afraid I have some bad news." Her voice broke as she told me that my father was in a car crash in El Paso, Texas. He was killed. The passenger, a woman, was unidentifiable because the car had burned. Martha reached for my hand. Aunt Flora took me in her arms. Martha clasped the two of us and we wept until it was time for dinner. My good school shirt was stained with tears. All that night and many nights that followed my mixed emotions swirled and counter swirled about in my head. I could not put even one wing on my feelings, they were so heavy they would sink like a rock. What I wanted most of all was to rewind the tape of my days with my father and edit the script and have my life come out right. Impossible to do. I had to live with memories of his rage and his sudden turn about. I had to tell him that I regretted sassing him and cursing him. I had to tell him that I forgave him. But it was too late. Whatever good he had was interred with his bones. After several weeks of being haunted by the picture of my father's inert body in a car crash, I finally attached wings to my tormented emotions and let them fly away. Weighing a ton, they dropped into the Atlantic where the swirling seas tossed them about until they broke into subatomic particles.

Sister Agatha was exceptionally kind to me during my travail. She told me to always carry God in my heart and my pain will go away. Of course, it did not but I remembered her tender words. Classmates who had ignored me and had even been hostile treated me decently. I wondered if they were sincere or afraid what Martha might do to them if they taunted me. She had a mean right jab—I knew that from experience. In those days of my rage and grief Martha and I walked to the school bus arm and arm. We did not have to speak because we understood one another.

Around Christmas time Aunt Flora gathered us together to tell us about Mr. Epstein's visit. She showed us the paper that gave her title to our house. Then she showed us another paper, her will. She bequeathed to Martha and me the house upon her death. We would be joint owners. According to her will neither of us could sell the house without the consent of the other. Any sale had to be by mutual consent. In the event that either of us marry the spouse had no rights of ownership. Those were tall orders for two eight year olds. We truly did not understand the implications of her will. In time we forgot the whole matter. Before New Year's Aunt Flora drove us to New York City to watch the New Year come in. The three of us were overwhelmed by the masses of humanity. We studied the skyscrapers, we went to a show at Radio City Music Hall, we went to the automat where we put in quarters to get soup and a ham and cheese sandwich on white bread—food Aunt Flora never served us. Exciting as it was nothing compared to the crush of humanity midnight at Times Square. Someone tried to snatch Aunt Flora's pocketbook. She waddled after him and whacked the back of his neck until he fell to the ground and surrendered the stolen goods. "Mama," Martha said, "we've had enough of New York City. Let's go home to peace and quiet and find Hozho." And we did but it was a memorable New Year's Eve. Martha and I seated in the back our Ford and, folded into each other, fell asleep.

The next year we were in Sister Stephen's third grade. She explained that Saint Stephen was the patron saint of bricklayers. Her father was a bricklayer, she changed her name from Bridget to Stephen to honor him. She would tell us stories of a father's love for his children, especially for Bridget who was forever getting into mischief. She added that at that stage of her life she was immature. "Immature class," she said, "from the Latin 'in' meaning not and 'mature' from the root to grow." She would often speak words and then analyze them. That year my vocabulary increased by leaps and bounds. She was heavy on homework and took no excuses for lateness.

She taught me the habit of punctuality—from the Latin 'punctum' point. Sister Stephen took especial interest in Martha. She told her that she has the makings of a journalist—jour in French meaning day, and newspapers were dailies. Martha started to write stories for the school newspaper. She interviewed townspeople about what brought them to our town; she talked with aging people in the retirement home; she interviewed patients in the hospital who talked about their terminal illnesses. She learned so much about people and we, too, all learned about them through Martha.

In summers we brought our jewelry to the Farmer's Market. Old Italian women, dressed in mourning black as was their custom, would gather around the pretty little girl selling jewelry and smile at her. Then Martha would say, "*Buon giorno madre.*" They would be so moved to hear their mother tongue spoken by a blond, blue-eyed Nordic type, that they would, in their broken English, tell her tales of the old country. She told them that their stories of Sicily were so intriguing that she wanted to visit as soon as she graduated from high school. They would kiss her forehead and buy necklaces that they would never wear. "Addio," they would say; "Addio," Martha would repeat. If Sister Stephen were there, she would explain that they were saying God be with you. Martha would then take out her notepad and jot down the main points of their stories which she would then transcribe into an article for the school newspaper. The next Columbus Day one of the Italian women invited Martha to her house for a real Italian meal. "Ah Santa Marta," she greeted her. She did not mean that Martha was a saint, but a very special girl filled with purity. They spoke in broken English and Italian. When Martha returned home she raved about the genuine Italian chocolate drink. For many years thereafter Martha was invited to Mrs. Spinelli's house on Columbus Day for a real Italian meal and gossip. It was at one of those meals that Martha learned about the rodent problem in the city. The mayor's brother-in-law had a contract to rid the town of rats. But he absconded with the funds and was living somewhere in Florida. The women took after the rats with their broomsticks. Martha submitted her article to the local newspaper which published it. Not only did she receive $25 for her article, but the story was picked up by a national syndicate. In no time at all the mayor was recalled. How surprised everyone was to learn that the journalist who brought down the mayor was not even ten years old.

When Martha was at one of those dinners, Victorborge and I went for a romp at the seashore. We listened to the rippling waters, so soothing. Victorborge lay by my side, and I told him a dog joke. How, I asked Victorborge can you tell today's weather? Send your dog outside. If he comes back wet it's probably raining; if his fur is ruffled, it's probably windy. If he doesn't come back it is either sunny or went to find another owner. I tickled Victorborge who would howl.

Sister Stephen was our teacher in the fourth grade. She taught how to use the dictionary and the encyclopedias. Martha and I already knew how. We would use our spare time in the school library looking up all kinds of information about science, art, and culture. For Christmas that year Aunt Flora had bought us the Encyclopedia Britannica. We devoured it. Both Martha and I had measles that March. Were it not for the encyclopedia we would not know what to do with ourselves. One day she would climb into my bed; another, I climbed into hers. We would read and then tell the other what we learned. When we returned to school we already knew algebra- the name derived from the ninth century Arabic book, *Hidab al-jabr wal-muqubala*. Seventh graders learned Algebra at our school. Sister Stephen told us that while we were sick she had the children write get well cards to us. She wrote our names on the blackboard and the word "measles" a word which came into English via the Dutch. That explained why Martha got a Get Well card from one of the children that said: "Dear Martha Measles get rid of the Dutch."

So much changed in the fifth grade. Sister Cecilia was our teacher and even meaner than my first grade teacher. "Sit up straight," she would bark. "Posture! posture! posture!" "No raising hands." "No library passes." "No bathroom privilege, Hold it in." It was "No" this and "No" that. This bothered both Martha and me and we would comfort one another with "put wings on it." Martha and I took out our anger in different ways. I would dribble hard and would shoot baskets in gym; Martha wrote horror stories. She did not make them up from her imagination. She wrote them based on newspaper items she read. She wrote of robberies, murders, fires, oppression of women, race riots. She even wrote about hockey games in which players slammed one another with their sticks and gave concussions. "You have a sick mind," said Sister Cecilia. Martha took it as a compliment. Sister Cecilia did get to Martha, though. Martha began to feign illness and wanted to stay in bed and study our encyclopedias. Aunt Flora, Martha's Momma Flora, squeezed out of Martha the real reason she did not want to go to school. One day while I was in school—and Martha was in bed—Aunt Flora came into the classroom and scolded Sister Cecilia in front of the class. "You should not be teaching children. You kill, yes kill, their desire to learn. You are a harsh, disagreeable women, a disgrace to your order. You should be on the docks with other longshoremen." The entire class clapped. It is so hard to mint a nun in the image of Mary, Mother of God. That was Sister Cecilia's last day in class. A lay substitute teacher came the next day. She was strict, too, but anyone was better than Sister Cecilia. Word got around school that my Aunt Flora, the Indian woman, was no one to mess with. Martha returned to school. She had no more sick days.

Toward the end of sixth grade both Martha and I were moving into adolescence. I couldn't help but notice her developing femininity. There was not only physical changes but some changes in her disposition. A day or two before grammar school graduation, she said, "Momma, I've had it with parochial school. Next year I want to go to public school. From now on call me Marty. Martha is a little girl's name and I am growing up." Aunt Flora did not protest. She thought it was a good idea to be exposed to cultural differences. Too often, Martha, now Marty, had commented on the gulf dividing people: Catholics against other religions, Democrats against Republicans, boys against girls, brothers and sisters against each other, city kids against country kids like us. "We only have one world," she said, "and we manufacture (manu-hand, fact-make) foolish differences that demolish its perfection."

The switch to public school was good for her. She made many new friends who looked upon her with respect, not like the parochial schoolgirls who made fun of her brain. I went on to Boys' Catholic. I did not need new friends although I met some boys with whom I would kid around. I had Aunt Flora, Marty, Victorborge, and my bantams with whom I was close. Especially, Marty. Something extraordinary did happen at Boys' Catholic that made a difference the rest of my life. Brother Leonard was my Phys. Ed. teacher. "Hey, beanpole," he said to me. "You have the build of a basketball player." He tossed the basketball to me and said, "Shoot". I eyed the basket and threw the ball in an arc. "In" he shouted. "Lucky shot? Maybe not. Try again." I made four baskets out of five throws. "I was right," he said. Then he proceeded to show me how to stand, hold the ball, and move my body to my best advantage. Aunt Flora put up a basket. An apple basket with a hole in it on our garage. I practiced when I had a chance. Marty practiced, too. In time we both became good at making baskets.

Everything went smoothly for me at Boys' Catholic. When I was ninth grade, I was given an independent study in physics. I particularly excelled in astrophysics. That year Brother Leonard tried me out against the school varsity team. I did O.K. but I realized that I still had much to learn. Marty had only one glitch in her ninth grade. While riding home on the bus Georgie Walsh came up behind her. Pulling her hair, he said, "I owe you". Then he fondled her breasts. She got up and punched him in the stomach and then gave him a black eye. "Did you see that?" he asked everyone on the bus. They were used to his antics and ignored him. Then he ran up to the bus driver who stopped the bus to investigate. "Yes, I did do what he said. He had it coming to him." Marty was irate. "I didn't do nuttin," Walsh protested meekly. Marty was reported to the principal who called Aunt Flora saying that Marty was about to be expelled for hitting a boy. Marty had given Aunt Flora all of the details. She told Marty that there are some feelings that need no wings. They should always be in her mind to keep her on guard against unwanted overtures. Aunt Flora, Marty, and I went to the principal's office for a conference. Georgie Walsh was there waiting tapping his feet and smirking. He took one look at me and told Marty that he was sorry and, remembering his first grade incident with me said that he would not do it again. "That's right," said the principal who expelled him.

There were many changes in our lives when we were in the eleventh grade. First, Marty had her own weekly column in the city newspaper. She called it MY TOWN. YOUR TOWN. OUR TOWN. Not only would she write about industry moving to North Carolina where the labor was cheaper and displacing many families, but she also wrote human interest stories about people who traced their ancestry to Germany, Sweden, Norway, Italy, Africa, and Asia. The citizens of our town began to look at each other differently. They realized all families have roots, have bugaboos, and have great moments of celebration. Some had criminals in their background; others, heroes. All people were different yet they were the same. Marty got paid $50 for each column. She knew about everyone's roots but her own. We all, momma (I started to call her that) and I and many anonymous readers knew that she had given something to the community that was lacking, mutual respect. When Victorborge died, we grieved for some time over his death. Momma said we could best celebrate his life by putting wings on our sadness and sending it out over the Atlantic. We dismantled the chicken coop and donated the bantams to the convent. I shudder to think what became of my dear bantams. Another thing that happened was that momma gave me driving lessons. After I passed my driver's test she bought me a Ford. Once I started driving I would pick Marty up at school and drive her home or wherever she needed to go.

Perhaps the most important thing that happened that year was that momma took us to her home in Arizona. We stayed with her brother David. He was among the Navajos in the Marine Corps during World War II who designed a code using Navajo words to express English words. Radio messages were sent using that code that befuddled the Japanese. Without that code the Marines might not have captured Iwo Jima in 1945. One day he took me on a long drive through Arizona. We met Zuni, Hopi, and other Navajo. I saw circles, hand, cross, lightning petroglyphs made by ancient ancestors. We tried to figure out what they meant. David said, "It beats me but they sure are pretty. Mebbee the Hopi understand them, but Navajo don't." While driving we stopped at a Navajo restaurant where David knew everyone.

He introduced me to several of the patrons. "From back East," he told them. While waiting for our meal to arrive he said he had something to tell me. His face turned serious. I listened intently. "Your father and I were buddies in the Marines. You may not know that or this either. My sister, the one you call Flora was engaged to Peter, another Navajo who was recruited just like me. Peter liked to drink. So did your father. You know that. Well Navajos don't hold their liquor too well. Peter got into a fight with another Marine who shot him. Shot him dead. Your father got so mad—I mean angry mad—that he grabbed that Marine and shoved his head against the wall. The guy lost consciousness, became confused, lost hand function and was eventually given a medical discharge. Your father felt bad, really bad and went on a binge. He kept on talking to himself that the guy deserved it. I took care of your father and made sure that he was never reported to the authorities. He said he would stop drinking and live a clean life. But he didn't. After the war we kept in contact with one another. When your birth mother died, he was downcast. He missed her. She kept him on the straight and narrow. But he needed someone to take care of you. Flora would marry no one. She missed Peter. I told her about your father and your father about her. Aunt Flora became your "aunt-momma." He then added that my father and his new wife visited him before they went to Mexico. I knew the rest. Wings were attaching to all of my feelings and fluttering around me like hummingbirds. "What was his wife's name?" I asked. He told me and then my turmoil boiled over. We had a soft drink and drove home. I was quiet, very quiet.

Flora and David had tearful goodbyes. We were all absorbed in our thoughts on the flight back. That next summer, the last one that I was home, Marty insisted I learn how to dance. She wanted me to take her to the senior prom. Momma urged me to learn. She said she would learn, too. "Why me? I asked her. She said that boys did not want to date a girl who was smarter than they. So I learned. Momma, learned too. During the Winter, Marty sewed her prom dress. Organdy. Apricot. I watched momma pin her up. I knew she would be stunning. And she was. In March, I rented a tux. Momma drove us to the prom. I was too young to drive at night. I had a much better time than I thought I would until Mr. Pirelli, a reedy man with a handlebar mustache came over to me while Marty was in the powder room. "I am going to steal your girl." I was ready to sock him when Marty returned. She said Angelo was her Geometry teacher. Angelo? I asked myself. They danced. Very close, I thought, for a smarmy Geometry teacher and his student. Momma drove us home. Marty was all smiles and I was sullen. "Whatever it is," momma said "Put wings on it."

Marty had given basketball up but she was at the games that I played. She cheered for me the loudest when Boys Catholic played City High, the school Marty went to. The last basket I made I was the proudest. I just spooned the ball into the basket. I could hear Marty yelling, "Bravo. Bravo." A chant started in the stands. My teammates lifted me up and the spectators clapped for me. Embarrassed, I took a bow and rushed off the court. Marty was there to greet me with a hug and a peck on the cheek. Momma was there, too. "We go out tonight to celebrate—with a steak."

I was accepted to the Naval Academy where I studied navigation. The review committee not only liked my academic record but my swimming, baseball, and basketball records. I did well at the Academy but I had to work hard at it. The other cadets were so much smarter than I. Marty refused a scholarship to go to Journalism school. Toward the end of our Senior year, Marty called and said she had something important to tell me and that I should come home right away. I got into my car and started my drive all the time wondering what she needed to tell me. When I arrived home she said, "I have good news and bad. Which do you want to hear first?" Before I had a chance to answer her she said, "The bad news is momma is dying; the good news is that I am marrying Angelo." Both were bad news so far as I was concerned. I ran to momma. She was having trouble breathing. "Will I ever see you again?" I asked. I know that was selfish of me. My dear mother dying, another mother dying, and all I could think of was myself. "We will meet on the other side of Time," she said. "My soul is returning to My Maker as one day will yours. On that day I will be there to take your hand and together we'll enter the Promised Land." I left the room disconsolate. "Angelo is a scum bag, a greaser. Ten years older than you." "But he's smart!" she protested. "He's a smart scum bag," I shot back in haste. Marty just shrugged her shoulders and left the room. The next time I saw her was at Momma's funeral. She invited me to her wedding but I did not attend. I knew she had made a bad choice.

While on board ship I got a call from Marty. It had been raining for three straight days and cloudy for two more. The weather was gloomy, and so was I. One is given to brooding in such weather. When I heard Marty's voice my heart thumped with joy. She had given birth to a baby girl, Flora Agatha Pirelli. I began to feel abdominal sensations as if I were having labor pains. I was overjoyed for her. But I was unhappy for myself, empty, unfulfilled. In my solitude I had had a steady diet of rolling seas, sunshine, rain, clouds and camaraderie. There is only so much forced friendship I could take. As navigation officer I had responsibility for charting the course. Instruments and Venus were my best friends. My mind was cluttered with facts and formulae. My soul was bleak and worthless, twined by loneliness and yearning. I felt useless. I did tell Venus my innermost secrets. That was just an excuse for a relationship. Venus shone before I was born and will shine after I die. Marty's call reminded me of how much I missed her and Momma Flora. Both women had connected me with meaning in life. I was haunted by memories of those who showed me love and whom I loved. "Please visit," she pleaded "the next time you are back in the states." How I would thrill to see Marty and Flora Agatha Pirelli but not her husband what's his name.

Just then I saw out of the corner of my eyes a flock of white birds flying south through the dark clouds in the sky. I imagined that they were carrying all of the anguish from North America and dropping them into the churning seas where they will roll about until they break up into small fragments, atoms, subatomic particles, then nothing.

Six months later I was granted leave. I went home dressed in my whites. I looked truly handsome but felt miserable beneath my skin. I went straight to her apartment. It was small and congested like my quarters aboard ship. I looked at her and my pulse quickened; my knees became jelly. I wanted to hug her like I used to, but she was a married woman. She greeted me with, "I am divorced." Not only was Angelo playing around with another student or two but he wanted to put his name down as co-owner of our house as a condition of remaining a faithful husband. "Not a chance," she said. He left the apartment with a black eye like she knew how to give. I held out my arms to embrace her but she held back. She pointed to the baby asleep in her cradle.

Flora Agatha was so beautiful. Marty called her a gift. I picked her up in my arms and she was soft, warm, and cuddly. I told her how sorry I was for the divorce-it was the proper thing to say but I didn't mean it. Sorry? I was glad she got rid of him. I called him repulsive (from the Latin *repulsum*) to drive back. Marty smiled and said he was scum but he gave me this beautiful little girl. How I would have liked to be her father. I told Marty—who called herself Martha again—that I would like to marry her. We knew each other better than most men and women know one another. We had been so close for so many years: living together under the same roof, feeding the bantams, walking Victorborge, beating up Georgie Walsh, studying the encyclopedia in bed with measles, going to New York City on New Years with Aunt Flora, catching a bluefish, making and selling silver beaded necklaces. We trusted ourselves and one another. We have always been there for each other. Life had taught us lessons that removed the rock setting up roadblocks on the path to happiness. "Sit down," she said. Her face turned serious. I sat holding the baby in my arms. "We can't marry. Before momma died she told me that you and I have the same father." I was crestfallen and confused. She went on, "That is a secret that I have had for some time." "I have a secret, too," I said. "One that David told me when we were driving in Arizona. It was your mother who died in the car crash with our father."

Potpourri

Wings from heaven clung to our smoldering anguish and, weeping, flapped their way to the Atlantic like a pair of mourning doves singing a dirge in harmony. They soared into the dark cloud that I saw on board ship the day Marty called me. Then they dropped their evil burdens and they fell into the roaring waters until they were smashed into nothing.

MY COUSIN'S FUNERAL

MY COUSIN, Albert, Bertie, became famous because of his singing. He started his career singing outside of Kaplan's pharmacy. So Izzy Kaplan chased him away because customers would gather round to listen to him. They'd forget the reason they came to Izzy: to buy medicines that improved the health of their loved ones. Bertie became cocky and would show his brothers how much he earned. Papa was proud of him. Sam and Sol not so. The brothers developed an envy that corroded their coronary valves. Bystanders stopped throwing quarters because Bertie found an agent and went professional.

One night all heard a thud. Upon investigating Father was found on the floor. He lost speech. Could only make grunting sounds. Bertie hugged him until life flowed from Papa's body. There was a funeral, but Sam and Saul refused to sit with their brother. Visitors left without giving condolence to the family. Bertie sat alone in his room until midnight when he packed his belongings and disappeared forever.

THE SOFT, SILVERED TONGUE OF AVON*

Hark! "... What light through yonder window breaks..."
It is the bard gathering kernels of brio

From every Time and every Place,
    From every region and every race
From every sphere, nook, and space
    From princes and scoundrels
From the belle and the beast
    From the very highest to the very least.
        From the wisest to the rudest
            And from the saintly to the lewdest.

Lovingly does he nurture their issue
    And harvests tragedy and comedy
        Embroidering their tracts with envy, beauty, grief,

Mystery, history, mist, fog, haze, daze, and maze,

    Trance, romance, dance
        Intrigue, revenge, quandary, subterfuge, and trickery,

        Through tempest and calm
            In verse of rhyme, in song sublime

The soft, silvered tongue of Avon
    Whose head was anointed by Erato
        Burnishes the soul with sonnets
            And polishes the mind with a lexicon unrivaled.

Wreathe'd, he is enshrined in the pantheon of poetry midst Dante and Petrarch.

The soft, silvered tongue of Avon enchants us

    With linguistic alchemy.
His verses will prevail through the ebb and flow of taste and style

   His weave of words, more lustrous than gold and sturdier than marble, will e'er beguile.

*Birth said to be April 23, 1564, death April 23, 1616.

HARK! HARK! HOW SPLENDID TO WATCH

How splendid it is to watch
The new day break
Returning from its circuit about the sun
This world remake.

What magic there is in the morning mist
That coats the earth in mystery.
Fluffy clouds of white
Blend with blue skies in celestial harmony.

Hearken closely and you will hear the sweet songs of children dear.
Songs that have been heard since yester year;
Songs to lonely hearts bring cheer. Their harmony delights the soul

And spreads good will with great elation.
Hearken closely and you will hear
Words of kindness throughout Creation.

Add your voice to tuneful songs;
To soften the hardest heart
And coalesce with all in this wonderful world
A new day to restart.

REQUEST

Tether thy soul to mine
And together we'll build a shrine.

GROWN UP AT NINE DURING WORLD WAR II

Days after Pearl Harbor I became an orphan. Not from the war. My father, an attorney for HIAS, was too old to be a soldier. After arriving in America, he worked as a day laborer and attended night school until he passed the bar. His was an accidental death. The crowded MATTAPAN Streetcar, that's the one with the wimple roof, swerved off icy tracks, hurtling passengers against and through windows. Dad was thrown against broken glass.

When I first got the news about his death I was sure it was a mistake. My mother sobbed, "no mistake," her tense, tortured face clouded over. Then I thought it was a bad dream. It was not that either. It was real. I still remember how it felt when Rabbi Cohen took a knife and made a gash in the only jacket I owned. It was like slashing my heart and making my soul bleed. He mumbled some words of *comfort*. 'Death is inevitable. Get used to it boychik.'

As a nine year old, I had to come to terms with loss and how it changed me and my family. I had made fun of my father's Yiddish accent a few times, too many times. His death, I told myself, was my punishment for dishonoring him, for violating the fourth of the ten commandments. 'My fault' for ridiculing my dad. My dreams were a seething overflowing river of rage and guilt. For one month night demons ravaged my sleep, wriggling, snapping, crackling, hissing like a snake, and shouting obscenities. Firecrackers exploded; lightening spikes crackled; automobiles collided; Nazi planes dropped bombs. People screaming for help taunted me and accused me of unimaginable crimes, my heart throbbed and pounded. I'd sweat profusely and grow weak. A river of rage flooded my rattled brain.

My gloomy night companions agitated my sleep and saturated me with a melancholy that I tried to hide from my mother. She had enough grief without adding mine to it. I found solace in reciting the kaddish, much against the advice of my rabbi. I was just praising God not for my father's death but for the greatness of Creation I would daily notice the sun in the morning and the stars at night as the song went.

I had argued with the rabbi to allow me to recite the mourner's prayer. He just threw up his hands in disgust. "A nine year old is too young to recite kaddish. It does not count because you are too young to be a part of the minyan. You are wiser than me, your rabbi? You are just a small fry," he sneered, red in the face.

How could my mother support us? That question was always on my mind. What she knew was how to cook, clean, and sew. So she hired herself out as a maid to a rich Jewish lady in Brookline. She would take trolleys and busses early in the morning and come home exhausted after eight o'clock. I had to fend for myself. That's when I learned to cook, clean, and sew. That's when I grew up.

Of course, I had my studies, too: Hebrew School and public school. Friends' mothers would take pity on me and would invite me to dinner. I was reprieved from meal preparation every now and then, but I could not do it too often as there was much to do at home. Much was expected of me and I fulfilled my obligations.

One day a tall elderly man knocked on my door and asked if he could rent a room. His posture was erect and he spoke English elegantly like a Shakespearean actor. His voice was robust but gentle. His eyebrows were white as snow. His nose was symmetrical. His suit was tailored and well cared for. His shoes reflected a high shine.

I called my mother at work and told her about the visitor. She was wary. "Is he in his forties or fifties?" she asked. I sized him up. "More like his late seventies," I said. "Does he want kitchen privileges?" she asked. I turned to the visitor and asked.

"Yes," he replied.

"He cooks for himself."

"Does he keep kosher?" she asked. I looked at his skullcap. I did not need to ask him. We settled on rent and the next day he arrived with boxes of books in Hebrew, English, French, and Italian. He asked if I would help him carry them in. I did. Otherwise he did not have much to say. We had no extra bookcases at the time so his books remained in cartons with the bindings showing.

That night he helped me prepare supper. He had exquisite recipes for preparing eggs. He prepared what he called 'omelette au fromage plus.' I grated cheddar cheese and cut up peppers and onions. I never knew that omelettes could be so tasty. My mother never fried onions or peppers. The spicy aromas surged through the kitchen. How I savored them. When she came home I introduced her to Mister Gorvich, the new lodger. She eyed him suspiciously but greeted him with the tired smile she now always wore. Mister Gorvich would never be considered a suitor. I knew that. He was not looking for companionship. What he wanted was a room and that's all.

That night my father's ghost loomed in my dream, dressed in the shroud he had been buried in. He spoke to me in fluent English just like Mr. Gorvich. In Heaven he had lost his accent. "Son," he said, "My death was a vehicular accident." He still spoke like a lawyer. "It was fate and not your doing." I felt absolved. There were no more bad dreams.

One Saturday, Mister Gorvich asked me if I would join him at the synagogue. I agreed. We looked like Mutt and Jeff as we walked past the heavy oaken door embossed with a Star of David. He was this tall, grand, imposing man and I, a short pip squeak. Unlike other men at the synagogue he was not one to *schmooze*. In fact, he had little to say most of the time. I was curious, though, what he was doing in Dorchester, the jewel in the crown of Boston's Jewry, as well as where he got the money to pay for rent, food and the like.

Immediately before the service ended, the men were removing their prayer shawls while singing Adon Olam. Singing? I mean bellowing. Mister Gorvich waited until the hymn ended before removing his prayer shawl. He was invited to have a *schnapps* and a *küchel*. He politely declined and we strolled home. As we were leaving the rabbi and his cronies were downing schnapps, sing—shouting Sabbath hymns and rhythmically pounding the table.

My mother had prepared a cholent for lunch. She never worked on the Sabbath. We sat very quietly and ate the potatoes and carrots soaked in meat gravy. She asked him where he came from. His answer was evasive. "Here and there, now from here."

"Do you have plans while you are here," my mother inquired.

"We'll see," he said. After the meal he recited the Grace silently and retired to his room. In time he and I became more comfortable with one another. One Saturday afternoon he invited me to his room. I was stunned. All of the books that had been in cartons were now on bookcases. He showed me copies of The Bible in different languages. I knew enough Hebrew to recite words but not understand them. In time I looked at the Hebrew and then the English. That's how I learned to translate.

My friends asked me if the tall man I sat with at the synagogue was a relative. I should have said that he was "a lodger" but I was starting to feel an almost familial bond with Mister Gorvich. I said he was my grandfather. "Why don't you call him Zaydeh then?" they asked. I said "because he prefers to speak English to me and his English is more elegant than any of my teachers and the rabbi combined."

One day he told me that he earned his money as a translator. "Were you always a translator?" I asked him when I felt at ease with him. "No, no," he replied. "I've been a chef, a waiter, a shoe salesman, and a lumberjack."

"A lumberjack?" I asked in disbelief. Then I, shamefaced, told him that I lied to my friends that he was my grandfather. He just guffawed. He put his arm around me and said that God will forgive my little transgression. Then chortling he said that since he never married, his being my grandfather would really make me illegitimate. "But," laughing louder he added, "that will be our little secret." Mister Gorvich was the kindest of men. Soft spoken. He would talk to the flowers, to dogs, and to the animals in the zoo.

When he saw a child cry for an ice cream that a mother would say she could not afford, he would buy it and watch the child lick the dripping cone and would smile. And when he parted his lips his gilded tooth glinted in the light.

When I was twelve I was of an age when my friends would start training for a bar mitsvah. I reminded my mother of this one Friday evening. She said that we could not afford the expense of a tutor or a party. Mister Gorvich asked if it would be all right with her if he taught me for free. My mother, always proud, said she would never accept charity. Mister Gorvich said it was not out of charity that he made his offer but because he was fond of me. It would be because of our friendship.

Reluctantly my mother agreed as long as there would be no party after-wards. That was fine with me. I just wanted a bar mitsvah; I just wanted the privilege of reading from the Torah and to be counted in the quorum. More than anything else I wanted to be counted. Mister Gorvich gave me lessons every Saturday afternoon. I found the cantillations he sang were not in the style I heard at my synagogue. I told him that. He said it was a "Yemenite vogue."

"But I am not Yemenite," I said.

"Neither am I," he smiled. "It is important to know that there are many acceptable Jewish traditions. We must broaden our outlooks."

I never told my mother for fear she would disapprove. I kept that secret, too. So I studied. My bar mitzvah portion was from Isaiah. Although the speech I was to give was in Hebrew I introduced the gist in English:

A tempest rose from Babylon tossing fireballs across the fields, Turning Israel's homes to ashes and melting David's shields. Our stomachs ached with hunger; our dreams and hopes were dashed. Our heroes fought with courage; their efforts, though, were smashed. Hearken to me Zion, sapphire in God's Sacred Crown, God Returns to Comfort you and you will not walk alone.

Triumphantly march to Jerusalem! Triumphantly declare God's Name! Triumphantly light Torah's torch and bless Its eternal flame.

Mister Gorvich never scolded me if I made a mistake in cantillation or in pronunciation. He would just say that was good, voice the correct sounds and say, "look how close you were." That was so different from my friends' teachers who would bang on the desk with a ruler and call them "stupid idiots" or "chamore", jackass.

The evening before my bar mitzvah my mother entered the dining room. She had been to the beauty parlor that morning and her long grey hair was cut and styled in waves. Her face was lightly rouged, her lips painted ruby red. She wore a tartan skirt and a black satin blouse. Around her neck was a strand of pearls, a gift from my late father. Before addressing the candles she recited a prayer.

During our weekly odyssey seeking serenity, storms brew; clouds scud; waves crash. As we approached Shabbat the storms abate; the clouds clear; the sun radiates warmth. Behold on the horizon is Shabbat, a sanctuary, resplendent with golden daffodils and releasing the scent of attar of roses. Glorious healing calm infuse sour souls.

Then her wrinkled hands circled the candle sticks she had inherited from her mother. They had been brought to America from a small village outside of Vilna. Her blessing completed, she smiled and kissed my forehead. Next to the candlesticks was a vase of fragrant red roses. She brought to the table a browned capon decorated with small, new potatoes, beets, and florets of broccoli. Parsley sprigs garnished the serving plate. For dessert she served a homemade apple pie. We were all stuffed.

Before the Grace we sang Sabbath hymns. I had never before heard her sweet, alto voice. "Thanks to you and to Mr. Gorvich," she whispered, "we are beginning a new time in our lives." There was a broad smile on her face. "Amen," Mr. Gorvich answered. So did I. What contentment reigned that evening. It was genuine Shabbat peace.

The next day, I was called to the Torah. I noticed the sun streaming through the stained-glass window, irradiating the ten commandments. It was a hot August morning and the windows were open, inviting several flies and a wasp that buzzed around a cup of wine placed on the reader's desk.

Mister Gorvich strode to the altar, shooed away the insects and stood by my side. He urged me to chant in slow, deliberate phrases. That would create a dramatic effect. It would make the day ever so meaningful in my memory. I recited the blessings. As I began chanting a tumult erupted. A young man in his late teens ran up to the bimah, took out a gun, and shot the eternal light. The glass shattered. Several congregants hid beneath the benches.

"Hand me the gun," Mister Gorvich demanded. "Don't take one step near me old man," the intruder yelled. "Because of you kikes my brother died on D-Day."

At that moment the women in the Lady's gallery ululated and flung bags of hard candies they had been saving for me. Pelted by bags of candy, the intruder was stunned. Mister Gorvich grabbed the intruder's arm so tightly that the gun dropped. When he scrambled to the floor to retrieve the gun, Mister Gorvich stepped on his hand.

"Let me go you crazy Kike," he screamed, "Your hurting me."

Mister Gorvich stepped on him all the harder. I recognized the man as the one who beat me up on Good Friday because he claimed that I had killed JC, his god.

Someone had sneaked out of the synagogue and phoned the police. After the police came and took the man away, the rabbi announced, "In light of the events that just transpired, we'll skip today's service and go home."

Then in a voice I have never heard Mister Gorvich use before he shouted, "this boy is to become a man today. He will chant his haftorah." The rabbi was petrified. He imagined he heard the Voice of God.

Mr. Gorvich nudged me to begin chanting. Then I began to sing the haftorah the way Mister Gorvich had taught me. Aaron Goldfarb, the undertaker, stood up and shrieked that mine was not a kosher rendition. He added that I was a *shaygetz*.

Then a small voice rose from the Women's Gallery saying, "the boy's rendering was of the ancient way. There is no one way to be Jewish." It was my mother.

Fuming, Goldfarb stomped out of the synagogue. "Good riddance," a voice of the "angel" called out from the Women's Gallery. At the conclusion of the service the rabbi shook my hand and asked me if I would teach others the Yemenite cantillation.

Mister Gorvich and I walked home together arm in arm. "Where did you get the gumption and strength to stop the intruder," I asked. He reminded me that he had been a lumberjack and was not afraid of anything or anybody.

Then my mother ran over to us and thanked him for all he did for me. Beaming, he just shrugged his shoulders.

The next day I showed him the headlines in the newspaper: "COPS FOIL KILLER IN SYNAGOGUE." Mister Gorvich just smiled and went to his room to study.

www.ingramcontent.com/pod-product-compliance
Lightning Source LLC
Chambersburg PA
CBHW071231300426
44116CB00008B/993